BULLDOZED AND BETRAYED

BULLDOZED AND BETRAYED

LOUISIANA AND THE STOLEN ELECTIONS OF 1876

ADAM FAIRCLOUGH

Louisiana State University Press
Baton Rouge

Published by Louisiana State University Press
lsupress.org

Manufactured in the United States of America

First printing
Designer: Laura Roubique Gleason
Typefaces: MillerText, text; Veneer Clean, display
Printer and binder: Sheridan Books

Maps created by Mary Lee Eggart

Jacket illustration: "The Potter Investigation Committee in Session in the Basement of the Old Capitol," *Frank Leslie's Illustrated Newspaper*, June 22, 1878.

Library of Congress Cataloging-in-Publication Data
Names: Fairclough, Adam, author.
Title: Bulldozed and betrayed : Louisiana and the stolen elections of 1876 / Adam Fairclough.
Description: Baton Rouge : Louisiana State University Press, [2021] Includes bibliographical references and index.
Identifiers: LCCN 2021006397 (print) | LCCN 2021006398 (ebook) | ISBN 978-0-8071-7559-0 (cloth) | ISBN 978-0-8071-7633-7 (pdf) | ISBN 978-0-8071-7634-4 (epub)
Subjects: LCSH: United States. Congress. House. Select Committee on Alleged Frauds in the Late Presidential Election. | Presidents—United States—Election—1876. | Contested elections—United States. | Elections—Corrupt practices—Southern States. | Voter intimidation—Southern States—History. | Voter suppression—Louisiana—History. | Political culture—United States—History—19th century. | United States—Politics and government—1869–1877.
Classification: LCC E680 .F185 2021 (print) | LCC E680 (ebook) | DDC 324.60975/09034—dc23
LC record available at https://lccn.loc.gov/2021006397
LC ebook record available at https://lccn.loc.gov/2021006398

To the memory of Dr. Mary L. Ellison,
mentor, inspiration, and friend

It is all history, except how it came to be history.

—Benjamin F. Butler

CONTENTS

ACKNOWLEDGMENTS

Completing this book amid a pandemic, when libraries and archives are closed to the public, I appreciate librarians and archivists more than ever. Since my first visit thirty-five years ago, it has always been a joy to work at the Manuscripts Division of the Library of Congress. Its friendly, helpful staff have remained friendly and helpful throughout the decades. At other archives I have met the same eagerness to make the researcher's lot a happy one: a heartfelt "thank you" to the staffs of the Historical Society of Pennsylvania in Philadelphia and the Louisiana and Lower Mississippi Valley Collection at Louisiana State University in Baton Rouge.

LSU Press has been a pleasure to work with. Editor in Chief Rand Dotson expressed confidence in this work from the outset and moved the publication process along smoothly and expeditiously. At every stage of that process, he was ready with practical suggestions and friendly encouragement. Kevin Brock, my copy editor, was a model of professionalism whose ear for language and eye for readability greatly improved the manuscript. He also spotted and eliminated any number of careless errors on my part.

Alexander Pope's observation that "fools rush in where angels fear to tread" often came to mind when I decided, some dozen years ago, to write about Reconstruction. And, indeed, I received one or two wallops (albeit anonymous ones) from scholars in the field who condemned my foolishness. My trepidation was therefore assuaged by the fact that other prominent scholars have encouraged my interest and helped me along the way. Mark W. Summers read an early draft of this book, offered constructive suggestions, and shared his unrivalled knowledge of the relevant sources. He has been exceedingly generous with his support. Paul D. Escott has been similarly unstinting in offering friendly encouragement and perceptive criticism in equal parts. Lawrence N. Powell has, for over thirty years now, been a friend and guide, showing interest in all my work and allowing me to exploit his deep knowledge of Louisiana history. At an early stage of my plunge into Reconstruction, a number of historians, including Michael Fitzgerald, Michael Perman, and J. Mills Thornton III, provided signposts and warning signs that proved of enormous assistance in helping me navigate this controversial field. More recently, I have benefited from exchanging ideas with Dr. David Ballantyne, a former postdoctoral researcher at Leiden and now a lecturer at Keele University. Needless to say, I absolve all of the above from any responsibility for this book's weaknesses. The mistakes are mine alone.

Four years into "retirement," I am very conscious of mentors who, whether or not I realized it at the time, helped direct my unfocused enthusiasm for American history toward serious scholarship and showed me how such endeavors could be immensely enjoyable and rewarding. At Hampton Grammar School Simon Williams and Ernest Badman were both superb teachers; at Oxford University John Walsh and Duncan McLeod guided me through historiographical debates over slavery, the Civil War, and Reconstruction. At Balliol College Maurice Keen, a medievalist, and John Prest, a scholar of Victorian England, were kind and sympathetic tutors who knew how to get the best from their students. What I owe to Mary Ellison of Keele University, to whose memory this book is dedicated, is hard to express in words. Suffice it to say that she was not only the perfect mentor for this doctoral student but also an engaged and enthusiastic scholar whose example of unselfish service continues to inspire me.

Mary Ellen Curtin, my wife, knows the story of the Potter Committee investigation in far more detail than she might have wished. Still, part of the enjoyment of researching and writing this book was the fact I had a fellow Americanist, and a scholar of race to boot, to converse with at the dinner table. Her love, companionship, patience, and good humor have sustained me throughout.

BULLDOZED AND BETRAYED

INTRODUCTION

On May 13, 1878, the House of Representatives ordered an investigation of the presidential election of 1876, a bitterly disputed contest that had taken four months to resolve. The Potter Committee, named after its chairman, Clarkson N. Potter, a Democrat from New York, commenced its work on June 1 and concluded it nine months later.

After questioning two hundred witnesses in Washington, New Orleans, Tallahassee, Atlantic City, and New York and accumulating a mass of documentary evidence, the committee left a published record comprising three thousand pages of closely printed text. A majority report charged Republicans with having stolen the election. A minority report asserted that Democrats had attempted to steal the election but failed. An opinion by Benjamin F. Butler held that the election in Louisiana had been so irregular that Congress ought to have rejected its electoral votes entirely.[1]

The House vote was, on the face of it, an odd move. Carried by that chamber's Democratic majority, it resurrected a controversy that had kept the nation in a state of suspense and anxiety. The country had breathed a collective sigh of relief when, on March 2, 1877, the two parties ended the impasse and Rutherford B. Hayes, the Republican candidate, was inaugurated without incident three days later. Throughout his single term of office, Democrats routinely referred to Hayes as "His Fraudulency." But few advocated removing him through impeachment, and virtually no one considered ousting him by extraconstitutional means. During the crisis, Georgia congressman Benjamin H. Hill poured cold water on talk of disunion, reminding fire-eaters of the "conservative influence of a fifteen-inch shell with the fuse in process of combustion."[2]

Congressional committees had gone over the contest between Hayes and Samuel J. Tilden, the Democratic candidate, with several fine-tooth combs. Those committees had drawn radically different conclusions, the Senate having a Republican majority, the House being controlled by Democrats. Nevertheless, between them they produced a mountain of evidence, published in a score of volumes, that made the Hayes-Tilden campaign and its aftermath the most closely examined and thoroughly investigated presidential election in the history of the United States. What more could possibly be discovered?

Plenty, Potter and his fellow Democrats believed. Former Republican officials in Florida and Louisiana would testify that they had lied about the intimidation of Black voters and had fraudulently manipulated the vote count. Republican-controlled state returning boards, clothed with the authority to exclude polls, conjured Hayes majorities by rejecting thousands of Tilden ballots, arguing that Black voters had been dragooned into voting Democratic or deterred from voting at all. Potter aimed to prove that their exclusion of Tilden votes constituted electoral fraud, which was aided and abetted by the "visiting statesmen." The latter were a group of eminent Republicans sent to Louisiana and Florida by President Ulysses S. Grant with a view to ensuring an honest count. But these visiting statesmen, Democrats asserted, did not act as impartial observers: they helped local Republicans steal the election.

The investigation singled out John Sherman, Hayes's secretary of the Treasury and a likely contender for the Republican nomination in 1880. In November 1876 Sherman, then a US senator from Ohio, had travelled to New Orleans along with two dozen other Republican worthies. Two weeks after the election, Democrats claimed, he had encouraged two Republican election officials, James E. Anderson and Don A. Weber, to falsely swear that Democrats had carried the majority Black parishes of East Feliciana and West Feliciana by threatening, whipping, and in some cases murdering Blacks, thereby suppressing the Republican vote. In reality, Democrats claimed, the election in those parishes had been peaceful and aboveboard, the Democratic majority fairly earned. Anderson and Weber had made no complaints when they forwarded the returns to New Orleans.

In order to steal the election, Democrats charged, the state's Republican leaders induced the two men to protest against nonexistent Democratic intimidation. This gave the Louisiana Returning Board, comprising four Republicans, a pretext to exclude two parishes that had chalked up overwhelming Democratic majorities. Democrats alleged that Sherman, despite knowing their election complaints to be false, helped Anderson and Weber overcome their scruples by promising them federal jobs as soon as Hayes became president—in effect, bribing the pair. According to Anderson, the Democrats' star witness, the senator even gave the two election supervisors a written guarantee of federal employment, a document that quickly gained notoriety as the "Sherman letter." The Potter Committee expended a good deal of time in a futile effort to track down this document.

Although some Democrats deluded themselves that the new investigation might cause Hayes to be impeached or to resign, most had more limited expectations. They were bent on a mission of political harassment, nothing more, for shortly after the committee began its hearings, the House voted not to dispute Hayes's title to the presidency. In creating the Potter Committee, therefore, Democrats sought not to oust Hayes from the White House but to embarrass the Republican Party in the run-up to the congressional elections of 1878. Some expected the investigation to pave the way for another presidential run by Tilden in 1880. Focusing on Louisiana (the Florida investigation never amounted to much), the Potter Committee attempted to prove that Hayes was the beneficiary of a crooked election that had been achieved by fraudulent counting, false testimony, and bribery.[3]

Rarely has an investigation backfired on the investigators in such an embarrassing fashion. No one could produce the original Sherman letter, only copies of dubious provenance, causing many to doubt that such a document had ever existed. The witnesses upon whom the Democrats relied turned out to be thoroughly untrustworthy. A few were eccentric, even insane. Some were double-dealers and self-confessed perjurers. Others revealed, when in the witness chair, that Democratic agents had tried to buy their testimony. Before the committee concluded its hearings, Anderson, the Democrats' principal witness, recanted his testimony. It then came out that the Tilden campaign had tried to bribe Republican returning-board members and presidential electors, thus forcing the committee to investigate *Democratic* shenanigans.

That the inquiry rebounded against the Democrats came as no surprise to some Tilden supporters. They knew that neither party had clean hands regarding the 1876 election and advised against setting up the investigation in the first place. If they were forced to testify, one of them warned Samuel J. Randall, Speaker of the House, the men around Tilden would either "commit perjury, or by telling the truth . . . disgrace themselves and ruin the party." The editor of the fervently Democratic *New York World* described the investigation as "an act of the greatest folly."[4]

The story of the Potter Committee is a convoluted tale of political skullduggery, with some form of truth eventually emerging. The hearings, observed the *New York Herald,* were "as full of surprises as a sensation play or novel." Hardened reporters listened spellbound as witnesses spun fantastic tales and dropped proverbial bombshells. Spectators in the committee room erupted in laughter at the unconscious cynicism of witnesses and the rapier-like repartee between questioners and questioned. Adding to the drama was the courtroom atmosphere. Congressional hearings of that time bore little resemblance to the soundbites and grandstanding that characterize today's televised hearings. Most members of the Potter Committee were experienced trial lawyers, and they cross-examined witnesses as a terrier shakes a rat. Goaded into outbursts of temper, forced to make damaging admissions or incredible denials, few witnesses escaped with reputations intact.[5]

Entertainment value aside, the Potter Committee hearings shone a light on the behind-the-scenes negotiations and political maneuvering that led to what became known as the Compromise of 1877. The talks between Hayes's confidantes and a number of southern Democrats, which commenced in December 1876 and concluded in February 1877, had been surrounded by rumor and speculation. What exactly transpired on February 26, when the two sides met at Washington's Wormley House hotel to nail down an agreement? Dribs and drabs of information had trickled out, but not the complete story.

What happened *after* the Wormley House meeting, however, was clear. First, Democrats in the House of Representatives ended the delaying tactics that had slowed Congress's counting of the electoral college votes, thus smoothing the way for Hayes's timely inauguration on March 5. Second, the new president, just weeks into his term of office, undermined Louisiana's Republican state legislature, withdrew military protection from Governor Stephen B. Packard, and recognized the Democratic claimants who had employed an illegal militia force to occupy New Orleans. The insurrectionists who installed an illegal legislature, seized the state supreme-court building, and inaugurated Francis R. T. Nicholls as governor thus became Louisiana's legal administration. The two actions—the counting in of Hayes and the latter's abandonment of Packard—looked suspiciously like a quid pro quo.

The men privy to the Wormley House talks therefore had every reason to keep mum, for the upshot of their agreement angered large swathes of their own political parties. The Republicans involved had promised to acquiesce in the Democratic coup d'état in Louisiana, and a great many other Republicans regarded that promise as a gross betrayal. The Democrats had agreed not to hold up Hayes's inauguration, even though Tilden had, on the basis of votes cast, easily carried Louisiana. A pragmatic response to a set of knotty political problems, the Wormley House talks were sensitive conversations, as the participants to it well knew, about which the less said the better.

Historians still debate whether these talks consummated a political deal or merely confirmed an inescapable reality. They differ, too, as to whether the Compromise of 1877 constituted a compromise at all in any substantive sense. Contemporaries, however, strongly suspected that some kind of behind-the-scenes agreement had been sealed. And their suspicions were correct. Southern Democrats conveyed the message to Hayes, just weeks after the election, that they were less interested in pressing Tilden's claim to the White House than in securing "home rule"—that is, ending Republican government in Louisiana and South Carolina and preventing further federal intervention in favor of southern Republicans. Hayes, for his part, indicated that he was willing to accede to this demand. He might have followed the policy he pursued regardless; we shall never know.[6]

The demand for the Potter inquiry came from Democrats still smarting over Tilden's defeat and Republicans who were angered by Hayes's abandonment of Reconstruction. The investigation thus proceeded on two tracks. In the first, the Democratic majority sought to demonstrate that the Republican Party had stolen the presidency from Tilden, with the Republican minority vigorously rebutting that charge. In the second, Ben Butler, a Republican congressman in the process of leaving his party, searched for evidence that Hayes had bought off Democratic obstructionists by promising to transfer political control of Louisiana from the legally elected Republican Party to the insurrectionary Democratic Party. Republican opposition to this dishonorable transaction, Butler believed, had been quieted with money and patronage.

The truth, as is usually the case, was more complicated. Neither Butler nor the Democratic committee members found the kind of documentary evidence that might have clinched their arguments. Still, the parade of witnesses that appeared before the Potter Committee revealed much about the nitty-gritty of Gilded Age politics—more, in some ways, than any number of party platforms or campaign speeches.

The history of the Potter Committee illustrates, too, the close connection between politics and journalism. Newspapers not only reported and commented on the hearings—reproducing column after closely printed column of verbatim testimony within twenty-four hours—but also shaped the investigation itself. Indeed, the partisan duel was as much a contest between two newspapers, the *New York Sun* and the *New York Tribune,* as between Democrats and Republicans on the committee.

With its history of lacerating criticism of the Grant administration and dogged pursuit of political scandal, the *Sun* became a repository for scuttlebutt and damaging information, much of it supplied by Republicans from Louisiana, regarding "the great fraud of 1876." The *Sun,* under editor Charles A. Dana, pushed hard for another congressional investigation. When that investigation began, the *Sun*'s Washington correspondent, Albert M. Gibson, who several years earlier had exposed the Crédit Mobilier bribery scandal, one of the great exposés of its time, acted as the committee's unofficial manager and adviser.[7]

The staunchly Republican *Tribune* not only ridiculed the investigation but also derailed it. In the summer of 1878, owner-editor Whitelaw Reid found himself the recipient of about four hundred telegrams that had passed between the managers of Tilden's presidential campaign in New York and their agents in Florida, South Carolina, and Louisiana. Half of the dispatches, written in plain English, were innocuous; the other half were written in code. These were passed to Reid by his friend William E. Chandler, a Republican from New Hampshire who, although holding no elective office, moved in the party's inner circles. It was Chandler, chiefly, who secured Florida for Hayes in the election, but he had since become the president's fiercest Republican critic. (The convoluted story of how he came into possession of the telegrams is told in chapter 7.) In the kind of scoop that editors dream about, the *Tribune* succeeded in deciphering the coded messages. These "cipher dispatches" furnished irrefutable evidence that Tilden's managers, including his own nephew, William T. Pelton, had tried to bribe Republican election officials in the disputed states.

The *Tribune*'s revelations sent shockwaves across the country. They compelled the Potter Committee to do the exact opposite of what its sponsors intended, forcing an investigation of the Democrats, including Tilden himself. If the testimony failed to conclusively prove the candidate's personal knowledge of his nephew's attempts at bribery, it was sufficiently damaging to scupper the New Yorker's chances of being renominated by the Democratic Party in 1880.

If the Potter Committee blew up in the faces of its Democratic sponsors and left Hayes and Sherman unscathed, its revelations presented both parties in a less than flattering light. The hearings showed that Hayes's surrogates were willing to take Louisiana's electoral votes to get their man into the White House while casting adrift the very Republicans who had delivered those votes. They showed that the Hayes administration, for all its talk of civil-service reform, made ruthless use of the spoils system to cover its tracks. They revealed Louisiana's Republican politicians as a set of amoral office seekers who gave little more than lip service to the interests of their Black constituents. The Democrats, however, were exposed as far more unscrupulous. They intimidated Black voters, engaged in bribery, suborned perjury, justified murder, and made promises they had no intention of keeping. The hearings lifted up a political stone, and what crawled underneath was not pretty.

The extremes to which each side resorted, however—coercion on the one side and fraud on the other—reflected the gravity of the issues in play. Political contests in the South were not a simple matter of "ins" and "outs" taking turns in government. Democrats were fighting to vindicate their "honor," which entailed restoring white supremacy by establishing their dominance over the Black population. That conception of "honor" justified a multitude of sins, including the resort to lies and violence. Once in power, Democrats had no intention of relinquishing it. Republicans were struggling to retain the perquisites of office, to be sure, but they believed themselves to be defending a Union dedicated to democracy and equal citizenship. Few thought that the Republican Party in the region could survive a Democratic victory: "carpetbaggers" would be forced to leave the South, Blacks would be subjected to further oppression, and election results would bear no resemblance to the way people actually voted, or might have voted if elections were free and fair. Both Republicans and Democrats convinced themselves that desperate times demanded desperate measures. "Nobody flinched on either side," observed "Gath" (George Alfred Townsend) of the *Cincinnati Enquirer*, "because at such times partisanship and patriotism are interchangeable terms."[8]

Republican fears were not misplaced. Hayes's inauguration, followed by his recognition of the Nicholls administration, left Louisiana's Republicans in a desperate position. The president not only abandoned the Republican state government but also awarded much of the federal patronage to Democratic jobseekers. True, he tried to cushion the blow by finding federal positions, many of them outside Louisiana, for the party's displaced leaders. But he could not accommodate the host of minor officials who now found themselves out in the cold. Nor could he protect those Republican witnesses, most of them Black, who had testified to Democratic intimidation. Some of them, afraid to return home, were marooned in New Orleans. Others went back to reclaim their homes and property and were murdered by vengeful Democrats. Still others believed that they had purchased Democratic "protection" by recanting their testimony and humbling themselves, only to be driven out again and, in at least one case, lynched. Hence the private talks that smoothed the way for Hayes's accession to the presidency facilitated a turning point in American history: the end of Congressional Reconstruction and the beginning of the Jim Crow era.

This is not a full account of the disputed presidential election of 1876. That controversy has been well covered in books by Paul Haworth, C. Vann Woodward, Keith Ian Polakoff, and Michael F. Holt as well in scholarly articles by Allan Peskin, Michael Les Benedict, and others. This study, rather, focuses on the Democratic-led investigation into the election in Louisiana. Then, as with the Potter hearings themselves, its spotlight shifts to the cipher dispatches and the sins of the Tilden campaign.

The Potter Committee consisted of white men, and most of the key witnesses were also white men. Yet the experience and testimony of Black citizens, including several women, provided the key to the investigation. It is therefore crucial to establish the extent to which that testimony confirmed the lived experience of the Black witnesses. Hence the first chapter examines the "facts on the ground" in East and West Feliciana Parishes during the two years leading up the election and how those facts comported with the allegations of James E. Anderson, the supervisor of registration for East Feliciana Parish. It was Anderson's untruthful complaint about Democratic intimidation, the majority report concluded, that enabled the Louisiana Returning Board to reject enough Democratic votes to elect Hayes. This logic resembled that of the old saying, "for the want of a nail . . . the battle was lost," with Anderson deliberately withholding the crucial nail. Yet his retrospective claim that the complaint had been a deliberate lie—one encouraged by Republican leaders up to and including Senator Sherman—could only be corroborated by his alleged partner-in-fraud, Don Weber, the supervisor of registration in West Feliciana Parish. And Weber, conveniently for Anderson, was dead.[9]

Politicians are fond of quoting a saying attributed to Otto von Bismarck: "Laws are like sausages—it is best not to see them being made." The observation could well be applied to politics in general. The politicians of that time were no more cynical, unprincipled, or dishonest than those of our own. The following study, however, focuses not on the sausage but on the sausage making.

As the title of this book suggests, that sausage making included multiple stolen elections. In carrying Louisiana through the application of "bulldozing," Democrats stole both the state and presidential elections. Through the machinations of the Louisiana Returning Board, Republicans stole them back. Louisiana's Democrats then seized power through force, a coup tolerated by Grant and confirmed by Hayes, making yet another mockery of the 1876 election. This fifth and final "steal" proved the most decisive in the long run, for the damage it wrought was irreversible. Nearly a hundred years would pass before Louisiana mounted a free and fair election based on universal suffrage.

1

BULLDOZERS

HOW DEMOCRATS STOLE THE LOUISIANA ELECTION

On August 28, 1876, James E. Anderson arrived in East Feliciana Parish to take up his position as supervisor of registration, which paid the princely sum of five dollars a day. The most striking thing about Anderson, upon a first view, was his hair. Everyone remarked upon his thick mat of russet curls and bushy red mustache. A little conversation revealed that this blue-eyed, boyish-looking twenty-nine-year-old was voluble, excitable, and quick tempered. Spend more time with him, and another characteristic was hard to miss: a fondness for whiskey, liberally indulged. Discounting the cliché of red-headed men having fiery tempers, the combination of whiskey and volatility made Anderson a fighting drunk. "I hold myself in readiness to shoot or drink," he boasted, "as the occasion may demand." One such occasion demanded a fistfight with the parish judge, Thomas B. Lyons, a Democrat. "I think he was the aggressor," Lyons recalled. "When he got two or three drinks he got bellicose."[1]

Don A. Weber, the supervisor of registration in neighboring West Feliciana Parish, was a man of more temperate habits and did not require alcohol to indulge his temper. In common with many native-born white Republicans ("scalawags"), he was loath to let a personal insult go unchallenged. The previous year he had engaged in a fistfight with Col. Robert H. Barrow, a Democrat, when the two men exchanged words in a store. "He beat the old man terribly," recalled Don's elder brother, Emile. Don and Emile—called "Big Weber and Little Weber" for their comparative height rather than their age—were the French-speaking sons of a German-born father and a Creole mother. Mainstays of the Republican Party in West Feliciana Parish since 1868, the Weber brothers were fiercely competitive and in 1872 had a bitter and very public falling-out. They "did not agree very well," remembered former governor William P. Kellogg in 1878. "For many years there was a feud between them." The estrangement abated somewhat when Don and Emile married sisters and became involved in their father-in-law's mercantile business. In 1876, moreover, political self-interest demanded a common front, especially when local Democrats threatened them both.[2]

As defined by state law, the duties of a supervisor of registration were to enroll voters during the two months preceding Election Day, arrange for polling places, and ensure an orderly and honest election. He could appoint two paid clerks to assist him, one or more special constables to keep order at each polling place, and three unpaid commissioners of elections (local citizens "from different political parties") to oversee the balloting in each ward. After the polls closed, the supervisor must tally the votes and then send the returns to New Orleans. If anything untoward took place during the registration period or on the polling day itself, he needed to accompany the returns with a report, commonly called a "protest," of what had occurred. Such reports must be attached to the returns "by paste, wax, or some adhesive substance" so that everything "can be kept together." A registrar's protest needed to be supported by three local citizens in the form of sworn affidavits.[3]

Then there were the unofficial duties. Like all the other registrars, Anderson and Weber owed their positions to the fact that they served the Republican Party. The Republican State Committee, a de facto arm of the state government, expected registrars to cooperate with their local party in fielding candidates and maximizing Republican turnout. Instructing them "to register and vote the full strength of the Republican party in your parish," the state committee assumed that virtually all Blacks were loyal Republicans and that "full strength" was equivalent to the number of voting-age Black men as recorded in the state census of 1875. In the "bad old days" of 1872, when renegade Republican governor Henry Clay Warmoth had brazenly rigged the election, many of the supervisors had been candidates for the state legislature, affording both the motive and the means to manipulate the vote. In 1876 the committee tried to motivate supervisors by promising "ample and generous recognition" to those who delivered the desired results. The recognition in question would take the form of a job in the US Custom House in New Orleans or some other state or federal sinecure.[4]

In accepting the position of supervisor, Don Weber took a calculated risk. Such was the poisonous political climate that few white Republicans living in the country parishes coveted the appointment. The danger was not that supervisors would suffer Democratic violence in the course of fulfilling their official duties, but rather that passions aroused by the campaign would leave them vulnerable to retaliation *after* the election. "Bulldozing"—the expulsion of Republican officials through the application of threats and violence—had become a common Democratic tactic. Even a temporary exile, if one was forced to flee, could be economically calamitous. The possibility of assassination was also real. Still, Don had an obvious incentive to mobilize the Republican vote in West Feliciana. In 1876 he was the parish tax collector (by appointment), while Emile (usually referred to as "E. L.") held a seat in the state senate representing the three-parish district of Pointe Coupee, East Feliciana, and West Feliciana.

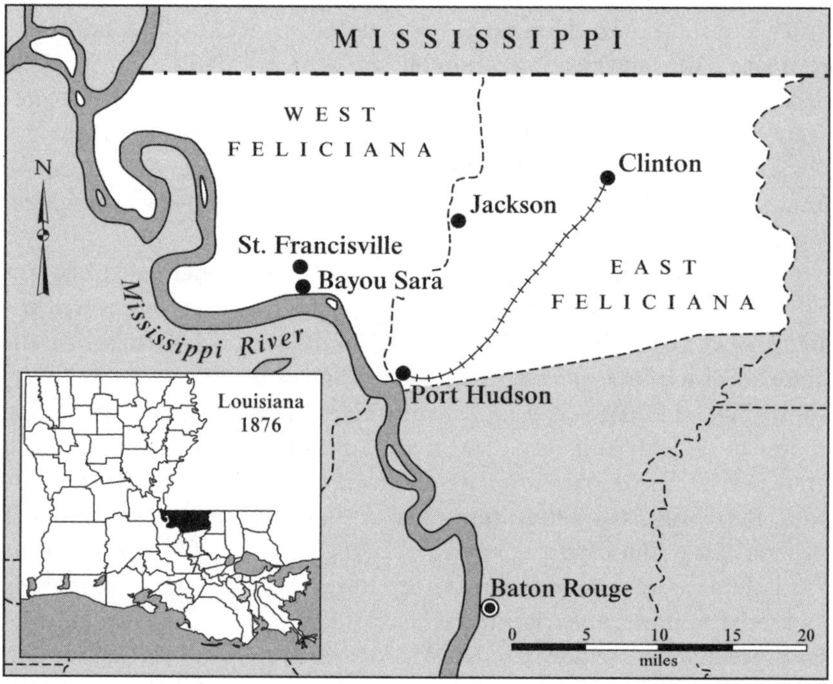

Anderson was more typical of the supervisors in 1876—a clerk in the New Orleans Custom House. This "granite pile," which occupied an entire city block near the foot of Canal Street, had become the employer of last resort for jobless journalists, unsuccessful lawyers, failed businessmen, displaced politicians, and general layabouts. The only qualification was loyalty to the Republican Party, as expressed by attending political conventions, taking part in campaigns, and paying "assessments" from their salary into party coffers. Born in Lancaster County, Pennsylvania,

Anderson had worked as a printer and then a journalist; he moved from Philadelphia to New Orleans at the urging of Congressman J. Hale Sypher, a fellow Pennsylvanian, to write for a Republican newspaper. For the past few years, he had rarely set foot outside the Crescent City except for a stint as Washington correspondent for the *New Orleans Republican.* Anderson's knowledge of Louisiana's rural hinterland was sketchy. But, having lost his position on the *Republican,* he was available. With nominal duties and few working hours, Custom House employees like Anderson stood ready to engage in political work whenever party leaders called upon them. For the Republican campaign managers, these men had another thing in their favor: they would be returning to New Orleans when the election was over. That made them less vulnerable to intimidation or reprisals by local Democrats.[5]

Anderson's temperament and habits made him singularly ill-suited for his assignment. East Feliciana Parish presented the most difficult challenge imaginable. Along with its westerly neighbor, it was the least hospitable parish to the Republican cause in the entire state. For more than a year before Anderson's arrival, Democrats had conducted a terrorist campaign against local Republicans. Calling for all-out political warfare, the *Clinton Patriot-Democrat* invoked "a higher law . . . the law of civilization," which justified whites "taking the control of public matters in their own hands." With the ability to mobilize mounted, well-armed bands at a moment's notice, and with the potential to enlist virtually every able-bodied white man in the locality, Democrats could overawe the Black majority and, if they saw fit, eliminate troublesome individuals. No longer would they permit Black officeholders to wield power. Blacks who continued to vote Republican were treated as enemies.[6]

Posing at first as nonpolitical "regulators" who sought to curb cotton stealing and the theft of livestock, bands of white men whipped Black sharecroppers and burned merchant's stores. The same armed bands, now known as "bulldozers," went on to all but destroy the Republican parish government. They forced Black elected officials to resign or flee; broke up the district court, warning the Republican judge never to return; and shot and wounded Sheriff Henry Smith, a Black man, driving him into exile.[7]

On October 13, 1875, a band of one hundred whites abducted a prisoner from a sheriff's posse and shot him to ribbons. The victim, John Gair, was a former state legislator and once the most influential Black politician in East Feliciana. The members of the lynching party had been so confident of their invincibility that they eschewed disguises. Later that night the body of Gair's sister-in-law, Catherine "Babe" Matthews, could be seen hanging from a tree in Clinton's courthouse square. Like Gair, the eighteen-year-old girl had been in custody before being lynched. Gair and Matthews were suspected of poisoning the latter's employer, Dr. J. W. Saunders, a prominent bulldozer who had been instrumental in driving Gair out of the parish. The alcoholic doctor, who survived the alleged poisoning, made sure that the pair never stood trial.[8]

At the beginning of 1876, Democrats in East Feliciana determined upon not merely defeating the Republican Party but also demolishing it. It was not enough that Black voters should be deterred from voting, they should be compelled to vote the Democratic ticket, thus making a double contribution to Republican defeat at the state level. To this end, white landlords dragooned their employees into Democratic "clubs." Their means of persuasion were not subtle. The experience of William Hansbury was typical, his employer addressing him thus: "If you fellows go to work here and vote for your radical government over us, do you reckon you are going to stay here amongst us? . . . The white men in this country are not going to stand for it. Why don't you attend the [Democratic] meetings?" Hansbury got the message. "I seen that I was protected by voting the Democratic ticket," he recalled. "I was afraid I wouldn't be allowed to stay on my place, and I went and joined a [Democratic] club."[9]

Democrats also employed more forceful methods. The most prominent Black Republicans—teachers, ward leaders, and potential candidates for office—were subjected to direct threats, nighttime visitations, whippings, and mock lynchings. Monroe Meyers, president of a ward club since 1868, refused at first to quit the Republican Party. But he joined a Democratic club after a band of armed men hauled him out of bed one night and browbeat him. "I wanted to lay down in peace and get up in peace," he later explained. "I had a family, and wanted to maintain them." The few holdouts went into hiding, fled to Pointe Coupee Parish on the other side of the Mississippi River, or traveled all the way to New Orleans.[10]

The mass conscription of Black voters stemmed from the flat failure of previous Democratic appeals for their support. Assembling in their own churches and ward clubs, Blacks had insulated themselves from the blandishments and threats of white Democrats. "They had their secret societies, and would not admit their old masters," explained parish judge Thomas B. Lyons. "They would listen to them on all other subjects but politics." In the Democratic clubs, however, Blacks constituted a captive audience; they did not *speak up* but were *spoken to*. Democratic speakers, often their employers, proffered stick and carrot. Blacks who stuck with the Republicans would face consequences (the threat did not need to be explicit), while those who sided with their Democratic "friends" could sleep safely in their beds. As Lyons put it, "The argument of protection had the greatest effect"—Democrats were proposing to shield Blacks from the very violence that Democrats were perpetrating. D. C. Hardee, a lawyer and former Confederate colonel, put the matter as delicately as he could: "I stated that disorder would continue to prevail under the government we had, and that we had to look for a good governor in order to get order and peace." It was a none-too-subtle version of "bad cop, good cop."[11]

Democrats threatened Republican leaders to their faces. Hardee advised ex-Freedman's Bureau agent James De Grey to quit politics. "You have been making officers and unmaking them for the last ten years," he told him, "and you must stop it." Otherwise, the Democrat added, De Grey's life "would not be worth a snap of his finger." Former state legislator James Law related that a Democrat named Camp Catlett warned him not to stand for reelection as treasurer of the state insane asylum. "We have decided that no more Republicans shall hold office in this parish."[12]

In August Judge Hugh J. Campbell of New Orleans visited East Feliciana Parish to discuss the upcoming campaign. Law was sufficiently nervous that he disguised his reason for traveling to Clinton, telling the president of the Democratic ward club merely that he "had some business" there. Two of the Black ward leaders in Jackson flatly refused to go at all: both men had joined Democratic clubs under duress; one had been tortured. The meeting with Campbell took place in the backroom of the tax collector's office, and Law tried to slip in and out unobserved. But Democrats in Jackson, including the town's mayor, knew about Campbell's mission and the reason for Law's absence. When confronted, Law promised to abandon all involvement with the Republican Party. He would not even vote. "I was afraid," he recalled. "I was absolutely afraid."[13]

The outlook for Republicans in neighboring West Feliciana Parish was, if anything, still bleaker. John S. Dula, the parish judge and son of a slave woman and her white owner, saw a mob burn down his merchant's store in October 1875. He fled the parish and stayed away for three months. In January 1876 Democrats held a mass meeting that demanded Dula's resignation, along with those of the sheriff, tax collector, state legislator, state senator, and "all ignorant and incompetent police jurors, justices of the peace, and constables." On May 1 fifty-some Democrats, "with pistols buckled outside their coats," crowded the courtroom at Saint Francisville and compelled four Republican police jurors to quit. The Republican sheriff sat by impotently. A nearby company of US troops did nothing. Blacks felt besieged.[14]

Retaliation proved very costly. On May 11 someone in a crowd of Black men shot and killed Max Aaronson, the owner of a merchant's store located along the railroad just inside the border with Mississippi. The homicide might have been unintentional, but the gang certainly wished to punish Aaronson for having beaten a sharecropper accused of cattle theft. Whites from West Feliciana, "every man who was able to bear a gun," thereupon rode into Mississippi and joined a sheriff's posse in hunting down the mob that killed Aaronson. Encountering an armed band that greeted them with gunfire, the whites responded with massive violence, killing between twenty and thirty people. Two of that group's leaders, Ben King and Duncan Gaines, were summarily hanged for Aaronson's murder after what the *New Orleans Daily Picayune* termed "a careful investigation" that lasted all of two days. Once again federal forces, this time the commander of the US Army post at Bayou Sara, Captain G. M. Bascom, did nothing. The disturbances took place in Mississippi, he explained, and he was uncertain as to his authority to act. Besides, the captain added, his men had no horses, and it would have taken them an entire day to march the twenty-two miles.[15]

Prominent Republicans fled. Teacher J. R. Watson closed his school on the Acklen estate at Tunica and took the boat to Bayou Sara. Finding that town full of armed whites, flush with triumph from their punitive expedition to Mississippi, he stayed on the boat until it docked in New Orleans. State Senator E. L. Weber, State Representative J. W. Armstead, and Deputy Sheriff George Swayze crossed the river to Pointe Coupee Parish and found refuge with Milton Jones, a Black farmer and member of the state legislature. Jones took Weber to a nearby landing, where he boarded a steamboat to New Orleans. The Weber brothers beseeched Governor Kellogg not to appoint any Democrats to the police juries of East and West Feliciana Parishes "when the courts and civil officers are powerless."[16]

White employers told their hands to quit the Republican Party and punished those who refused. Captain John J. Barrow instructed the manager of Greenwood plantation to assemble the men and tell them to join his Democratic club. Sixty-three of seventy-five employees affixed their signatures to the membership roll or made their marks. Three of the twelve holdouts were whipped by regulators. A fourth, L. T. Cotton, the Republican leader in the Tenth Ward, was threatened by Barrow himself. Cotton reluctantly signed up and told the others to do the same. "The boys did as I instructed them to do," he later explained. "They had to do it to save their lives." Barrow insisted that Cotton, a preacher, give Democratic speeches, which he did reluctantly. Asked later why he put up with Barrow's browbeating, Cotton explained southern realities to US Senator Samuel J. R. McMillan, a Republican from Minnesota: "A man's life in that parish at that time was not worth any more than that [snapping his finger and thumb]. . . . I was afraid to resent anything."[17]

The suppression of Republican clubs continued apace. Meeting after church on a Sunday evening early in July, a dozen young men from the Flower, Smith, and Barrow plantations decided to organize a ward club. One of the group told his employer, Charles Barrow, that the club, headed by Gilbert Carter, proposed to shoot the chief regulators at the next "dark of the moon." The intended victims, the informant claimed, included Barrow himself. Taken to the army post by Barrow's elderly father, the informant repeated his story to Captain Bascom, who declared that this was not a matter for the army. The officer raised no objection, however, when Barrow suggested that local whites deal with the matter themselves. Despite the proposed action being "irregular," the captain reasoned, the party would consist of "gentlemen . . . of character, education, and property." He ordered one of his lieutenants to accompany them.

On the night of July 11, a fifty-strong party of whites raided cabins on the Flower place. Beating down doors and dragging men from their beds, they demanded to know who was involved in the alleged plot. Riley Norfliss found himself astride a horse, a rope connecting his neck to a tree limb, a cocked pistol pointed at his face, and the man with the gun telling him, "By God, say your prayers." Norfliss protested that he "didn't hear nothing about killing white men." Carter, too, was subjected to a mock lynching. The whites then marched Norfliss, Carter, Isaac Vessel, Thomas Stewart, and Daniel Johnson to Charles Barrow's place. When one of the guards asked, "Where's the best place to hang these sons of bitches?," three of the captives made a break for it. Norfliss and Vessel got away, but a double blast from a shotgun felled Carter. "Hallo, by God, this fellow's pulse is beating yet," one of the whites noticed, whereupon Barrow coolly shot him in the head. The following day Vessel surrendered to Barrow, the latter wringing from him a confession that Carter's club had been bent on murder and mayhem. Taken before Captain Bascom, Vessel repeated this false statement. "I knew that I was swearing to a lie," he later explained, "but to save my life I did it."[18]

Fifty years later, shortly before he died, Charles Barrow boasted of how his gang of bulldozers had kept Blacks in a permanent state of apprehension by riding through the various plantations at night, yelling, banging on doors, and discharging firearms. "Occasionally there were a few necks broken," he admitted, "and straps used against the worst." So intimidating were these nocturnal visitations that the sight of a dozen or more white men on horseback, whatever the time of day, caused some Blacks to down tools and run, others to freeze "like they appeared to be scared to death." Some took to sleeping in the woods. As many as two hundred Black Republicans from the Feliciana parishes sought refuge across the river or in New Orleans.[19]

In the months leading up to his appointment as supervisor, Don Weber faced mounting pressure from Democrats to remove himself from politics. At the beginning of 1876, a mass meeting of Democrats demanded his resignation as tax collector and delegated the Rev. A. G. Bakewell, pastor of Saint John's Episcopal Church, to urge him to leave. If he refused to step down and remained in the parish, the minister warned, his life would be in danger. Weber refused to be "bulldozed," but he took precautions. "I never went out after dark. I bought side-arms. I had a shot-gun which I repaired." On the first day of registration, John Barrow bluntly told Weber that no Republican leaders would be permitted to canvass.[20]

James Anderson adopted a tone of jaunty bravado when he reported on the anxiety felt by Republicans in East Feliciana Parish. Democrats appeared to think that "fear of what may occur in the future would induce anyone living in the parish to do as they might dictate," he wrote Lieutenant Governor C. C. Antoine. But Anderson assured Antoine that he was made of sterner stuff. Registration was proceeding slowly, he confessed, but "I am getting the party together . . . and will soon have a parish ticket in the field." The Democrats would like to run him out, he claimed, but they realized that bulldozing the registrar would only damage their cause. "I am going to win this fight," he vowed.[21]

Behind this display of optimism, however, Anderson was despondent. "It is simply impossible to organize our party in this parish," he complained to Don Weber. The Democrats were thoroughly organized and "working like beavers," while local Republicans appeared unwilling or unable to get up a slate of candidates. Anderson attributed this paralysis to disagreements between the party's white and Black leaders—the whites insisting that "the 'niggers' are kept in the background," the Blacks refusing to submit to white leaders whom they distrusted. The tension reflected lingering bitterness caused by a violent faction fight that had split the party two years earlier, the history of which Anderson appeared ignorant. But the dominant factor was the one he identified in his report to Antoine—fear.[22]

"We could not organize a Republican club," De Grey recalled. "I don't think it would have been safe." Henry Marston, an eighty-two-year-old merchant and banker, a pillar of East Feliciana's white community for fifty years, affirmed the veracity of the many Republicans who later testified to congressional committees. When a congressman asked him if Black men were intimidated, Marston simply referred him to their testimony: "Didn't one man tell you the other day that if he had not voted the Democratic ticket he would have been driven out of the parish?" Daniel J. Wedge, a staunch Democrat, admitted, "There have been some cases [of whipping] where the motive could be traced to political causes."[23]

Wounded and frightened Blacks took their stories to the army post at Clinton, where a company had been stationed since July. They told of being compelled to join Democratic clubs, of being too afraid to sleep in their homes, of being threatened, and of being whipped. Captain Benjamin H. Rogers saw one man, whom he had previously listened to and sent on his way, return two days later displaying a badly beaten head. Another man, Zeke Glover, was whipped so severely that his back "was almost cut to pieces." His offense had been to collect Republican newspapers from the post office shortly before the election and read them to Blacks on the plantations. Lieutenant William S. Davies saw the same parade of scared and battered people, many of them too apprehensive to make out formal complaints. As to the feasibility of mounting a Republican campaign, Davies stated, "I would not have done it myself without my uniform."[24]

The sole public meeting held by Republicans in East Feliciana Parish took place on September 15 in Clinton. This was a stop in the statewide canvass by gubernatorial candidate Stephen B. Packard and his team of speakers. After arriving the previous afternoon, Packard's group became apprehensive. Local Republicans had done nothing to publicize the event, leaving it to James Lewis, the only Black member of the candidate's team, to send messengers into the countryside to drum up a crowd.[25]

J. P. Harris, one of the visiting speakers, got a further insight into what

Republicans were up against when he found himself in a local drugstore surrounded by hostile Democrats. He was acting as the emissary of Anderson, who had gotten himself into a quarrel with a "drummer," or traveling salesman. After the ritual back-and-forth of notes demanding that the other man apologize, Anderson demanded "satisfaction" (southern code-of-honor talk for a duel), and Harris agreed to carry his challenge to the drummer. After Harris entered Collins's drugstore, which doubled as the Democratic campaign headquarters, the leading bulldozers of the parish trooped in and proceeded to browbeat him. "If you raise a row here," warned Dr. Saunders, "there is not one of you who will get away alive." Withdrawing Anderson's challenge and apologizing profusely, Harris managed to extricate himself. Apart from making Harris sweat, the incident supplied further evidence of Anderson's unfitness for his job as registrar. "When under the influence of strong liquors," Democratic leaders complained, he became "turbulent, quarrelsome, and insulting."[26]

When they heard Harris's account of this one-sided confrontation, Packard's party became thoroughly alarmed. J. Henri Burch of Baton Rouge, a Black man and state senator, sought refuge at the army post and never gave his speech. Others stayed up all night lest they be attacked while asleep. De Grey and John C. Reilly, the most prominent white Republicans in the parish, declined to chair the meeting, leaving that job to James Law.[27]

About four hundred Blacks showed up at the courthouse square the following morning. Almost as many whites were present, many displaying pistols and a good few inebriated. These Democrats had come to "spot" (identify) any Blacks at the meeting, but mostly they came to disrupt and intimidate. They interrupted, heckled, jeered, and insulted the speakers. One man "pulled out his pistol," Harris recalled, "calling me a d——d liar."[28]

The most tense moment came when Lewis, in the course of his speech, stated that Blacks had no desire to intrude upon whites socially, but they did not wish whites to intrude upon them either, "as they used to do before the war, unbidden." This reference to the sexual exploitation of enslaved women drew the drunken ire of Dr. Saunders. "You are a damned liar," he bellowed, "you just take it back." It was hardly a secret that white men had fathered children with slaves, and Lewis, pointing out his light skin, referenced his own provenance as the son of a Mississippi slaveholder. "It don't make no difference, damn you," Saunders retorted. "You must not tell these niggers anything of that kind." Lewis "thought it advisable" to retract his statement. He might not have recognized Saunders as a leading bulldozer, whose alleged poisoning had prompted the killings of two innocent Blacks, but knew that Babe Matthews, one of the two, had been lynched in the very square in which he was speaking.[29]

"It was not pleasant at all," recalled Reilly, a Presbyterian minister, of that mass meeting. Packard and his team agreed. They had planned to go on to Jackson for another rally, but they wanted out of East Feliciana Parish. Telegraphing for a special train to collect them in Clinton, they proceeded to Port Hudson.[30]

In an effort to palliate Democratic opposition and secure at least some Republican representation, Anderson and De Grey offered local Democrats a "mixed ticket." They suggested that Republicans would support a Democrat for the position of parish judge if Democrats permitted Republicans to run for minor offices. Democrats rejected the offer. Having staged a primary election that excluded Black voters, they had already signaled their determination to bring about a clean sweep. And they could only achieve that result by completely suppressing the Republican vote. Democrats felt confident that they would carry the parish with a majority of one thousand votes—a majority that would consist of ballots cast by Blacks.[31]

Making the same prediction, Anderson tried to negotiate his own deal with the Democrats. As early as September 1—a mere three days into his job as supervisor of registration—he confided to a friend, "nothing but a desire to help Nash's interests induces me to remain." Charles E. Nash, a Black Union veteran who had lost a leg in the war, was the Republican congressman who represented Louisiana's Sixth District. He looked to Anderson to promote his reelection. If successful, and if Hayes won the presidency, Nash would reward him with a lucrative federal sinecure. Anderson was angling for the plum position of naval officer in New Orleans. He proposed to local Democrats that he deliver East Feliciana's Black vote to all the Democratic candidates for parish offices as well as their candidate for the state senate. In return, he asked them to back Nash's reelection. They would be a "set of damn fools," he told Colonel S. J. N. Smith, a member of the Democratic state campaign committee, if they refused his offer. The Returning Board, he explained, would throw out the East Feliciana returns in their entirety if the Republican vote were suppressed. But the Democrats rejected his overture. They had Black voters thoroughly cowed: why concede anything, especially a prize such as a seat in Congress?[32]

On October 12 Anderson abruptly resigned his position and returned to New Orleans. A few days earlier, he explained, he and another Republican, John Pilant, had set off in a buggy from Jackson to Clinton when someone tried to assassinate the supervisor. According to Anderson, a shot rang out in the dark, the horse reared, the carriage veered off the road, and he tumbled out. Another shot then holed his coat. Pilant drove off in the buggy, leaving him hiding in a ditch. Anderson made his way to Clinton on foot and reported the incident to the sheriff.[33]

Republicans and Democrats alike were baffled by Anderson's story. Sheriff James Monahan inspected the site of the alleged attack in the company of Captain Rogers and local Republicans De Grey and Frank Powers. They came away none the wiser. Anderson asserted that a bullet had gone through his coat and pierced some letters he was carrying, but his claim evoked skepticism. How could a bullet trace such a trajectory without touching his body? Rogers tried on the jacket to see if it could be done and decided that it might just be possible. But he knew of Anderson's tenuous relationship with the truth—"I could not believe him under oath in any way, shape, or form"—and was disinclined to give him the benefit of the doubt. This was a man, he later testified, who was "liable to shoot at his own coat in order to make political capital out of it." The fact that Pilant and Anderson were inebriated at the time of the alleged attack—they had imbibed all afternoon and left Jackson with two bottles of whiskey between them—made Anderson's claim doubly implausible. The sheriff found it hard to get a sensible word out of Pilant: he "looked like a man who had been on a terrible spree. . . . He almost had delirium tremens." Anderson's state can readily be imagined.[34]

The story became even murkier when Democrats voiced the suspicion that one of Anderson's clerks, Pierce C. Butler, might have been the shooter. Butler was certainly capable of murder. This former Confederate soldier had a justified reputation for being one of the most violent men in the parish. During the Republican faction fight of 1874, he had acted as a "hired bully" for John Gair, on one occasion shooting up a rival mass meeting and wounding eight men. He was also a killer. His claim to have shot twenty-three men (the number varied in the telling) might have been an exaggeration, but it was not pure braggadocio. Adept with pistol, knife, and cane, Butler once stabbed a man twenty-two times in the space of three minutes. He had recently shot one man dead and wounded another who happened to have been in his line of fire. Anderson described him as "hell on the end of a poker."[35]

How Butler came to occupy the position of assistant registrar is puzzling. A less suitable candidate could scarcely have been found. Perhaps local Republicans thought he could provide Anderson with personal protection. If so, the appointment backfired. Given the pugnacity and drinking habits of both men, the two were bound to clash. Butler was even more of a menace than his boss when drunk: he shot and wounded two fellow Republicans when not even trying. He was not a man to tangle with—but tangle Anderson did. When Butler heard that he was being talked about as Anderson's would-be assassin, he confronted the supervisor. A challenge followed. When Anderson declined it, Butler concluded that he would be justified (according to the southern code) in shooting him on sight. Anderson had had enough: "Finding that there was a determination . . . to get me killed, I made up my mind to leave."[36]

Nobody believed Anderson's account of the nighttime shooting incident. Complaining of the supervisor's absence to Isaac W. Patton, president of the Democratic State Central Committee, Lyons reported that "Anderson himself fired the shot by which his coat was injured" and that "the other shots were fired by a friendly accomplice." Lyons and others attributed Anderson's departure to his "personal difficulty" with Butler, "a rather desperate character." Democrats joked that he had tried to "bull-doze himself."[37]

Republicans, too, found it impossible to swallow Anderson's story. Governor Kellogg forwarded his affidavit to the *New Orleans Republican.* The newspaper normally played up such incidents, but in this case it ridiculed Anderson's story.

> [The] thrilling account of his waylaying, of volleys and musketry fired at him and through his garments, of harsh epithets applied by mysterious horsemen, which whether true or not, have plainly done him no more serious harm than the infliction of a terrible scare. We are sorry that Anderson's feelings have been so torn and mutilated. . . . To take so much time and trouble to accomplish so little damage . . . is calculated to weaken respect for the prowess of the East Feliciana bull-dozers, and we have no reasons for believing that they waste time in that manner.

One of his friends, fellow journalist John Leet, summed up Republican skepticism: "The story seemed like a dime novel."[38]

Representative C. B. Darrall came across Anderson on board the steamboat to New Orleans. "He was really in a terrible condition at that time in every respect, mentally and physically," the congressman recalled. Back in the city, he spent the following two weeks, to quote Darrall again, in a "much dissipated" condition. For all his bravado about refusing to be intimidated, Anderson's flight revealed that he was not only a braggart but also a windbag. Explaining his presence in New Orleans, he told all who had ears to listen that no Republican could be safe in East Feliciana.[39]

But party leaders wanted him back there. US Marshal J. R. G. Pitkin tried to shame Anderson, pointing out that his absence from the parish could be interpreted as cowardice. It made no difference. Kellogg ordered him to resume his supervisor duties and gave him $50 (equivalent to about $1,200 in 2020) to cover his expenses; he drank and gambled the money away. Discovering that Anderson was still in the city on October 31, with the election only a week away, Kellogg gave him a peremptory order, in writing, to return to East Feliciana Parish forthwith. Still he lingered. "I am not going back without money," Anderson confided to a Custom House employee.[40]

In an effort to save face and dispel the imputation of cowardice, Anderson concocted a story that he later told to the Potter Committee. He claimed that the *Republicans,* not the Democrats, had driven him out of East Feliciana and that Kellogg, despite ordering him to return, was determined to keep him in New Orleans. Knowing that the Democrats would carry the parish, Kellogg conspired with De Grey and other local Republicans to have no election, thereby nullifying the solid Democratic vote that would otherwise be cast. As Anderson repeated his story, this alleged conspiracy became ever more sinister. Kellogg, he claimed—the governor of Louisiana!—had ordered his attempted assassination on the road between Jackson and Clinton. According to Anderson, Kellogg was so bent on preventing his return to East Feliciana that he put a man on his tail, instructing the shadow, Lorenzo B. Jenks, to arrest him (any trumped-up charge would do) if he tried to leave the city.[41]

The origins of this fantastic tale can be traced to a comment contained in Anderson's report to Lieutenant Governor Antoine. Democrats in East Feliciana, he wrote on September 3, "are under the impression (conveyed by yours truly) that I was sent here for the express purpose of being killed, in order to make political capital." It was a cynical conviction among Republicans, often expressed in gallows humor, that the party reaped political dividends when they could "wave the bloody shirt." Anderson once joked to J. Henri Burch that "every Negro that was killed in the South was worth $50,000 to the Republicans of the North." Kellogg purportedly told Leet that Anderson would make a "first-class martyr." From such thin threads did Anderson spin the story that the governor coldheartedly sent him to East Feliciana for the purpose of getting killed. Whether he actually believed this story is beside the point: Anderson had a casual approach to truth, equating it with whatever he said at any given time. And whatever the story was, he had to be at its center, an honest soul surrounded by scoundrels.[42]

Kellogg did indeed employ Jenks, a Union veteran and former state senator, to stick close to Anderson. His purpose was to get the supervisor back to East Feliciana Parish so he could organize the election there. When Law saw Kellogg to report on the plight of local Republicans, the governor exploded in frustration, describing Anderson as a "god-damned, red-headed rascal" who "ought to go back up there" but was "scared to death." As things stood, the governor complained, Democrats had everything their own way—"What the hell is the matter with you all up there?"[43]

The notion that Kellogg wanted no election in the parish is only plausible if one rejects the testimony of Law and half a dozen other witnesses, or if one supposes that the governor's protestations were the elaborate performances of a skilled actor. Kellogg, a wily political survivor, certainly knew all the tricks of his trade. But there was no advantage to be gained by not holding an election in East Feliciana. As he later told the Potter Committee, the best strategy would have been to concentrate Republican voters at a single polling place; the Returning Board could then let those votes stand while disallowing the other predominantly Democratic polls. The governor, state senator, district judge, and congressman all needed votes from East Feliciana. Without an election, the parish would not contribute a single Republican ballot. In short, Kellogg had nothing to gain from East Feliciana Parish holding no election.[44]

What, then, accounted for the failure of Republicans in East Feliciana Parish to nominate any candidates? The reason was straightforward—fear. At the urging of Kellogg and others, Union veteran E. A. Rigby, who had fled East Feliciana on July 28, agreed to return in an effort to organize Black voters. The mission took on the character of a clandestine trip not unlike that of a resistance organizer in German-occupied France during World War II. A former police juror as well as a brother-in-law of the murdered Matthews and Gair, Rigby was a well-known Republican. During a week in October, he traveled the parish by night and "went through the fields in the day-time." His visit confirmed Law's assessment. At the mercy of bulldozers, and with the army doing nothing to protect them, Blacks saw no other option but to vote Democrat. "They didn't say intimidation," Rigby recalled, "they said they were afraid for their lives." Andrew J. Dumont, who headed the Republican state executive committee, asked Law if Republican ballots papers could be forwarded to De Grey. "De Grey is scared out of his breeches," he replied. "He won't touch a Republican ticket."[45]

If further evidence were needed to contradict Anderson's claim, West Feliciana Parish supplied it. There, the bulldozing was every bit as savage as in East Feliciana. On September 28, on the way home from a "protracted meeting" at the church he pastored, Julius Green encountered Charles Barrow's gang of eight. He broke and ran, Barrow and his men shooting as he fled. The gang then visited the nearby home of Green's brother-in-law, Isaac Mitchell, who had refused to join a Democratic club. "We came to break up this damned radical hole," they told his wife when she opened the door. Amy Mitchell protested, "Isaac is not in here," as her husband hid under a pile of seed cotton. Barrow's men entered the house, found Mitchell, dragged him outside, and proceeded to beat him with their pistols. Barrow then shot him three times. Mitchell died the following morning.[46]

Yet in West Feliciana Parish, the Republican Party managed to hold two public meetings *and* field a ticket. Strong leadership made the difference. Big Weber and Little Weber may have detested each other, but they stood firm in the face of Democratic threats. So did the Black Republicans who took up arms in self-defense. Three weeks before the election, E. L. Weber, accompanied by white Republican Thomas H. Jenks and Black legislator George Swayze, asked Kellogg for weapons. A few days later two crates arrived in Bayou Sara containing ten Springfield rifles and 100 rounds of ammunition. The shipment doubled the stock of firearms at Weber's house, which Black Republicans used as a safe haven; armed guards stood watch day and night. Swayze, who stayed there often, "took one of the guns and carried it to my home." Bulldozing in West Feliciana was not a risk-free activity. Four days before the election, a bulldozing gang led by Thomas C. West, the Democratic candidate for sheriff, attempted to burn out Black Republican Thomas Rice. Rice shot West and killed him.[47]

West Feliciana also had a Republican sheriff. Dr. P. G. A. Kaufman had served as a surgeon in the Prussian army before emigrating to the United States and settling in Louisiana. Kellogg appointed him in 1875 after Democratic obstructionism prevented Thomas Dalton, a Black man, from qualifying. At sixty-two he was too old for the job, and Democrats repeatedly undermined him. When attempting to make arrests, his deputies were obstructed or driven away. But Kaufman was stubborn. Refusing to resign, he utilized whatever scraps of authority he could muster. After Isaac Mitchell's murder, the parish coroner, a Democrat, sent a deputy to New Orleans to arrest and bring back Amy Mitchell and two other witnesses. The trio had been spirited out of West Feliciana by E. L. Weber and were lodged in a hotel guarded by L. B. Jenks. Kaufman wired the city's chief of police and asked him to prevent the arrests, which he did. Remaining in New Orleans, the witnesses made out affidavits identifying Charles Barrow as Mitchell's killer—something they would never have done in West Feliciana.[48]

Democrats in East Feliciana, determined to record a thumping majority, were desperate for Anderson to return. Several hundred whites remained unregistered. Without a supervisor there could be no election, and the months of forcing Black voters into Democratic clubs would be wasted. In the absence of an election, moreover, a Republican governor could appoint all the parish officials. In fact, the Democrats had much more to lose from Anderson's absence than did the Republicans, who as yet had no candidates and, even if they did, were likely to lose heavily.

Anderson did not propose to return, however, unless he could profit thereby. He approached the two leading officials of the Democratic state organization, E. A. Burke and I. W. Patton, to see what their party would offer. As noted, he pressed his idea of delivering a large majority for the Democratic ticket if the Democrats helped reelect Nash, his political patron, to Congress. Patton declined the proposition, doubting in any case that Anderson "had the power which he seemed to fancy he possessed."

Negotiations dragged on for two weeks. Judge Lyons, accompanied by attorneys Charles McVea and D. J. Wedge, came down from East Feliciana and pressed Anderson to return. As Patton remembered it, the latter kept raising objections; as the Democrats answered one objection, he raised another. Anderson had a personal difficulty with Butler; his life would be in danger; he needed cash; if he tried to leave New Orleans, "Kellogg would have me arrested." Anderson "half-way agreed to go back," Lyons recalled, once the Democrats agreed to pay him $350 cash (rather than depreciated parish warrants) and guaranteed his safety. The triumvirate from East Feliciana twice saw Kellogg to make sure that Anderson fulfilled his duties. Twice the governor agreed to send him back. McVea arranged for Anderson to go upriver with him on board the *Governor Allen.* When the lawyer arrived at the landing at the appointed hour, however, Anderson failed to appear. "He was not a very truthful man," Judge Lyons remembered.[49]

Later the same evening, Patton received an unexpected visitor at Democratic Central Committee headquarters. Agnes D. Jenks, a woman soon to become famous through her appearances before the Potter Committee, was the witty, charming, and politically knowledgeable wife of Captain Thomas H. Jenks, late of the US Navy and formerly the Republican tax collector in East Feliciana. Mrs. Jenks suggested that Patton come to her mother's house, where Anderson was lodging, the following day. Together, she promised, "we can get him to go back." Patton agreed to the rendezvous. He paid Anderson's lodging bill and arranged for a buggy to take him to Carrolton, a suburb of New Orleans, where he could board the steamboat *Pargoud.* It was an unscheduled stop for the boat; the captain had a skiff row to shore to collect the supervisor.[50]

The cloak-and-dagger departure catered to Anderson's insistence that Kellogg was intent upon confining him to New Orleans. "He was such a peculiar, whimsical, fussy kind of fellow," Wedge recalled, that the Democrats felt obliged to mollify him. Captain Jenks accompanied him on the *Pargoud,* acting as a kind of minder. As Mrs. Jenks told Patton, Anderson was weak willed and unreliable, especially when drunk. Her husband would "keep [him] straight, stiffen him up, and he would not be allowed to be bull-dozed into doing wrong." When the supervisor disembarked at Port Hudson, a handcar transported him by rail to Clinton.

Back in harness as supervisor, Anderson lost no time in getting into a scrape. Offended by "scurrilous abuse" in the pages of the *Clinton Patriot-Democrat,* he "wrote the editor a challenge." When the editor declined to accept, Anderson marched into his office and, calling him a liar and a coward, vowed to shoot the top of his head off as soon as he met him on the street. The editor replied simply, "We'll settle your hash after the election."[51]

Election Day, November 7, passed off peacefully throughout Louisiana. In the Felicianas, the Democratic strategy of frontloading intimidation and violence paid off. The Democrats "commenced some time before the election," explained white Republican George T. Norwood, "so as not to have the charge raised on election-day." By then, "the colored people [were] so badly scared that they would do anything that they told them." Virtually all the Black officeholders and Republican ward leaders had been driven into exile or pressed into Democratic clubs.[52]

In East Feliciana, Black voters marched to the polls in their Democratic clubs to vote in what appeared to be a free and fair election. With no Republican ticket, the Democratic vote of 1,740 constituted the majority. Two years earlier the Republican Party had carried the parish by 841 votes—about the number of Black voters who cast Democratic ballots in 1876. The switch was not entirely coerced. Numerous Blacks testified that they voted Democrat of their own free will and gave cogent reasons for doing so. "The Republicans promised us . . . two mules and forty acres of land to vote for them," explained forty-four-year-old Isaac Guy. "Well, I voted for them, but I got tired of being fooled." And contrary to Republican claims, the number of Blacks who always voted the Democratic ticket was larger than a handful. Without Democratic bulldozing, however, the Republican Party would have racked up another decisive majority in a parish where Blacks outnumbered whites two to one.[53]

Anderson, despite his later claim to the contrary, was not fooled by the Election Day calm. Fearing for his own safety, he insisted that he would only sign the returns once he was out of the parish. He also requested an escort of US soldiers. But no troops were needed: Anderson and Thomas Jenks traveled by buggy to Baton Rouge in the protective company of two prominent Democrats, D. J. Wedge and Joseph A. Norwood. The latter headed the bulldozers—he had commanded the squad that killed Gair. After mailing the returns from Baton Rouge, Anderson collected $350 from Wedge and took the boat to New Orleans. He never set foot in East Feliciana Parish again.[54]

Democrats also carried West Feliciana, but they did not have things entirely their own way. Speaking at a final Republican barbecue, E. L. Weber told Blacks to vote in Saint Francisville, where Don Weber had set up three polling places. There, they would enjoy safety in numbers and be close to the army post at Bayou Sara. On the day before the election, about six hundred Republican voters gathered in Saint Francisville; Democrats then deployed pickets around the town to prevent further arrivals.

Don Weber wired Kellogg explaining the problem: "If you can get a guard for us at St. Francisville tonight all will be well. Bascom refuses to do anything for us." Kellogg immediately wired the information to the chairman of the Republican National Committee (RNC), Zachariah Chandler, in New York, so that Weber's report could at least be publicized in northern newspapers. But the army commander in Louisiana, Brigadier General C. C. Augur, issued no new orders, while Captain Bascom, whose Democratic sympathies were plain and who detested Weber, sat on his hands. On Election Day US soldiers were nowhere to be seen. "I visited no polls," Bascom remembered. "I had my men all . . . confined to their quarters."[55]

The wisdom of concentrating Black voters in Saint Francisville was evident when the ballots were counted. The Republican ticket gained 776 votes, all but 154 of them cast in the town. Of the 1,248 Democratic ballots, well over half were deposited by Black voters at polls outside Saint Francisville. At the Brick Church polling station in Ward Ten, for example, every Black voter but one cast a Democratic ballot: their employers simply "marched them up and voted them." Blacks were afraid to ask Washington Spooner, the Republican ward leader, for Republican tickets, and he was afraid to distribute them—Spooner voted Democrat himself. The sole exception, a brave man named Jesse Dunbar, "went up bold as a lion" and deposited his Republican ticket in the ballot box.[56]

After mailing the returns, Don Weber, like supervisors across the state, headed to New Orleans. In the spacious rotunda of the Saint Charles Hotel, which served as the state's informal political marketplace for the next few weeks, Weber ran into Samuel J. Powell, an attorney from Saint Francisville who represented West Feliciana on the Democratic State Committee. "I have done something for which you fellows will give me no credit," Powell remembered Weber telling him. "I have filed my return without any protest. I now intend to go home and not have anything more to do with this business; pick up my gun and go in the swamps and hunt ducks." On his return journey upriver, Weber told fellow passenger John H. Kennard, another Democratic attorney, substantially the same thing.[57]

Anderson had not attached a "protest" to the East Feliciana returns either. In fact, not a single supervisor across the state included any written complaint about the fairness of the election. As the preliminary results poured in, Democrats claimed to have won the presidential vote in Louisiana by a majority of between 8,000 and 15,000 ballots. The fact that every supervisor had signed his parish returns without comment furnished conclusive evidence, they claimed, that the election had been, in the words of the relevant statute, free from "riot, tumult, acts of violence, intimidation, armed disturbance, bribery, or corrupt influence." The Returning Board had merely to confirm the Democrats' victory.[58]

The likelihood of the Returning Board ratifying the popular vote, however, was close to nil. It was as "certain as any future event can be, that the vote of Louisiana will be returned for the Republican party," Congressman Randall Lee Gibson, a Democrat, had predicted back in March. Democrats might claim that Tilden had won the presidency, but Hayes's campaign managers begged to differ. As soon as it became clear that Tilden, in order to win, needed the electoral votes of Florida, South Carolina, and Louisiana, Republicans refused to concede defeat.[59]

On the morning of November 8, RNC chairman Chandler informed the press that "Hayes has 185 [electoral] votes and is elected." The claim was, writes Michael F. Holt, "amazingly brazen." The calculation behind it, however, was clear. The three crucial southern states had Republican governors and Republican-controlled returning boards; the latter could overturn the Democratic majorities in each one. Telegrams flew back and forth between the Hayes campaign's headquarters in New York and Republican officials in Tallahassee, Columbia, and New Orleans. "Grave importance attaches to the electoral vote of your State," Chandler wired Governor Kellogg the day after the election. Another telegram the same day reminded gubernatorial candidate Stephen B. Packard, "We are now absolutely certain of 185 votes for Hayes if your State is safe."[60]

Louisiana was key. In the two other contested states, the claimed Democratic majorities were razor thin, and in South Carolina, as the full returns came in, Hayes edged ahead of Tilden. Republicans and Democrats alike realized that, to quote the *New York Herald,* "it may chance that Louisiana's vote shall be needed to decide the election." There, once all the returns were in, the Democratic ticket had a majority of at least 7,000 in terms of actual ballots cast. As the pro-Democratic *Cincinnati Enquirer* recognized, "Everything depends on Louisiana to elect Tilden," nervously praying that the state's Democrats "will not permit us to be counted out."[61]

If Louisiana held the key to the White House, the bulldozed parishes of Ouachita, Morehouse, East Baton Rouge, East Feliciana, and West Feliciana held the key to the state. In these five parishes, Kellogg told the *New York Tribune,* the evidence was "perfectly conclusive" that Democrats had engaged in a "systematic course of murder, intimidation, and terrorism." How else to account for a Democratic majority of about 4,500 when those same parishes had registered a Republican majority of over 4,000 voters two years earlier? "These parishes were picked out and raided, the officers of election and the colored people overawed, and things generally smashed," the governor wired Senator John A. Logan of Illinois. From the moment the polls closed on November 7, therefore, Louisiana's Republican leaders claimed victory on the assumption that these lopsided Democratic majorities—results that differed so markedly from all the other majority Black parishes—would never pass muster with the Returning Board. "Be easy so far as Louisiana is concerned," Kellogg reassured northern Republicans. "You can bet your bottom dollar on Louisiana for Hayes."[62]

If the five bulldozed parishes were the key to Louisiana, the two Feliciana parishes (and here is where a kind of reverse "for the want of a nail" proverb is appropriate) were *absolutely crucial.* Between them, they delivered a majority of about 2,500 votes for Tilden, 2,000 of which came from East Feliciana alone. It made sense, therefore, to highlight those parishes as the most egregious and easily provable examples of Democratic bulldozing tactics. "No Republican ticket was allowed to be put in the field," Kellogg told the *New York Tribune* on November 8. "The supervisor of election was run out of the parish, and . . . not one Republican vote was allowed to be polled." This somewhat misleading statement did not allow that Anderson had returned to the parish, albeit reluctantly and very late. The following day the *New Orleans Republican* published the even more misleading claim that Anderson "was run off, and an election was held in violation of all the forms of law."[63]

Republicans looked to the Returning Board to wrest victory from the jaws of defeat. As Pitkin explained to US Senator J. R. West in a coded telegram, "State cannot carry unless fraudulent parishes are rejected." In order to exclude polls, however, the Returning Board required evidence, and lots of it, in the form of protests from supervisors and affidavits from Republican voters, all signed and sworn to in legal form. Three days after the election, Pitkin's deputy, J. B. Stockton, wired Chairman Chandler to send funds so that witnesses could be brought to New Orleans to swear that they had been deterred from voting "by violence and intimidation." Stockton suggested that affidavits be taken from 10,000 to 12,000 people, a figure apparently calculated to overcome the Democratic majority. It was an absurdly unrealistic number, but Chandler did send funds, and the process of collecting affidavits began. Democrats started gathering their own affidavits, in situ rather than in New Orleans, from Blacks who swore that they had voted of their own free will. A week after the election, Democrats in East Feliciana had accumulated 149 such statements.[64]

Republican affidavits were worthless, however, unless the supervisors of election filed "protests" with the Returning Board that substantiated the charge of violence and intimidation. Protests made in New Orleans days *after* the election would not conform to the letter of the law, which, as we have seen, required them to be attached to the returns immediately after the election. But Republican managers did not worry overmuch about this technicality; they assumed, correctly as it turned out, that the Returning Board would accept late-arriving protests anyhow. They explained that no protests accompanied the returns for the simple reason that supervisors in the bulldozed parishes had been too frightened to file them.[65]

On the morning of November 10, after disembarking from the steamboat, Anderson marched into the marshal's office at the New Orleans Custom House. Surprised by the supervisor's friendly disposition, their previous meeting having ended on a sour note, Pitkin asked if he had filed a protest with his returns. When Anderson replied in the negative, Pitkin made his pitch. "Jim, I do not want you to do anything which your conscience does not warrant you in doing, but there is a crisis here, and it looks as if the Presidency is going to hinge on Louisiana, and if you can conscientiously make a protest against your parish, I wish you would do it." Anderson went off with a sheet of paper and returned half an hour later with a written statement. Pitkin saw that it would not pass muster as a legal document, but he had Anderson sign and swear to it anyway. Aware of Anderson's contacts with Burke and Patton, he wanted something from him on paper "in case he subsequently yielded to Democratic overtures."

Judge Hugh Campbell had drafted a template, a form with some boilerplate text and blanks to fill in, in order to couch protests in the appropriate legal style. At Pitkin's request the judge gave one to Anderson. The latter balked at "certain general sweeping statements . . . that I recommended," Campbell recalled, and when he left Pitkin's office, Anderson was still "discussing and objecting." Nevertheless, the supervisor returned to the marshal's office later that day with a new version that, according to Thomas Jenks, he and Anderson had gone through "sentence by sentence." Campbell witnessed Anderson's signature and oath. Jenks, Norwood, and Hansbury, Republicans from East Feliciana Parish, supplied the three supporting affidavits required by law. Pitkin surmised that Anderson was trying to get back into the good graces of the Republican Party but distrusted the man, asking the head of the Metropolitan police, Colonel W. F. Loan, to have him followed.[66]

Don Weber made out a protest on November 15. He did so with foreboding. Supervisors who lived in their assigned parishes were in an entirely different position from Custom House employees like Anderson. Their protests were sure to make bitter enemies of local Democrats, who had assumed that supervisors, in declining to include protests in their returns, had given the election a clean bill of health. Weber would make a protest, he told J. P. Harris, if it helped Packard and Hayes win. He asked Harris to inform him by telegram if and when the latter lodged his statement with the Returning Board: "I thought it would be unsafe for me to remain there after it became known that I had filed the protest." Wondering whether he had done the right thing, Weber consoled himself at the bar of the Saint Charles Hotel, with the journalist Leet as a drinking companion. "There were some Democrats in the State that he did hate so cordially," Leet remembered him saying, "that he would rather risk his life in order to beat them than to see them come in." The reporter had to restrain Weber from picking a fight with Henry J. Hearsey, the bibulous, pugnacious, and venomously anti-Republican editor of the *New Orleans Times*.[67]

Anderson, meanwhile, was having second thoughts about his own protest. As the nation's attention focused on Louisiana, with the outcome of the presidential election hanging in the balance, he berated himself for not being more assertive in dealing with the Republican managers. The arrival in New Orleans of senior politicians from both major parties to keep tabs on the Returning Board—the press dubbed them "visiting statesmen"—underlined the enormous stakes. His protest might make Hayes president, yet Anderson had received no promise of reward. If his own party neglected to give him something better than his current position, a lowly clerk at the Custom House, then perhaps the Democrats would provide for him if he could somehow ensure that the returns from East Feliciana withstood the scrutiny of the Returning Board. In a classic case of closing the doors of the stable after the horse had bolted, Anderson decided to deny the very testimony that he had signed and sworn to.

2

VISITING STATESMEN

HOW REPUBLICANS STOLE THE ELECTION BACK

A week after polling day, two dozen prominent Republicans from the North, responding to a request from President Grant, arrived in New Orleans. Their official assignment was to observe the count and report anything untoward. Their unofficial assignment was to provide the Returning Board with political protection so that it felt confident about bending and breaking rules. Few of the Republicans relished their mission. "I am almost sorry that I came," John Sherman wrote his wife, Cecilia. "This whole business is a thankless ungracious task not entirely free of danger." Still, the senator had a strong incentive to see Hayes returned: he nurtured his own ambition to become president. Hayes, if elected, would almost certainly appoint him secretary of the Treasury, and from that position Sherman could allocate hundreds, if not thousands, of jobs to political supporters. The most senior among them, Sherman was the acknowledged leader of the Republican group.[1]

For a someone who enjoyed such a long career in national politics, Sherman is the invisible man of American history. A founding member of the Republican Party, he sat in Congress for forty-two years, served as secretary of the Treasury and secretary of State, and left his imprint on the key legislation of his age. In terms of intellect, many thought he outclassed Hayes and James A. Garfield. Yet biographies are thin on the ground; the last one appeared in 1908. The fact that he never served as president (although he came close) explains much of this neglect. The rest of the explanation lies in Sherman's character. In stark contrast to his Republican contemporary James G. Blaine, he was utterly devoid of what is now called "charisma." Respected he might be; loved he was not. A biography published in 1884, written by an Episcopal minister who knew him well, tried to humanize Sherman but soon gave up. "Most of those who know him regard him as a 'cold' man," the Rev. S. A. Bronson reported, "which, I am happy to say, he is."[2]

Physically, Sherman cut an impressive and somewhat intimidating figure. At six feet, two inches and "as thin as a rail," he towered over most of his contemporaries. His bearded visage resembled that of his famous brother, General William T. Sherman, but his personality was very different. The general was excitable, garrulous, and full of nervous energy. The senator was calm, collected, and tight lipped. Known for his brains rather than his voice, he was a grimly serious man who rarely laughed or joked. "No man ever controlled himself more perfectly," wrote Bronson. "The man does not live who can bore him for any length of time." With his stern expression and piercing eyes, Sherman attracted the nickname "Ohio Icicle."[3]

A centrist, moderate, cautious politician, Sherman gained the reputation of a man with no strong views, a compromiser who adroitly advanced his career by moving in step with, but never ahead of, public opinion. Keeping his emotions in check and his political calculations to himself, he "covered his trail and hid his tracks." Newspaper correspondent "Gath," one of the most astute political commentators of the day, analyzed Sherman's role during the crucial Senate debates over Reconstruction. The Ohioan possessed a "managing mind," he wrote, rather than an "executive mind." The former "crosses a muddy street successfully"; the latter "mends it." Sherman was an "adroit puller of wires" and one whose "deepest convictions [were] no deeper than expediency, his standard of statesmanship no higher than Disraeli's." In a brilliant aperçu, Gath tried to nail down the essence of the man: "One of Shakespeare's great characters remarked, 'I am what I am!' But John Sherman is most what he is not."[4]

There were, however, hidden depths. "There was much of the iceberg to John Sherman," another reporter recalled. "Still, the ice was more apparent than real. It was on the surface. Within, Sherman was warm, at times tropical." Once, early in his political career, during the height of the conflict over "Bleeding Kansas," he let down his guard and revealed the fire within. After Sherman concluded a speech in the House of Representatives, Congressman John Wright, a Democrat from Tennessee, called him a liar. The next day, after Sherman invoked personal privilege to comment on the insult, the Tennessean made as if to assault him, whereupon the Ohioan "picked up a cup of wafers, such as lay on the desk of every member at that time, and threw the contents in his face." Wright reached for his pistol, but fellow Democrats restrained him. "There was every expectation of a duel or an affray," Sherman recalled. "I was no duelist, but . . . I got a pistol . . . and I made up my mind the instant Wright approached me with a hostile intention, I would shoot him dead." The rencontre blew over, but it showed the stern stuff of which Sherman was made.[5]

When the Republican visiting statesmen checked into their accommodations at the Saint Charles Hotel, they found that a group of Democratic "visiting statesmen" had preceded them. Fearing that the Returning Board would manipulate the results in Hayes's favor, Abram S. Hewitt, chairman of the Democratic National Committee (DNC), prevailed upon two dozen senior party supporters to travel to New Orleans to witness the count. Anxious to present the delegation as high-minded statesmen rather than rabid partisans, he took care to include several former Republicans, of whom ex-senator Lyman Trumbull, author of the 1866 Civil Rights Bill, and John M. Palmer, a former Union general and one-time Republican governor of Illinois, were the most prominent. The Democrats aimed to expose the board to public scrutiny in the hope of deterring it from blatantly "counting out" Tilden.[6]

The Democratic visiting statesmen lost no time in homing in on East Feliciana Parish. Where was the proof of bulldozing, they asked Governor Kellogg. Why had Supervisor Anderson been absent from the parish, thereby denying registration to several hundred Democrats? In reply, Kellogg cited the murders of John Gair and Babe Matthews, and the subsequent "reign of terror" for which, he claimed, evidence was "so overwhelming as to remove all doubt on the subject." He "emphatically denied" that he had contrived to keep Anderson out of East Feliciana. As for the Returning Board, the governor insisted that he had no power to influence it one way or the other.[7]

The Democrats' references to Anderson and East Feliciana Parish had an obvious source: Anderson himself. The ink was scarcely dry on his protest when the ex-supervisor made overtures to the opposing party. Spotting him in the rotunda of the Saint Charles Hotel, a hive of political gossip and intrigue, Democrat S. J. N. Smith offered him a drink, "which he didn't refuse." When Anderson asked for an introduction to Pennsylvania congressman Samuel J. Randall, the Speaker of the House, Smith half-jokingly announced him as "one of the 'bull-dozed' supervisors." Anderson took umbrage. He had not been bulldozed at all, he insisted. "Some damn radicals" wanted him to state that he had been afraid, "but he would be going back on his manhood if he did, and he didn't propose to do it."[8]

Charles E. Whitney of the *New York Herald* caught wind of Anderson's blustering and sought him out. Anderson regaled the reporter with complaints about the ingratitude of the Republican Party, which had reneged on its promises to reward him with either money or high office. He proposed to see what the Democrats would offer, asking Whitney to introduce him to E. A. Burke, one of Democratic gubernatorial candidate Nicholls's campaign managers. Over dinner with Burke at Denechaud's restaurant, Anderson admitted to signing a protest on November 10 but explained it away by stating that he had been drunk at the time. According to Burke, the election official claimed that "he could place in my possession such evidence that would undoubtedly prevent the throwing out" of the East Feliciana Parish returns. After further meetings, Burke offered him $4,000 in cash and a position worth $1,800 a year. But the negotiations were never concluded. "We did not have the money," Burke explained.[9]

Anderson's bargaining position was weakened by the fact that, first, he possessed no documentary evidence (letters, telegrams, or witnesses, for example) to support his claims and, second, that he had already protested against the Democratic sweep in East Feliciana Parish by the time he met Burke. How could he possibly guarantee that the Returning Board would certify the result?

His first attempt to solve this conundrum was brazenly direct. On November 14 Anderson marched into Pitkin's office and demanded the return of his protest. The marshal replied that it was no longer in his possession. Even if it had been, he had no intention of giving it back in order for Anderson to "destroy his protest in the Democratic interest." A blazing row ensued, with both men resorting to what Pitkin called "unbolted English." Threatened with being thrown out of the office, Anderson stormed off, leaving a wake of threats and curses. Stewing, he told anyone who cared to listen how ill-treated he had been, how ungrateful the Republican Party was, and how Pitkin had better watch out because he would shoot him on sight. The marshal recalled that Custom House employee James Casey, "a large brawny man," offered to "mash" Anderson. "I told him I thought it was not necessary, that I could take care of myself." Pitkin took the precaution of acquiring a pistol.[10]

Having failed to retrieve his protest, Anderson changed tack. He now tried to discredit his own statement. Back at the bar of the Saint Charles Hotel, he told Whitney of the *New York Herald* that Kellogg was bent on throwing out the vote of East Feliciana Parish on the spurious grounds of intimidation. The reporter recognized a story when he heard one, and immediately wired his copy to New York. The following day the *Herald* reported Anderson's claim that "the election [in East Feliciana] was peaceably and fairly conducted . . . , that the large Democratic gains were legitimate, and that he had signed the returns to that effect, because they were true."[11]

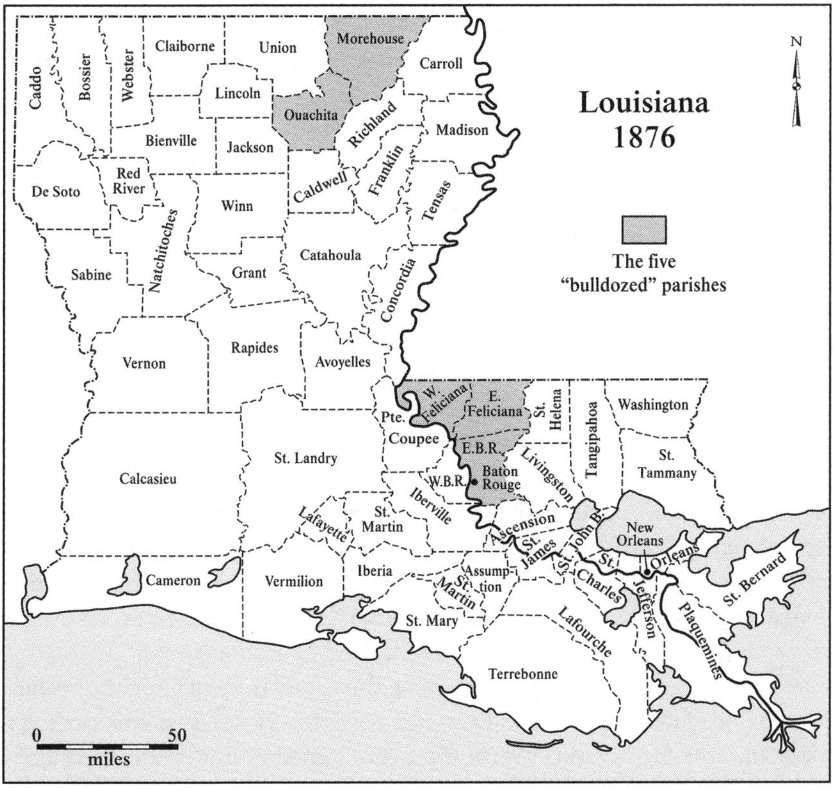

Kellogg could hardly miss the *Herald*'s story, and that may well have been Anderson's intention. "He was bidding . . . for an office from one side or another," thought Whitney. Anderson's claim directly contradicted the content of his supervisor's protest, but it nevertheless complicated, in a most unwelcome way, the Republican narrative of Democratic intimidation. It also smacked of extortion: what would the Republican Party offer him to stick to his protest? Kellogg, however, was in no mood to offer Anderson anything, and instead berated him for treachery. According to Anderson's highly colored account, the governor threatened to fasten a halter round his neck. Ever the braggart, Anderson told Whitney that he "would have killed Kellogg, or knocked him down, had not the steps of the Custom House been filled with Custom House strikers, who would have shot him." The *Herald* duly reported this "sharp exchange," adding that "three or four other supervisors have evinced a disposition to kick in the harness, all of whom the Democrats are actively and assiduously courting."[12]

A handful of supervisors did indeed hesitate to sign protests. Their reluctance, however, stemmed from fear. Like Don Weber, who before writing his protest told D. J. M. A. Jewett, "my head is a damned sight more important to me than Packard's being governor," supervisors who conducted the election in their home parishes were not so much tempted by Democratic bribes as afraid of Democratic wrath. Jewett recalled that M. J. Grady of Ouachita Parish complained that if he protested the returns, "it would subject him and his family . . . to great personal danger." Grady eventually made the sought-after statement, but "it required a good deal of persuasion." F. M. Grant of Morehouse told Jewett that "he was a man of family and property; that he was obliged to remain in his parish, and that he did not dare to do it if he made a protest." Kellogg summoned Grant to his private residence, with Jewett in tow, to help stiffen the supervisor's backbone. There, Grant assented to the desired protest. J. F. Kelley of Richland Parish proved especially recalcitrant, refusing to sign a protest despite the combined arm twisting of Jewett, Kellogg, and Campbell. "I saw no intimidation during the registration or election myself." he explained, "I knew it only from hearsay." The governor instructed him to return to Richland Parish to obtain witnesses. Upon his return Kelley finally signed a protest drafted by Kellogg.[13]

When Burke proved unable to raise the $4,000 he promised, Anderson rowed back toward the Republican Party. It seemed increasingly likely that the legerdemain of the Returning Board would produce majorities for Packard and Hayes. "The parish will be thrown out, and nothing I could have done or can do will prevent it," he lamented. In that case, Anderson calculated, his best chance of financial reward lay with the Republicans. The presence of the Republican visiting statesmen would enable him to bypass Kellogg, Jewett, and the other state leaders and approach powerful men who had a direct line to Rutherford B. Hayes.[14]

The two groups of visiting statesmen, most of them lodged in the Saint Charles Hotel, eyed each other warily. "There is but little intimacy between men of the opposite parties," Sherman wrote his wife. As if to emphasize the partisan divide, the Republicans rejected a request from the

Democrats that the two groups confer and cooperate to ensure an impartial "canvass of the votes actually cast." Cheekily citing their wish to respect "states' rights"—a Democratic shibboleth—they stated that it would be wrong to interfere with decisions of the Returning Board. Congressman Garfield considered the exchange "a pretty good piece of thrust and parry." As the days passed by, however, the partisan cold war thawed. "A Kentucky friend sent me a demijohn of . . . very old Bourbon," recalled Henry Watterson, the editor of the *Louisville Courier-Times* and a visiting Democrat, "and I divided it with 'our friends the enemy.'"[15]

For many of the visiting statesmen, New Orleans seemed strange and exotic. Watterson again: "We attended the places of amusement, lived in the restaurants, and saw the sights as if we had been tourists in a foreign land." Several, to their subsequent embarrassment, attended a quadroon ball, dancing with "creamy and peach-tinted" mixed-race women who were renowned for their grace, beauty, and availability.[16]

But the city also aroused negative impressions. "Strange that in the land of flowers so cold a day should look down upon roses and orange groves," Garfield wrote his wife. "The weather seems to have imparted its fickleness to the people, who smile in the morning and murder at night." At a time when Mexico was a byword for political instability, Louisiana seemed the closest US equivalent. Garfield found his "old opinion of the Latin races" confirmed: "they have not the genius for self-government." Sherman, too, found "the spirit of politics" in Louisiana utterly alien. "The history and conduct of politics here . . . alarms me for the peace of the whole country."[17]

The fact that the presidential election turned on Louisiana made the Republican visitors acutely uncomfortable. In an age of loose ethics and brass knuckles, Louisiana stood out for corruption, violence, and electoral fraud. The behavior of the state's Republican leaders, who had governed since 1868, consistently embarrassed the national party. Between 1870 and 1873, faction fights tore the party asunder, produced much brawling, and caused at least one death. A disputed election in 1872 resulted in two governors and two legislatures, a political mess that President Grant tried to clean up by coming down firmly on the side of the Republican Kellogg, using soldiers to install his administration.

Once in office, however, Kellogg proved incapable of establishing his authority. In 1873 in Grant Parish, armed Democrats defeated an ad hoc Black militia and massacred at least eighty men after they had surrendered. In 1874 the 5,000-strong White League, the Democrats' extralegal militia, routed the state militia in open battle and seized control of New Orleans. Kellogg fled to the Custom House, a federal safe haven. Only the intervention of troops, again acting on Grant's orders, forced the insurgents to disband and restored Kellogg to office. Numerous congressional committees traveled to Louisiana to examine the state's "political troubles." None could offer a solution. Grant's repeated use of military force to shore up Kellogg's government united Democrats in condemnation and evoked spirited criticism from many Republicans. Members of the president's own cabinet considered the state's Republican leaders corrupt, incompetent, and cowardly.[18]

The Louisiana Returning Board had an unsavory reputation. Created in 1870 in response to a wave of Democratic terrorism during the presidential campaign of 1868, it had become synonymous with political trickery. A Republican legislature endowed it with the power to set aside any polls it deemed to be tainted by fraud and intimidation. But the board had done little to improve the integrity of the electoral process. The chaotic election of 1872 produced no fewer than *four* returning boards, none of which showed any interest in an honest count, each of which served as the tool of a rival faction. After the election of 1874, the board excluded polls to elect certain Republicans who had been beaten fairly and squarely. Yet this body, consisting of four Republican placemen who made little pretense of impartiality, might now determine Grant's successor. "I feel a great repugnance toward accepting any assistance in the election of Hayes from that quarter," a Republican voter wrote Sherman. Political necessity, however, compelled the national party to rely on this deeply flawed instrument. Regardless of his distaste for the Returning Board, Grant was determined that it should be protected from Democratic intimidation.[19]

The possibility of violence could not be discounted. Politics in the North was a rough-and-tumble affair, but in Louisiana it was often deadly. "The condition of our country is very different from that here," the chairman of the Returning Board, James Madison Wells, explained to a congressional committee in Washington. "The people are forced with the bullet; the bullet is swapped for the ballot." Since 1865 dozens of Republican politicians, white and Black, had been assassinated; many more had been forced to resign or flee under the threat of being lynched. More than a thousand Black voters had been murdered, most of them victims of organized campaigns of terror that Louisiana's Democrats encouraged and even directed. The state also boasted a culture of personal violence that could quickly turn political quarrels into physical confrontations.

The "code of honor" bred into the South's white men meant that an offensive comment, or an innocuous remark misconstrued, could spark a duel, knife fight, or brawl. When asked how many men in Louisiana carried revolvers, Wells replied, "It is part of a man's wardrobe." Heavy consumption of whiskey fueled many a gunfight, even as it diminished the imbibers' ability to shoot straight.[20]

The most serious danger came from the White League. Although it had yielded to federal troops in 1874, it never truly disbanded, maintaining a clandestine organization that could be mobilized overnight. According to US Marshal Pitkin, the League possessed 15,000 stands of arms, including 1,800 rifles, and two twelve-pounder howitzers—all stolen from the US arsenal. Knowing that precipitate action would antagonize the president and jeopardize Tilden's cause, the White League hung fire. But it had no intention of allowing the Republican Packard to become Louisiana's next governor. Grant ordered the army to "preserve peace and good order" and to see to it that the members of the Returning Board went "unmolested in the performance of their duties."[21]

These were necessary precautions. Wells, sixty-eight years old, was a man of undoubted personal courage. An unwavering Unionist during the Civil War, he had repeatedly risked his life as Confederates tried to hunt him down. Elevated to the governorship of Union-occupied Louisiana shortly before the surrender of Confederate forces west of the Mississippi River, Wells had tried to ingratiate himself with his former enemies, aiming to create a white conservative party that would sustain him after the war. But after being elected governor in the state's first postwar election, he found himself stymied by a hostile legislature dominated by ex-Confederates. Wells then joined the Republican Party and became a proponent of Black suffrage, which he had previously opposed, a switch that many attributed to political opportunism. Removing him from office after the New Orleans riot of July 1866, Major General Philip H. Sheridan described Wells as a "political trickster and a dishonest man." The characterization was unfair. True, Wells had switched sides, but in the confusing and rapidly evolving politics of that time, such changes of allegiance were common. Certainly, nobody attributed his actions to cowardice. As the state's most prominent scalawag—the term Democrats applied to all southern-born white Republicans—he was a constant target of insults and threats. A bantam cock who stood at five feet, one inch tall, Wells never ran away from a fight and, when it came to abuse, gave as good as he got.

As the one individual who could deprive Democrats of both statehouse and White House, Wells had even greater cause for apprehension. Setting out from his home in Rapides Parish for New Orleans, he received word that if he boarded the steamboat in Alexandria, he would be assassinated. Accompanied by two friends and two of his sons, all of them armed, he rode to an obscure landing at the mouth of the Red River and boarded there instead. When he called the Returning Board into session at the Saint Louis Hotel on November 17, soldiers guarded the building inside and out. Sherman, who noted with relief that he and the other visiting statesmen had received no threats or insults, conjectured that "our presence here is a restraint upon violence to the Board."[22]

Sherman and his colleagues were purportedly in New Orleans as impartial observers, their goal simply to ensure fair play when the Returning Board canvassed the votes. "We want you to be nothing but a looker on," President Grant emphasized, "and note anything that you may think . . . improper." They simply wanted an honest count, Garfield echoed. Sherman took a similarly high-minded view of their role. He and his colleagues were acting "only as witnesses," not as Republican partisans. Hayes piously informed Sherman, "We must not allow our friends to defeat one outrage and fraud by another," insisting that "there must be nothing crooked on our part." The visiting statesman adopted a hands-off approach to the Returning Board and claimed that the outcome of its deliberations was never predetermined.[23]

But these visitors were not entirely passive. They knew that they could not confer legitimacy on the Returning Board simply by their mere presence. Closed-door proceedings, Garfield feared, would inflame public opinion and create an indelible suspicion that the board was "determined to count a Republican majority, right or wrong." At the Republicans' insistence, the board permitted each set of visiting statesmen to select five of their number to witness its daily sessions. That would at least foster the appearance of transparency.[24]

The Republicans also had to justify the Returning Board's actions when they came under national scrutiny. They might not be able to persuade Democrats, who were bound to cry foul, but they wanted a respectable case to defend not only before the general public but also before fellow Republicans who wished to restore integrity to the party after the scandals of the Grant administration. Congressman Jacob D. Cox, a former Union general and ex-governor of Ohio, warned Hayes, a personal friend, that it would be a fatal error to resort to "fraudulent returns." Carl Schurz, a political ally, shared similar misgivings. He was especially troubled by the fact that the Returning Board, which was supposed to have five members, with representation from both parties, consisted of only four Republicans. Garfield confessed to his wife, "to satisfy our incredulous and suspicious public opinion will be a task most difficult." It was not enough, therefore, for the Republican visiting statesmen merely to observe. They had to make out a case. "To do this," Garfield explained, "it is necessary to examine the recent political history [not only] of the state, but also of the special parishes where violence and intimidation have vitiated the result of the election."[25]

As local Republicans compiled evidence of intimidation, bringing more than three hundred witnesses to New Orleans and taking a mass of affidavits, the visiting statesmen examined the written evidence and interviewed many of the witnesses. Such was the volume of documentation that Sherman, as chairman of the group, assigned each of the five bulldozed parishes to one of his colleagues, with the aim of producing a report that would show, in Garfield's words, "our northern people how justly the [Democratic] vote can be thrown out." Garfield took charge of West Feliciana; Cortlandt Parker, a judge from New Jersey, handled East Feliciana. Twenty soldiers "worked day and night . . . for about two days" copying the affidavits for the perusal of the visiting statesmen.[26]

The evidence that made the strongest impression was furnished by a live witness, Eliza Pinkston, a sharecropper, one of several Black Republicans from Ouachita Parish who narrated their experiences of Democratic bulldozing. Carried into the committee room on a chair, the battered and wounded woman described her recent ordeal. Three weeks earlier, she recounted, shortly before the election, a group of white men murdered her husband and killed her baby. Eliza fought off the attackers, who shot and stabbed her before leaving. "At this point she unfastened her dress and revealed the wounds, which were a terrible sight to look at," the *New York Tribune* reported. There were deep gashes to her thigh and breast; her neck had been cut and some of her teeth knocked out. The visiting statesmen were horrified. George Julian, formerly a Republican but now a Democrat, could not bear to look. Overnight, Pinkston's story became a national sensation. No matter how hard Democrats impugned her character and nitpicked her testimony, the evidence of her wounds spoke volumes.[27]

The northern Republicans quickly convinced themselves that Hayes had a solid claim to Louisiana's vote. After a week in New Orleans, Sherman wrote Cecilia, "We have already heard enough to show in some of the

Parishes the most extraordinary system of intimidation and violence it is possible to conceive." Garfield, answering the objections of a close friend, laid out the case for the Returning Board overturning the Democratic majority: "Making all allowances for the exaggeration which partisanship and the sense of personal wrong may naturally make, I know of nothing in modern history so destructive of popular government and so shocking to humanity as the conduct of the Rebel Democracy during the four months that preceded the late election in Louisiana. They acted upon a preconcerted plan and intended to do just as much violence and murder to accomplish their purpose and no more." In their zeal to suppress the Republican vote, however, the Democrats' bulldozing had been so egregious, Garfield added, that it furnished ample grounds for the board to adjust the results by way of compensation.[28]

Despite the appearance of keeping their distance from the Returning Board, personal contact with its members undoubtedly influenced Sherman and his colleagues. Dining with Wells and Thomas C. Anderson, the board's two white members, shortly after their arrival helped dispel their unfavorable impressions of the four-man body. As Garfield confided to his diary after the dinner, "My opinion of the Returning Board is far better than it was before I came here." Sherman professed to be similarly impressed. "They are firm, judicious, and, as far as I can tell, thoroughly honest," he told to Hayes.[29]

Whatever their initial doubts, the Republicans endorsed the actions of the Returning Board, even when contrary to law. The relevant statute, as we have seen, required that supervisors' protests be attached to the returns, supported by at least three accompanying affidavits. But the board decided not only to accept protests and affidavits submitted after polling day but also to consider protests by Republican candidates, including a "general protest" by Stephen Packard that covered several parishes. One of the most egregious acts of the Returning Board was its decision to *add* votes to the Republican total in certain parishes where, through sheer incompetence, the Republican ballot had failed to list all eight presidential electors, creating a shortfall that threatened to defeat one or two of them (Hayes needed all of Louisiana's eight electors to beat Tilden). Democrats objected. Republicans, however, found no fault with any of these decisions.[30]

The Democratic visiting statesmen were reduced to the role of frustrated observers, impotently protesting the unfairness of the proceedings. "All is perfectly tranquil here," Watterson wired Tilden. "Well organized plan supported by troops to cheat us." The deck seemed stacked: Republicans controlled the federal government, the army, the state government, and the Returning Board. Democrats realized that the result was a foregone conclusion. Julian predicted that "the board will turn us all out in a day or so, go into secret session, and declare the result in favor of Hayes." And so it proved. After throwing out over 13,000 Democratic ballots, along with 2,415 Republican ones, the board announced that the Hayes electors had a majority of at least 3,437 over the Tilden electors and that Packard was elected governor over Nicholls by an even larger majority.[31]

Democrats charged that the Republican visiting statesmen had connived with the Returning Board to steal the election. Later, after Hayes was inaugurated, they elaborated on this allegation: Through the promise of lucrative federal employment, the visiting statesmen had induced supervisors to fabricate accounts of intimidation and encouraged members of the Returning Board to discount Democratic polls on spurious grounds. These federal appointments, Democrats charged, amounted to bribes. The charge of illegitimate influence bore most heavily on Sherman, who, according to James Anderson, used federal patronage to persuade him and Don Weber to stand by their protests *although he knew the protests to be false.*

While Anderson recounted his story before the Potter Committee in June 1878, it belongs here in this narrative, for the events he described, whether remembered or imagined, took place in November 1876 shortly after the election. On November 14, it will be recalled, Anderson tried and failed to retrieve his protest from US Marshal Pitkin and angrily vented to a *New York Herald* reporter to the effect that the election in East Feliciana Parish had been free and fair. But he realized that if the Returning Board were to throw out the returns no matter what, he had little chance of striking a deal with Democrats. Anderson therefore looked to the Republican Party to reward him for standing by his protest. Yet he doubted that he could secure the financial reward he considered his due without giving party managers a strong inducement to pay him off. He needed to engage in extortion and wanted to involve Don Weber in his scheme.

In order to avoid a tedious repetition of the word "alleged" and its various synonyms, the reader should bear in mind that the following account is based solely upon Anderson's uncorroborated testimony. On the same day that Weber signed his own protest, Anderson proposed that the two supervisors swear that the Democratic majorities in East and West Feliciana Parishes had been "secured by legitimate means" and were due to the "disgust and hatred" with which many Black voters regarded the Republican state government. They had protested the results—protests they knew to be false—in order to carry Louisiana for Hayes, and they had done so at the suggestion of Packard, Kellogg, Pitkin, and Nash. The following day, November 15, they signed their joint statement before a notary public in the presence of two witnesses. This was their insurance policy, Anderson reasoned, a document the party would pay them to suppress.[32]

On November 17, the day the *Herald* floated Anderson's trial balloon, E. L. Weber told the supervisor that some of the Republican visiting statesmen wished to see him. Anderson declined. The following day Don Weber told Anderson that Sherman himself was asking after him. The two supervisors called upon the senator at the Saint Charles Hotel "but failed to see him." Trying again on the nineteenth, the pair spotted Sherman through the window of Moreau's restaurant while on their way to the hotel. Stepping inside, they introduced themselves to the Ohioan, who was dining with Edwin W. Stoughton, a New York lawyer and fellow visiting statesman.

Sherman explained that he wanted to see the men because he understood that there was "some difficulty in reference to your parishes." The country was in a crisis, he went on, and "we want and expect every Republican and every true patriot to stand by us." Weber replied that his life would be in danger if he returned to West Feliciana; Sherman reassured him that he could be "provided for" outside Louisiana. Weber pointed out that he and Anderson had made enemies of Kellogg and Packard, who would be loath to offer them positions. Sherman quickly disposed of this objection. As president, he explained, Hayes would control the federal patronage, and he would undoubtedly reward those who stood by the Republican party in its "hour of peril." Anderson interjected that he was liable to be prosecuted for perjury, "for they are going to throw out my parish on a forged protest." That was not a matter he wished to discuss, Sherman responded, but he promised that if the supervisors stood firm, they would have no cause to regret it. With this, the interview concluded, and the two men left the restaurant and went their separate ways.[33]

Mulling over what Sherman had said to them, Anderson wondered if they could trust his verbal assurances. "Unless we get a written guarantee that we shall be taken care of," he wrote Weber, "I am unwilling to go a step further." After conferring on the morning of November 20, the two men drafted the following note:

> Sir: We have carefully considered the arguments advanced by you in our interview. Your assurance that we should be taken care of is scarcely specific enough. In case we pursue the course suggested by you we would be obliged to leave the State. Will you, therefore, state in writing who we shall look to for the fulfilment of those promises.

From the Cross Saloon, witness to many a political plot, Weber had someone deliver the note to Sherman at the Saint Charles Hotel. A reply was not long in coming. Meeting Anderson at the corner of Saint Charles and Canal Streets, Weber displayed an envelope addressed to them both. The note inside, bearing Sherman's signature, met the supervisors' request:

> Gentlemen: Your note of even date has just been received. Neither Mr. Hayes, myself, the gentlemen who accompany me, or the country at large can ever forget the obligation under which you will have placed us should you stand firm in the position you have taken. From a long and intimate acquaintance with Gov. Hayes, I am justified in assuming responsibility for promises made, and will guarantee that you shall be provided for as soon after 4th March as may be practicable, and in such manner as will enable you both to leave Louisiana should you deem it necessary.

Few missives have generated as much public controversy as this alleged (the word cannot be avoided) letter.[34]

But Anderson was not through with his scheming. Still nurturing the illusion that Nash might, through the efforts of the Returning Board, overturn a Democratic majority against him of 6,000 votes, he had the congressman cosign a document whereby he, Anderson, undertook to "suppress evidence showing that the . . . parish of East Feliciana was fairly carried by the Democratic party." In return Nash agreed, if reelected, to have Anderson appointed to the position of naval officer at the Port of New Orleans. Two Custom House employees witnessed Nash's and Anderson's signatures. In contrast to the Sherman letter, the authenticity of this document was never in question: Nash admitted to signing it. Former congressman Chester B. Darrall, who read it much later, called the agreement "something extraordinary," adding "even for Louisiana."[35]

For Louisiana's Republican leaders. James Anderson was, as yet, a minor nuisance. Their more serious worry was that Democrats might bribe the Returning Board or one of the presidential electors. The Republican visiting statesmen shared that disquiet. "A great many people express[ed] concern that the board would be tampered with," Garfield recalled.

"There were apprehensions and rumors constantly flying about." On November 22, for example, Sherman received an anonymous letter stating that the Tilden campaign had offered "a bribe of some consequence" to Louis M. Kenner, one of the board's two Black members. Other bribery attempts certainly took place. Board member Anderson testified that Dr. W. A. Robertson, a state senator, suggested "that I could get $200,000 if I could insure the State for the Democratic party." Robertson's weak denial was unconvincing.[36]

The man who chaired the board, however, caused Republicans the most anxiety. J. M. Wells, a political survivor with nerves of steel and the ability to land on his feet, was so politically flexible that Sheridan, in ousting him from the governor's chair in 1866, had likened his usual course of action to the marks in the dust left by a snake. Since his ignominious dismissal, however, Wells had become a Republican warhorse. He was both the chairman of the Returning Board and its dominant figure. Given that the presidential election turned upon his decisions, he now faced immense pressure. As Garfield put it in a letter to his wife: "You can imagine the stress and strain of the hour and how much steadiness of mind and nerve are needed to bear one's self through it and keep his head level."[37]

As the board opened the parish returns, Wells's task became even more daunting. The assumption that simply throwing out Democratic polls in the five bulldozed parishes would bring about a Republican majority turned out to be erroneous. Republicans therefore challenged polls in numerous other parishes, none of them previously considered objectionable. But a further difficulty arose. Merely engineering a majority for Packard would not elect Hayes, for in several parishes, as explained above, Republican ballots had failed to list all eight presidential electors. Wells somehow had to make up for a shortfall of about 2,000 votes in order to knock out two Tilden electors. The board considered yet more protests against yet more polls in yet more parishes. The chairman had to do all this while maintaining the fiction that the board considered each case on its merits without regard to which party would benefit or how individual decisions would affect the outcome.[38]

That Wells wavered under the pressure is no surprise. If he delivered Louisiana to Hayes and Packard, all the anger and bitterness of the Democratic Party would be directed toward him. On November 19, Democrat Duncan F. Kenner, one of the wealthiest planters in the state, bluntly warned him that he would incur the "hatred of every [white] man in the community" if he used his position to count in Packard. If he confirmed Nicholls's victory, on the other hand, grateful Democrats would reward him. Kenner asked Wells to name his price, but the latter emphasized his loyalty to the Republican Party and pointed to compelling evidence of preelection bulldozing. Eleven days later, however, Wells, according to Kenner's account, proposed letting Nicholls's majority stand in return for $200,000 "cash in hand." Kenner began to raise a bribery fund, but he never came close to accumulating such a sum, so nothing came of the scheme. Whether Wells would have accepted $200,000 had it been offered is a moot point. He denied ever soliciting a bribe; even if he did, he may have been playing the Democrats all along. Still, as the Returning Board went into closed session to make the crucial decisions about which polls to reject and which to let stand, Packard voiced the common suspicion that "old Wells is trying to get what he can" and "would sell out to either side."[39]

The day after his first meeting with Kenner, Wells reached out to the Grant administration through an intermediary, Joseph H. Maddox, a Treasury Department employee whom he had known for decades. According to Maddox, the board chairman wanted $200,000 each for himself and Thomas Anderson and smaller amounts for the two Black board members. Armed with Wells's letter of introduction, he traveled to Washington and informed Grant that the board chairman was in danger and needed personal protection from the US military. He then saw Don Cameron, the secretary of war, and delivered the second part of Wells's message: a request for a "large amount of money." Maddox suggested a figure of $1,000,000. Cameron turned him down.

Maddox, whose allegiance to the Republican Party was purely nominal, then took it upon himself to negotiate with the Democratic Party. Wells had urged him to enlist the aid of Republican senator J. R. West, to whom he addressed a letter stating that "millions [of dollars] have been sent here in the interest of Tilden" and warning that without "some countermove" by the Republican Party, the "results will be disastrous." Instead of seeing West, however, the duplicitous Maddox withheld Wells's letter and recruited a confederate, John T. Pickett, to meet DNC Chairman Hewitt in New York. Pickett set out Wells's million-dollar price tag—which included a tidy percentage that he and Maddox expected to take from any bribe they negotiated—but Hewitt also said no. The pair then tried to secure the money locally, again without success, a failure that reflected the would-be bribers' inability to come up with the stupendous sum demanded more than any moral compunction against paying bribes. As Kenner later testified, "none of us thought we were doing wrong."[40]

When a congressional committee revealed evidence of the bribery attempts, producing letters and telegrams that could hardly be more incriminating, Wells denied ever contemplating making a corrupt bargain with the opposition. "Republicans are not easy bought," he told Congressman David Dudley Field. "They may trade among themselves, but when a Democrat comes in to buy them they are not there." Field pounced: "You mean to say that they sell out to each other?" Wells laughed, unfazed by the question. "If it is necessary," he replied. The logic of Republicans "selling out to each other" was explained by US Marshal Jack Wharton: "I do not consider it bribery to give a man $100 to keep him from blowing my brains out." In the end, Wells had to make do with a promise of federal patronage if and when Hayes became president.[41]

For whatever reason (and some Republicans never doubted his loyalty), Wells came through for his party. Days before the Returning Board officially finalized the results, Pitkin informed West by telegram, in code: "Have seen Wells, who says board will return Hayes sure. Have no fear." As Jewett recalled in 1878, "it was a matter of general confidence that we would come out all right."[42]

Having failed to sway the Returning Board, Democrats sent an agent to offer presidential elector Aaron B. Levisee $40,000 to refrain from casting his ballot, suggesting that he justify his refusal "on a high moral ground." Levisee asked for $200,000—ostensibly to string the Democrats along by asking the impossible—and reported the approach to his party. Levisee claimed never to have been tempted. Be that as it may, he duly voted for Hayes.[43]

The visiting statesmen left New Orleans at the beginning of December, when the Returning Board went into closed session. From the mass of protests and affidavits, and from the notes of their many personal interviews with witnesses, the Republican group put together a report that Sherman submitted to President Grant. Hurriedly prepared (much of it drafted by Garfield during his return train journey), the "Sherman Report" asserted that the Democrats had implemented a "predetermined and settled plan" to suppress the Republican majorities in Ouachita, Morehouse, East Baton Rouge, West Feliciana, and East Feliciana Parishes by employing "violent and terrible means." Stressing the independence of the Returning Board, the necessity for its existence, and the respectability of its four members, the report urged that "its determination should be respected."[44]

Rising in the Senate on December 6, the same day that Louisiana cast its vote for Hayes, Sherman demanded that the report be published so as to "show how narrowly the people of the United States have escaped the danger of having a President elected by violence and murder." In a fiery speech that day, and in returning to the topic over the weeks following, he defended Louisiana's Republicans. He had arrived in the state, he confessed, with a marked "distaste of the turbulence and disturbance we had heard about them." But when he learned what they were up against, he came to appreciate their courage. There may be some "rascals among them . . . , but they have stood by the rights of the humble and the lowly, by the poor Negro who has been armed with political rights." The supervisors who had lodged protests, Sherman insisted, were decent men who were doing their duty. Democrats had ridiculed one of them for having run a snake show in New Orleans, but "he is not dishonest simply because he shows snakes." As for James Anderson, he was a "very good man in every respect, a worthy man; no imputation was cast on him." That was a stretch to say the least, but Sherman was doing his best to make a silk purse of a sow's ear. He knew, of course, that the Returning Board had engaged in sharp practice.[45]

Lewis V. Bogy of Missouri, one of the Democratic visiting statesmen, replied with vitriol. There had been no intimidation of Black voters by Democrats, he asserted. The affidavits alleging such were "made by unknown vagabonds and perjured villains . . . , not one of whom could read a word of what had been written for them." The murders of Dr. Dinkgrave, Henry Pinkston, and John Gair had nothing to do with politics but were carried out "for other purposes or by blacks themselves." The entirety of Eliza Pinkston's testimony was "founded in falsehood." The protests of Weber and Anderson, from which Sherman had liberally quoted, were worthless, the former being a "dog of low degree" who was "bribed to lie," while the latter was "the fellow who shot himself" and then blamed the deed on Democrats. The Returning Board had accepted protests long after the day of the election, had refused to appoint a Democrat to the panel, and was in any case illegitimate. Should the election really be decided by three scoundrels—Wells, Anderson and Kenner—and an ignoramus, Gustave Casanave (the fourth member of the board)? "The thing is too absurd."

Sherman advised Bogy to "keep cool and sit still" as he airily dismissed the Returning's Board's rule bending. Supervisors submitted their protests in New Orleans because they had been afraid to make them in the bulldozed parishes. The fact that the board consisted of four Republicans did not negate its authority. Amid derisive laughter from the Democratic senators, he praised Wells and Anderson for having "conducted themselves with manly courage." The violence and intimidation had been real, Sherman insisted. Dr. Saunders, whose alleged poisoning had led to Gair's and Matthews's lynchings, was alive and well. When Pinkston testified, "her wounds were yet bleeding and her dead husband and child buried like dogs without inquest or examination." If Tilden were inaugurated president, "the blood of hundreds of men would rest upon his skirt."[46]

The arguments over Louisiana helped each side rally their troops. But they did nothing to resolve the electoral crisis, which simply moved into a new phase after Republican returning boards gave the votes of Florida and South Carolina (along with Louisiana) to Hayes. With these, the chances of Tilden coming out on top slowly faded as the candidate exhibited a passivity and indecision that bewildered his supporters. Democratic hopes rose again in January 1877 when Congress created the Electoral Commission to rule on the disputed electoral college votes of the three southern states and Oregon. The commission comprised fifteen members: five from the House, five from the Senate, and five from the Supreme Court. Its composition, eight Republicans and seven Democrats, suggested that the panel, if voting along party lines, would confirm the Hayes electors. But one of the justices, David Davis of Illinois, had the reputation of being "studiously independent." Democrats persuaded themselves that he might support Tilden's case; the selection of Davis, in fact, largely influenced their decision to back the legislation creating the commission.[47]

It was now the Republicans' turn to sweat. The Electoral Bill had passed with strong Democratic support, but most Republicans, regarding it as a needless concession that weakened their position, voted against it. Representative Ben Butler of Massachusetts called the measure unconstitutional and unnecessary: Hayes had 185 electoral votes, and the Constitution provided that the president of the Senate should count them. "We think we hold a good hand . . . and that the Democrats want a new deal," an Ohio Republican wrote Garfield. "Don't give it to them!" Garfield himself, having strenuously opposed the measure, tried to make the best of the situation. "While the bill surrenders a great advantage, it will not necessarily defeat us," he wrote Hayes. "Probably it leaves us an even chance—possibly more."[48]

Those odds improved significantly when Davis, upon his election to the US Senate by the Illinois legislature, announced that he would not be serving on the commission after all. Democrats were appalled by this turn of events, but the blame lay within their own ranks. Encouraged by William T. Pelton, Tilden's nephew, Democratic legislators had voted with Independents to elect Davis. Pelton had naively assumed that, in Michael Holt's words, "a grateful Davis . . . would award enough disputed electoral votes to Tilden to make him a winner." It was a colossal miscalculation. The punctilious (or perhaps devious) Davis at once recused himself. Justice Joseph P. Bradley, a Republican, took his place.[49]

Neither side could be sure how Bradley would vote. Democrats took heart from the fact that he was no Radical. They had cheered his ruling in *US v. Cruikshank,* which weakened the antiterrorist Enforcement Acts and drastically narrowed the reach of the Fourteenth Amendment. Writing many years later, Eppa Hunton recalled that he and the other Democrats on the commission "firmly believed" that Bradley would support Tilden's case. Republicans thought otherwise: Bradley was one of them, and partisan lines were tightly drawn at this time. He would be as reliable as the two other Republican justices, William Chandler told Hayes.[50]

When the Louisiana case came before the Electoral Commission, ex–Supreme Court justice Joseph A. Campbell, arguing for the Democrats, spoke for two solid hours, prompting Garfield to reflect, "I doubt if any Louisiana man is competent to discuss this question wisely." The Republican members emitted an audible sigh of relief when the commission voted 8 to 7 to confirm the Hayes electors.[51]

Bradley supplied the crucial vote on each of the four states (the fourth was Oregon, where the qualifications of a Republican elector were in doubt). The votes were all 8 to 7. Crucially, the commission voted not to "go behind the returns." This meant that it would not relitigate the fairness or unfairness of the elections in question, ostensibly out of deference to states' rights. As Bradley put it, the appointment of presidential electors was solely a matter for the states, and if those electors were chosen through fraudulent elections or crooked returning boards, Congress could do nothing. The honesty or dishonesty of Louisiana's board was irrelevant, he argued. "The motives of the members may have been bad motives, corrupt, fraudulent, what not; but with improprieties and with the motives of the members we have nothing to do." Democrats suspected, and some openly asserted, that Bradley had intended to support Tilden's case but was bribed to change his vote. They could never substantiate that charge.[52]

Pelton nursed the hope that the Senate would reject the commission's verdict on Louisiana: he was counting on Roscoe Conkling, the powerful senator from New York, to lead a Republican revolt. Conkling, in the parlance of the time, was a "spoilsman" and a "stalwart": he believed in appointing Republicans to federal jobs and supported Congressional Reconstruction. He therefore despised Hayes, a self-styled reformer who was eager to woo southern Democrats. Convinced that Tilden had won the election, Conkling backed the Electoral Bill. He also assured Hewitt that he would denounce the Louisiana Returning Board when the Senate considered the electoral votes of that state. On the day the Senate took up the Louisiana case, however, Conkling absented himself; the anticipated Republican revolt failed to materialize. If Conkling expected Hayes to express gratitude, he was to be disappointed. Deprived of the recognition and patronage he felt due to him, the New Yorker later struck back at Hayes through the Potter Committee.[53]

With Hayes's election assured, Louisiana's Republicans looked forward to four more years in state power. Once again, however, for the third time in four years, the Democratic Party took the law into its own hands. Mobilizing the paramilitary White League, it set up its own legislature and, on January 9, 1877, inaugurated Francis Nicholls as governor. To underline his government's power, Nicholls ordered the White League to seize control of the state arsenal, the police stations, and, forcibly ejecting Republican judges, the state supreme court. Packard, inaugurated the previous day, found himself besieged in the Saint Louis Hotel, the state capitol, by an armed mob.

Packard, Pitkin, Campbell, US Attorney J. R. Beckwith, and others implored Grant to declare his support for the Republican state government and, using troops if necessary, order the Nicholls forces to stand down. "For God's sake act," wired Pitkin. "Packard will hold state house until death."[54]

Grant answered their pleas with a refusal to recognize either government. He would not allow armed Democrats to eject Packard and the Republican legislators from the statehouse, where federal troops protected them, but he would not help them regain control of the city. Instructing General Augur to "maintain the present status quo," the president told him to intervene only "if armed bodies threaten peace and safety." Nicholls, anxious at all costs to avoid provoking Grant, assured Augur that he would keep the White League under control, refrain from violence, and lift the siege of the statehouse. He agreed, too, not to install Democratic officials in the country parishes if it meant forcibly displacing Republicans.[55]

The ostensible reason for Grant's neutrality was that he should make no decision pending the outcome of two congressional investigations of the Louisiana election. The explanation was unconvincing. For one thing, the two committees, one with a Democratic majority and the other dominated by Republicans, were never likely to agree on the fairness of the election or on which candidates deserved to win; as expected, they ultimately reached radically different conclusions. For another, the witnesses called by the Republican Party provided detailed, consistent, and voluminous evidence that violence and intimidation had been central to the Democratic campaign. Anderson, appearing before the Senate committee chaired by Republican Timothy O. Howe, stood by his supervisor's protest. Weber, testifying before the same committee, identified the principal bulldozers in West Feliciana by name and spoke about the threats against his own life. True, Democrats furnished numerous Black witnesses who testified that they voted freely. The accumulated testimony of the two committees, however, suggested that the five bulldozed parishes fully merited that description.[56]

Secretary of War Cameron, unhappy with Grant's refusal to recognize Packard, half-jokingly suggested, "we must wait then until a shot is fired, and then we can act." In distant New Hampshire, William Chandler had the same thought. "Act with more courage," he unhelpfully wired Kellogg. "You and Packard cannot die a better death than resisting rebels and revolutionists." In reply, Packard explained the futility of such a gesture. "I have one musket when the White League have one hundred." A violent clash might provide the occasion for the federal government to intervene, but Packard and his crew were unlikely to instigate one. "Our fellows down there won't fight," complained Cameron. Nicholls, meanwhile, went to great lengths to restrain Democrats from committing any acts of violence.[57]

Grant's apparent evenhandedness could not but help Nicholls and further isolate Packard. The Democrats "have substantial possession of the city," Augur wired the secretary of war. As the standoff dragged on into February, Nicholls's position only grew stronger, Packard's weaker. The latter's opponents were "numerous, united and aggressive, his friends few, unorganized, and furnish no moral or material support," the general reported. The Republican state government, he believed, could "only be maintained by use of U.S. troops."[58]

That is precisely what Grant was determined to avoid. He did not wish to tie his successor's hands by supporting either Packard or Nicholls—that was for Hayes to decide. Privately, however, he concluded that the least undesirable outcome would be the disappearance of Packard's government and the eventual recognition of Nicholls's regime. The president had, in fact, lost patience with Louisiana's Republican Party. His intervention two years earlier had provoked a barrage of criticism, much of it from fellow Republicans. He did not wish to repeat the experience, especially when he believed that Tilden had carried Louisiana fairly and that the Returning Board—an "outrageous contrivance" whose record had been "tainted with suspicion, if not with actual fraud"—had reversed the true result. The fact that Grant knew about Wells's demand for money did nothing to temper that view. But it was not so much the corruption of Louisiana's Republicans that bred contempt as their fecklessness—a far worse political sin. "They are always in trouble," Grant complained, "and always wanting the U.S. to send troops."[59]

As the electoral crisis wore on, Grant's attitude hardened. In cabinet he characterized Louisiana's Republican leaders as stereotypical carpetbaggers: northerners who had no interest in Louisiana other than to hold office and would leave the state, or be driven out, as soon as they lost it. When former Confederate general James Longstreet, now a Republican, urged him to recognize Nicholls as the winner, Grant read his letter to the cabinet. Longstreet told his old-army friend that Nicholls had been "fairly elected" and that his Democratic administration would not contest the Returning Board's award of the state to Hayes. On February 20 Grant told a delegation of Louisiana Democrats that he would recognize neither Nicholls nor Packard but intimated that his sympathies lay with the former. During a cabinet meeting three days later, Secretary of State Hamilton Fish recorded, the president stated "with a great deal of emphasis" that "*we will not sustain Legislatures by military force.*"[60]

Shortly before Hayes's inauguration, the retiring president made his position unmistakably clear. In response to another plea from Packard, Grant had his private secretary, C. C. Sniffen, inform him that the president "feels it his duty to state frankly that he does not believe that public opinion will [any] longer support the maintenance of State Government in Louisiana by the use of the military, and that he must concur in this manifest feeling."[61]

The "Sniffen Telegram" shocked Louisiana Republicans. Kellogg had blithely assumed that either Grant or Hayes would recognize Packard's government. That was the least that the state's partisans could expect as a reward for the incredible feat of converting a Democratic majority of 8,000 votes into a Republican victory margin of over 3,000. As Kellogg put it, Louisiana was "the corner-stone" of Hayes's victory. Garfield, after hearing Grant denigrate the Packard government, was bewildered by the president's prediction that Nicholls would come out on top. "I don't see how Packard can be overthrown without destroying the authority which gave the electoral vote of that State to Hayes," he confided to his diary. "I don't see how the vote for Electors and the vote for Governor can be separated." In any case, he added, "this seems to be a bad outlook for our friends in Louisiana."[62]

Quite how bad those "friends" did not yet appreciate. Although Grant had left office with US soldiers still protecting the Louisiana statehouse, it would be difficult for Hayes, even if he wished it, to reverse his predecessor's policy and recognize Packard. In fact, he was just as convinced as Grant that the use of military power to prop up Republican governments in the South must cease.

Publicly, Hayes had been careful not to explicitly commit himself to abandoning Packard; he confined himself to vague, general, and ambiguous statements about pursuing a "wise and liberal policy" that secured to southerners "the blessings of honest and capable local government" as well as "the rights of all." That elastic formula gave Hayes plenty of wiggle room. Throughout the electoral crisis, he stuck to the same vagueness and ambiguity in his statements. His inaugural address on March 5 stuck to the theme of supporting the right of states to "self-government" while insisting that "it must be a government which guards the interests of both races . . . [and] which submits loyally and heartily to the Constitution."[63]

Behind the scenes, however, Hayes's surrogates had assured a group of Louisiana Democrats—Nicholls's personal representative E. A. Burke and Congressmen E. John Ellis, Gibson, and William M. Levy—that the incoming president would confine the soldiers to barracks and allow Packard's government to fall. The fact that those surrogates included fellow Ohioans Charles Foster and Stanley Matthews, Hayes's brother-in-law, persuaded the Democrats that they spoke for the president. Just as important was the participation of Sherman and Garfield in the culminating discussions on February 26 at Washington's Wormley House hotel; their involvement helped convince the Louisianans that Hayes would be able to carry his own party with him. In order to assuage Republican fears, the Nicholls legislature passed, at the urging of Burke, a set of resolutions pledging to respect the Constitution, enforce the law impartially, and refrain from persecuting people "for past political conduct." Taking these promises at face value, Senator Oliver P. Morton, one of the staunchest supporters of Congressional Reconstruction, signaled his assent to the "just and conciliatory policy" advocated by Hayes. As a quid pro quo, Burke advised Democrats in the House of Representatives to end the parliamentary delaying tactics that had prevented the counting of all of Hayes's electoral votes. On March 2 the count was finally completed.[64]

The day after the Wormley House meeting, Matthews wrote to Packard urging him to resign. As soon as the troops were withdrawn, he told the beleaguered governor, "the Nicholls government will be the only existing government, and will have to be recognized as such." To maintain Packard's regime by force of federal arms, he added, "will be impossible for a Republican [that is, Hayes] administration." Packard refused, obtusely noting that Matthews was expressing a "personal opinion" that did not necessarily coincide with that of Hayes. Besides, he would not betray Louisiana's 70,000 Republican voters or the "hundreds of Republicans who have given their lives as a sacrifice to the cause of liberty and free government." Packard vowed to go down fighting rather yield to force and violence.[65]

The prospect of Packard as a Republican martyr held no appeal for Hayes. In cabinet he discussed what to do about Louisiana as if it were still an open question, but the lack of support for maintaining Packard's government strengthened his conviction that "it is not the duty of the President . . . to use the military power of the Nation to decide contested elections in the States." Yet a precipitate withdrawal of troops risked splitting the Republican Party and placing Packard and his supporters in mortal danger. It might also reveal an embarrassing truth: Hayes had already, privately if indirectly, assured Democrats that he would ditch Packard. The president needed time to finesse the problem. Extinguishing Republican rule in Louisiana required some kind of compromise, at least something that could be presented as a compromise. To this end, Hayes announced that he would send a five-man commission to Louisiana—another set of visiting statesmen.[66]

Democrats greeted the commission with a marked lack of enthusiasm, fearing it would engineer a compromise that would deprive them of full state power. Astute commentators, however, discerned the purpose of the commission from its composition: John M. Harlan, was a Kentucky Unionist and law partner of Benjamin Bristow, Grant's secretary of the Treasury and a critic of military intervention. Having delivered Kentucky's delegates to Hayes at the Republican National Convention, Harlan coveted the seat on the Supreme Court recently vacated by David Davis. Wayne MacVeagh, a Philadelphia lawyer who had served as Grant's ambassador to the Ottoman Empire, was a conservative Republican, as was C. B. Lawrence, lately of the Illinois Supreme Court. Joseph R. Hawley, a former governor of Connecticut and now the owner of that state's leading Republican newspaper, firmly supported Hayes's policy of conciliating white southerners. The fifth member, John C. Brown, a prewar governor of Tennessee, was a Democrat. All five commissioners "had strong personal, family, or military relationships" with Representative Gibson. It was not an especially high-powered group (several more-prominent Republicans declined to serve), but it could be counted upon to carry out its assignment.[67]

Arriving in New Orleans on April 5, the commissioners made it clear from the outset that they were not in Louisiana to relitigate the election or adjudicate the contending claims of Nicholls and Packard. Rather, they were instructed by Secretary of State William M. Evarts to clear away the obstacles to the formation of a unitary state government under Nicholls.

That was no easy task. "Of all the States I have ever visited," Harlan wrote Bristow, "this beats all. Its politics are an utter confusion, and it will puzzle any one to get at the exact truth." One stumbling block was the intransigence of the Democrats, who, Harlan explained, "infer that if they stand fast they will secure an early withdrawal of the troops and the consequent disappearance of the Packard government." Further complicating the problem were the numerous Democratic aspirants to the US Senate, who judged every proposal to reconfigure the legislature according to how it might affect their own chances of being elected. The Republicans, for their part, pressed their claim to be the only legal state government, still hoping that Hayes would support them.[68]

The commissioners concluded that the only way to convince Packard to abandon his claim was to undermine the Republican legislature, thereby presenting him with a fait accompli. They reasoned that the Democratic-controlled assembly would have unassailable legitimacy if the majority of its members had been certified by the Republican-controlled Returning Board. To achieve this "Returning Board quorum," members of the Republican legislature were offered financial inducements—their accumulated mileage and per diem, plus under-the-table cash bribes—to join the

Nicholls body. By April 18, however, the eighty-three-strong Republican caucus, despite a few defections, refused to disband. Insisting that Republicans should replace three Democrats from New Orleans who had clearly been defeated, it rejected the commissioners' "plan of adjustment."[69]

But the Democrats would concede nothing. Unseating these three lawmakers would hand control of the House to the Republicans; it would also be a tacit admission that the Democratic-controlled legislature had never possessed a legal quorum in the first place. Given their contention that the state legislature canvassed the vote for governor, such an admission would cast doubt upon the legitimacy of Nicholls's title. It would also undermine the legal rationale that Matthews had offered for distinguishing between the vote for president and the vote for governor—Hayes taking Louisiana's electoral college votes while at the same time abandoning Packard.

With state Republicans refusing to give way, the commissioners gave them an ultimatum. On April 18 Harlan and MacVeagh met a delegation of twelve from the Packard legislature. If anyone "entertains the most lingering idea that the troops are going to remain," MacVeagh declared, "for God's sake disabuse him of that idea, for they are going to be removed." According to State Senator Swayze, MacVeagh warned that the Democrats "will hang every one of you to the lamp posts" if Republicans offered resistance. The following day twelve of the caucus moved to the Nicholls legislature; the dam had given way. The Packard legislature dwindled to a rump of ten people. In order to persuade key Republican politicians to acquiesce in their loss of state power, Harlan promised them federal patronage positions.[70]

On April 24, acting on Hayes's instructions, General Augur ordered the troops who had been protecting the statehouse to return to their barracks. Packard resigned, and in 1878 sailed off to Liverpool, where he took up the post of US consul. Louisiana would not elect another Republican governor until 1980.

For native Republicans who had fled the Felicianas, many exiled in New Orleans, Hayes's southern policy was catastrophic. Hayes and Matthews set great store by pledges of good behavior from Louisiana's Democratic Party. They hoped that by "conciliating" the South's white conservatives, the latter might be persuaded to accept the legitimacy of a two-party political system that embraced the civil and political equality of the Black population. And, indeed, Nicholls and his state legislature promised to protect Blacks' constitutional rights, including the right to vote and hold office, and to refrain from persecuting Republicans "for past political conduct." But the Democrats had made similar pledges before—in 1872, 1874, and 1876—and there was little to suggest that this latest iteration was any more sincere. As a Republican pointed out to the *New York Tribune*, "Democratic promises are the cheapest and most worthless things we have in Louisiana."[71]

No sooner had they laid their hands on the machinery of justice than state and parish authorities prosecuted several leading Republicans, including Judge Henry C. Myers of Natchitoches Parish, Judge Henry C. Dibble of New Orleans, and all four members of the Returning Board. In West Feliciana Parish the schoolboard indicted E. L. Weber for embezzlement. Some Democrats, Governor Nicholls among them, deplored these prosecutions. The so-called Bourbon wing of their party, however, applauded them. No Republican, the *New Orleans Daily Democrat* thundered, "has any right to expect generous treatment from this people; and they may rest assured that we are in no temper to display any toward them." Without an "aggressive policy" of prosecuting "able and unscrupulous" Republicans, the *Democrat* added, such men would "reorganize the ignorant and facile negroes."[72]

Democrats in the Feliciana parishes had no intention of allowing the local Republican Party to recover. Black refugees were put on notice that they would be permitted to return only if they prostrated themselves. Lucius Early, for example, published a groveling "card" in which he apologized for having taken up his seat in the Packard legislature and begged for forgiveness. "I fully acknowledge my error. . . . [I]t is a dereliction of duty that can never occur to me again."[73]

Democrats also prevented Blacks from holding public office. When the postmaster general appointed John Dula and Samuel Chapman to run the post offices in Saint Francisville and Clinton, respectively, they vowed to block them. Dula was a "vile, unconscionable wretch, a moral leper," raved the *West Feliciana Sentinel;* Chapman was "an ignorant field hand." Both men hesitated for months before attempting to install themselves in office, finally presenting their commissions in May 1877. Despite Governor Nicholls's assurance that they had nothing to fear, neither man stayed long. Dula found a small coffin, six inches long, on the porch of his house, with a note admonishing him to leave West Feliciana Parish by June 1. In Clinton Chapman was confronted by two leading Democrats who engaged in the "good cop-bad cop" routine: they had nothing against him themselves, but the white people of the parish found him "obnoxious" for having testified before the Howe Committee. "They said that so far as they were able they would protect me, but added, 'There is no law that will protect you from a mob in case you attempt to take possession of the office.'"[74]

If either Dula or Chapman harbored any doubts about what lay in store for them, the murder of James Law settled the matter. The most prominent Black Republican in East Feliciana Parish, Law had fled to New Orleans and, in his testimony before the Morrison Committee, named the two men who had set fire to his store in Jackson. He did so reluctantly, however, telling senators that if he returned to the parish, "I might be killed for it." He did return, and on May 19 assassins "found him sitting on his porch in the company of his mother and shot him dead." Dula and Chapman resigned their commissions. A few days later a party of whites "waited on" Joseph Armstead, Julius Green, Valentine Emory, and Riley Norfliss, telling them to leave West Feliciana Parish. All had been stalwart Republicans and had testified before one or both of the congressional committees investigating the recent election.[75]

Don Weber received no reward for his part in securing Louisiana for Hayes. Returning to his home in West Feliciana Parish in late January 1877, he felt he was a marked man. Democrats were incensed by his "protest" over the conduct of the election. They burned with indignation over his testimony before the Howe Committee. They felt affronted by the "swaggering insolence" with which Republican senators had interrogated Democratic witnesses. Weber, the *West Feliciana Sentinel* stated on February 10, had maliciously abused and vilified the "good people" of West Feliciana, "branding the whole community as perpetrators of heinous crimes and misdemeanors." The man was a "a rascal and a dog of low degree."[76]

Weber tried to assuage those "good people" by offering to support the Democratic claimants to parish offices. "It is a notorious fact," he wrote Packard on February 24, "that at the late election . . . several persons were elected who did not enjoy the confidence of the tax-payers." These "obnoxious persons" were willing to resign in favor of men who did. Such a change, he promised, would ensure "no more trouble" in West Feliciana. He was writing, he explained, at the behest of "several gentlemen who own large pecuniary interests in the parish."[77]

On March 3, 1877, the day before Hayes's inauguration, Weber wrote to Republican senator Samuel J. R. McMillan of Minnesota, who had served on the Howe Committee. Since testifying before that body, Weber stated, "I have been at home cooped up in the house, unable to appear on the streets without incurring danger." He pleaded with the senator to use his influence with the incoming administration, and persuade other Republican senators to do likewise, to secure the president's recognition of Packard's government. "Our lives, our property, and the security of our families depend on you."[78]

Five days later Weber's body was found riddled with buckshot, lying in a ditch opposite the courthouse in Saint Francisville. He had been gunned down in broad daylight by, in the words of the coroner's jury, "two or more persons unknown." Only thirty years old, he left a widow and three children, the youngest a three-week-old baby.[79]

Bereft and without any means of support, Mrs. Weber abandoned the family home and moved to Donaldsonville, in Ascension Parish, where her father and mother-in-law operated merchant's stores. Her brother-in-law, E. L. Weber, also moved to Donaldsonville. From the safety of a majority Black town in a majority Black parish that Republicans still controlled, Weber publicly implicated Charles M. Barrow, the Democratic clerk of court, and John J. Barrow, the Democratic sheriff, in his brother's murder. The former was a known killer, he stated: Republican witnesses named him as the man who fatally shot Gilbert Carter and Isaac Mitchell. The other Barrow was a "noted bull-dozer." The Barrows had both the motive and the means to kill Don Weber. Both men had been inside the courthouse at the time of the shooting.[80]

Governor Nicholls offered a reward of $5,000 for information leading to the arrest of Weber's killers. Nobody claimed the money. Rather than regret the murder, many Democrats justified it. Weber "had made himself odious to a number of our citizens," explained the *West Feliciana Sentinel*. He had been "an incendiary spirit of the worst kind, and has several times tried to instigate race riots," charged the *Louisville Courier-Journal*. "It is only a wonder he has lived so long." He and his brother "were bold bad men," declared a Mississippi paper, "who should have been put to death by an outraged community long ago."[81]

In his plea to McMillan, Weber made no mention of the supposed Sherman letter. Nor did he ever write to Senator Sherman to demand the office that the latter had, according to James Anderson, promised. If Weber had ever possessed a letter from Sherman, he kept that fact hidden from his wife, Emilie; his brother, Emile; and his brother-in-law, former congressman Joseph P. Newsham. In fact, he never mentioned it to a living soul.

The Jenkses, living in Agnes's mother's house, felt unable to return to their home in Jackson. E. L. Weber abandoned his property in West Feliciana and was afraid to set foot in the parish. "I am already bankrupted," he complained to William Chandler, "and I do not know what I shall do to furnish bread and meat for my family if we are not let alone." These Republicans, who had been in the political firing line both figuratively and literally, knew better than most the naïveté of Hayes's southern policy. "We are altogether left out in the cold," Agnes Jenks griped to Anderson. "I can't help laughing when I think what fools we have been."[82]

3

BIPARTISAN FURY

SEEKING REVENGE AGAINST RUTHERFORD B. HAYES

James Anderson, meanwhile, had not been idle. Still a clerk in the New Orleans Custom House, where his duties were so negligible that they appeared not to have required his presence, he set his sights on a position that was loftier, better paid, and far from Louisiana.

The day after Hayes's inauguration, the editor of the Steubenville, Ohio, *Herald* recommended Anderson to the president as a "worthy young man and a staunch Republican" who, as the supervisor of East Feliciana Parish, was "in a great measure instrumental in saving us the State." Armed with additional recommendations from Congressmen C. B. Darrall and J. E. Leonard, ex-governor Kellogg, and former congressman Charles Nash, Anderson joined the army of office seekers who thronged the White House hoping to catch the president's ear. With Darrall and Nash in tow, he made his case to Hayes in person, presenting himself as a loyal Republican who had risked his life for the party.[1]

Hayes was sympathetic. Anderson "appeared intelligent and capable," he recalled. "He represented that his wife's health required him to go to a warm climate." It seemed an open-and-shut case of a deserving Republican who had the support of his Republican congressional delegation. Hayes endorsed Anderson's application with a note to Secretary of State Evarts: "Please appoint this gentleman to a consulship in a warm climate. This is a special case." Anderson filed his application with the State Department, where it joined a growing backlog of jobseekers' letters.[2]

Anderson then tried his luck with the Treasury Department. Three times he asked to see Secretary of the Treasury Sherman, who was either absent or too busy. He then turned up at Sherman's private residence, presenting his card according to the custom of the time. By Anderson's account, the Treasury secretary came out to see him but made no acknowledgement that they had previously met and offered no help. "He neither proposed to use his influence for me in his department nor in any other department." Anderson took his leave without ever mentioning the purported Sherman letter.[3]

Nothing if not determined, Anderson took a train to Cincinnati and introduced himself to Stanley Matthews, who had replaced Sherman in the US Senate. He told the senator about his heroic role in the election in East Feliciana Parish and complained that Kellogg and Packard had failed to fulfil their promises to him. He pressed for a federal appointment that matched his sterling services and, referring to his wife's delicate health, stated that a consulate somewhere warm would suffice. A sympathetic Matthews promised to do what he could. He told Anderson to proceed to New Orleans and present his case to John M. Harlan, who had the important but unstated task of doling out federal patronage in order to mollify Louisiana's ousted Republican leaders. As their discussion ended, Anderson gave Matthews the original copy of his agreement with Nash. He explained that despite the document's wording, he had no actual evidence to suppress, did not covet the naval office, and had merely wished to possess a document that gave him a "hold" on Nash.[4]

Anderson and Matthews both left descriptions of this meeting, and they tallied except in one crucial respect. The senator denied that Anderson said anything about the Returning Board throwing out the East Feliciana returns on a "forged protest," while Anderson claimed that he told Matthews all about it. On one crucial fact, however, their accounts agreed: Anderson neither referred to the Sherman letter nor mentioned Sherman's name.[5]

When Harlan arrived in New Orleans on April 5, Anderson was waiting with the senator's letter of introduction. The bearer "may desire to communicate with you confidentially," Matthews wrote Harlan. Anderson, according to his own account, gave the Kentuckian "a complete history of how the election had been manipulated in Louisiana." He supplemented his account by providing copies of his agreements with Nash and Don Weber. He did *not* give him a copy of the Sherman letter. At Harlan's suggestion, Anderson wrote to Matthews regarding the consulship in Callao, Peru, where the death of the incumbent had created a vacancy. On April 14 Hayes forwarded Anderson's application to Evarts at the State Department, with a note that Matthews "requests that this appointment be made for important reasons."[6]

Despite the best efforts of Matthews and Harlan, and despite several meetings with the president himself, Anderson secured neither the consulship he craved nor the deputy collectorship at the New Orleans Custom House that he considered an acceptable consolation. Part of the problem was that the number of office seekers far exceeded the number of available offices. Yet despite the relative weakness of his claim, Anderson proved impossible to satisfy. When finally offered a consulship in Funchal, a town on the Portuguese island of Madeira, he turned it down. As one historian puts it, such postings "offered little more than poverty in an exotic setting."[7]

By now Hayes suspected that Anderson was not the deserving case he had first thought. A letter from J. A. Straight of the Government Printing Office urged him to bar Anderson's appointment: in Louisiana, Straight informed the president, Anderson "tried to sell out to the Democrats and did everything that was low and dishonorable." While in Washington, he added, the applicant had been "blowing around among his acquaintances in my presence that he will 'feather his nest' while he is in office." Hayes instructed Evarts to make no decision on Anderson's application "until further enquiries as to [his] character are instituted." When Anderson saw the president on June 1, he left the White House emptyhanded and furious. "Come here and settle this affair," he wired Matthews, "or you can all face the music."[8]

Despite this threat, or perhaps because of it, Matthews interceded with Hayes to secure Anderson a position in the Treasury Department. But Anderson disdained the position of Custom House clerk (the equivalent of his old position in New Orleans) and insisted on seeing the president to explain that Matthews had promised him something better. Thomas H. C. Smith, the Treasury Department's appointments secretary, accompanied Anderson to the White House, but Hayes declined to see him. "I told Smith I believed Anderson was a great scoundrel," he recalled, "and that I wouldn't see him and wanted nothing further to do with him." Still, while the president saw no reason to award Anderson a "larger place," he did not bar him from "ordinary employment." Anderson seemed content with the offer of inspector of customs in Baltimore.[9]

Upon discovering that the job involved hard work, however, Anderson contemptuously rejected it. The position was suitable for a "ward-bummer," he complained. The pay was derisory, and the job entailed "stand[ing] under a broiling sun" for twelve hours a day in order to "prevent a rascally lot of sailors from smuggling." Anderson was now trying Matthews's patience. "If he does not choose to take what you choose to offer," the senator wrote Smith on June 22, "drop him." Yet Anderson subsequently went to the Treasury Building and asked Smith to appoint his brother John to the same position that he himself had declined. After consulting Matthews in Cincinnati, Smith complied. Finally, upon securing a job for his brother, Anderson assured Smith, "this will be satisfactory to me."[10]

The trouble Matthews took to placate Anderson was inexplicable if the latter were a run-of-the-mill jobseeker. His solicitude was even more extraordinary in light of Anderson's insolent behavior. "Something must be done immediately," he wired Matthews on May 5. After his fruitless meeting with Hayes, he wired, "I want no more correspondence and no more nonsense." Threats followed. He possessed further knowledge of "rascality during the campaign," Anderson told the senator; anti-Hayes Republicans were urging him to release "documents damaging to the Administration." On June 19 he warned, "you shall hear from me before the October election." A week later he repeated the threat, telling Matthews that he "had nothing further to ask of you or of the monumental fraud who occupies the White House."[11] On June 26 he demanded that the senator return the Nash and Weber agreements. "If you refuse [I] will publish your letters and show how Louisiana was carried for Hayes."[12]

Matthews, it is clear, wanted to keep Anderson quiet. The Nash agreement furnished evidence of disreputable dealings in the Louisiana election. Anderson had also sent him his agreement with Don Weber, which, if authentic, could also be damaging. Matthews wanted to ensure that these documents never saw the light of day. Their publication, he later explained, would reinforce the Democrats' "false and injurious" narrative of a stolen election. Better to put up with Anderson's insulting behavior and fix him up with a job.[13]

In his meetings with Matthews, Harlan, Hayes, and Sherman himself, Anderson never mentioned any written pledge from Sherman. The suspicion that he had never received such a promise is heightened by the fact he never referred to one until June 10, 1877. Even then he failed to mention Sherman by name. "When those Republican 'dead-beats' came to Louisiana last fall to have a 'fair count,'" he wrote Thomas Jenks, "Don Weber and I refused to fall into line until we secured a written guarantee that we would be provided for." Weber had taken possession of the letter, he claimed, and probably had it in his jacket pocket when murdered. "If we can get possession of it, we will make this administration hum." Reluctant to set foot again in Louisiana lest the state indict him for perjury,

Anderson pressed Jenks to find it. "It was enclosed in a white envelope," he told him. "If you can secure it our case is made."[14]

Agnes Jenks, Thomas's resourceful wife, got to work. Taking a train from New Orleans to Donaldsonville, she questioned Emilie "Millie" Weber about the letter. Don's widow denied any knowledge of it but agreed to go through his papers that were stored in her father's warehouse. Nothing turned up. When Thomas reported that Agnes had drawn a blank, Anderson asked if anybody had searched Weber's body after he was gunned down. He guaranteed "a cool thousand dollars if you do get it." Taking up his suggestion, Agnes promised Millie that she would be "remunerated well" if she could lay her hands on the letter; "I feel sure it must be among Mr. Weber's papers, as he had it in his pocket." Millie replied that she had gone through her husband's effects but failed to find anything of the kind.[15]

Anderson was drawing the Jenkses into a scheme to extort federal appointments from the Hayes administration. On May 11, the day Anderson departed New Orleans for good, Thomas swore to an affidavit that corroborated the former's story of the election in East Feliciana Parish: Kellogg had tried to prevent an election by keeping Anderson in New Orleans; the election, when it took place, had been fair and square; and he and Anderson had falsely alleged intimidation in order to secure Hayes's election. Jenks's affidavit, written down by Anderson, made no reference to any promise from Sherman or any other of the visiting statesmen. Anderson promised to show it to Matthews "for the purpose of getting Jenks a place."[16]

On July 2, when he was still seeking favors from the administration, Anderson mailed copies of his letters to Don Weber to Charles A. Dana, editor of the *New York Sun* and strong Tilden supporter. These documents, he explained, provided "an interesting inside history of the last election in Louisiana." Two weeks later Anderson met William Chandler of New Hampshire, a member of the Republican National Committee, and spilled out the story of his "forged protest." Now, *for the first time,* he referred to promises allegedly made to him, in writing, by John Sherman.[17]

Chandler listened sympathetically. Thoroughly opposed to Hayes's southern policy, he was eager to find ammunition to use against the president. But he was also an experienced lawyer: he wanted documentary evidence. Showing Chandler his letters from Matthews, Anderson demonstrated the latter's eagerness to find him a federal position—solicitude that struck Chandler as telling. In a memorandum for the record, he noted that Anderson "is to all outward appearances an ordinary carpetbag place-seeker whose party loyalty was under a cloud." That being the case, Chandler added, "these letters have a significance of their own." Why would the Ohio senator go out of his way to assist such a political hack—"begging him to keep quiet, [and] telling him promises would be kept"—unless Anderson possessed damaging information about Hayes's election?[18]

Yet Chandler also noted the documents that Anderson did *not* produce. The latter claimed to have made a memorandum of his conversation with Sherman at Moreau's restaurant on November 19, 1876. "This memo," Chandler noted, "I have not seen." Above all, Anderson could not produce the Sherman letter itself. He had given it to Don Weber for safekeeping, he explained, because he worried that he might lose it while out on a drinking spree. "It is Anderson's firm belief," Chandler recorded, "that [Weber] was shot by John Sherman's orders and that he now has the letter." This fantastic claim surely dumbfounded the New Hampshire Republican, especially when Anderson immediately contradicted it by saying that Captain Jenks, acting on his behalf, was hunting for the original. Much as he wished to discredit Hayes, Chandler realized that Anderson's testimony would have little value without that document. That eight months had elapsed between his supposed receipt of a written guarantee from the Ohioan and his first mention of that fact suggests that the Sherman letter was a product of Anderson's fertile imagination.[19]

Anderson claimed to have discovered a copy of the Sherman letter, as well as his own letters to Weber, when he visited New Orleans in early April 1877. He tracked them down to an iron safe in the dry-goods store of Katz and Barnitz, he related, where Weber had supposedly placed them for security. Perhaps this discovery among Weber's papers had prompted his sudden readiness to disclose its existence. Even if his story were true, it seems strange that he failed to give a copy to Harlan when he met the latter a few days later. After all, Anderson provided him with copies of the Nash and Weber agreements. Why hold back the much more significant—to a man seeking a federal appointment—Sherman letter? By his own account, moreover, Anderson had already made two copies back in November 1876. If so, the copy he claimed to have located in April 1877 was superfluous. Did he, either alone or in concert with Agnes Jenks, concoct the letter and its accompanying origin story in the summer of 1877?[20]

Fictitious or not, Anderson ensured that the public knew about it. In early September, a month after he lost his job at the Custom House—for which he had done no work since April—he told his Feliciana story to the *Philadelphia Times,* claiming that he and Don Weber had been given a written promise of employment "by a member of the Republican committee." The article failed to name that individual, but the alleged Sherman letter soon became, in Kellogg's words, a "matter of speculation, scandal, and gossip."[21]

Sherman's alleged bribery of Anderson and Weber was but one of many rumors about Returning Board shenanigans. Nevertheless, Republican malcontents recognized its potential value. Office seekers hoped to exploit it as a means of gaining patronage; enemies of Hayes saw it as a means of embarrassing the administration. There were plenty of men in both groups, and some were ready to make common cause with Democrats in order to question the legitimacy of the presidential title. This was, after all, a political culture in which intraparty faction fights were often little more than quarrels over the distribution of spoils.

In this instance, however, Republican opposition to Hayes ran deeper. Having exerted might and main to elect him, Louisiana Republicans felt betrayed by Hayes's abandonment of Packard. They felt doubly betrayed when the new president, in a futile effort to increase the party's white support in the South, placed Democrats in key positions. Hayes tamped down dissent by rewarding party bigwigs with patronage plums. When facilitating the destruction of the Packard legislature in April 1877, Harlan had promised that "all the leading Republicans who have borne the brunt of this work shall be taken care of." But federal positions were limited, and most of the small fry—even some of the bigger fry—got nothing. Small wonder, then, that displaced and exiled Republicans felt no compunction in attacking Hayes with any weapon that came to hand.[22]

Former US marshal Pitkin was happy to fall in with Anderson's scheme. The two men had parted on acrimonious terms in November 1876, but in July 1877 Anderson approached him outside Willard's Hotel in Washington, having traveled from Philadelphia to show Pitkin some documents. The latter was interested: eager to discredit the Hayes administration, he possessed the high-level connections to ensure that, by disseminating Anderson's documents to the right people, he could inflict maximum political damage.[23]

Pitkin had turned against the administration when Attorney General Charles Devens asked for his resignation. He refused to go quietly and accused the president of ingratitude. Hayes "would not have received the vote he did but for my ceaseless energy . . . in getting our ranks into discipline," he immodestly but not inaccurately claimed. Pitkin had also arranged to bring hundreds of Republican witnesses to New Orleans when the party was accumulating affidavits to present to the Returning Board. "I labored under the delusion that I had helped to elect a Republican president who would naturally respect those who had befriended him." Lambasting Hayes's southern policy, Pitkin belittled the president's "pathetic weep over the poor colored man whose votes he now forgets he got."[24]

Perusing Anderson's documents, Pitkin was struck by the letters from Matthews. They seemed damning: the senator appeared to have "enmeshed himself" in a "seriously compromising" situation. And it was Matthews, along with Wayne MacVeagh and John Harlan, whom Pitkin most wished to punish. This triumvirate had done more to destroy Packard's government, in his view, than anyone else barring Hayes himself. MacVeagh was a lawyer in private practice and could not be touched. But Matthews sat in the Senate, and Harlan was angling for an appointment to the Supreme Court. Pitkin deemed them vulnerable. Through the threat of publishing his letters to Anderson, Pitkin believed, "Mr. Matthews might be held by the bridle a little." He might be induced, for example, to thwart Harlan's elevation to the nation's highest tribunal.

Pitkin traveled to Philadelphia to consult with J. R. Sypher, Anderson's attorney. He then arranged for Sypher to meet Senator Conkling, Republican of New York and a political enemy of Hayes, at the Capitol. The attorney summarized Anderson's story and went over the documents. The purpose of the meeting, Pitkin later explained, was to give ammunition to the Republican senators who opposed Hayes's southern policy. On Anderson's claim that he had made his supervisor's protest while drunk, however, Pitkin demurred. Retrieving Anderson's original handwritten statement, he mailed it to Conkling, stating, "I did not wish it to appear that I had taken advantage of a man who was inebriated."[25]

Agnes Jenks, in the meantime, was losing faith in Anderson's ability to arrange a federal appointment for her husband. With Thomas unemployed, and her mother hard pressed to meet the mortgage payments on her New Orleans home, she struck out on her own. Without telling Anderson, she decided to throw in her lot with Packard and Kellogg—the former a candidate for collector of customs in New Orleans, the latter awaiting confirmation as a US senator. Whereas Anderson seemed to relish his ability to levy blackmail regardless of damage to party, Jenks presented herself as a tried and true Republican. Party loyalty aside, she may simply have concluded that without the Sherman letter, blackmail would not work. Better to ingratiate herself with Republican leaders than continue as Anderson's accomplice.

Kellogg had picked up the rumor that Anderson was threatening to publish a certain document that could scupper his chances of being seated by the Senate. When he wrote Jenks to ask if the ex-supervisor was referring to the Sherman letter, she assured him that Anderson's threat of exposure was empty. "He is not in possession of the document and you may be sure *he shall never get it.*" Underlining her own party loyalty, she described him as a "poor fool . . . [who] seems to think that honors, friends, and political principle are up for bargain and sale." Kellogg not illogically inferred that she had the letter in her possession. Calling on him at the Saint Charles Hotel on New Year's Eve, 1877, Jenks summarized the letter's substance without explicitly stating that she held the original. Packard, whom she visited on the same day, claimed to have been unimpressed. "She talked mysteriously about the letter," he recalled, but Jenks "never would state . . . who had it." He drew the conclusion that "she did not know anything about it, but was trying to give herself some importance."[26]

In mid-January 1878 Jenks followed Kellogg and Packard to Washington to press her husband's claims through the agency of these men. She made little headway. Although Packard was still in the running for the collectorship, his prospects were fading. And Kellogg, who had been confirmed by the Senate and was now out of danger, had yet to establish any control over Louisiana's federal patronage, much of which had already been doled out by Harlan. Besides, so many claimants for office were clamoring for his support that the case of Thomas Jenks, while deserving, was low on his list. Neither Kellogg nor Packard, moreover, considered the Sherman letter to be particularly egregious. They seemed disinclined to intercede with the Treasury secretary on behalf of Jenks.

Tired of kicking her heels, and with her money running out, Agnes Jenks seized the bull by the horns. On the afternoon of January 19, she walked into the Treasury Building, wearing a heavy veil over her face, and asked to see Sherman. The meeting did not go well. When admitted to his office, she asked to see him alone. Sherman insisted that his private secretary remain in the room. She explained that she possessed information about the election in the Feliciana parishes, whereupon Sherman retorted that the country was tired of Louisiana matters and that he was in any case too busy to grant her an interview. His mood scarcely improved when Jenks mentioned, in his words, "a letter I was said to have written." Declining to discuss the matter, Sherman ended the conversation by telling her, in effect, to publish and be damned.[27]

Jenks thereafter made her presence in Washington felt. Her lodging house attracted a stream of reporters and politicians, whom she entertained with her razor-sharp repartee and enthralled with her pretended knowledge of the Sherman letter. "She is a woman of great shrewdness," related the *New York Times,* "and possesses a thorough knowledge of the politics of Louisiana." The "mysterious lady," whom the article left nameless, was in Washington to secure a position for her husband in the New Orleans Custom House, and she possessed "secret information" of interest to the Treasury secretary. The *Times* hesitated to accuse her of blackmailing Sherman but reported that she "claims to have in her possession evidence which implicates him . . . in questionable practices connected with the Louisiana count."[28]

The story of the Sherman letter was by now the worst-kept secret in Washington. Jenks had convinced Kellogg, Packard, Darrall, and several others that she alone knew its whereabouts, sometimes hinting that Millie Weber had it in her safekeeping, at other times stating that the letter was securely locked away in New Orleans. Anderson, too, spoke of it incessantly, although he never claimed to possess the original. Meanwhile, lawyer Sypher was negotiating with Representative Clarkson N. Potter regarding a possible congressional investigation that would target Sherman. If such an inquiry took place, Sypher stated, he wished to be paid an attorney's fee. The *Washington Post,* a Democratic paper, exulted that "the downfall of John Sherman is at hand."[29]

Sherman reacted angrily to these reports. He told the *New York Times* that he regarded Jenks and Anderson as blackmailers. Writing to a friend, he classed the pair along with the "multitude of claim agents, custom house brokers, extreme silver and inflation advocates, and the host of men who crowd around the Treasury to obtain money improperly." He had made no promises to Anderson, had never written to him, and never "did anything in Louisiana which could ever be construed into wrong." The *Times* published this letter, as the secretary no doubt intended.[30]

Anderson was aghast. "You have 'put your foot in it' badly," he scolded Jenks. Sherman's categorical denial contradicted all that she had told him about the letter as well as undercutting what he had supposed was a joint effort to secure a position for Captain Jenks. Sherman had not only denounced them as blackmailers but also challenged her to put up or shut up. "If, as you say, it is in your possession," Anderson told Jenks, "it is very easy to prove that Mr. Sherman states what is false." Betraying something close to panic, he wrote to Millie Weber and asked her if Jenks really had the Sherman letter; if not, could she say where it could be found? Tastelessly, he reminded her that the Ohioan's title to office was "stained by your husband's blood."[31]

Morris Marks of Ascension Parish had known Millie Weber since she was a child. She had grown up in Donaldsonville, Marks's home, and she returned there after her husband's murder. A former parish judge, district attorney, and presidential elector, he was on familiar terms with Louisiana's Republican leaders. He was also personally acquainted with John Sherman.

Reading the *New York Times* piece about "the mysterious lady from Louisiana," Marks noted that Sherman's letter to Don Weber was "now in the possession of his widow." He immediately visited Millie to ascertain the letter's whereabouts. Millie assured him "that she had never seen or heard of any such document," adding that Jenks had made a perfect nuisance of herself when she came looking for it the previous July. In light of Millie's pitiable situation as a widow with three young children, Marks offered to help her secure an appointment as the postmistress of Donaldsonville. He then asked her brother-in-law, E. L. Weber, to draft a letter on her behalf (a French-speaking Creole, Millie knew limited English) denying any knowledge of the Sherman letter. Weber demurred. According to Marks, he questioned the wisdom of having her name "dragged into the public press."[32]

More likely, Weber's reluctance had another source. Marks's sudden visit convinced him that the Sherman letter might be genuine; if found, he could benefit thereby. Writing to his "runner" Robert Morris, he contemplated how to turn the document, if he could discover it, to financial advantage. Marks, Weber related, had told him that Jenks "threatens Hayes, Sherman, and Co,. with exposures if they don't dance up to her with large sums of money." The Hayes administration wished to suppress the letter, he speculated, and had instructed Marks to find out if Millie possessed it. "I know that this document . . . must be in existence," he told Morris. "I would like to know now what could be done with it." Weber asked him to visit the Jenkses in New Orleans and find out what they were up to. He also suggested approaching the Democrats, as neither he nor Morris had any interest in protecting the Hayes administration—"they don't care for us anymore."[33]

Weber also reached out to William Chandler, now thoroughly alienated from Hayes. He complained that he had been banished and persecuted while his brother's assassins "roam at large in pastures fresh and green." These murderers had been empowered by Hayes, whose title to the presidency was "tainted with the blood of my brother." Weber's situation was indeed unenviable. As long as the threat of prosecution in West Feliciana hung over his head—and the schoolboard showed no sign of relenting—his property there remained vulnerable to seizure, and he dare not set foot in the parish.[34]

Chandler expressed sympathy over Weber's "unfortunate condition." What interested him most, however, was the Sherman letter: "Write me all you know about it." Weber assured him that the letter "has been in existence, and must yet be," but he confessed, "I cannot just now tell you where it is." As they continued to correspond, Chandler kept pressing him. "You do not inform me why you think the supposed letter is genuine nor where you think it is," he wrote in March. Two months later he tried again: "You have not given me any information about the original letter I mentioned." Weber never could produce it, even though he put it about in Washington that he had it in his hands.[35]

Agnes Jenks, in the meantime, having been named and shamed as a blackmailer, wrote to the *New York Times* disclaiming any knowledge of the matter. Mrs. Weber had told her that she knew nothing about any letter to her husband from Sherman. Jenks rebutted the charge that she was engaged in blackmail: "I most earnestly assure you that I have not one letter or document in my possession in the least detrimental to or that could reflect on the honor of Secretary Sherman either as an honest statesman or a true gentleman. Nor have I any 'secret information to dispose of' that would in any way affect the Louisiana case." She added (ingenuously), "I have no knowledge whatever of Louisiana politics."[36]

In private, however, Jenks was putting out an entirely different story. When Anderson visited her on February 16, 1878, accompanied by a reporter from the *Baltimore Gazette,* she insisted that the letter "was in safe-keeping in New Orleans." She said much the same thing to Chandler in early March. It was hardly surprising, therefore, that the press refused to take her public denial as definitive—indeed, they took it as a given that the Sherman letter was, or had been, genuine. Newspapers reported that Jenks had disposed of the original to Sherman. Any number of people claimed that, if they had not seen the original themselves, they knew someone who had. In June, when the Potter Committee hearings were underway, the *National Republican* speculated that "Mrs. Jenks has guarded it safely, and . . . has it in readiness to be produced when called for."[37]

When he read her *New York Times* denial, Alfred G. Haley, a fellow lodger at her Washington boardinghouse, reminded Jenks that she had told him that the Sherman letter existed and that she knew where to obtain it. Jenks offered him a telling explanation of this apparent contradiction. Like Talleyrand, she reasoned, she had used language that, while literally true, conveyed a false impression. She had denied having the Sherman letter (present tense) in her possession (physical)—a true statement at the time of writing, assuming the letter to be in New Orleans. This kind of semantics brings to mind Bill Clinton's "it depends upon what the meaning of the word 'is' is," and it foreshadowed the tricky wordplay with which Jenks amused, baffled, and infuriated the members of the Potter Committee. The simple truth is that she never possessed the Sherman letter and never knew—if it had ever existed in the first place—where to find it.[38]

Frustrated by Sherman's rebuff and embarrassed by his public scolding, Jenks delivered a letter, by hand, to the secretary's private residence. She addressed it to Sherman's wife, Cecilia, for the purpose of what we now call "plausible deniability"—she could thus claim that she never wrote to John Sherman.

Jenks explained that her pretended knowledge of the Sherman letter was a ruse. She had traveled to Washington merely to secure a position for her husband through the advocacy of Packard and Kellogg. But having been led to believe that she possessed the document, those men told her that they needed it in order to secure the New Orleans collectorship for Packard. Only in that way could they help her husband find a position in the Custom House. Jenks thus found herself maintaining the fiction that she could obtain it. Yet the document was wholly imaginary, she confessed, "I had it not to give." If it had ever been in her possession, "I would have given it to you . . . long since without question." Enclosed with her letter were two others: the letter from Anderson in which he observed that Sherman had pronounced her a blackmailer and the draft of her letter to the *New York Times* rebutting that charge. She promised to call back later in the day in the hope that Sherman would give her a recommendation on behalf of her husband.[39]

Returning that evening, Jenks finally gained an audience with Secretary Sherman. The last thing on her mind was blackmail, she explained. She merely intended to request—not demand—a position for her spouse. Sherman expressed his sympathy but noted that Jenks's public statements "had made it impossible . . . for me to render her assistance or aid."[40]

Jenks nonetheless persisted. She saw Senator Matthews and asked him to intercede with the Treasury secretary. She told her story to William Chandler. Through it all, she kept writing to Sherman, describing her circumstances, and those of her family, as pitiable. Staunch Republicans, they had been compelled to flee East Feliciana: "My brother was shot, I was fired at through my window at night, [and] my husband was threatened with assassination." Her mother had been forced to mortgage her home in New Orleans, and a note of $500 was pressing. Her own position in Washington was "truly awful," she complained. "I had to remain so much longer than I had expected that my means were exhausted—so far from home—without a change of clothes for many days, without even car fare, or the wherewithal to get food."[41]

The better to win Sherman's trust, Jenks disassociated herself from Anderson. As it dawned on the latter that she had misled him as to the Sherman letter—that she had lied "most damnably"—the correspondence between them became acrimonious. "They do say that Sherman fooled you badly," taunted Anderson, "that you gave him that letter on promises to pay, and that after getting it he told you to whistle for your 'dingbats.'" Jenks forwarded Anderson's letters to Sherman, contrasting his blackmailing proclivities—his professed desire "to carry consternation generally to the administration"—with her own loyalty and integrity. Anderson, she wrote Sherman, was "devoid of all principles, or sense of honor, a man who I *know* received money from the Democrats, in fact was in *their* pay." Her own actions, on the other hand, had been guided by "honor and good faith."[42]

Sherman's attitude to Jenks softened. Perhaps her sob stories and application of soft soap had an effect on this notoriously cold man. Perhaps her declarations of loyalty convinced him that she might be a useful witness on his behalf if, as appeared likely, the House of Representatives authorized an investigation. For whatever reason, Sherman penned a letter—the only one he ever sent her—apologizing for his blackmail accusation and acknowledging, "I did you an injustice." He assured Jenks that he knew how cruelly many Republicans in Louisiana "have suffered and are now suffering." He still gave no promise of a job for Thomas, but he did not rule it out.[43]

Other Louisiana Republicans, however, had no compunction about resorting to blackmail. D. J. M. A. Jewett had occupied a key position in the 1876 campaign. As secretary of the Republican State Election Committee, he strove to maximize Black registration and turnout. After the election he helped Pitkin organize the taking of registrars' protests and witness affidavits. But having helped secure Louisiana for Hayes, he found himself, like Pitkin, out in the cold.

As reports of the Sherman letter circulated in September 1877, Jewett threatened to expose postelection wrongdoing. "It was a big struggle to get Hayes in on Packard's coat-tails," he told the *Cincinnati Enquirer*, a result that could only be achieved by doctoring the returns of the election supervisors. As a reward for their creative counting, he alleged, the white members of the Returning Board, Thomas Anderson and Chairman Wells, had been promised control of the federal patronage in Louisiana, most of which became Sherman's to dispose of upon becoming secretary of the Treasury. Later, as the Potter Committee investigation unfolded, Jewett warned Kellogg that unless the senator consulted him over appointments in Louisiana, he would use "my knowledge of the frauds committed to carry Louisiana" in order to ruin his political career. "I have screened the administration and yourself in many ways," he reminded the ex-governor.[44]

Darrall, a three-term congressman, also resorted to blackmail. He coveted a federal appointment because, having been reelected to Congress from Louisiana's Third District in November 1876, the House of Representatives upheld the challenge of his Democratic opponent, Joseph H. Acklen, and in February 1878 unseated him. Eying the office of collector of customs for the Port of New Orleans, he enlisted James Anderson to press his case with Matthews, using as leverage the senator's "desire to avoid the scandal" of seeing his letters published. Ramping up the pressure, Darrall warned the Ohioan that the Democrats were trying to work up an investigation and sought Anderson's cooperation. If he were appointed to the collectorship, he would be able to keep disaffected Republicans on their side by employing them in the Custom House. And, of course, the appointment would ensure his own silence: Anderson would surrender the incriminating papers, which Matthews could then destroy. When writing to the senator, Darrall advised Anderson, "put it strong."[45]

Anderson now demanded, in peremptory fashion, Darrall's appointment as collector, his brother's promotion to a higher-paid position at the Baltimore Custom House, and a job at the Philadelphia Custom House for a friend of his. If he got his way on these matters, he wrote Matthews, "I will consider my claims satisfied." Encountering the senator at the Capitol one day, an inebriated Anderson demanded to know, in a "very abrupt and insolent manner," why Darrall had not been appointed, giving him a week to arrange things or face the consequences.[46]

Matthews demonstrated astonishing forbearance. Here was a US senator, the brother-in-law of the president, going out of his way to satisfy the demands of a low-level former office holder who was no longer an active Republican, certainly not a loyal one. Moreover, Anderson had turned down a position in 1877 and was now employed by the *Philadelphia North American*. If he no longer sought a federal position for himself, why did the senator give him the time of day, meeting with him not once during the early months of 1878 but repeatedly? The most benign explanation, expressed by Kentucky Democrat Henry Watterson, his nephew, held that Matthews had been impelled by charitable motives. "He thought Anderson . . . a meritorious poor fellow, and he tried to help him. After he had committed himself he discovered his mistake, and then he tried to get him and his dangerous knowledge in his possession out of the country."[47]

One piece of "dangerous knowledge" that Matthews wished to suppress could prove especially damaging to Hayes. In April 1877 Anderson had informed the senator, in writing, that three of Louisiana's Republican presidential electors had not been present to sign the electoral certificates: someone had forged their signatures. Unlike other allegations of election skullduggery, this one had never reached the public. Garfield only learned of it on May 7, 1878, whereupon he immediately informed Hayes.[48]

In the event, all of Matthews's efforts to placate Anderson came to naught. By May Darrall had lost his bid for the collectorship, and the office seeker turned into a seeker after revenge. With the Potter Committee about to begin hearings, Darrall advised Anderson to give the Democrats the ammunition they needed—his testimony and his documents—to discredit Hayes, Sherman, and Matthews. "Don't spare them," he encouraged Anderson. "They are the most unmitigated scoundrels I have ever met—a miserable, hypocritical, psalm-singing, cold-blooded set, whom it would be doing the country a service to expose."[49]

Republican hostility toward the president had been building for months. Indeed, Hayes had barely settled into the White House when James G. Blaine, in his first speech as a senator, demanded that he uphold the Republican government of Louisiana. The same Returning Board that elected Hayes, he pointed out, had also elected a Republican legislature and a Republican governor. To abandon Packard would be to discredit himself. There were rumors, Blaine complained, that "some kind of arrangement had been made by which Packard was not to be recognized and upheld." If the rumors were true, then he wished to know "who had the authority to make such an arrangement." The chasm between North and South was far too deep to be bridged by appeasing the Democrats, Blaine told Garfield. "I can't go the new policy," he wrote Whitelaw Reid of the *New York Tribune*. "Every instinct of my nature rebels against it." After Hayes went ahead and abandoned the Republicans in Louisiana and South Carolina, Blaine refused to have any dealings with him.

Hayes's appointment of a Democrat, David M. Key, as postmaster general and his naming of southern conservatives to federal positions across the South swelled Republican opposition. The president appeared oblivious to the fact that such appointments did nothing to persuade Democrats to switch parties. Far from reciprocating his conciliatory gestures, Democrats simply accepted them and carried on as normal. The oppression of Blacks continued, as did the repression of the Republican Party in large swathes of the region. One of the surviving Republican senators from the South explained that the president's policy meant "the abandonment of political friends to conciliate political foes." The assumption that large numbers of former Whigs were ripe for the picking turned out to be mistaken. Reporting from Louisiana after the collapse of Packard's government, Hayes's close friend James Comley wrote that his search for ex-Whigs had come up empty. "The 'old Whig' sentiment . . . petered out before I reached New Orleans."

Hayes's aloofness, vanity, and self-righteousness prevented him from admitting his error. Garfield thought that his highly publicized tours of the South, in which the president lapped up the praise of white southerners, deceived him. "When the South praised him," Garfield told Hayes to his face, "it dispraised the [Republican] party." Within a year of becoming president, Hayes was widely disliked within his own party. After his first annual message to Congress on December 3, 1877, in which the president smugly affirmed the effectiveness of his southern policy, Chandler published a withering riposte that instigated an open revolt.[50]

The thirty-two-year-old Chandler came from a small state, New Hampshire, and had never served in Congress. Since resigning as assistant secretary of the Treasury in 1867, concluding a three-year stint working for the federal government, he had been a private citizen. Yet Chandler exercised outsize influence within the Republican Party. He had taken part in every national campaign since 1864. His Washington, DC, law practice, which made him rich, placed him at the center of the political world and facilitated his friendships with Blaine, Butler, and other leading Republicans. His prominence in New Hampshire politics, boosted by his position as a newspaper proprietor, placed him on the RNC. His legal skills, mastery of detail, appetite for work, and combative personality made him a highly effective political tactician. In 1876 he threw himself into the Hayes campaign. After the election he headed the Republican visiting statesmen in Florida, doing more than anyone else to land that state for Hayes.[51]

Chandler is sometimes dismissed as a spoilsman, along with the likes of Conkling and Butler—men whose opposition to Hayes stemmed from their inability to influence federal appointments. But this label, with its connotations of "corrupt" and "unprincipled," is unhelpful. For one thing, the "reformers" were often just as ready to use appointments for political purposes; in this regard Hayes was as much of a spoilsman as any other politician. For another thing, Chandler saw no conflict between patronage and principle. A party man through and through, he regarded patronage as the glue that bound Republicans together, a legitimate means of rewarding faithful political service. He therefore looked on with horror as the president cultivated southern Democrats and appointed them to office. The ingratitude and hypocrisy of the man disgusted him. Highly strung and vulnerable to breakdowns brought on by overwork, Chandler relished a fight. He also, according to his biographer, had a "taste for mischief."[52]

In an open letter to the Republicans of New Hampshire, Chandler charged Hayes with adopting a policy toward the South, formulated in secret, that abandoned the 1876 party platform. The essence of that policy, he asserted, had been hammered out by Hayes's Ohio associates with a small group of southern Democrats, the agreement being sealed with a written agreement at the Wormley House discussions of February 26,

1877. The terms of the bargain, in Chandler's summary, were simple: The Democratic negotiators agreed to end the filibuster in the House of Representatives that was holding up the electoral count, thereby permitting Hayes's timely inauguration. In return, the new administration undertook to destroy the Republican state governments of Louisiana and South Carolina by withdrawing military protection, thus allowing the insurrectionary Democrats to assume power. Democrats who had gained high office "through the blood of murdered Republicans" now basked in the president's favor. In the case of Louisiana, Chandler added, Hayes sent an unconstitutional commission to deliver the coup de grâce to the legally elected Republican legislature. The result of Hayes's southern policy, which the Wormley House agreement foreshadowed, had been the virtual destruction of the Republican Party in the South.[53]

Chandler reserved his most stinging criticism for Matthews, Sherman, and Garfield, who had "urged the Louisiana Republicans to do their duty courageously and sold them out even before the vote of the State was counted for Hayes." The pledges they made to the Democrats at Wormley House were "cowardly and disgraceful." No legalistic quibbling could justify their insisting on Hayes's title to the presidency while rejecting Packard's claim to the governorship. If the votes of Louisiana had elected the one, those same votes must have elected the other.[54]

Chandler's letter, and others that followed, delighted many Republicans. "We all bless you here," Pitkin wrote from New Orleans, "for your grand arraignment of Hayes and his co-traders. . . . I trust you will drive the knife to the hilt into the Presidential huckster." Along with Jewett and others, Pitkin was only too happy to supply Chandler with derogatory information about E. A. Burke, the chief Democratic negotiator during the electoral crisis.[55]

Another formidable opponent now joined the anti-Hayes revolt. Speaking in Boston on Christmas Eve, Ben Butler, the party's leading Radical in Congress since the death of Oliver Morton, explained that he had swallowed his doubts about president's southern policy in order to give it a chance to work. Now, he no longer believed it could succeed. Less vituperative than Chandler, he testified to Hayes's sincerity. But on every major issue—not just the southern question but also civil-service reform, the tariff, and the gold standard—the congressman opposed the president. As the *New York Herald* put it, Butler "emptied his hat of those bricks which he has been holding back for so long." Early in the New Year, reports surfaced that the representative from Massachusetts was preparing a resolution calling for an inquiry into the presidential election in Louisiana. Hayes claimed to be unperturbed. "I hate the corruptionists of whom Butler is leader," he confided to his diary. While the president wanted to drive him out of the party, Butler wished to drive Hayes from the White House.[56]

Events in New Orleans gave fresh ammunition to critics of Hayes. In January 1878 state authorities scheduled trials for the four former members of the Returning Board, charging them with fraudulently altering the returns from Vernon Parish. Thomas Anderson, Gustave Casanave, and Louis Kenner took refuge in the Custom House; Madison Wells boarded a train that took him to a station near the border with Mississippi and went into hiding. The first three were incarcerated after US Marshal Wharton, acting on advice from Attorney General Devens, allowed the local sheriff to enter the Custom House to arrest them. Wells, having endured "two days of cold and rain" and in danger of contracting pneumonia, surrendered to the local sheriff and a few days later joined the others in jail. Anderson, the first to be tried, received a sentence of two years at hard labor after a jury took only forty minutes to find him guilty. The other defendants expected the same treatment.[57]

If Democratic leaders in Louisiana had deliberately set out to embarrass Hayes, they could hardly have done better. Republicans condemned the prosecutions as a flagrant breach of the pledges that Governor Nicholls and his legislature gave in February 1877 and reiterated two months later. Anderson's conviction proved especially discomfiting to Sherman, Garfield, and the other visiting statesman, all of whom had publicly endorsed the Returning Board's integrity. "You are falsely accused and maliciously persecuted," they wired Anderson. Sherman asked the president to intercede with the governor, decrying the prosecutions as "a shameless abuse of the judicial process to gratify partisan hate and prejudice." Hayes found the case disturbing and discomforting. "I put it as a simple question of good faith, of honor, on the part of Louisiana," his diary recorded. But his trust in the good faith of Louisiana's Democrats appeared misplaced.[58]

In the House of Representatives, a debate over the contested election between Darrall and Acklen quickly veered off into an argument over the Returning Board prosecutions. Republicans were incensed by the refusal of Louisiana congressmen Gibson and Ellis, both parties to the Wormley House agreement, to criticize the trials. The two Democrats rejected Republican accusations of bad faith. Ellis, who privately deplored Anderson's conviction as "unwise and impolitic," described him as a scoundrel who merited punishment. A furious Eugene Hale, one of the Republican visiting statesmen to Louisiana, contrasted the state's pursuit of the Returning Board with its inaction over the murder of Don Weber and other Republicans.[59]

Garfield struggled to defend Hayes's southern policy. The Democrats of Louisiana, he confessed, "were not meeting the President in the same spirit in which he went to them." And yet he felt duty bound to support the president, even if, as he believed, Packard had been honestly elected. Hayes had endeavored to end the "semi-military" phase of the conflict between North and South; "he had no right to maintain an armed force in the room of the governor of a state to keep him in his office." In Garfield's telling, Hayes withdrew military protection from Packard not because of political necessity, nor even as a means of conciliating the South, but "as a matter of constitutional duty." Chandler, in another public letter, was unsparing. In making such a strained argument and denying the obvious, he wrote, Garfield "further degrades himself."[60]

In mid-March the Louisiana Supreme Court overturned Anderson's conviction, thus sparing Nicholls from having to issue a pardon that would attract the wrath of fellow Democrats. (Anderson expressed his appreciation by recommending the son-in-law of Chief Justice Manning for a clerkship in the Custom House.) That decision lanced this particular boil and allowed Hayes to delude himself that "pacification begins to tell." But it did not tamp down opposition to the president's southern policy. It also kept in view two issues that the Hayes administration would have preferred to keep out of sight—the shady actions of Louisiana's Returning Board and the underhand role of the Harlan-MacVeagh commission in disposing of Packard.[61]

Barely a week after Anderson's release from jail, Senator Timothy O. Howe of Wisconsin launched a full-throated attack on Hayes. The southern policy, he told the Senate, had not only "subverted and trampled upon" the express will of Louisiana's voters but also "surrendered a national prerogative vital to our institutions." It was one thing to acquiesce, in the case of Louisiana, "in what seemed to be a disagreeable necessity." It was quite another, and much worse, he declared, to state that the federal government would never again intervene in a disputed state election. Such a disavowal "proclaimed license to insurrection" and would merely encourage the further oppression of southern Republicans. "The effect is

. . . plainly to be seen," Howe concluded. "The Republican party has disappeared in the South."[62]

Garfield considered Howe's attack "trenchant, bitter, [and] useless." But he privately acknowledged that Hayes "has less force and nerve than I supposed" and that "the current of public sentiment is turning against him." According to Conkling, barely half a dozen Republican senators now supported Hayes, and the senator from New York himself was most decidedly not of that number. Harking back to the Wormley House agreement, Conkling told a reporter from the *New York World* that "everyone knew that there was intrigue going on between the Southern Democracy and the friends of Hayes." Matthews and Sherman were privy to the resulting bargain, and Hayes, he alleged, was apprised of all that was being negotiated on his behalf. When the facts came to light, Conkling believed, "the whole country will be appalled by the dishonor of this Administration." When the *World* published his interview, the senator "repudiated" it, explaining that "the conversations were all in confidence." But he did not deny its substance, and it accurately reflected his views.[63]

Tilden, meanwhile, having accepted his defeat with apparent good grace, stewed over the injustice done to him by the verdict of the Electoral Commission. A coterie of close supporters encouraged his resentment and urged him not to let the matter drop. With his tacit assent, they assailed the Democratic leaders who voted to create the commission as political fools who had acted in defiance of Tilden's wishes. From the editor's chair of the *Louisville Courier-Journal,* Watterson singled out former DNC chairman Hewitt for a particularly vituperative attack, spewing out epithets such as "charlatan," "falsifier," and "snake in the grass." In July 1877, before departing for an extended visit to Europe, Tilden had publicly questioned the legitimacy of the commission and, in an oblique reference to the Returning Board indictments, predicted that the Republican frauds in Louisiana would surely be exposed. In late October, upon his return from Europe, he denounced Hayes's victory as a triumph of fraud. "The crime will never be condoned, and it never should be."[64]

Tilden refrained from explicitly calling upon Congress to investigate the election—the *New York Sun* articulated that demand for him. The paper's editor, Republican-turned-Democrat Dana, was in receipt of James Anderson's package of documents; he instructed A. M. Gibson, his star reporter, to follow them up by ferreting out more evidence in Louisiana. An ardent Tilden man, Dana ensured that the *Sun* never mentioned

Hayes without calling him the "fraudulent president." From the summer of 1877 on, the paper pressed for an inquiry into Republican frauds in Florida and Louisiana with a view to challenging Hayes's title. As Gibson noted, Dana was "not one of the forgiving kind."[65]

Gibson approached his assignment with zeal. The author of Tilden's 1876 campaign handbook, he was convinced that the Democratic candidate had been cheated out of the presidency. During two lengthy trips to the Pelican State, he prepared the ground for an investigation by lining up potential witnesses. By February 1878 he felt sufficiently confident to tell Representative Ellis that "in about a week the whole question of the Presidential Election will be reopened by Congress." He asked Ellis if he could locate the Sherman letter, confidant that "Weber's wife or mother at Donaldsonville" had it.[66]

Evidence from Florida was also accumulating. In early March Pelton, Tilden's nephew, received an extensive report from Alfred Morton, a Florida Republican who had turned against Hayes. The report detailed ballot-box stuffing, fraudulent returns, false affidavits, and the bribing of Returning Board members. It also listed dozens of Republicans who, feeling betrayed by the administration, were prepared to testify regarding their knowledge of, and participation in, these frauds. Two of the witnesses, county election supervisor L. G. Dennis and Returning Board chairman Samuel B. McLin, went public with their confessions. Both claimed that Florida had gone for Tilden.[67]

Like Anderson, the pair from Florida were aggrieved that they had not received adequate reward for their part in electing Hayes. "He is a traitor to the party that put him" in the White House, declared Dennis, who had received, but then lost, a minor position in Washington. In a vengeful mood, he predicted that his testimony would lead to the president's downfall. McLin's was a sad case. Appointed to the supreme court of New Mexico, he was forced to step down when the Senate refused to confirm him. During his brief spell in the West, he lost one child to illness and another to an accident. He himself was dying of tuberculosis. Volunteering a mea culpa in the form of an affidavit, he complained that Hayes "basely betrayed and mercilessly destroyed the Republican party of the South."[68]

Winning support for a congressional inquiry, however, proved an uphill struggle. "We are without a leader," William M. Springer complained to Tilden on March 10. "We seem to be floating about, or drifting along without a plan or without a chart." The Illinois congressman, one of Tilden's most ardent advocates, met with resistance when he pressed his colleagues to back an investigation. More than a few Democrats, he reported, "prefer Hayes to the expense and little excitement which might unseat him."[69]

That sentiment was fully displayed in April, when the House debated a proposal to appeal the decision of the Electoral Commission to the Supreme Court. Congress declined to reopen the dispute over the presidency, with Democrats describing it as a dead issue and a useless distraction. Many stated that however bruised they felt about the manner in which Hayes had entered the White House, they had forfeited their right to protest when Congress approved the creation of the commission. They must abide by the commission's decision, albeit through gritted teeth. "I am opposed to this everlasting ding-dong about the Presidency," a Massachusetts Democrat told the *New York Herald*. "I do not want to hear the subject mentioned again." Of the Democrats interviewed by the newspaper, twenty-four senators and ninety-four representatives echoed that view. This group easily outnumbered the dozen who unequivocally supported a challenge to Hayes's legitimacy. Even among the sixty or so Democrats whom the *Herald* classified as "on the fence," few leaned toward investigation.[70]

Springer and his allies did not give up. They calculated that by proposing a more narrowly focused investigation, and by disavowing any plan to force Hayes's resignation, they could win the backing of the House. In mid-May Representative Potter of New York introduced a resolution to investigate the conduct of the election in Louisiana and Florida. Rather than relitigate the entire contest, a practical impossibility, the proposed inquiry would examine specific allegations of fraud made by Republican officials in those two states. Anderson's testimony would provide the foundation for the Louisiana probe, Dennis and McLin's for the Florida one.[71]

The Republican minority tried to stymie Potter's resolution through delaying tactics. It was the custom at that time to define a House quorum in terms of the number of congressmen voting, not the number of members present in the chamber. Simply by refusing to vote, the Republicans rendered the House inquorate, bringing business to standstill. The required quorum of 147 votes could have been supplied exclusively by Democrats, who numbered 152. The shortfall indicated continuing opposition to the inquiry from within their caucus. Alexander H. Stephens of Georgia, the former vice president of the Confederacy, complained that the proposed investigation, which focused solely on alleged Republican misdeeds, would result in "mischief, disturbance, and disaster." But when he supported an amendment offered by Representative Hale of Maine, a Republican, for a "more exhaustive and searching investigation," the wheelchair-bound Georgian was shouted down by fellow Democrats. Potter maintained that nothing the Democrats did had influenced the outcome of the election; he refused to entertain any amendments.[72]

With his colleagues under intense pressure to close ranks—"The Country Expects Every Democrat to Do His Duty!" the *Washington Post* demanded—the Speaker shut the doors of the chamber and ordered the arrest of absent members. Potter finally made a quorum and passed his resolution.[73]

Democrats supported in May what they had opposed in April because the resolution did not directly challenge Hayes's title. The inquiry was so framed, moreover, to prevent any investigation of Democratic "bulldozing" or of alleged attempts by Tilden's agents to improperly influence the election results in Oregon and South Carolina. The resolution singled out John Sherman and E. F. Noyes by name for their role, as visiting statesmen in Louisiana and Florida, respectively, in persuading election officials to commit the alleged frauds.

Hayes suspected the malign influence of Congressman Butler and Senator Conkling. The only Republican to vote in favor of the inquiry, Butler relished the opportunity to embarrass the president by questioning his legitimacy. Conkling showed his hand when he refused to sign a public statement by Senate Republicans deploring the inquiry. According to George F. Hoar of Massachusetts, who drafted the document, the senator from New York "spoke with great severity of President Hayes, and said that he hoped it would be the last time that any man in the United States would attempt to steal the Presidency." Without Conkling's backing, the Republican caucus shelved the declaration.[74]

Republican support for the investigation extended far beyond Butler and Conkling, however. Few were as outspoken as Senator George E. Spencer of Alabama, who declared of Hayes, "If he is an honest man it is his duty to abdicate." But many southern Republicans silently indulged the schadenfreude of seeing the president discomforted. Kellogg, now in the Senate, remained outwardly loyal but did little to mask his resentment over the president's ingratitude: "Mr. Hayes should have some sense of respect for those who helped to put him where he is."[75]

Writing to Tilden, Springer confessed that he could not predict where the investigation might lead. "We have been so accustomed to strange things that it is impossible to tell what effect a given state of facts would produce." Having divorced the inquiry from the issue of impeaching Hayes, he hoped nevertheless that when the frauds were exposed, "every man, woman, and child in the land would unite in demanding that Hayes and Wheeler should at once relinquish the offices which they have held solely through bribery, forgery, and perjury!"[76]

This was wishful thinking. The majority of Democrats in Congress had not changed their minds about the foolishness of attempting to unseat Hayes. Southerners, in particular, had little to complain about: Hayes had, after all, restored "home rule" and abjured further military intervention, a change of policy that was all the more decisive for having been effected by a Republican president. Most Democrats, within Congress and without, viewed the investigation as a means of embarrassing Hayes and making the stolen election of 1876 a Democratic rallying point. "We are willing for this Congressional investigation in order that we may make capital for the next campaign," a Georgia Democrat wrote Tilden. "But we are opposed to it, if it is designed to oust Hayes."[77]

There were also Democrats who regarded the investigation as a thoroughly bad idea. Charles W. Woolley warned Speaker Randall that it would be "folly." As one of the visiting statesmen in Florida, Woolley knew whereof he spoke. The problem, he explained, was that the messy aftermath of the 1876 election had left both parties with soiled hands. If the truth came to light, it would not be pretty: reputations might be ruined, including that of Tilden himself. On this point Woolley agreed with the staunchly Republican *New York Tribune*. When Potter set out on his fishing expedition, warned that paper, he had better be careful not to cast his line "in the neighborhood of Gramercy Park" lest it "get caught in the trousers seat of a statesman who is now out of politics."[78]

Sherman and Noyes professed themselves unfazed at the prospect of being investigated. Noyes, now serving as minister to France, wired from Paris that he wanted the Potter Committee to immediately subpoena him. Sherman, too, appeared to be in a fighting mood. "I do not fear them," he stated. "The Democrats are heartily welcome to do their worst."[79]

Still, Sherman took precautions. The persistent lobbying of Agnes Jenks had persuaded him to offer her husband a post in the New Orleans Custom House, which had the benefit of binding wife and husband to his cause. He could count on both to contradict Anderson's testimony before the Potter Committee. The Treasury secretary also approved a position for

E. L. Weber. Samuel Shellabarger, Sherman's personal attorney, assumed that Weber could be trusted and, through Morris Marks, asked him to supply a list of potential witnesses who could attest to "bulldozing" in the Feliciana parishes. Marks assured Weber that the postmastership that his widowed sister-in-law sought would soon be hers. "She is certain to be a witness; so are you," he explained. "Have you received your appointment? If not, let me know at once."[80]

On the same day that Marks wrote his letter to Weber, Agnes Jenks was in Donaldsonville, bearing a letter for Millie Weber from Lionel A. Sheldon, a former congressman (and friend of Garfield) who lived in New Orleans. The letter was cryptic—a mere two lines—but the import was clear. Sheldon stated that it was important for Mrs. Weber to proceed to Washington immediately so that she could testify before the Potter Committee; Mrs. Jenks would explain the situation more fully. The request did not go down well with Don Weber's widow. She resented the reappearance of Agnes Jenks and bristled at her peremptory tone. She declined to accompany Jenks to New Orleans. Sherman's team wanted Weber to testify, it seems, so that she could deny any knowledge of the Sherman letter.[81]

Millie's brother-in-law, however, had different ideas. Unbeknown to Shellabarger, who was preparing Sherman's defense, E. L. Weber was toying with the idea of testifying on behalf of the Democrats. Weber apprised Chandler of Jenks's visit and assured him that "Mrs. D. A. will not move without my consent." And having applied for a position at the Custom House, he now turned the job offer down, telling Marks that accepting the appointment "might subject my future actions . . . to the charge of being or having been improperly influenced." Weber put it about that *he* was in possession of the Sherman letter.[82]

Marks had taken upon himself the role of Sherman's political firefighter. He had good reason to make himself useful to the Treasury secretary. Having been elected a district judge in 1876, he had to vacate the position when, in February 1878, the Louisiana Supreme Court disqualified him. He was now waiting upon a federal appointment, collector of internal revenue for Louisiana, a lucrative position that was in Sherman's gift.[83]

On May 25, a week before the Potter Committee opened its hearings, Marks arranged for James Anderson to meet Sherman at the Treasury Building. Accompanied by Michael Hahn, another Republican from Louisiana—also, worthy of note, an applicant for a position in the Treasury Department—Marks took Anderson from the Willard Hotel to the Treasury Building. Sherman refused at first to see Anderson, describing him as a scoundrel, but he relented when Marks fetched Shellabarger, who advised that there would be no harm in hearing what Anderson had to say.[84]

Entering Sherman's office, Anderson saw the secretary, sitting behind a large desk and flanked by Shellabarger and a stenographer, at the end of a long room. After an awkward silence (he was notoriously taciturn), Sherman asked Anderson if they had ever met before and, if so, where. He replied that they had met twice: the first time at Moreau's restaurant in New Orleans, the second time at the secretary's private residence in Washington, when Sherman had abruptly stated that he had no position for him.

The meeting then went off the rails. The sight of the stenographer taking notes made something inside Anderson snap. When Sherman asked if they had transacted any business in New Orleans, he jumped up and, in Shellabarger's words, "began to talk pretty loud" and got ready to leave. When Marks pointed out that he had come to the meeting of his own accord, Anderson angrily insisted that attending had been Marks's idea, not his. Cursing and shouting, he took his hat and cane and stalked out of the room. Outside the Treasury Building, Anderson rounded on Marks, calling him "everything mean and contemptible that could be thought of." The row attracted a crowd of onlookers, one of whom intervened to stop a brawl from breaking out. Back at the bar of the Willard Hotel, Anderson continued to rant and rave. "God damn Sherman," he declaimed. "He has tried to trap me." Marks and Hahn attempted to calm him, but the more Anderson talked, the angrier he became. Shellabarger attributed this performance to alcohol. The man was half-drunk, he told the *Washington Post*. "That's the truth about it."

What was this meeting all about? Anderson gave a typically self-aggrandizing account to the *New York Sun*'s Gibson. In Anderson's telling, he was lured into seeing Sherman by Marks, who told him that instead of going before the Potter Committee and testifying for the Democrats, "by taking our advice you can make something." Once there, however, he discovered that the Republicans were attempting to find out what he intended testifying to, creating a written record that might be quoted against him. There is no evidence that Sherman, either directly or indirectly, offered Anderson any inducement. It is entirely plausible, however, that he and Shellabarger wished to gain foreknowledge of Anderson's planned testimony or simply to size him up. Why else grant him an audience at all? Sherman could now truthfully claim, as he did a week later, that Anderson had never mentioned the alleged letter.[85]

As Anderson prepared to appear before the Potter Committee, Democratic newspapers were giddy with anticipation. He would produce a photographic copy of the Sherman letter; he could prove that Sherman paid Agnes Jenks to surrender the original; his testimony would "tear Sherman all to pieces." Anderson did nothing to lower these expectations. If the Republicans thought he would stand by them, he told the *New York Herald,* they had another think coming. "Why did they not remember me when I needed them?" When he testified, Anderson teased reporters, expect fireworks: "I've got enough here to burst the whole thing," he declared. "I believe we can make Sherman come down from his high horse."[86]

4

THE COMMITTEE

JAMES ANDERSON AND THE SHERMAN LETTER

The room in the Capitol now occupied by the Potter Committee had witnessed the unravelling, in 1873, of the most notorious scandal in recent history. Exposed by the *New York Sun* and dissected in congressional hearings, the Crédit Mobilier affair besmirched the reputations of several leading Republicans, including James Garfield. Many now anticipated a similar splash. The hearings would be "sensational," predicted Henry Van Ness Boynton, the well-connected Washington correspondent of the *Cincinnati Gazette*. The Democrats, he confided to a friend, "have a good many affidavits ready to print, and rough charges which they will make plausible against Sherman and Matthews." Senator Conkling, he added, was in possession of the letters between Senator Matthews and James Anderson "and will fire them at the first fitting opportunity."[1]

The room was far too small for the number of occupants. Anderson seated himself halfway along a table that stood lengthwise in front of the far window. The eleven committee members, seven Democrats and four Republicans, occupied the rest of the table, most of them sitting on the same side as the witness, facing the audience, with scarcely enough elbow room between them. A small table with six chairs was wholly inadequate to accommodate the thirty or so reporters who covered the proceedings. Newsmen and members of the general public jammed the remaining space.

This was a high-powered committee. At one end of the long table sat the chairman, Potter, "whiskered and bland." A native of Schenectady, Potter had worked as a civil engineer before switching to the law, the practice of which made him a wealthy man. Elected to Congress in 1868, he was now serving his fourth term as a representative from the city of New York. Ambitious to be elected governor, Potter maintained good relations with both "Honest John" Kelly, the leader of Tammany Hall, and Tilden, who headed his own party faction. Although a next-door neighbor of Tilden in the swish Gramercy Park neighborhood of Manhattan, the two men were political allies, not personal friends; a notoriously cold man, Tilden had few intimates. But Potter, according to former DNC chairman Hewitt, "possessed his confidence so far as any person might be said to have had it." It was rumored that he was a reluctant chairman. The New Yorker certainly had no stomach for using the investigation as a means of ousting Hayes. Being a good soldier, however, he did his best to substantiate Tilden's complaint that he had been cheated of the presidency. Potter turned out to be fair-minded chairman, respected by both sides.[2]

William R. Morrison, an Illinois Democrat, was a gruff, taciturn man—a workhorse, not a show horse. He had served as a private during the Mexican War and a colonel during the Civil War. Wounded at Fort Donelson while leading the 49th Illinois Infantry, he resigned his commission at the end of 1862 after being elected to Congress. Defeated in 1864 and again in 1868, he returned to the House in 1872 and remained there for four more terms. In 1876–77 he chaired the House committee investigating the Louisiana election, an experience that made him well equipped for another inquiry focusing on that state. He had been a tough, no-nonsense chairman: when the Returning Board refused to hand over requested documents, he cited the four members for contempt of Congress and had them taken to Washington and confined in the Capitol. Although the report he produced was thoroughly partisan, politicians on both sides of the aisle respected Morrison as thoughtful, industrious, and trustworthy. As a committee member, however, he was eclipsed by colleagues with louder voices and more assertive personalities. Unlike Potter, one of Congress's snappiest dressers, Morrison was known for his shabby coat and battered hat. By 1878 he had been a practicing lawyer for a quarter of a century.[3]

John A. McMahon, a Democrat from Ohio elected to the House in 1874, had spent his early career as the law partner of his uncle, Clement Vallandigham, one of the most controversial politicians of the Civil War years. The unofficial head of the antiwar "Copperhead" faction of the Democratic Party, Vallandigham's vehement criticism of the Lincoln administration and undisguised sympathy for the Confederacy moved Major General Ambrose Burnside to have him arrested for treason and banished to the Confederate lines. Nevertheless, McMahon learned his trade from a master: Vallandigham was a skilled trial lawyer. "There is no man . . . abler to dig a pit for a witness and sweetly coax him into it," one colleague said of him. Having served on the Morrison Committee, McMahon's knowledge of the election in Louisiana made him a natural choice for the new investigation.[4]

William M. Springer also entered the House in 1875, the beginning of a twenty-year stint as a congressman from Illinois. He had made a name for himself by refusing to pay federal income tax, arguing that the law under which it was levied, passed in 1864, was unconstitutional. Rather than back down, Springer took his fight to the Supreme Court. Although he lost his case and saw his home seized by the tax man, his resolute stand endeared him to Democrats. During the electoral crisis, he had been one of Tilden's most ardent advocates and a leader of the Democratic filibuster that delayed the counting of Hayes's votes. Springer had never reconciled himself to the verdict of the Electoral Commission and entertained the hope—a fantasy, really—of driving Hayes from the White House.[5]

William S. Stenger of Pennsylvania, another of the 1875 freshmen, served but two terms in the House before defeat ended his political career. His experience as the district attorney for Franklin County, a position he held for ten years, made him a seasoned prosecutor who knew how to interrogate witnesses. Potter selected Stenger to chair the subcommittee that held hearings in New Orleans. The Pennsylvanian "keeps his clear blue eyes fixed upon those of the witness," noted the *New York Times*. So quiet was his manner "that often the witness is thrown off his guard."[6]

The two other Democratic committeemen, Joseph C. S. Blackburn of Kentucky and Eppa Hunton of Virginia, were both Confederate veterans. Blackburn joined the rebel army as a private and ended his service as a lieutenant colonel. Another member of the class of 1875, he went on to serve three more terms in the House and then three in the Senate. Like the others, he was an experienced trial lawyer. In 1876 he served as one of the House managers during the impeachment trial of William W. Belknap, Grant's bribe-collecting secretary of war (who escaped conviction). Through his service on the Morrison Committee, Blackburn had acquired extensive knowledge of the 1876 election in Louisiana.[7]

Hunton, a somewhat older man, had taught in a rural schoolhouse before being admitted to the bar. In 1849 he was elected commonwealth's attorney (equivalent to district attorney), a position he held for twelve years. He served in the Confederate army throughout the Civil War, first leading a regiment and then a brigade. At Gettysburg he suffered a wound on the third day of the battle. First elected to Congress in 1872, he served four terms. In 1876 he chaired the committee that investigated charges of corruption against Representative James G. Blaine. As a member of the Electoral Commission in 1877, Hunton vigorously pressed Tilden's claim to the presidency but, like many supporters, was sorely disappointed by the candidate's want of "nerve."

Shortly after the Potter Committee set to work, Hunton became embroiled in a personal spat that moved him to demand a duel. The manner in which he sent the challenge occasioned much satirical comment from the *New York Times.* Likening Hunton to a figure from Sir Walter's Scott's fictional world of medieval chivalry—a "noble knight of high degree"—the *Times* complained about the incongruously modern manner of his throwing down the gauntlet: "He telegraphed to his foe to go to the Post Office and find a challenge at the Registered Letter Department of that useful branch of the postal service." The quarrel blew over without any shots fired.[8]

The four Republicans on the committee could scarcely have been more dissimilar. Jacob D. Cox was a man of many parts: lawyer, general, politician, historian, and microbiologist. As a student at Oberlin College, a progressive institution that admitted both Blacks and women, he had come under the influence of Charles G. Finney, the leading figure of the revivalist movement known as the Second Great Awakening and a passionate abolitionist. Marrying Finney's daughter, Cox studied theology with the intention of becoming a minister. After falling out with Finney, however, he made a career in law and threw himself into Ohio's nascent Republican Party. During the Civil War, he led a division, then a corps, in both the eastern and western theaters, attaining the rank of major general. After serving one term as governor of Ohio (1866–68), Grant appointed Cox secretary of the interior. He lasted barely eighteen months: his instincts as a reformer who opposed the spoils system alienated him from Grant, who gladly accepted his resignation. Cox had never been a Radical. Sympathetic to Andrew Johnson, he had opposed Black suffrage and once advocated colonizing the freed people in a separate territory along the southeastern coast. In 1878, during his single term in Congress, he was the only committee member close to Hayes personally.[9]

Thomas B. Reed of Maine stood at the threshold of a stellar congressional career that culminated with his election as Speaker of the House at the end of the century, a position he strengthened immeasurably by ending the ability of the minority party to filibuster. "A big boyish-looking man, with a bright eye and good brains," the freshman congressman from Maine stood six feet, two inches tall, with a bald head atop a massive frame. Not yet forty years old, he had taught at a boys' school before being admitted to the bar in 1863. After serving briefly in the US Navy during the Civil War, his political ascent had been swift. Elected to Maine's lower house in 1868 and the state senate in 1870, he served as the state's attorney general for two years and, after three years in private practice, was elected to Congress in 1876. His imposing physical presence aside, what truly impressed was Reed's sharpness of mind and lacerating wit. As one of his biographers put it, "He could make opponents appear ridiculous by use of the mock-heroic."[10]

Frank Hiscock of New York was serving the first of his four terms in the House; a single term in the Senate closed out his political career. Originally an antislavery Democrat, he navigated his way through the political minefields of the 1850s by migrating first to the Free-Soil Party, and then to the Republican Party. With his brother he founded a law firm in Syracuse that exists to this day. Like several other committee members, he had experience as a prosecutor, having served for three years as the district attorney of Onondaga County. The *New York Sun* judged him as "that type of adroit, clear lawyer of which central New York is so full." He showed himself to be a formidable cross-examiner.[11]

Last but by no means least, Ben Butler of Massachusetts was one of the best-known, most-feared, and most-maligned politicians of his time. Senator Hoar, a longtime foe, devoted an entire chapter of his autobiography to attacking Butler as a bullying, vindictive, dishonest, demagogic political chameleon, placing him alongside Benedict Arnold, Aaron Burr, and Robespierre as an awful example of talent gone bad. The disdain of the Boston Brahmins, however, revealed a great deal about their own snobbishness. Reared in his mother's boardinghouse in Lowell, a thriving manufacturing town, Butler grew to know the laborers, many of them Irish immigrants, who worked in the textile mills. Throughout his political career, he sympathized with these laborers: fighting for the ten-hour day and universal suffrage while opposing the anti-Catholic and anti-immigrant "Know Nothing" Party. Even Hoar had to acknowledge Butler's popularity "with the poorer class of foreign immigrants"; his gift for "clear, racy and simple speech"; and his ability to "convey his thoughts to the apprehension of common men."[12]

Butler began his political life as a Jacksonian Democrat. In 1860 he voted to nominate Jefferson Davis for president. With the outbreak of war, however, his devotion to the Union and experience as an officer in the state militia earned him an appointment as a brigadier general and later a commission from Lincoln as a major general. His military record, like that of many such appointed "political generals," has been much derided. Yet he achieved a good deal more than some of the West Point–trained professionals. In 1861, when Washington was virtually undefended and endangered from the north by secessionist sympathizers in Maryland, Butler acted decisively to secure the safety of the capital. After troops en route from Massachusetts to Washington were attacked by a mob in Baltimore, he took a thousand soldiers to the latter city and imposed federal control. He also secured Annapolis and safeguarded the railway between the state capital and Washington.

Later that year, as the US commander at Fort Monroe, Virginia, Butler declared that slaves who fled to the Union lines were "contraband of war" and should not be returned to their owners. This bold decision gave the Union war effort a firm push in the direction of emancipation. Appointed military governor of New Orleans after Union forces captured the city in May 1862, he earned the sobriquet "Beast" for his stern measures against public expressions of secessionist sentiment, which included hanging a man who had torn down the Stars and Stripes and designating women who insulted Union soldiers as "women of the town plying their avocation." But he established firm US control over the vital Mississippi and Gulf port. He also gave New Orleans an efficient administration that cleaned up the streets, kept yellow fever at bay, and provided rations to poor people who had been slowly starving.[13]

There Butler had also added the first Black regiments, composed of free people of color, to the Union army. His experience with Black soldiers profoundly influenced his views on race. At first reluctant to recruit former slaves, he quickly became convinced of their fighting qualities. While other Union generals viewed Black soldiers with contempt, Butler did not hesitate to use them in combat. After witnessing their courage and determination at the battle of New Market Heights in September 1864, he had a special medal struck and decorated nearly two hundred soldiers for gallantry. Riding over a field strewn with Black dead and wounded, he recalled in old age, "I swore to myself an oath . . . that they and their race should be cared for and protected by me to the extent of my power so long as I lived."[14]

By the war's end Butler had switched his political allegiance to the Republican Party. He joined the ranks of the Radicals, those most committed to punishing Confederate leaders and ensuring civil rights for the freed people. Elected to Congress in 1866, he played a leading role in the impeachment of President Johnson, the return of the South to military rule, and the implementation of Black suffrage. Over the next decade his support for Black equality never wavered. In 1871 he steered the Ku Klux Klan Act through the House; three years later he championed the proposal that became the Civil Rights Act of 1875. The term "waving the bloody shirt"—encouraging support for Congressional Reconstruction by emphasizing atrocities against southern Republicans—was inspired by Butler exhibiting that eponymous garment during a debate in the House.[15]

A man of great personal charm in private, Butler was a bruiser in public. He had the ability, one biographer observed, "to change in an instant from a well-mannered, affectionate gentleman to an insolent brazen bully." When he got into a political fight, he was a no-holds-barred, below-the-belt slugger, "known for his acid tongue, sarcastic wit, and facile way of routing his enemies in debate." Yet his brains, ability, and phenomenal memory were universally acknowledged. Reed described Butler as "powerful, effective, courageous and full of resources." Hayes, who regarded him as a "wicked demagogue," conceded that he was a man of "energy and ability."[16]

Amassing substantial wealth from business investments, including ownership of a textile mill, Butler built up a lucrative law practice, specializing in criminal defense. "As one of the nation's top trial lawyers," writes one biographer, "he possessed both brutal cross-examination skills and intimate knowledge of courtroom tactics." A cartoonist's delight, Butler's corpulent body, spindly legs, drooping left eyelid, bald pate, stringy hair, and perpetual cigar (usually unlit) made him instantly recognizable. Of the eleven committee members, he was the undoubted heavyweight. While many of the others served reluctantly, Butler relished his appointment. His determination to embarrass Hayes by discrediting both the Wormley House agreement and the MacVeagh commission led to fierce clashes with the other Republicans, especially Hiscock.[17]

The first witness, upon whose testimony the Democrats laid great store, made a favorable first impression. Smartly dressed in a dark-blue frockcoat and pinstripe trousers, James Anderson "took his seat with a jaunty, self-possessed air," the *New York Herald* reported. "He was exceedingly glib of tongue and rattled out his story." The *Washington Evening Star* thought that the neatly dressed young man "demeaned himself with proper composure." Even the *National Republican* found him "cool and determined," adding that his testimony "was well put together, and presented at first blush as fair a case . . . as the fraud-seekers could have expected."[18]

This, of course, was the easy part. Guided by McMahon, Anderson recounted his tale of Republican perfidy. Kellogg and Jewett had planned to prevent the election in East Feliciana Parish from taking place because they knew that the Democrats would win. They drove Anderson out of the parish by arranging for him to be ambushed on the road from Jackson to Clinton. When Democrats pleaded for his return, Kellogg ordered him back but secretly instructed L. B. Jenks to keep him in New Orleans, even if that meant having him arrested. Escaping the city with the assistance of Colonel Patton, a Democrat, he supervised the election in the parish.

Anderson further claimed that upon his return to New Orleans, Marshal Pitkin, taking advantage of his inebriated state, induced him to protest the returns, despite the fact that the Democrats had carried East Feliciana fairly and squarely. Later, when Anderson asked to retract his protest, Pitkin refused. Someone then doctored the protest to make it stronger, forged the jurat, and submitted it to the Returning Board. Worried that he had placed his life in danger by swearing falsely, Anderson enlisted Don Weber as his confederate in order to secure federal appointments for them both. Approaching John Sherman in Moreau's restaurant, the pair asked for a guarantee that they would receive employment, outside Louisiana if need be. Not trusting Sherman's verbal promise, they asked for—and received—a written commitment. Weber took the Sherman letter with him when he returned to West Feliciana Parish. It was never seen again.

Such, in short, was Anderson's opening testimony, much of which he had trailed in the press for months. It lasted almost seven hours. Reporters struggled to take it all down, their task hindered by the witness's clipped diction—"he swallowed his own words as if accustomed to the dose"—and the murmur of spectators who, the committee room being full, thronged the passageway outside.

To buttress his testimony, Anderson submitted the letters he wrote to Weber before and after the election, copies of the Nash and Weber agreements, and his correspondence with Senator Matthews. He recounted his futile quest for a satisfactory federal position, his meetings with President Hayes, and his dealings with Agnes Jenks, who fully convinced him that she possessed the original Sherman letter.[19]

The four Republicans objected to Anderson's copy of the Sherman letter being accepted in evidence. If the existence of a genuine original depended upon Anderson's word, they contended, his copy had no evidentiary value and should be excluded. "It would not be received in a case where only ten cents was involved," complained Hiscock. Morrison conceded that the copy "will not amount to much as evidence" but argued for its admissibility nevertheless. Even if the original had been a forgery, Anderson might have *believed* it to be genuine and acted accordingly. Potter agreed. Before receiving the copy, however, he accepted Butler's suggestion that Sherman should have the opportunity to confirm or deny that he had written such a note. A telegram was duly sent from the Capitol to the Treasury Building. Half an hour later, Sherman elbowed his way through the spectators outside the committee room and took a seat at the table. "He was cool," reported the *New York Sun*. "There was no fuss about the man. There never is."[20]

Borrowing a pair of spectacles from Cox, Sherman perused the dog-eared slip of paper that Potter handed him. Holding it up to the light and scrutinizing it closely, he pronounced his verdict. "I do not believe I ever wrote that letter," he stated. "At the same time there are things in the letter that I would have written to these or any other men who were engaged in the performance of what I believe to be their duty, if I had been asked; but I do not believe I wrote that letter." He thereupon left the committee room. Anderson resumed his testimony.[21]

Sherman's equivocation disappointed Republicans and delighted Democrats. He had previously denied, both publicly and privately, giving any such written guarantee. Why the hesitation now? "Considering his reputation for shrewdness," commented the *New York Times*, "his course is inexplicable." He could have vindicated himself by either explaining why he wrote the letter or repudiating it as a forgery. "Before the committee he did neither." The verdict of the *Boston Post*, a Democratic organ, was harsher. The "choking hesitation" of his denial had created "the almost universal impression that Sherman lied."[22]

Did Sherman fear that somebody might produce the original and so left himself enough wiggle room if that happened? His previous denials had not been made under oath: lying to a congressional committee would be a more serious matter. Sherman, the *National Republican* noted, was a cautious and prudent lawyer. "Under no circumstances could his answer be perjury," agreed the *New York Sun*. "He is safe there." When Hiscock asked Anderson whether he knew "of any photographic copy of the original letter being made," Blackburn objected: "If Mr. Sherman wants any signpost, anything to guide him, he cannot get it that way." Republicans, who had expected either a firm denial or a frank avowal, told themselves that the letter, even if genuine, did not incriminate Sherman. To promise jobs for political services was standard practice. It would only be unethical if he had known at the time of writing that Anderson's protest had been a lie.[23]

The Treasury secretary's less-than-Shermanesque statement sparked another round of speculation about the whereabouts of the original letter. Democrats put it about that Millie Weber had given it to Agnes Jenks "to be used in her negotiations with Sherman." Jenks had made photocopies and held the original "in readiness to be produced when called for."[24]

It did not take an Inspector Dupin, however, to spot the weaknesses and contradictions in Anderson's testimony. His account of the conspiracy to keep him out of East Feliciana Parish seemed farfetched. Jewett, he claimed, wanted to prevent elections in the five bulldozed parishes, yet elections took place in all of them. The notion that Kellogg wanted him killed—hence the alleged assassination attempt—seemed fantastic. And if the governor was so determined to prevent him returning to East Feliciana after his flight to New Orleans, why did the *New Orleans Republican* publish an article imputing cowardice, a charge calculated to spur Anderson's return? The Jenkses, he claimed, were parties to the alleged conspiracy to keep him in New Orleans. Yet Agnes met with Colonel Patton to facilitate his return.

It also appeared odd that Anderson had failed to utilize the Sherman letter when seeking a high-paying federal position. Even if he only possessed a copy, surely he would have deployed it. When he met Harlan in New Orleans, he confessed, "I did not mention Mr. Sherman's letter at all." He did not mention it to Hayes or Matthews either. Even when he forced his way into Sherman's office, he never referred to it. "If Mr. Sherman would carry out his original agreement and give me a position," he weakly explained, " it might excite comment."[25]

At least one thing was clear: Anderson was hardly a model witness. His testimony showed that he had signed a protest of his own free will on November 10, 1876. Even if he had been under the influence of alcohol at the time—hardly a character recommendation—was he so blind drunk that he did not know what he was doing? His own words revealed that he had offered himself for sale to the Democrats and would have accepted their money had they come up with the cash. His letters to Matthews showed him engaging in extortion. The *New York Herald*'s description of him as "an adventurer and political trader" was no more than the truth.[26]

After Anderson completed his opening testimony, Republican committee members began the cross-examination. Their purpose was straightforward: to discredit the witness by portraying him as a liar, a perjurer, and a forger. Butler led for the Republicans, and even the *Sun* could not but admire his forensic skill. "For fully half an hour Anderson was subjected to a most rigorous cross-examination. It was not manifestly unfriendly, neither was it manifestly friendly. It was evidently the effort of an expert to find the truth. The point of attack was the Sherman letter. . . . All of this was minutely and exhaustively dissected by the greatest cross-examiner of the age."[27]

Butler homed in on the note that Anderson and Weber sent to Sherman seeking a written guarantee of employment and Sherman's letter in reply. Anderson described both documents as exact copies of the originals. But under questioning he revealed that they were anything but that. The note, ostensibly the "original draft," had been altered. "The words 'New Orleans' and the date were evidently written at a different time and by another pencil," Butler observed. "I guess I must have sharpened it," Anderson responded, a less than persuasive explanation. Butler then noted, and Anderson had to agree, that the wording of the note had also been changed. Clearly this was not the "original draft" but a later version. As for Sherman's reply, Anderson admitted that the version he presented in evidence had been a second copy, which he had written down from Weber's reading of a first copy. Butler pounced: "This copy was made by reading from a copy, which was made by reading from a copy, which was made by reading from the supposed original?" "Yes," a deflated Anderson replied.[28]

Butler's attack was damaging but not fatal. It was enough, however, for William Chandler to lose any faith in Anderson's claims about the Sherman letter and, by extension, E. L. Weber's claims about the same. As much as he opposed Hayes, this astute lawyer recognized the significance of Sherman's denial. He knew also that Anderson's testimony must have caused Democrats on the committee to doubt the letter's existence—hence Potter's decision not to examine Millie Weber, the one person who might be able to confirm or deny that Don Weber had ever possessed it. Chandler advised E. L. Weber to get himself a good attorney and, if called as a witness, "to testify to the exact truth—whether it hurts or helps friend or foe, Republican or Democrat."[29]

From the White House, Hayes dismissed Anderson as a disappointed office seeker and a "great scoundrel." When he recommended him for a position, the president told his diary, he had no inkling that there was anything amiss in his conduct as supervisor. If Anderson had ever told him that he was guilty of sharp practice, "it was on one of those occasions when he was under the influence of liquor and excited."[30]

Sherman, speaking to a reporter from the *New York Tribune,* repeated his denial—this time more forcefully—that the letter Anderson attributed to him ever existed. He would never commit the solecism of writing "neither . . . or." He would prove that the "spurious document" was a forgery.[31]

When the hearings resumed on June 4 after a two-day break, Reed took over the cross-examination. He started by reading excerpts from Anderson's testimony to the Howe Committee in January 1877. Given that the witness was now repudiating that testimony, Anderson had little choice but to admit that he had deliberately deceived the senators. He quibbled over the word "perjury," but it did not matter. "I intended to leave them with a false impression," he confessed. "I did not state all the truth. . . . I carefully suppressed a good deal." In falsely testifying to Democratic intimidation, he explained, he was carrying out his "implied agreement with Mr. Sherman." The implication of these admissions was obvious to all: if Anderson had lied to the Howe Committee, how could he be trusted to tell the truth to the Potter Committee?[32]

Having plunged a knife into Anderson's credibility, Reed twisted it. He elicited admissions that undercut the ex-supervisor's assertion that the election in East Feliciana had been free and fair. Yes, he did propose to Democrats that they should permit the Republicans "to organize their party without fear." Yes, he did inform Kellogg that the Republicans were afraid to nominate a ticket and that "there won't be a fair election." Yes, the Democratic district attorney did warn him that it would be dangerous for the Republican district judge to hold court in Clinton. And yes, he did state that he failed to affix his protest to the returns "because he would have been in danger of his life to have done so at the time." Indeed, Anderson had added that sentence in his own handwriting: whatever Pitkin or others may have done to "improve" the protest, the statement was indubitably Anderson's.[33]

Further damaging admissions followed. According to their alleged agreement, Anderson and Weber had filed protests at the instigation of

Pitkin, Kellogg, Packard, and Nash. But now Anderson conceded that he never discussed his protest with those last three men. In the agreement with Nash, he had undertaken to "suppress evidence" that the Democrats had carried East Feliciana fairly. He now confessed that he had possessed no such evidence.[34]

Anderson's attempts to adjust his answers were comically obvious. During his conversation with Sherman in Moreau's restaurant, he testified, the senator's dinner partner, E. W. Stoughton, heard nothing of the conversation because he was engaged in reading a newspaper, his back turned to them. "How far was he from you and Mr. Sherman?" Reed asked. About the width of the committee-room table, Anderson replied. Realizing that so small a distance would hardly put people beyond hearing range, he added that perhaps the table in the restaurant was somewhat wider, also noting that Stoughton "was a small distance away from the table, and we were a little out from the table."[35]

Turning to the alleged Anderson-Weber agreement, Reed moved in for the kill. Quizzed about the two sets of signatures on the document, Anderson displayed a foggy memory. He could not be certain when and where they had signed the first set: in the Custom House, the office of the claim agents who witnessed the signatures, or the office of the notary public who signed and sealed the jurat. Neither could Anderson recall whether he or Weber signed first.

Reed then handed him the original document, the one he had mailed to Matthews in April 1877. Anderson examined it, held the paper up to the light, read it again, and held it up to the light again. He then pronounced it a forgery. Asked why he considered it counterfeit, he explained that the paper on which the original agreement had been written had been disfigured by two spots of red ink, "one on the top and one below the middle of the page." He had taken an eraser and erased those blotches. The paper Reed gave him showed no sign of any erasures. "This denial of the inevitable caused a titter among the audience," reported the *New York Times*.[36]

This was the moment the Republicans had been waiting for. The *New York Sun* reported that "Reed laughed outright. Everybody either smiled, laughed, or looked annoyed." It was also the moment that Anderson lost his composure. "Reserve your smiles until after the investigation is over," he snapped, glaring at Reed, "and perhaps you will smile on the other side of your face." Amid the ensuing hubbub, Potter gaveled for order.[37]

Anderson had walked into a carefully laid trap. Suspecting that Don Weber's signature on the Anderson-Weber agreement might not be genuine, Matthews had shown the document to Kellogg, who as governor of Louisiana had received many letters from Weber. The signature was not, Kellogg deduced, that of the murdered man. Sherman, too, had received a letter from Weber and concurred that the signature was a "plain and palpable forgery." He alerted Reed to the fact and suggested that the congressman collect the original document from Matthews so that he could confront Anderson with it. Meanwhile, Matthews ensured that the newspapers reported Republicans' suspicion that Weber had had nothing to do with the so-called agreement. Anderson undoubtedly picked up these reports. Having assured the Potter Committee that the document he had sent to Matthews was the original, he realized that his position was now untenable. The Republicans could show that someone—presumably Anderson—had added Weber's signature after the notary had signed and stamped the document. If they could make their case stick, Anderson would be exposed as a perjurer and forger. He decided not to take the risk.[38]

Anderson's description of the entire document as counterfeit, however, defied belief. He had failed to recall when and where he and Weber signed the agreement. He could not describe the clerk at Katz and Barnitz who supposedly gave him the envelope containing Weber's papers. Yet he now described in exact detail the sheet of paper upon which he had written the Anderson-Weber agreement twenty months ago. Not only that, he recalled that the ink-marked sheet was the last piece of paper in his drawer and that, having failed to locate a fresh supply, he had made do with the soiled sheet by erasing the ink marks. The counterfeit was so good, moreover, that only the absence of erasure marks indicated to Anderson that it was not the original. He was stumped, however, when it came to explaining how a counterfeit document could bear the notary public's seal and signature, both of which, he acknowledged, appeared genuine.[39]

Reed, assisted by Cox, pressed home the Republicans' advantage. The name "D. A. Weber" had evidently been added to the statement, "Sworn before me . . . by the within-mentioned James E. Anderson." The fact that it was written in a different ink reinforced the impression that it was a later addition. Weber's signature, also in the different ink, appeared on the same line as that of the notary, not above it, raising the suspicion that it had also been added later.[40]

Two men who had witnessed the first set of signatures were summoned, as was the notary public. All three testified that Anderson had been accompanied by a man he introduced as "Weber." But none would swear to having seen this "Weber" actually sign the document. Moreover, they described the man they saw as a having a dark complexion and being of a similar height to Anderson's five feet, six inches. None of them knew Don Weber, who was several inches taller than Anderson and had blond hair.[41]

Reed questioned Thomas Jenks about Weber's signature. Handing him several documents, he asked the former navy captain if he recognized Weber's signature. The witness affirmed that the signatures appeared genuine. Then Reed gave him the Anderson-Weber agreement. "I do not think that this is Mr. Weber's signature," Jenks responded. It was a nice piece of theater, for which Jenks might well have been prepared by Sherman's attorney, Shellabarger, who had met him when he arrived in Washington and conferred with him half a dozen times. "Mr. Shellabarger is a very interesting gentleman," Jenks lamely explained, when Butler enquired as to what the two men had discussed. "I went to converse with him . . . generally on matters and things." Rehearsed or not, Jenks's refusal to confirm Don Weber's signature cast further doubt upon Anderson's testimony.[42]

Why, indeed, would Weber swear to a statement that contradicted his own bitter experience, as attested to in his verbal and written testimony? True, he had hesitated to file a protest after the election. But this reluctance stemmed, as we have seen, from fear of Democratic retaliation when he returned home. Weber already understood that his protest had placed his life in jeopardy. Anderson might possibly have persuaded him that in jointly swearing their protests to have been false, they were hedging their bets on the outcome of the election. Yet unlike Anderson's weak performance before the Howe Committee, Weber's robust testimony provided a detailed account of Democratic bulldozing in West Feliciana Parish.

Confronted by Weber's testimony, Anderson could only respond by denying any personal knowledge of the allegations and claiming that Weber never mentioned them to him. He had already undercut his own position, however, by admitting that Weber had good reason to protest the election in West Feliciana. "I felt sure that D. A. was acting in the line of duty by putting his name to the protest," he told the *New York Herald,* "because in one part of the parish, there was a small body of disorderly roughs, who interfered with the negroes." The implication was clear: Weber's supposed claim that the election had been free and fair was false, not his protest.[43]

The press had a field day. The committee's first witness, the *Herald* pointed out, was "a drunken 'dead beat'" whose unsupported testimony amounted to "worthless rubbish." What possible motive, it asked, could Matthews have had in arranging for the production of a forged document that Anderson had consistently represented, until now, as the genuine article? By denying the evidence of his own handwriting, Anderson had "quite disarmed himself from further mischief." The *New York Tribune* agreed: "Anderson a Lying Witness" read the headline above its report of the day's proceedings. Even the *New York Sun* acknowledged the damage inflicted upon Anderson's credibility: the Republicans had done their homework; their cross-examination was "masterful."[44]

The possibility that Anderson forged Weber's signature on the Anderson-Weber agreement suggests that Weber might have had no involvement whatever in his plot. The only evidence that he was a confederate, aside from the dubious "agreement" of November 15, 1876, and Anderson's own word, were Anderson's letters to Weber dated before and shortly after the election. None of these missives, however, had accompanying envelopes with postmarks or bore any marks or annotations in Weber's own hand. There was, in short, no external evidence to confirm that any of these letters were genuine: Anderson might have forged them all.

Tellingly, Anderson produced no letters *from* Weber—nothing in the murdered supervisor's handwriting at all. His wife, Laura, Anderson implausibly explained, had destroyed all of his incoming correspondence. Yet he *had* preserved all the letters and telegrams sent by Matthews. Given his blackmailing proclivities, to which his use of the Matthews correspondence bore testimony, why would he permit letters from Weber, if he had received any, to be destroyed? Such documents could only have strengthened his hand—or not, which was perhaps the point. Then there was the fact that Anderson produced no letters *to* Weber between November 19, 1876, and March 7, 1877, the date of Weber's murder. His claim that he and Don Weber had been "close, intimate, personal friends" made the absence of such correspondence all the more puzzling. The two men were very poor coconspirators if they exchanged no letters during the four and a half months following their receipt of Sherman's alleged written promise.[45]

No one was more delighted by the results of Anderson's cross-examination than Stanley Matthews. His correspondence with Anderson, now blazoned across the newspapers, caused him severe embarrassment. The lengths to which he had gone to placate the faithless carpetbagger, putting up with his insulting telegrams and brazen threats, made him look like a political ingénue who was being played for a fool or, worse, a man submitting to blackmail in order to cover up a crime. The *New York Sun* reveled in his discomfort. "For two months he and Matthews exchanged letters—this vagabond, as he is now called, imperious and aggressive; this Senator, apologetic and anxious. At last Anderson sent a dispatch with this phrase, 'Come here and arrange the affair or you can all face the music.' Matthews came!"[46]

The testimony of former congressman Chester B. Darrall did nothing to alleviate Matthews's plight. Darrall detailed his efforts to obtain the senator's support in his quest to be appointed collector of customs for the Port of New Orleans. He had pressured the senator though Anderson, he explained, believing that "we could cause Mr. Matthews to render efficient assistance" if they threatened to publish his letters. (Darrall's euphemism for blackmail triggered an eruption of "great laughter" in the committee room.) In return for Matthews's support, Darrall went on, Anderson would return the letters as well as hand over his copy of the Sherman letter. The senator, notwithstanding his bruising experience of the previous year, agreed to meet Anderson in order to satisfy his "claims on the administration." Once again Anderson's insulting behavior caused Matthews to regret his involvement with the man. When the ex-supervisor blackmailed the senator to his face, threatening to publish his documents, Matthews told him to go to hell and had nothing more to do with him. Still, his indulgence of this "drunken, miserable fellow" (Butler's apposite description) had many Republicans scratching their heads. "This makes a singular showing for Matthews," Garfield confessed to his diary, "but his testimony may clear it up."[47]

Subpoenaed by the Potter Committee, however, Matthews refused to appear. Butler's personal animus against him made fair treatment impossible, he complained; besides, a committee of the House had no right to investigate a sitting senator. Butler rebutted both points but had no real power to compel Matthews to attend. The latter, rising on a point of privilege, asked the Senate to appoint a select committee to examine his conduct in respect to Anderson. Better to be investigated by this Republican-controlled chamber than by the hostile House.[48]

A seven-man committee, chaired by William B. Allison of Iowa, summoned Anderson to appear on June 21. The man who had caused Matthews so much grief showed up but refused point blank to answer any questions. He explained that he would only testify if the committee allowed him to be represented by a lawyer, or, alternatively, if Matthews agreed to testify before the Potter Committee. As the Senate was no longer in session, the committee was powerless to cite Anderson for contempt. The committee kicked the can down the road, postponing its business indefinitely.[49]

His Republican colleagues protected Matthews from interrogation by Democratic senators, but they could not shield him from public scorn. The kindest verdict was that, to quote the *New York Tribune*, his "foolish letters" showed only "political stupidity." The *New York Times* judged that his "easy tolerance of rascality" demonstrated a "sense of self-respect [that] is quite as elastic as his political conscience." As for his refusal to appear before the Potter Committee, "Privilege has its uses, but the concealment of truth is not one of them." The *New York Herald* scolded Matthews for his "extraordinary lack of judgment," noting that "innocence does not take refuge in such technicalities."[50]

Spared the ordeal of cross-examination, Matthews gave a short explanation to the Senate of his dealings with Anderson, a defense he elaborated in comments to the press. His sole motivation for agreeing to help the former supervisor was humanitarian, he claimed, believing "that he had rendered honest, honorable, lawful, and efficient service to the Republican cause in Louisiana, at the sacrifice of time and money and peril to his person." Anderson never told him that he had lied about intimidation in East Feliciana, the facts of which were "notorious and indisputable." The senator's assistance occurred long after the Returning Board delivered Louisiana's electoral votes to Hayes, and he had no knowledge of any promises made by Sherman or anyone else. Only later did he realize that Anderson was out to cause trouble. From that point on, he confessed, his efforts to help were driven by a desire to keep him quiet, to remove any temptation to "make mischief."[51]

When Anderson, confronted with the so-called Anderson-Weber agreement, denied the evidence of his own handwriting, Matthews turned the tables on his tormenter. Anderson denied the authenticity of the document that he had sent him, the senator told the *National Republican*, because he realized that the Republicans on the Potter Committee could show that Weber's signature was a fake. "There never was such a joint agreement," Matthews explained. "The one he gave me was a forgery as regards Weber's name. Weber never signed it."[52]

After Reed's lacerating cross-examination, Anderson was of little further use as a Democratic witness. Moreover, Darrall's testimony, while embarrassing to Matthews, further undercut Anderson's credibility. He had never intimated that his election protest had been false; rather, he told Darrall that "no Republican was safe there for a moment. . . . [and] that he thought then that no Republican vote could be pulled there at all." The Potter Committee's first witness, gloated the *New York Herald,* only convicted "himself of perjury in the testimony which he gives."[53]

The Republicans' next witness, Aaron B. Levisee, although a loyal party man, proved a gift for the Democrats. A native of Ohio, he had settled in Shreveport in 1855 and practiced law there. After serving in the Confederate army, he became a staunch Republican, serving a term as district judge. In 1876 he was listed on Republican ballot papers as one of eight presidential electors.[54]

McMahon asked Levisee to recount what had happened after the presidential election, when a banker, acting for unnamed Democrats, offered him a bribe in exchange for casting his electoral vote for Tilden. Levisee had given all the details in his testimony before the Howe Committee eighteen months earlier, but he went through the story again. There was nothing new here, apart from some amusing badinage between McMahon and the witness. A sample: Approached by the Democrats' go-between, who offered him $40,000, Levisee asked him to find $200,000 instead, though only "with the view of putting myself beyond temptation as regards my political virtue"—reasoning that such a gigantic sum would be far beyond the Democrats' financial resources. When McMahon suggested that he had indeed solicited a $200,000 bribe and would have taken such if offered, Levisee admitted, "you may think it strange that a man should be talking about political virtue in regard to Louisiana politics." It did indeed seem strange, McMahon agreed. "You know that Louisiana virtue needs to be carefully watched," Levisee riposted. The witness's repartee was entertaining, but it added nothing to the record.[55]

What came next, however, left the audience "looking on in open-mouthed wonder." McMahon took four sets of papers from four envelopes and handed one set to Levisee. He then asked the witness to examine what appeared to be his signature. Levisee perused it closely and, his face betraying astonishment, stated in a voice that betrayed no doubt, "That is not my signature. I never wrote it." The document in question was the certificate of electoral votes from Louisiana. It turned out that someone had forged his signature as well as that of another presidential elector, Oscar Joffrion.[56]

Why the forged signatures? On December 6, 1876, the day the Returning Board declared a majority for Hayes, the eight Republican electors met to sign electoral certificates in triplicate. The first set was deposited with US District Judge E. C. Billings, the second sent to Washington by mail, and the third carried to Washington by courier. The man charged with the third errand, board member Thomas C. Anderson, did not leave New Orleans until December 21, arriving in the nation's capital three days later. Yet when he presented the electoral certificate to Senator Thomas Ferry, president of the Senate, on Christmas morning, Ferry pointed out that the electors had not signed the outside of the envelope containing the certificate, as required by law. The error was trivial, but a panic-stricken Anderson immediately departed, taking the package with him, and boarded a train for New Orleans in order to put matters right. In the meantime, opening the envelope, he discovered another irregularity. The certificate showed one set of signatures on a single piece of paper, whereas the rules required separate certificates with two sets of signatures, one the vote for president and the other the vote for vice president.

When he arrived back in New Orleans on December 28, Louisiana's Republican electors had only days—the deadline was January 3, 1877—to get the corrected certificates to Washington. The six electors who lived in the city, or close to it, signed new certificates. Two others, however, were beyond easy reach: Joffrion in Pointe Coupee Parish and Levisee in Shreveport. With time running out, somebody forged their signatures six times—one each for the three sets of certificates. One set, backdated to December 6, was mailed on the twenty-ninth. Republican official Charles Hill carried a second set, similarly backdated, by train to Washington.[57]

To the Democrats, the discovery of the forged certificates was a godsend after the disastrous performance of James Anderson. It comported with their narrative that Hayes was fraudulently elected. And in seeking to identify the forger or forgers, it gave them a line of inquiry that could only reinforce the impression that Louisiana's Republicans were a set of scoundrels.

Levisee's sensational testimony also provided another disgruntled Republican with an opportunity to levy blackmail. Thomas S. Kelly, described by one reporter as a "spruce and intelligent mulatto," had served in the Louisiana House as one of Kellogg's messengers. He now eked out a living as a cornet player in a brass band and an itinerant music teacher. On June 9 he wrote to Potter professing his knowledge of the forged signatures and offering to testify before the committee. He would be able to identify the offending signatures, he promised, and name "the men who forged them."[58]

Potter immediately arranged for Kelly to be subpoenaed to appear before a subcommittee that was due to begin hearings in New Orleans. In the meantime, while the subpoena was on its way, E. A. Burke of Louisiana's Democratic Central Committee dispatched his trusted agent James B. Kelley, a former captain on the New Orleans police force, to Lake Providence. The white Kelley tried to persuade the brown Kelly to accompany him to New Orleans voluntarily.

Kellogg, however, who appeared to have advance knowledge of Kelly's approach to Potter, took steps to prevent him from testifying. The former governor either knew the identity of the forger or, if he did not, suspected that Kelly actually did. He therefore instructed James D. Kennedy, a friend of Kelly and a former member of his brass band now employed in the US Senate as an assistant doorkeeper, to take a leave of absence in order to track him down and bring him to Washington. Traveling to New Orleans by train and then taking a steamboat upriver, Kennedy found Kelly in Lake Providence, East Carroll Parish. He discovered that the Democratic agent Kelley had arrived before him. But Kelly and Kennedy slipped away in the night. Kelley telegraphed a private-detective agency in Cincinnati with a view to tracing their whereabouts. The detectives reported that the pair had arrived by steamboat and boarded a Washington-bound train. When Kelly arrived in the nation's capital, he made himself scarce.[59]

An ineffective governor but a tenacious political survivor, Kellogg was adept at covering his tracks. Unlike Henry Warmoth, his gubernatorial predecessor, whose extensive political correspondence is of inestimable value to historians, Kellogg's papers are virtually useless. Warmoth preserved everything, Kellogg almost nothing. "I destroy all my letters as fast as I read them," he told the Potter Committee. "If they are black-mailing letters, such as I frequently get, or letters pretending to know about rumors, I destroy them." When he told the committee that he had nothing to do with Kennedy's journey to Lake Providence, there was therefore no documentary evidence to contradict him.[60]

Kellogg's denial evoked skepticism. Kennedy was his protégé; they had known each other for ten years. While in New Orleans before traveling upriver, Kennedy undertook some political errands for the senator, including lining up witnesses for the subcommittee. That he brought Kelly to Washington on his own initiative seems unlikely. Kellogg, moreover, had every reason to keep him quiet. He knew that Kelly was a "sorehead"—a Republican who felt aggrieved that he had not received a federal appointment. As Kelly confessed when asked why he had offered information to Potter, "Mr. Hayes was not treating us exactly as he ought to have done, and considering the circumstances under which he was elected, I thought I would return the compliment if I could."[61]

According to A. M. Gibson—a hostile journalist, to be sure, but according to C. Vann Woodward "an extraordinarily well-informed" one—Kellogg paid Kelly's bills in Washington for eighteen months, using money furnished by John A. Walsh, a banker and speculator, formerly of New Orleans. Kellogg and Walsh were old friends and political allies; the former later testified that he had rendered the latter "one unbroken line of favors, running through the years." Walsh, then in receipt of a munificently lucrative contract from the US Postal Service, had good reason to return those favors. In December 1879 Kellogg finally secured an appointment for Kelly in the New Orleans Custom House, a job that required neither his presence in New Orleans nor the performance of actual work. Four months later Kelly was appointed to a clerkship in the Treasury Department.[62]

At the New Orleans hearings of the Louisiana subcommittee, two handwriting experts studied Kelly's letter to Potter; they both concluded that Kelly had forged the two signatures on the electoral certificates. When he finally appeared before the full committee in January 1879, Kelly refused either to confirm or deny his authorship. Three days later, pressed hard to give an answer, he attributed the deed to P. F. Blanchard. When he added that Blanchard had died of yellow fever in August 1878, the room fell silent. "Then Butler laughed a little. Then Potter, then Reed with his deep base, then the spectators, and, finally, there was a royal horse-laugh all around." The answer was risible; no one believed it.[63]

Butler, cross-examining, asked him to write the name "Oscar Joffrion." Kelly refused. Shown the forged signatures and the genuine ones, he could not tell them apart. By the time Butler got through with him, no one could pretend that Kelly was a trustworthy witness. After the committee adjourned, Butler showed the *Washington Post* correspondent Kelly's letter to Potter. The reporter compared how Kelly had written "Oscar Joffrion" with the forged signature on the second electoral certificate. "They were almost precisely alike." Gibson surmised that Kelly covered up his own guilt, probably at Kellogg's suggestion, by laying the blame on a dead man. Asked by Butler if it had ever occurred to him "that it was pretty bad" for someone to forge a man's signature, Kelly batted away the question. "It was just like any political matter."[64]

The whole affair, truth be told, was a tempest in a teapot. As Senator Ferry explained to the committee, the electoral returns of ten other states failed to show the electors' signatures on the envelope, and those of a dozen more states betrayed some other form of irregularity. The rival Democratic returns from Louisiana—as well as those from Florida, South Carolina, and Oregon—also departed from the required format. In short, there had been no need to forge signatures because the original certificate would have sufficed. He would have accepted it, Ferry explained, had not T. C. Anderson rushed off with the envelope, certificate and all. The defective first certificate, in fact, was the one the Electoral Commission decided, after a party-line vote, to accept. Louisiana's Republicans, Ferry noted, had alarmed themselves unduly and put themselves to a great deal of unnecessary trouble. Yet it was characteristic that their first resort was to skullduggery even when the situation did not require it.[65]

By the second week of June, the Potter Committee was floundering. Newspapers of both political persuasions agreed that the hearings underlined the shady character of Louisiana's Republicans. But what the *New York Times* called "the utter depravity of Louisiana politics" was hardly news. Moreover, the testimony of Anderson and Levisee indicated that the state's Democrats, with their professed willingness to engage in bribery, were equally debased. More important, the hearings had failed to impeach Sherman, let alone demonstrate Hayes's involvement in any electoral fraud. Indeed, the Democrats' star witness had flamed out in a welter of lies and inconsistencies.[66]

If Tilden had believed that the investigation might trigger a movement to get him into the White House by removing Hayes—and apparently he did—no such movement materialized. The electoral crisis of 1876–77 had revealed the "Sage of Gramercy Park" to be vacillating and ineffective. "The great New York leader has proven himself without a plan and without a policy," complained Louisiana congressman Ellis at the time. "His chosen agents were men without capacity, or brains, or nerve." Tilden's reputation never recovered. In the brutal assessment of banker and former DNC chairman August Belmont, "Any movement connected with Tilden is doomed to defeat." Democrats welcomed the investigation as a means of making political capital for the 1880 campaign, but most opposed any effort to oust Hayes before then. Indeed, Potter privately claimed that Tilden was so unpopular that a large portion of the Democratic Party would rather have no investigation at all than one that "might even indirectly advantage him."[67]

Hayes himself made it crystal clear that he would respond forcefully to any "revolutionary" attempt to eject him from the White House. If Tilden tried it, he declared, he would order him "arrested and shot." The remark was offered in private, but "Gath" overheard and published it, and Hayes neither confirmed nor denied it—which the press took as a confirmation.[68]

To remove any doubt about the matter, on June 14 the House passed a resolution stating that the 45th Congress had no right to question the decision of the 44th Congress in recognizing Hayes as duly elected. The *New York Sun* pointed out that nothing would prevent Congress from impeaching Hayes if the Potter Committee tied the president to fraud. Butler declared that the resolution did not abolish judicial review and insisted that Hayes's title could still be challenged before the Supreme Court. The political reality, however, was that Hayes had no need to worry about having his term of office cut short.[69]

Republican newspapers depicted the investigation as pointless and encouraged a rumor that Potter himself was tiring of the business. They also resorted to ridicule. The term "banana republic" had not yet been coined, but Louisiana evoked comparisons with the nineteenth-century equivalent, Mexico, then notorious for political turbulence and instability. The *New York Herald* "Mexicanized" the proceedings by referring to "El Capitano Butlero," "Excelencia Pottero, Tilderano's Nuncio," and so on. The *New York Tribune* affected boredom. The investigation "reminded the looker-on of the employment of a forty horse-power engine to run an ordinary domestic sewing-machine."[70]

The committee's greatest failure and biggest embarrassment was its inability to unearth the Sherman letter. So far, the only evidence for its existence was James Anderson's unreliable word. The Republicans, moreover, were about to go on the offensive. They had lined up a string of witnesses to directly contradict Anderson's testimony. The visiting statesmen declared themselves ready and willing to defend their actions in Louisiana. "We have nothing to fear from investigation," Stoughton wired Sherman from Saint Petersburg, where he served as the US minister to Russia.[71]

The Republicans' first rebuttal witnesses were Thomas and Agnes Jenks. Born in Florida, Thomas had a peripatetic childhood, following his parents to Alabama, Mississippi, Alabama again, and then New Orleans. In 1862, as a fifteen-year-old, he joined the US Navy and served in that branch until 1869. He then received an appointment from Governor Warmoth as tax collector for East Feliciana Parish. There he met Agnes, and in 1870 they married. The couple lived in Jackson, with Agnes's widowed mother and two younger siblings, a sister and a brother. The Jenkses appeared devoted to each other—Agnes affectionately referred to Thomas as "the Captain"—their domestic happiness marred only by the fact that none of their children had thus far survived infancy. Thomas looked the part of the grizzled sea captain that he was. On land, however, he was out of his element.[72]

Born in Glasgow, Agnes D. Murdoch had emigrated to the United States with her Scottish parents. Her father died during the first year of the Civil War, and the Murdochs found themselves in a part of Louisiana that was subject to both Confederate impressment parties and Union raiding parties. Their status as British citizens enabled them to maintain a shaky neutrality, at least for a while. "While living in Jackson," wrote a friend of the family, "they kept open house for both Confederates and Federals." Then disaster struck. After Union authorities cracked down on trade between the lines, the Murdochs were arrested and taken to New Orleans. Following the war, acting on behalf of her mother, Agnes filed a claim against the federal government for the destruction of family property in Jackson by Union forces. In 1874 the Mixed Commission on British and Canadian Claims awarded her mother $1,848.[73]

Thomas Jenks proved an incompetent tax collector. Owing his appointment to a distant relative, Lorenzo B. Jenks, a Union veteran and state senator, he allowed the latter to draw upon parish funds for his own political use. Having taken the money as loans, however, Lorenzo failed to pay it back, and in 1871 a police jury discovered a shortfall of $15,000 in the tax receipts of the parish. Thomas did his best to make restitution and managed to avoid prosecution. Throughout his difficulties, Agnes worked diligently to clear his name by writing letters in his defense and interceding with legislators.[74]

After his botched service as tax collector, Thomas went back to sea, serving in the merchant navy, while Agnes helped make ends meet by securing a temporary appointment as a clerk in the Treasury Department through the assistance of Senator J. R. West. Forced to leave East Feliciana Parish in 1876, the couple moved into a house in New Orleans that Agnes's mother had purchased. Their economic situation was precarious.

Staunch Republicans, they were disgusted by Hayes's betrayal of the Louisiana party and allied themselves with Anderson in his scheme to "bulldoze" the administration. But now, having broken with Anderson, they looked to Sherman for assistance.

Thomas Jenks's testimony impressed no one. It was easy enough to refute Anderson's claim that the Democrats had carried East Feliciana without intimidation or violence. He could also truthfully testify that Anderson had signed his supervisor's protest of his own free will. Other Republicans would be summoned to support these statements, and there was plenty of documentary evidence to back them up.

In denying that he jointly swore an affidavit with Anderson, however, Jenks pitted his word not only against that of Anderson but also against that of Thomas Seymour, the notary who affixed his seal on the document, as well as other witnesses. Moreover, his claim that he did not know Seymour—that he saw him for the first time shortly before testifying—was flatly contradicted by Seymour and others. Whereas the notary did not positively identify Weber, who was a stranger to him, he professed certainty about the identity of Jenks. The latter, of course, had little choice but to claim that someone forged his signature. If he admitted to signing the document, which attested to a free and fair election, he would be confessing that his postelection affidavit in support of Anderson's protest amounted to perjury. Such a confession would have exposed him to indictment by vengeful state prosecutors when he returned to Louisiana. On this one point at least, Anderson's testimony that Jenks had indeed signed a joint affidavit rang true.[75]

Jenks's denials became still less persuasive when he disclaimed any knowledge of the Sherman letter until January 1878. Anderson had written him four times between June and September 1877 urging Jenks to find the "letter," a written "guarantee" that he and Weber had secured from the visiting statesmen. His wife had visited Donaldsonville in search of the letter and had talked about it to E. L. Weber and Joseph P. Newsham. In October 1877 Agnes had written to Millie Weber to again ask after the letter, explaining that Don Weber "had it in his pocket when he left for Bayou Sara the last time as Mr. Anderson and Captain Jenks went to the boat with him, and they were speaking of it."

Jenks did his best to explain away these inconvenient facts. He and Agnes had had no inkling that the "document" Anderson asked them to find was the Sherman letter—"it might have been a letter of invitation for all I know." He denied having accompanied Weber to the landing when the latter took the boat to Bayou Sara. He and Agnes had never discussed the Sherman letter. He professed ignorance as to why his wife had felt it necessary to travel to Washington in January 1878 and spend several weeks there.

Butler was at his sarcastic best (or worst) in his cross-examination. Why did Agnes tell Millie that he had accompanied Don to the landing unless he, Thomas, had told her so—where else could she have gleaned this information? "After the first kiss on her return" from Donaldsonville, did he not ask his wife what kind of document she had gone to look for? Did he never ask Anderson, in light of the value he evidently placed upon it, "'what is this important document'"? Was he not curious as to the purpose of his wife's trip to Washington? "Not having a stupendous income you were yet going to pay your wife's expenses . . . on an errand that you knew nothing about; now didn't you make enquiries before you undertook that expenditure?" Butler's questions exposed the absurdity of Jenks's denials, which, the *New York Times* noted, "created the impression that he was not telling the truth."[76]

The *New York Sun* was predictably, and in this case justifiably, scathing: Jenks not only lied but lied without skill. His attempt to conceal the purpose of Agnes's Washington sojourn "was the most serious of the many serious blunders made by him in presenting his story." It added, cruelly, that he was "somewhat below the average Louisiana witness in the matter of brains." Whatever Thomas Jenks lacked in brainpower, however, Agnes Jenks, the next witness, more than made up for.[77]

Republican Rutherford B. Hayes needed Louisiana's electoral votes to win the presidency. Once in the White House, he abandoned the state's Republicans.

Photograph circa 1879. Library of Congress Prints and Photographs Division.

Democrat Samuel J. Tilden would have been elected president had all the votes been counted.

Photograph circa 1876. Library of Congress Prints and Photographs Division.

Senator John Sherman helped secure Louisiana for Hayes. Democrats alleged that he bribed election officials to give false statements.

Photograph circa 1875. Library of Congress Prints and Photographs Division.

Congressman James A. Garfield argued that the Democrats carried Louisiana by "bulldozing" Black voters and Republican officials.

Photograph circa 1880. Library of Congress Prints and Photographs Division.

Philadelphia lawyer Wayne MacVeagh headed the Hayes-appointed commission that demolished Louisiana's Republican state government.

Photograph circa 1875. Library of Congress Prints and Photographs Division.

Kentucky Republican John M. Harlan helped undermine Louisiana's Republican state legislature. Hayes rewarded him with a seat on the US Supreme Court.

Photograph circa 1880. Library of Congress Prints and Photographs Division.

Republican Thomas B. Reed leavened his devastating cross-examinations with coruscating wit.

Photograph circa 1880. Library of Congress Prints and Photographs Division.

A reluctant committee member, Republican Jacob D. Cox discredited E. L. Weber's testimony with brutal efficiency.

Photograph circa 1870s. Library of Congress Prints and Photographs Division.

Republican Frank Hiscock tilted at Samuel Tilden and clashed with Ben Butler.

Photograph 1878. Library of Congress Prints and Photographs Division.

Chairman Clarkson N. Potter suffered the embarrassment of having to investigate Tilden, his next-door neighbor, over the cipher telegrams.

Photograph circa late 1870s. Library of Congress Prints and Photographs Division.

Former Confederate general Eppa Hunton of Virginia proved a relaxed and fair-minded subcommittee chairman.

Photograph circa 1880. Library of Congress Prints and Photographs Division.

J. C. S. Blackburn of Kentucky, an ardent Tildenite, was forced to play defense as the Democratic case collapsed.

Photograph circa 1870s. Library of Congress Prints and Photographs Division.

Democrat William S. Stenger chaired the Louisiana subcommittee. He was falsely accused of preventing the appearance of Republican witnesses.

Photograph circa 1870s. Library of Congress Prints and Photographs Division.

William E. Chandler labored mightily to elect Hayes and was outraged when the president undermined the Republicans who had given him the victory.

Photograph circa 1870s. Library of Congress Prints and Photographs Division.

Whitelaw Reid, editor of the *New York Tribune*, pulled off the scoop of a lifetime when his paper translated and published the Tilden campaign's cipher dispatches.

Photograph circa 1870s. National Portrait Gallery, Smithsonian Institution.

New York Sun editor Charles A. Dana not only championed the Potter Committee but also, through reporter A. M. Gibson, influenced its proceedings.

Photograph circa 1870. National Portrait Gallery, Smithsonian Institution; gift of Robert L. Drapkin.

The mercurial James E. Anderson, the committee's first witness, turned out to be thoroughly untrustworthy.

From *Harper's Weekly*, June 29, 1878, p. 516.

An early breakthrough for the Republicans came when Congressman Reed (*extreme left*) cross-examined Anderson. Seated at the table, from Reed's left: McMahon, Anderson, Butler, Springer, Potter, Morrison, Hunton, Blackburn, Stenger, and Hiscock.

Theo. R. Davis, *The Potter Committee Room,* from *Harper's Weekly,* June 29, 1878, p. 516.

Agnes Jenks ran rings around one of America's most feared trial lawyers. Here, a deflated Butler throws in the towel.

Mrs. Jenks and the General, 1878. Miriam and Ira D. Wallach Division of Art, Prints and Photographs: Print Collection, New York Public Library.

THE TRAPPER—TRAPPED.

Senator Stanley Matthews was sorely embarrassed when his correspondence with James Anderson came to light.

Thomas Nast, *The Trapper—Trapped,* from *Harper's Weekly,* June 29, 1878, front cover.

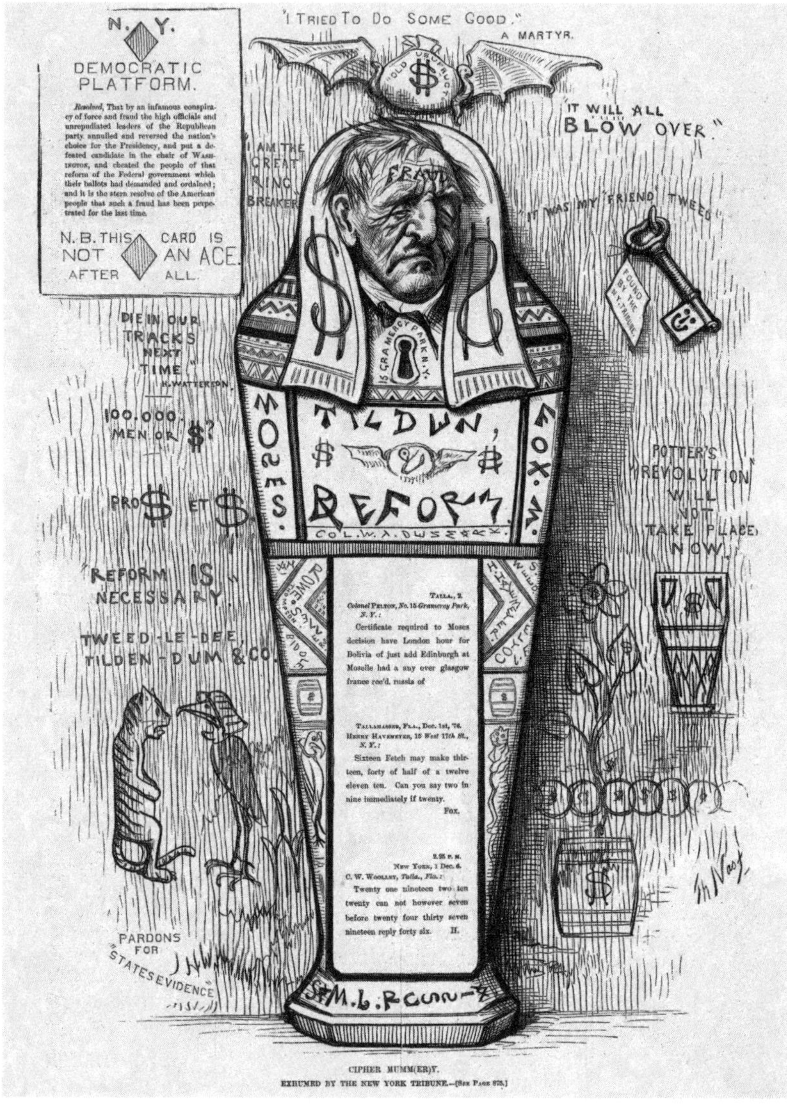

CIPHER MUMM(ER)Y.
EXHUMED BY THE NEW YORK TRIBUNE.—(SEE PAGE 875.)

Thomas Nast here depicts the decrepit Tilden as an Egyptian mummy, his sarcophagus inscribed with quotations from the cipher dispatches.

Nast, *Cipher Mumm(er)y,* from *Harper's Weekly,* November 2, 1878, p. 869.

5

"NO ORDINARY WOMAN"

AGNES JENKS AMUSES AND BAMBOOZLES

It was Saturday, June 23, 1878, and Agnes Jenks kept the Potter Committee waiting. Her late entrance, befitting a drama queen, foreshadowed the performance that followed. "She came to the witness chair with an air of conscious superiority," reported the *New Orleans Daily Picayune,* and "assumed the attitude of a disdainful coquette." A. M. Gibson of the *New York Sun* detected a touch of stage fright, but she soon had it under control. Looking demure as she stood for the oath, Jenks settled back in her chair, looking "wonderfully self-possessed."[1]

Her appearance before the committee was the most highly anticipated event of the hearings. After arriving in Washington in January, Jenks had spoken freely with reporters and politicians, conveying the impression that she knew all about the Sherman letter and other "questionable transactions in the Louisiana count." She also let slip that she had met Sherman himself. In February the *New York Times* described her variously as the "lady from New Orleans," the "remarkable lady from New Orleans," and the "mysterious lady from Louisiana." By June she had become "the famous Mrs. Jenks."

Reporters found her captivating. One described Jenks as a "bright, chipper person . . . bordering on thirty-five years of age, and possessed of mature beauty, not the least attractive feature of which is a pair of dark-blue eyes. Her head is well poised, well shaped, indicative of intellectual capacity, and crowned with clustering ringlets of dark-brown hair." Intelligence, vivacity, and wit, combined with striking good looks, made a potent combination.[2]

The audience in the packed committee room was not disappointed. Her five hours of testimony had reporters struggling for words. She "had the audience . . . almost breathless," wrote one. "A more dramatic scene was never witnessed in a committee room," claimed another. The *New*

York Herald's man confessed that his powers of description were inadequate: "A mere verbal report . . . can give only a faint idea of the scene." In one reporter's opinion, "This country has never before witnessed such a spectacle."[3]

That last judgment might well have been literally true. America was becoming accustomed to seeing women play important roles in the public life of the nation. Harriet Beecher Stowe, Sojourner Truth, Dorothea Dix, Clara Barton, Elizabeth Cady Stanton, Victoria Woodhull, and others had achieved prominence in the fields of literature, abolitionism, nursing, and women's rights. And if it was rare for women to appear before congressional committees, such appearances were not unknown. Eliza Pinkston, for example, created a sensation when she related her harrowing experiences of Democratic violence during the 1876 election campaign in Ouachita Parish.

For a woman to appear before a congressional committee and testify in the manner that Agnes Jenks did, however, was a novelty. She displayed extensive knowledge of politics, a male domain, and conducted herself "with most irritating self-possession." Her theatrical manner and quick repartee had the audience "convulsed with laughter." Reporters "looked on with open-mouthed wonder." She became an overnight sensation.[4]

Butler kicked off the questioning and got straight to the point: What did Jenks know about the "Sherman letter" and when did she know it? It immediately became apparent that her answers would be anything but direct. She evaded, obfuscated, bantered, played word games, pretended not to understand, and feigned indignation. To Butler's evident skepticism, she claimed that the first she had heard of the letter was when Marshal Pitkin mentioned it to her husband in January, shortly before she left New Orleans for Washington. Until then, she had no idea that the document Anderson had been so keen to lay his hands on was the Sherman letter. When a disbelieving Butler asked if she had not known about it earlier, she deployed her tactic of verbal fencing.

JENKS: I may have known about it, but I did not think much about it.

BUTLER: Did you know about it?

JENKS: I did not think about it.

BUTLER: Did you know that there was such a document?

JENKS: If I had thought about it I might have known it.

BUTLER: Did you know it?

JENKS: Well, if a person does not think about anything he does not know it.

Spectators laughed appreciatively, the *New York Sun* recorded. "Two members of the committee roared, then snickered like giddy girls." After much verbal sparring, Jenks conceded, "I did see a document."[5]

Jenks paused for effect. "I wish to state in the presence of this august committee, and of the country at large," pausing again before launching into a soliloquy. She alone knew the truth about the "so-called Anderson and Weber guarantee." Sherman had nothing to do with it either directly or indirectly; he was entirely blameless. Anderson, although a "magnificently sublime scoundrel," sincerely believed the letter was genuine—"that is a single ray of light admitted to the darkness that surrounds him." But no one, she repeated, "knows aught of that document save myself."[6]

Committee and audience were stupefied. A pokerfaced Butler fixed Jenks with a steady stare. Cox appeared discomfited, Reed nonplussed, and Hiscock chagrined. McMahon "watched the witness as a cat watches a mouse." Morrison tried to look composed. Hunton and Springer struggled not to laugh. The spectators watched "in open-mouthed wonder." When Jenks ended her declamation, "committee, audience, and reporters broke into a loud guffaw." When the laughter died down, Springer intoned: "Now let the curtain drop. The act is finished." Jenks's performance, the *New York Times* wrote, "would do credit to a trained actress."[7]

Butler pressed on. Bit by bit, he extracted from Jenks an explanation of how the "so-called" Sherman letter came into existence. To cut a long story short—something Butler proved incapable of inducing her to do—Jenks claimed that she faked it.

Her improbable story went like this. On November 20, 1876, she encountered D. A. Weber on his way to the Saint Charles Hotel bearing a note for Senator Sherman. Weber explained the import of the note: he and Anderson were asking Sherman for a written guarantee of federal employment. Jenks asked why they would doubt the word of so respected a Republican as Sherman. "I do not care so much about it myself," Weber replied, "but Anderson thinks we had better have it." She offered to deliver the note, and Weber handed it to her.

Entering the hotel, Jenks enquired after Sherman. Informed that he was not in his room but might be somewhere upstairs, she went into the ladies' reception room and, quite involuntarily, bit the end off of the envelope, thereby rendering it unpresentable. She then "quite unconsciously read" the note inside. Its contents shocked her. "It contained an insult to Mr. Sherman. . . . I was disgusted at their asking for his assurance that they should be provided for, and stating that his word was scarcely specific enough." She decided not to deliver it. Instead, she went into Parlor P, the hotel's main public room, and concocted a reply. She did not write it down herself; rather, she dictated the text to a local politician of her acquaintance who (conveniently for her story) had since died. She then left the hotel, met Weber as previously arranged, and handed him Sherman's supposed reply. "I was simply maintaining the dignity of the party," she explained, by shielding the visiting statesmen from the "contemptible stratum of humanity that we had in Louisiana politics at that time."[8]

When Butler handed her a copy of the Sherman letter, Jenks set it aside, turned to face the audience, and repeated its contents from memory, giving a word-perfect rendition. Her manner, the *New York Times* thought, "showed thorough study of the meaning as well as the words of the text."[9]

Questioned about her motives, Jenks explained that she produced the letter "for the honor of the party," acting on her own initiative. Her missive to Anderson and Weber had "poured oil on troubled waters"; it "made them feel better, and it kept them quiet." She confessed to being a supreme political realist. "There is nothing impossible in politics, you know," she lectured Butler (of all people). "If it is possible it may be done, and if it is impossible it shall be done. . . . It is said that 'the end justifies the means,' and in Louisiana politics it is well to adopt that rule."[10]

Jenks's story was so farfetched that Butler seized upon its most obvious flaws. Why had she traveled to Donaldsonville the previous summer to ask Millie Weber if she knew of the letter's whereabouts? Did she not realize that the document Anderson wished to procure—the "written guarantee" from the "dead-beats" that he and Weber would be provided for—was, in fact, the Sherman letter? Why, in October 1877, had she asked Millie to make another effort to find it? If she had forged the letter herself, why did she even bother? When she assured Kellogg in November that "the letter you wot of," the one that Anderson "values highly," was not in the latter's possession, what else could she and Kellogg have been referring to?

As Butler probed the inconsistencies in her account, Jenks played the verbal equivalent of rope-a-dope. "The witness first evaded," the *New York Sun* reported, "and then began to fence." When she eventually provided answers, they defied belief. It had never occurred to her that Anderson could have been referring to the Sherman letter when he asked the Jenkses to search for the "written guarantee." She assumed it must have been some other document and that the "dead-beats" to which he referred were members of the MacVeagh commission. Had she known it was the Sherman letter, she "would not have taken the trouble to go to Donaldsonville for it." The problem with this explanation, of course, was that the MacVeagh commission could not have given a "written guarantee" to Anderson and Weber—by the time the commissioners arrived in New Orleans, Don Weber had been dead for over a month. Moreover, Anderson had dated the written guarantee to "last fall," making it plain that the "dead-beats" he had in mind were the Republican visiting statesmen, of whom Sherman was the most prominent.[11]

Jenks also struggled to explain away why, in writing to Millie Weber in October, she disclosed that her late husband had carried the letter in his pocket "when he left for Bayou Sara the last time as Mr. Anderson and Captain Jenks went to the boat with him."

But she was equal to the challenge. Thomas never had accompanied Don Weber to the boat, she claimed. That piece of information came from Anderson, and she ought to have placed his words in quotation marks when relaying them to Millie. Jenks was squaring her testimony with that of "the Captain," who had made the same denial that morning. The explanation, while impossible to disprove, was nevertheless implausible.[12]

When Butler tried to identify the source of the various Sherman letter "copies" that had mysteriously surfaced, Jenks put on a bravura display of deliberate obtuseness.

> BUTLER: Have you since the 20th of November, 1876, ever written any letter of the same purport substantially as that letter which we have here and put John Sherman's name to it?
> JENKS: Why should I do so?
> BUTLER: I do not know why, but did you?
> JENKS: Why should I do so at any time?
> BUTLER: I do not see, but I am asking if you did so.
> JENKS: There has been no protest entered since that time, and there has been no occasion for any guarantee. . . .
> BUTLER: Have you or have you not?
> JENKS: Why should I do so?
> BUTLER: Will you please answer the question?
> JENKS: I generally know what I am about. There was no occasion to write such a letter to anybody else. I am not the amanuensis of Senator Sherman.

BUTLER: Have you or have you not?
JENKS: What do you want to know?

And so it went on. After pushing him to the edge of apoplexy, Jenks finally gave Butler a plain denial. "How long it took to get that piece of truth!" exclaimed the exasperated congressman. "Well, you do not ask your questions right," parried the witness. Exhausted and somewhat crestfallen, Butler, to quote the *New York Herald,* "retired from the unequal contest leaving the enemy in the field."[13]

McMahon fared little better. The more impatient his questions, the more frivolous and insolent Jenks's replies. "What business is it of yours?" she retorted when the congressman asked why she had visited Washington at the beginning of the year. "I was devoted to the nation," she flippantly replied when he pressed her further. Changing tack, the congressman asked about her meetings with Packard—what had they discussed? "We had consultations about the Eastern question," Jenks quipped. McMahon could hardly believe his ears. "About the Turkish question?" "Yes, sir." When the congressman suggested that Sherman "bluffed you off," she put on a marvelous show of faux indignation.

JENKS: I don't understand your expression.
MCMAHON: "Bluffed" is an English word.
JENKS: Yes; but it is slang. It may be a Democratic expression.
MCMAHON: No, it is English.
JENKS: Well, I object to it.
MCMAHON: Well, I withdraw it.
JENKS: All right.

The congressman was slow to learn. His suggestion that she had met Sherman in order to "blow up the Sherman letter" provided Jenks with another opening: "I have no dynamite, not a bit if it." "You have more than you think," riposted McMahon. "Then it must be an unseen force," came back the reply. Insisting on the last word was another string to her verbal bow, a handy method of keeping her interrogators off balance.[14]

On Monday, as members of the public besieged the committee room to witness the Agnes Jenks show, it was Springer's turn to "extract some truth from the artful female dodger." He largely failed. Once again Jenks played the actress-comedienne. She bowed to the audience as she took her chair. She then "hesitated and equivocated," refused to answer questions she did not like, and quibbled over words as if they injured her amour propre. She took offense at Springer's description of the Sherman letter as "bogus." She also objected to "counterfeit" and was equally unhappy with "forged." When he asked her to name the person to whom she dictated the letter, she answered, absurdly, "a pen is a mechanical instrument, you know." "You dictated it to a pen?" "Yes; someone might have been holding the pen, though." Who that someone was, however, she declined to say. She refused, too, to copy the Sherman letter in front of the committee, placing her elbows on the table and supporting her head in her hand "as if to show that she was determined not to write." Her extended stonewalling tried Springer's patience, "and the more she noticed this the more provokingly impudent she became."[15]

Butler and McMahon again tried, but their questions merely elicited frivolous badinage that had the audience in stitches but revealed nothing new. Asked by McMahon to explain what she had meant, in writing to Kellogg, by "the letter you wot of," she replied, "Doubtless it was a letter, and thereby hangs a tale." "I want to get hold of that tale," McMahon patiently explained, thereby inviting the inevitable riposte: "Do you? Well, I presume it will a tale unfold." Even the unflappable Butler struggled to maintain his sangfroid in the face of Jenks's provocations.

BUTLER: Will you produce—

JENKS: Now, compose yourself, General.

BUTLER: I have neither anxiety or emotion on the subject, madam; now let me see those letters. I want the Anderson letters.

JENKS: The Anderson letters are not couched in such a style as would edify you; I know you are flowery. [Laughter; a pause]. Have you anything else to ask me?

The witness "succeeded in baffling and beating Butler till his head swam," wrote one reporter. She "snatched his questions out of his mouth before they were fairly uttered, and returned them to him like so many boomerangs." Jenks once again outfoxed the committee in a most entertaining way.[16]

The press, almost without exception, loved Agnes Jenks. The sheer novelty of seeing a woman discoursing on politics fascinated reporters. As Dr. Johnson remarked of a woman preaching: "[It] is like a dog walking on his hind legs. It is not done well, but you are surprised to find it done at all." In this case, however, Jenks performed exceedingly well. Here was a type "not found in northern politics," marveled the *New York Tribune,* "and a rare specimen even in the South." The *Washington Post* reckoned her to be "the ablest politician that Louisiana has yet produced." The *New York Times* was effusive: Jenks "cannot be judged as an ordinary woman. She was active and prominent in Louisiana politics, and . . . worked with more boldness and sagacity than is usually displayed by many masculine leaders." Even the *New York Sun* agreed that her "mental quickness, and readiness at repartee," showed Jenks to be "not an ordinary woman intellectually."[17]

And, of course, she provided the press with priceless entertainment. As the *New York World* put it, "her testimony relieves the waste of Washington politics like an outburst of opera bouffe." Reporters watched with delight as she outwitted the committee members, conducting herself "like a shrewd and brilliant lawyer." The *Tribune,* which did its daily best to trivialize the investigation, had to acknowledge that this "diverting, ingenious witness" was "the equal of the sharpest member of the committee, a match for General Butler himself." She displayed "a certain Machiavellian finesse," the *Times* editorialized, "which, superadded to her native shrewdness and tenacity of purpose, makes her character a highly piquant compound." Even her diction, which the *Tribune* thought "weird" but to the *Times*'s man fell "pleasantly upon the ear," captivated the press. "Her gay, vivacious manner and ready command of language," observed the *Post,* "proclaim what her slight accent would betray, a French origin." Once again, however, Jenks had the reporters fooled. Her accent was Scottish, not French, an error that caused considerable merriment in Louisiana.[18]

The *Post* called her the "legendary, mythical Mrs. Jenks." She was not merely a news item but also that recognizably modern type—a "personality." Reporters found her combination of playfulness and strong opinions irresistible; she enjoyed their attention and gave them what they wanted. "I have quite a talent for drawing," she told the man from the *Post,* "and I mean to make a picture someday. On one side will be the Returning Board, visiting statesmen and prominent men of the country; on the other will stand Anderson and Weber. I will stand in the middle, holding in one hand the Sherman letter and in the other a mace." The smitten reporter described her as a "handsome, well-preserved lady . . . with a full round face, bright sparkling eyes and a piquant, dashing expression." She began to attract fan mail. "I receive almost daily a sonnet or poem about myself." Jenks had become "the most famous woman in America," the *Tribune* declared. "Oh, but she enjoys it!"[19]

Agnes Jenks's dazzling performance, however, could not disguise the fact that much of her testimony challenged credulity. Unless an original document turned up—a genuine one—her claim that she forged the Sherman letter could not be disproved. But it depended upon her word alone; there was not one iota of corroborating evidence. The *New York Times* tried to give her the benefit of the doubt: "It was a clever trick, and no one who knows Mrs. Jenks doubts she has the capacity to invent and the boldness to execute an act of this kind." Her sheer lack of scruple, the *New York Herald* thought, made her "equal to the task of fabricating the letter which has caused all this fuss and turmoil."[20]

But the cleverness that so impressed her audience was a talent she pressed into the service of evasion and equivocation. As the *Herald* put it, "The same qualities which render Mrs. Jenks so diverting a witness throw suspicion upon all she says." Her search for the Sherman letter in the summer and autumn of 1877 made no sense if she had forged the document in November 1876. Her claim that she had no idea that the document in question was the Sherman letter struck the *Times* as "too unreasonable to be true." For someone who claimed to possess a photographic memory, Jenks proved vague about the circumstances in which she composed the forgery. She could not recall the type and size of the paper she used. She was unable to name a single person who was present in the Saint Charles Hotel during her visit there. She adamantly refused to name the "local politician" to whom she dictated the letter.[21]

Skeptics also pointed to the wording of the letter: it was terse and businesslike. "How did this flighty, erratic, loquacious magpie of a woman succeed in composing such a letter?" the *Herald* wondered. The *New York Tribune,* too, noted the "painful dissimilarity in style" between Jenks's florid letters to Anderson and "the letter she 'dictated' to the unknown amanuensis in Parlor P." The words "your note of even date" seemed especially incongruous. McMahon asked her if she ever used that phrase; she claimed that she did. He then asked her to produce a letter in which she had used it. She could not. Every word of the Sherman letter, the *New York Sun* argued, "bears internal evidence of being written by a man of affairs, and those familiar with the style of John Sherman can hardly mistake its paternity. The style is the man in miniature."[22]

If most of Jenks's claims were unprovable but also impossible to disprove, her flagrant denial that she had ever claimed possession of the Sherman letter—or, at least, knew where to find it—was easily contradicted. At least half a dozen witnesses, including Anderson, Darrall, Kellogg, Packard, and Samuel P. Butler of the *Baltimore Gazette,* all testified to hearing Jenks refer to the letter in a manner that suggested, for all her circumlocutions, that she could produce it. Visiting William Chandler in March, Jenks flatly stated that "she had the letter . . . safely deposited in New Orleans."[23]

It seems, in fact, that she could hardly stop talking about it during her stay in Washington. Alfred Haley, a Confederate veteran and fellow boarder who made no secret of his unbounded admiration for Jenks's wit, intelligence, and handsome looks, nonetheless rebutted her denial. She "not only admitted its existence" but also claimed "that the letter was where she could find it." Even the landlord of the boardinghouse heard her talk about the letter: she claimed to have obtained it from Millie Weber and that it was now in New Orleans. Haley confessed to being hard of hearing, but he was not so deaf as to be unable to follow a conversation.[24]

Recalled before the committee, Jenks flatly denied Haley's testimony. "Now," she rhetorically asked McMahon, "have you any more deaf, dumb, lame, halt, or blind witnesses to be called in this investigation?" This cruel reference to Haley's deafness provoked considerable amusement. For once, however, McMahon got in the last word. "There are none so blind, Mrs. Jenks, as those who won't see."[25]

The only new piece of information that Springer coaxed from the witness was a claim that the reply she gave to D. A. Weber was actually a second draft, the first draft having been, on reflection, too specific in its offer of employment. Asked what happened to that initial version, she could not resist going for the laugh. Like Anderson and Weber's note to Sherman, "It was scattered over boundless space, where the eye of Omniscience could not find it, nor the power of Omnipotence put it together again." Pressed to identify the Republican politician to whom she dictated the second draft—the one person who might substantiate her claim to have forged the Sherman letter—Jenks again refused. "I did see him a little over six months ago," she asserted. "He may be dead," she speculated. "I know not."[26]

Her penultimate appearance before the Potter Committee, on June 29, took place on an insufferably hot day. "A mere hole in the wall it is at best," the *New York Sun* complained of the committee room, "and in it fifty persons sweltering." The fact that half the men were smoking cigars added to the foul air. Still, Jenks alleviated the discomfort and ennui by adding some light relief.[27]

Quizzed by Potter, she mixed flippancy with sneers and snobbery. Asked about her visits to Donaldsonville, she referred to Millie Weber as a "French dago" who lacked intelligence, then implied that E. L. Weber, Millie's brother-in-law, was a coward for being "too much afraid of assassination to go out of his front door." When Potter enquired if she had discussed matters with A. J. Reynolds, an acquaintance who escorted her to her hotel, she quipped, "I am not accustomed to converse with common people." Reminded that Reynolds was a newspaper editor, she retorted, "That did not make him any better."[28]

Jenks was now treating the committee with undisguised contempt. Every question elicited a facetious response. What was her occupation? "I am a general genius." And that of her husband? "His occupation is as a witness before this august tribunal." Potter, whom she chided for being "very dull of comprehension," became so irritated that he lost his temper. When Springer alluded to the fact that the hearings had made her famous, Jenks shot back, "I have made you famous; you have not made me so." The session brought out no new information. She again refused to name her coconspirator in forgery: to do so would be a "violation of trust." Her swansong on July 1 was more of the same. To Potter's incredulity, she claimed not to know if her brother was employed in the New Orleans Custom House. "Do you mean to swear that you do not know—" Jenks cut him off: "I am not swearing at all; you are doing all the swearing."[29]

She had one more brief appearance, this time at her own request. Witnesses normally made such requests in order to correct their previous testimony. Jenks did it to correct another witness's testimony. The correspondent of the *Baltimore Gazette* had attributed to her the words, in speaking of Sherman's reaction to her mention of the Felicianas, "those names operated on him like a red rag to a bull." She indignantly denied that she would ever use such an expression—"as if I acted as a picador in a Spanish arena." Having once again underlined her punctilious regard for the English language, she stood up and, striking a dramatic pose, thanked the committee for its courtesy. "The scene was so ridiculous that it evoked laughter from all present." Her departure from the stage, the *New York Times* lamented, was an "irreparable loss to the comic company."[30]

Jenks's testimony, while amusing, was utterly unreliable. In private correspondence with Sherman, Jenks admitted that she had made up the story of possessing "some imaginary letter" after arriving in Washington in January. She also revealed that her aptitude for hairsplitting enabled her to lie without, in her own mind at least, committing perjury. When Potter asked if she had received any letters from Sherman, she replied in the negative. "I said *no,*" she explained to Sherman, "because I had but one *letter.*" Potter also wanted to know if she had written to Sherman; she denied that she had. "I did not deem it necessary to state to the committee that I had sent letters to Madame your wife." She even denied being called as a witness on behalf of Sherman when she had actually offered to so testify.[31]

Still, her story of having forged the Sherman letter, however farfetched, proved a boon to the Treasury secretary. It cleverly vitiated Anderson's testimony without factually contradicting it. "The cunning and unscrupulous Anderson . . . was himself only the deluded fool and tool of Mrs. Jenks!" marveled one observer. Republicans could hardly suppress their smiles. A delighted congressman wrote to congratulate Sherman: Jenks's "marvelous" testimony "justified not only all you did, but all you said before the same committee." A relieved Sherman told the *New York Tribune* that the only doubt he had harbored was whether Anderson forged the letter himself or someone else did. After Jenks's testimony he leaned toward the latter explanation.[32]

Their hopes of finding the Sherman letter fading, Democrats now produced a witness who rebutted Jenks's claim to have forged it. Emile Weber, who testified on July 2, 1878, provided an incontrovertible explanation of why nobody could produce the original Sherman letter. The document was genuine, he told the Potter Committee, but he had destroyed it with his own hands in the summer of 1877. Weber added a sensational twist to an already convoluted story. "One could have heard a pin drop as he spoke," reported the New Orleans Daily Picayune.[33]

According to Weber, his brother, Don, had not wanted to file a protest because he regarded the election in West Feliciana as free and fair. Against his better judgment, however, party higher-ups persuaded him to protest the result. Among those leading him astray was Emile, whom the unholy trinity of Kellogg, Packard, and Thomas Anderson induced to exercise his influence over his younger brother. Stricken by remorse, Don reluctantly allowed his protest to stand after Emile conveyed a message from Sherman that he would be "protected and provided for."

Weber recounted his eyewitness view of the meeting between his brother, James Anderson, and Sherman. On November 20, happening to pass by Moreau's, Emile glanced through the window and saw Anderson and his brother inside the restaurant, engaged in conversation with Sherman. Afterward, Don revealed that he and Anderson had received verbal and written assurances from the senator. He handed Sherman's written guarantee to his brother. Emile read it over carefully; he recognized the handwriting as Sherman's because he had seen the senator scribbling at a desk in the Custom House. After Agnes Jenks came looking for the letter in July 1877, he rummaged among his brother's effects and found it inside a shoebox. He decided to destroy it because the letter had become a "subject of mortification to Mrs. D. A. Weber and myself and to the members of my family." Tearing it up seemed "the best and easiest way to have the matter disappear from public notice."[34]

Weber's bombshell testimony, however, betrayed as many improbabilities as that of Anderson and Jenks. His alleged conversations with his brother and with Sherman could not be corroborated by third parties. Don, of course, was in his grave, and Sherman denied ever confiding in Emile or discussing Don's protest with him. Weber's assertion that he recognized the handwriting on the letter from the one time that he saw the Ohioan writing was implausible; it became shakier still when Sherman denied ever having sat down to write at the Custom House. As to his destruction of the Sherman letter in the summer of 1877, Weber was hard put to explain why he had never mentioned the fact to anyone—not even Don's widow—before testifying to it a year later. Indeed, when Jenks was in Washington putting it about that she had the letter under lock and key, Weber was claiming that *he* had possession of it. As the *New York Times* sarcastically commented, "There seemed to be no point in connection with this mysterious letter that this man was not prepared to swear to."[35]

Sherman was scathing. He poured scorn on Weber's story—"concocted within ten days"—of having destroyed the nonexistent letter. "No one acquainted with the darkness of Louisiana politics" would believe it. It was indeed absurd. A letter that Weber wrote to his close associate Robert Morris in February 1878, which the subcommittee compelled him to produce, suggested that Weber had never seen the Sherman letter, let alone destroyed it. "There is a woman in Washington now," he told Morris, "who . . . says she has the document that John Sherman, Stanley Matthews, Foster, & Co. signed to D. A. Weber and J. E. Anderson." Clearly unfamiliar with the letter, he was nevertheless keen to obtain and exploit it. The following month he informed William Chandler that the letter "has been in existence, and must yet be, but I cannot just now tell you where it is."[36]

As Democratic hopes of finding the Sherman letter faded, Republican committee members were emboldened to deny its existence. From the evidence thus far presented, Butler argued, no inference "could be legally or logically drawn that Mr. Sherman ever wrote the so-called Sherman letter."[37]

Their search for the letter a wild-goose chase, Democrats abandoned it. Weber's main value to them now was his testimony concerning the elections in the Felicianas, and in that regard he did not disappoint. Like Anderson, he denied Republican charges of bulldozing on the part of local Democrats. True, he conceded, there had been much violence since the Civil War, but there had been violence before the war as well, most of it inspired by "personal difficulties" that had nothing to do with politics. As for the "regulators" who had roamed at will in 1875–76, these were simply "clubs formed by citizens of both colors to protect themselves against thefts of cotton seed, chicken and stock." Miscreants had been whipped, and this "sometimes led to retaliation between the parties." But this kind of vigilante justice was "not political" and in any case had died down by November. In fact, for six months preceding the election, "quiet and order" had prevailed, with "good feeling . . . among all classes."[38]

Weber's claims about Republican machinations to steal the election were startling in their breadth. Kellogg had not only conspired to keep Anderson out of East Feliciana, he asserted, but also tried to prevent local Republicans from mounting a campaign in West Feliciana. In fact, in Weber's telling, Republican leaders decided in advance of the election that, whatever the actual vote, the Returning Board would declare that their ticket had carried the state. To this end they set aside "legitimate Democratic majorities" in the Felicianas, induced election supervisors to sign baseless protests, and, when it became evident that the Hayes vote was lagging behind the vote for Packard, concocted further spurious protests in order to set aside Democratic polls in a dozen more parishes. Without the connivance of Sherman and the other the visiting statesmen, he contended, Louisiana's Republican leaders would never have manipulated the returns so recklessly.[39]

Weber's testimony ought to have carried more weight than Anderson's. A native of Louisiana, he was thoroughly familiar with the Feliciana parishes. As a former state senator, he had an insider's knowledge of the Louisiana Republican Party.

That knowledge and experience, however, had left a trail of documentary evidence that contradicted everything Weber was now telling the Potter Committee. His testimony before the Boutwell Committee in June 1876 regarding the terror induced by regulators; his telegram to Kellogg, a month before the election, reporting an attempt on his life; his subsequent request for a supply of arms to equip the men who guarded his house; and his postelection affidavit in support of his brother's protest all described the threats, whippings, and other forms of violence that Democrats employed to intimidate Republican leaders and silence Black voters.

Weber struggled to explain why he now disavowed all these statements, his clarifications amounting to one long mea culpa. His testimony to the Boutwell Committee was inaccurate, designed for political effect, and he should not have so testified. He had believed his life to be in danger, but he had since learned that he was mistaken. His postelection affidavit had been drafted by L. B. Jenks and was not truthful; "I inconsiderately signed this incorrect statement of fact" without even reading it, a mistake for which "I have no defense to make."[40]

His most abject retraction concerned the letter he wrote on March 24, 1877, intended for publication, in which he blamed his brother's murder on Democrats who now held public office, three of whom had been in the courthouse when the fatal shotgun blasts issued from the building. He confessed to the committee that he had done those men an injustice. His letter had been written for "political effect," and he had got his facts wrong: "I ought not to have made that statement. . . . I have no excuse for making it." He now understood that his brother's death had had nothing to do with politics. Don Weber had many personal enemies; the proximate cause of his murder was that he caused mortal offense to some of them by announcing his intention to publish the names of delinquent taxpayers in the *West Feliciana Ledger.* Cox could hardly believe his ears. "Are you testifying that you believe that the mere threat of publishing in an authorized newspaper a list of people who had not paid their taxes is regarded as a sufficient matter to kill a man in West Feliciana?" Apparently so, replied Weber: "Those parties named in it might think so."[41]

Weber knew how flagrantly this letter contradicted his current testimony and implored the committee not to introduce it as evidence. To Republicans, however, it spoke for itself. Weber's claim that he wrote it "to make political capital out of his brother's assassination," the *New York Times* commented, "disgusted even the Democrats." The *New York Tribune* dismissed Weber's explanation as "ridiculous." The document whose threatened publication supposedly signed Don Weber's death warrant was "nothing more than an ordinary county delinquent tax list," the kind published every month, as mandated by state law, in selected newspapers. With his wholesale retraction of all his previous statements regarding Democratic bulldozing, Weber condemned himself out of his own mouth. "Anderson was reluctant to admit that he had committed perjury before. But this fellow is actually eager to prove himself an habitual liar."[42]

Weber's lamentable performance betrayed a woeful lack of coordination on the part of the committee's Democratic managers. Potter had left much of the business of finding and preparing the Louisiana witnesses to the *New York Sun*'s Gibson, who left a revealing memorandum about the negotiations that took place regarding Weber's appearance. The talks involved Weber, Potter, Gibson himself, and Senator William H. Barnum, chairman of the DNC. Gibson and Barnum had assured Weber that he would be examined in New Orleans, not Washington, and that the Louisiana subcommittee would be thoroughly briefed "as to what he would testify to." But on June 29 Gibson learned that Weber had been subpoenaed to appear in Washington, without adequate time to prepare his testimony and in violation of this agreement. Moreover, the subcommittee had already left for New Orleans "without any knowledge of [the] case to be made there." In his absence, Gibson feared, Stenger and Blackburn would fail to ask the right questions, and some witnesses might offer testimony that injured the Democrats' case. Feeling ambushed by the subpoena, Weber threatened not to testify; if he failed to appear, Gibson warned, "I must abandon the case."

The reporter mollified Weber—it seems that money changed hands—but the latter's shakiness in the witness chair was painfully obvious during his appearance on July 2. As soon as the committee dismissed him, Weber and Gibson departed for New Orleans.[43]

To an extent that few appreciated at the time, Gibson orchestrated the business of the Louisiana subcommittee. It was he who prepared the groundwork for the investigation, consulting local Democrats about whom to call upon to testify. When the hearings got underway, the journalist furnished Stenger and Blackburn with documents, witness statements, and tactical advice. During the hearings Gibson sat beside Stenger, the subcommittee chairman, and whispered suggestions in his ear. "To separate my duties as a correspondent and as a quasi-adviser . . . would be a pretty difficult thing for me to do," he later admitted.[44]

Gibson relied on Weber to recruit Black witnesses, and he used his influence with Stenger to have Sam St. Martin, Weber's sidekick and bodyguard, appointed a deputy sergeant at arms. St. Martin then went into the countryside and served the committee's subpoenas. Once in New Orleans, witnesses were cloistered in a boardinghouse, where Weber and St. Martin never let them out of their sight. "It was unsafe to bring any colored witnesses from the country within the shadow of the Custom-House," explained James H. Maddox, whom Gibson employed as his assistant.[45]

Maddox, ostensibly a Republican, was a man of nebulous political principles for whom double-dealing was second nature. During the war he had supplied military information to both sides—and both sides imprisoned him for disloyalty—while accumulating a tidy fortune trading between the lines. He served the Grant administration as a special agent of the Treasury Department, a post that afforded him ample opportunity for political intrigue. After Louisianans voted in 1876, it will be recalled, he solicited a bribe on behalf of Madison Wells, a scheme that caused Maddox acute embarrassment when forced to describe his actions to a congressional committee in January 1877. At Gibson's behest, Maddox now saw the witnesses as they arrived in the city and prepared their testimony in affidavit form.[46]

Tendering Weber legal advice was George W. Carter, another apparent Republican. A former Confederate from Texas, Carter had entered Louisiana politics in 1870 as a political ally of Governor Warmoth, only to fall out with his sponsor when, as speaker of the Louisiana House, he sided with the "Custom House faction" in the convulsive intraparty dispute of 1871–73. Crushed by Warmoth, his career in Louisiana politics ignominiously truncated, Carter tended to his law practice and family property. He claimed that he simply represented Weber in his legal troubles and had no interest in furthering the Democratic cause. "I do not like to do dirty work," he explained. "I do not often do it for my own party, and never for others." In truth, Carter had long colluded with Louisiana's Democrats. "He is nominally a Republican," Representative Ellis told his brother in 1876. "But he is disgusted with Radicalism and when the time comes he will repent. Better for us now if he seems to remain on that side."[47]

The Republican side was not idle. Sherman proposed calling witnesses who would testify to Democratic bulldozing, sending Potter a list of people who had testified before the Howe Committee. He intended to prove beyond peradventure that the elections in East and West Feliciana had been preceded by a campaign of violence and intimidation that was "political and directed by Democrats against Republicans." He also asked Potter to subpoena the Republican visiting statesman. As for Weber, Sherman's attorney in New Orleans, John Ray, gathered an array of evidence that would, he predicted, discredit him. A veteran Republican who was thoroughly familiar with Louisiana politics, Ray knew Weber to be a bribe taker—not so different from the run of politicians but one whose lack of scruples could be easily demonstrated. Ray had another card up his sleeve: he had found witnesses who would testify that Anderson forged Don Weber's signature on the so-called Anderson-Weber agreement.[48]

Thoroughly briefed by Ray, Cox took on the job of cross-examining Weber, whom he demolished with clinical efficiency. All he needed to do was quote the witness's words back to him. First, Cox cited his testimony before the Boutwell Committee, to which Weber responded, unconvincingly, "I have since learned that those reports were incorrect. . . . I had no knowledge whatever of what I spoke." He then quoted Weber's reports about attempts on his life. His statements had been "exaggerated and incorrect," the witness responded. True, he had testified that a party of mounted men loosed a volley at his house, but he had since learned that "the volley was fired in the opposite direction." Yes, he had kept a small arsenal in his house, but he had never asked for the weapons and did not need them. As for the armed guards around his home before the election, they had served "more to protect themselves than to protect me." What about his testimony that Democratic regulators had ridden their horses into his brother-in-law's store in Bayou Sara, consumed drinks without paying for them, and behaved in a threatening manner? "I have understood that they were personal friends of mine," Weber explained, "and that they had come in there and taken . . . two of three friendly drinks with him." Had he not stated that he left West Feliciana because his life was in danger? "It was my wife who was in fear." Had he not explained his absence from a court hearing in Clinton by telling the judge, "I thought my life was in danger?" Yes, but only on the advice of his attorney—it was not true.[49]

Cox then confronted Weber with evidence of his bribe taking during the period of rival legislatures in early 1877. Weber admitted that he took $1,000 to assist Pinkney Pinchback's election to the US Senate: along with two others, he absented himself from the legislature in order to rob the state senate of a quorum, with the aim of preventing the election of Kellogg, Pinchback's rival. But this was not a bribe, Weber insisted, because he needed the money to defray his expenses—drinks, suppers, dinners, and such. He then rejoined the legislature after State Senator Marshall Twitchell promised him $10,000 in state warrants. Until the assembly issued the warrants, however, Weber insisted on a "guarantee of good faith," a bird in the hand being preferable to two in the bush. Twitchell handed him $4,300 in existing warrants and signed over a "due bill" worth $1,840. This did not constitute a bribe either, Weber explained, but more of a "personal favor." He believed that his action in restoring the senate quorum "was worth something."[50]

Weber volunteered more evidence of skullduggery that, if damaging to the reputation of Louisiana's Republicans, reflected no credit on him. In 1875–76, he related, a "ring" of nineteen state senators, of whom he was one, demanded bribes for passing legislation—$1,000 each for a levee bill, $1,000 for a bill to construct a new state capitol, and so on. "Whenever money was to be paid I was to get a share of the plunder." He was confessing to past misdeeds because he wished to "make a clean breast of the whole thing" and expose Republican rascality. In 1876, he explained, "I was blind; I was a partisan; I had a self-interest; I was working under the advice of others."[51]

Cox baited Weber relentlessly on his epiphany: When did he see the light and embrace morality? When were his eyes opened? When did he decide to expose his brother's villainy in making an untruthful protest? Weber became visibly agitated by Cox's needling. "If there was any villainy in this thing," he riposted, "Mr. John Sherman and the visiting statesmen . . . were the ones guilty of the villainy." The outburst drew applause from the audience, which consisted mainly of white Democrats. Protesting that Cox was insulting and browbeating him, Weber lost his composure entirely. He shouted, gesticulated, and pounded his fist on the table: "I don't want you to talk about my moral character. You have ruined me, and now I will ruin them all. If I am to go down, they all have to go down, by God! . . . If I am a rascal they are worse rascals. They corrupted me; I was young and inexperienced—they corrupted me; they led me into these wrongs; they did it."[52]

A dozen witnesses then testified about the election in the Felicianas. The first few followed the Democratic script. Corroborating Weber's testimony, they denied statements they had sworn to in postelection affidavits or told under oath to congressional committees. Henry Reid, a Boston-born sailor who moved to the parish in 1865, affirmed that "there never was a more peaceable election" than that of 1876. A Custom House scribe had inserted allegations of Democratic intimidation without his knowledge; he signed the affidavit without reading it over or having it read back to him. And so it went with Andrew Duncan, Joseph Armstead, Thomas Steward, T. W. Dalton, Riley Norfliss, and Julius Green. They all took back the statements attributed to them in their affidavits, explaining away their testimony before the Morrison and Howe Committees. Nobody had forced Blacks to join Democratic clubs; nobody had been compelled to vote the Democratic ticket; they had not been threatened; the only armed and mounted bands they knew of had been formed to stop the illegal trade in seed cotton.[53]

The most pathetic retraction was that of Amy Mitchell, who had described in great detail how her husband, Isaac, had been murdered by a gang of Democrats led by Charles Barrow. Having been brought to New Orleans by E. L. Weber as a material witness, she had subsisted in that city by washing and ironing, leaving two of her three children with their grandmother on a West Feliciana plantation. Now she claimed that she had seen nothing and heard nothing; awakened by gunshots, she had hidden inside her house. When Cox read her testimony back to her, she took refuge in memory loss—"I 'done forgot' all that was done there"—or claimed that she simply repeated lines that had been fed to her. "What I did say I didn't know myself; they just put it down as the folks told me to say it."[54]

Chairman Stenger could not resist a joke at the Republicans' expense. If he had "gone through all the horrors" described in his affidavit, he suggested to Steward, "your face would have blanched white and your hair gray." "Well, I would have been dead," Steward agreed.[55]

Short of calling the witnesses liars, Cox could do little but exude skepticism at their inability to recall the things they had described in such detail eighteen months earlier. In one exchange, however, he coaxed a frivolous but revealing admission. In a statement that seemed too good to be true—one that he had failed to make previously—Duncan claimed that Don Weber, after the election, disclosed to him "that Mr. Sherman had got him to stick up for Mr. Packard and that he wouldn't need anything after this."

> COX: Is it not strange that you can remember that conversation with D. A. Weber so well, and cannot remember any of the conversation that you had here when you made the affidavit?
>
> DUNCAN: No, sir; I was promised to be taken care of and I was not, and I did not care to remember.

COX: That failure to take care of you affected your memory?
DUNCAN: Yes, sir.

The audience chuckled appreciatively. The full significance of Duncan's playful admission, however, soon became apparent.[56]

John S. Dula was an important witness. The son of a slave and her male owner, he had served as parish recorder and then parish judge in West Feliciana. He had also operated a merchant's store until December 1875, when whites burned it down. He was educated and articulate. Weber expected him to retract his postelection affidavit as agreed.

To the Democrats' consternation, however, Dula stood by every word of his affidavit. "Everything was done in perfect order. It was done accurately." He then dropped a bombshell: he had been promised $500 "if I changed my affidavit [and] went with the boys." Weber had disclosed that a man from New York (presumably Gibson) had come with money and assured Dula that, if he retracted his previous testimony, he could have an appointment as a schoolteacher in West Feliciana Parish. Dula asked for a down payment—"promises are not worth a cent"—and received $45. He buttressed this account by stating that St. Martin witnessed the transaction. Since taking the money, however, he had suffered pangs of conscience and decided to testify truthfully. As he recounted his story, Dula twisted in his chair and tried to avoid looking at Weber, who was staring at him from the other side of the table. After leaving the committee room, he was jostled and kicked as he exited the Saint Charles Hotel.[57]

Astonished by Dula's revelation, Stenger asked St. Martin if there were any truth in it. "Not a damn word," the latter replied. At the chairman's urging, St. Martin, fortified by a couple of drinks, rebutted the allegation. The $45 was a loan, he testified, which Weber had borrowed from him. Weber, recalled as a witness, also described the money as a loan. Dula had been pestering him "to have something" for his testimony, he added, but he slapped down the suggestion. "I stated to him that there was no way in the world by which he could get money to go back on his affidavit."[58]

But the cat was out of the bag, and two other witnesses, Tony Clark and George Swayze, kept the creature in full view. According to Clark, who had fled East Feliciana in 1875, Dula told him that they could procure money from Weber—"money sent here from New York"—in exchange for their testimony. "The Republican party is gone up," Weber reasoned, "and there is no use of hanging on to it any longer, and you had better come with us in this thing." He promised to give Clark $175 and have him appointed to a job in the state government that paid $75 a month. But Clark stood by his previous testimony regarding Democratic intimidation. Pressed by Blackburn to substantiate his claim that Blacks in East Feliciana were still being whipped, however, he refused to give names. If he identified the victims, he explained, "they would be dealt with immediately."[59]

Swayze recounted a similar conversation with Weber. "Hayes has sold out the Republican party in the State," the former state senator told him, "and I do not see any other stand but to get on the Lord's side, and you had better come and go with me." But the ex-legislator refused to go back on his previous affidavits. "Said I, 'I won't do it; I was honest when I made them, and if I was not I should not have made them.'" Since he claimed Weber as a friend, Swayze declined to say if there had been any discussion of money. He had no such hesitation, however, in rehearsing his testimony before the Boutwell and Howe Committees, including his own brushes with Democratic bulldozers. Swayze swatted away Stenger's efforts to impugn his testimony. Of course polling day had been peaceful: months of bulldozing had already created a state of terror among Republicans. Of course he did not personally witness all the incidents he described in his testimony, but they were direct reports that convinced him that "nine-tenths of the colored men . . . were threatened." No, of course he would not disclose names—that would place people's lives in jeopardy. Why had he left the parish? Because he was a leading Republican, of course: "There was no trouble but my politics."[60]

Swayze offered Stenger and Blackburn, whose questions betrayed a mixture of naïveté, willful ignorance, and callous indifference, a tutorial in political reality. After 1875, he told them, he had rarely ventured outside Bayou Sara for fear of getting his head shot off. He, Weber, and Thomas Jenks had asked Kellogg for guns because their lives were in danger. Any Republican who testified truthfully faced Democratic wrath, and it was idle to suppose that the visiting congressmen could afford them any protection if they returned home. "You don't amount to much down here," Swayze lectured Stenger. Prompted by Cox, he explained the obvious: no white man was ever convicted for killing a Black man; "I don't know if I will be strung up for testifying as I am now doing." The *Picayune* characterized Swayze's manner as "violent and insolent." Translation: a forceful and articulate witness who displayed no deference toward the committee members.[61]

Democrats suffered a further setback when their efforts to secure the testimony of Eliza Pinkston came to nothing. The dramatic appearance before the Returning Board of a scarred and wounded Pinkston had been a nationwide sensation, providing powerful support to Republican charges of bulldozing. Democrats desperately wished to erase that blot. They had tried, with indifferent success, to portray Pinkston as a lewd and lying woman. Now they tried a different approach. Visiting her in Madison County, Mississippi, where she and her new husband worked as sharecroppers, Colonel F. C. Zacharie of the state Democratic committee persuaded her to swear to an affidavit contradicting her previous testimony. Her former husband had not been killed by bulldozers, she now stated, but by a colored man, the result of a personal quarrel that had nothing to do with politics. Republicans had paid her to give a false account, she explained, and arranged for her to be carried into the committee on a sofa for dramatic effect, although she had been perfectly capable of walking unaided. If she repeated those claims before the subcommittee, Democrats could present the most famous victim of bulldozing as a perjurer.[62]

Ray knew that Pinkston's testimony could greatly embarrass the Republican case. But he also recognized that her recantation was insincere. "She is now in the midst of the most violent bulldozing elements in the South," he wrote Sherman, "and I have no doubt but that she and her present husband will say anything they are asked whilst under their influence." She had made her affidavit in the presence of four white men, of whom one was her landlord. If Pinkston testified in New Orleans, however, beyond the reach of her Democratic handlers, Ray was confident that she would testify truthfully. Before that could happen, Henry R. Smith, the Republican postmaster of Canton, Mississippi, secured a retraction of her retraction. Zacharie had promised her $200, she told Smith, if she testified for the Democrats, but she was now prepared "to swear that her former testimony was true and that Mr. Zacharie has attempted to bribe her to tell a different story." The Democrats decided not to subpoena Pinkston after all.[63]

Earlier, Representative Cox had performed brilliantly in discrediting E. L. Weber's testimony. He was rather less successful, however, in establishing that the agreement between Weber's brother and James Anderson was a fake. Ray lined up several witnesses who testified that Don Weber never signed the so-called Anderson-Weber agreement. A. J. Reynolds, the printer who worked on the late Weber's *West Feliciana Ledger,* stated that he did not recognize Weber's purported signature. But the men Ray put on the stand to contradict the testimony of the notary, Seymour, and the witnesses to the affidavit, Wilder and Dicks, proved less than convincing. Three witnesses claimed that they had heard Wilder and Dicks admit that Weber had never signed, but that hardly constituted persuasive evidence. One of them revealed his confusion about the date of Weber's murder, enabling Stenger and Blackburn to tangle him in knots. A fourth witness, Hiram Smedley, who kept a coffeehouse on Exchange Alley, made the astonishing claim that a notary public named J. W. Jones had forged Weber's signature in his presence while Anderson waited nervously outside. Needless to say, Smedley had no idea of Jones's whereabouts and suspected that he was dead. The Democrats called half a dozen witnesses to testify that Smedley was a scoundrel. "The witness stand is not the best place to acquire a good character," the *New York Sun* noted. "If there are any dark spots on a witness's past record, the keen eyes of a Congressional investigator will very soon single them out."[64]

Smedley's testimony did provide moments of light relief. Recounting his employment history, the witness divulged that he had served on the New Orleans police force for several months. "Did you perform any police duty?" asked Stenger. "I did not," replied Smedley. "Did you get paid for doing nothing?" He admitted, "Yes, sir." The witness also instructed the congressman on the meaning of the term "coffeehouse." He did not actually sell any coffee, explained Smedley: "That is what people call drinking saloons in New Orleans." Indeed, much of the testimony taken in New Orleans involved witnesses going in and out of saloons in varying degrees of intoxication. Drunkenness, it seems, covered a multitude of sins, including false testimony.[65]

Still, the efforts of Stenger and Blackburn to disprove Republican allegations of bulldozing had backfired. The pair was no doubt relieved when Potter, in light of the yellow-fever epidemic sweeping through New Orleans, ordered the subcommittee to return to Washington.[66]

The main committee, in the meantime, had moved to Atlantic City, New Jersey, the "heat and foul air in the crowded committee room" in the Capitol having become intolerable. Cooled by ocean breezes, the committee finally heard from Sherman and the other Republican visiting statesmen.[67]

The secretary of the Treasury came out swinging. He forcefully and categorically denied authorship of the Sherman letter. He admitted to a faint recollection of James Anderson introducing Don Weber to him at Moreau's restaurant on November 19, 1876, but he flatly contradicted

Anderson's version of the ensuing conversation. He knew that the pair had been election supervisors in the Felicianas, which he understood to be "the two most bulldozed parishes" in Louisiana. He was aware, too, that both men had filed protests. But neither man intimated that he had stretched the truth or made things up, and neither spoke of having incurred the enmity of Kellogg, Packard, or other Republican leaders. He never offered them "any inducement or gave any assurance whatever of a reward or hope of reward" in connection with the 1876 election. Their conversation had been "of the most general and casual character in plain hearing of Stoughton." As to his giving Anderson and Weber a written guarantee of employment, it never happened. Anderson's claim that they had sent him a note requesting such a guarantee was a "palpable lie."

Sherman was not content, however, with making a denial, no matter how emphatically stated. He knew that his word alone would not silence the doubters. He therefore offered a detailed argument, the kind that a lawyer pitches to a jury, to demonstrate the absurdity of Anderson's story. He offered, as strong circumstantial evidence that he could not have written the damning letter, the fact that Anderson never mentioned it when, between March and June 1877, he met with Harlan, Matthews, Hayes, and Sherman himself in his quest for a federal appointment. "I consider that a strong reason to prove that it did not exist."

Knowing that invoking his own integrity would cut little ice, the Ohioan emphasized his political sagacity in language that the men on the committee might understand. Every elected politician used patronage to reward supporters and buy off opponents. But few were so foolish as to make written promises on behalf of an as-yet-unelected president. As for Anderson and Weber asking him, in writing, for such a promise, "That I would have regarded as insulting—certainly exceedingly improper. . . . Now, gentlemen, all of you in public life know very well that no public man could have received such a note without recollecting it."

Sherman rebutted the various allegations, widely reported in the press, that he had bought Agnes Jenks's silence by purchasing the "original" Sherman letter from her. His account of his dealings with Jenks, and the fuller version he put into a written memorandum, accord precisely with the evidence of his private papers: he avoided contact with her, and his wife was present on the only occasion when he granted Jenks an interview. "As to a trade with her, it is simply absurd."

The witness struggled, however, to account for his failure to straightforwardly deny authorship of the Sherman letter when the committee gave him an opportunity to do so on June 1. "I was called upon suddenly without notice," he explained, "in ignorance of the testimony of Mr. Anderson, illy informed as to his character and credibility." Moreover, the existence of the alleged letter had been proclaimed by the newspapers, which reported "that [the] original was to be produced, and that other people had said that such a letter was in existence." Given those circumstances, Sherman told the committee, his denial was "as emphatic as any man could have made." Since then, however, his recollection had been "refreshed," enabling him to state with assurance that the Sherman letter never came from his pen.[68]

He had done his utmost to lay the matter to rest. But his explanation was not entirely persuasive. In denying that he had received a note from Anderson and Weber, Sherman asserted that "no public man could have received such a note without recollecting it." Possibly so. But if that were the case, would not a "public man" recollect, even more vividly, if he had *replied* to such a note? "He now remembers that he did not write the famous letter," the *New York Sun* sarcastically noted, suggesting that the appointment of Levisee, Marks, and Thomas Jenks to federal positions might have refreshed his memory.[69]

A careful listener, moreover, might have noticed that Sherman's fresh denial left open the possibility that he gave a *verbal* assurance of federal employment to Anderson and Weber. He had given them no promises or inducements *"in connection with the election"* (emphasis added). But if by filing protests these men had simply done their duty—and he harbored no doubts about the violence and intimidation to which they attested—he saw nothing wrong with rewarding them. After all, the election was over, and their protests already signed. "I did say to friend and foe alike," Sherman affirmed, "that the Republicans in Louisiana who stood by their guns there deserved credit." Pressed as to why so many of the men involved in the Louisiana election had been given federal employment, the Ohioan was unrepentant. "I would undoubtedly appoint an honest man in Louisiana who had suffered . . . for his political opinions. . . . I would not desert men because they are cried down for doing what they believed to be their duty."[70]

Sherman concluded his testimony by indulging in a little "bloody shirt" rhetoric.

> Now, in regard to pressure. The whole pressure in Louisiana at that time . . . was against the Republicans. . . . Every influence of fear, favor, or affec-

> tion—everything that would tempt a bad man to do wrong or that would swerve a good man from doing right—was against the Republicans. Fear, hope, every animating influence calculated to move the human heart was at work against the Republicans and in favor of the Democrats, and the feelings of fear and intimidation which filled the atmosphere in New Orleans even then, after the election was over, was just as potent and apparent to every intelligent mind as it could be.

Had he been a citizen of Louisiana, Sherman claimed, he would have resisted the Democratic rifle clubs and gone down fighting. His verbal heroics prompted applause—"muffled" according to the *New York Sun,* "loud" according to the *New York Times.*[71]

A parade of Republican visiting statesmen came to Atlantic City to affirm their integrity and corroborate Sherman's testimony concerning Democratic intimidation. Garfield, charged with summarizing the affidavit evidence from West Feliciana, had come to Louisiana with a dim view of that state's Republican Party, assuming that "there must be a good deal of lying." He therefore tested the Republican affidavits by speaking to the men and women who had signed them, asking them to tell their stories in their own words. The result was something of a revelation: these people seemed sincere and credible. He found Amy Mitchell "quite an intelligent person," her account of her husband's murder wholly believable. Garfield also interviewed Don Weber, who impressed him as a "brave, sincere, and truthful man." He found no reason to doubt Weber's account of the bulldozing in West Feliciana, especially when he provided many more details than those contained in his relatively brief protest. The witnesses from East Feliciana made a similar impression upon Cortlandt Parker. When he interviewed James Anderson, the latter gave no hint that his affidavit was in any way false or inaccurate. It would have been strange, of course, if Garfield and Parker had testified other than they did. They had their reputations and careers to protect.[72]

Democrats produced two more witnesses in the fading hope of establishing the authenticity of the Sherman letter. Former congressman J. Hale Sypher, a brother of J. R. Sypher, Anderson's attorney, testified that Don Weber had actually shown him the letter. He refused to swear positively, however, that he had recognized Sherman's handwriting. It was difficult to set much store by his claim, moreover, when he admitted that he had never mentioned the letter to anyone else, save a brother in Louisiana, who did not testify. That he never asked his brother in Philadelphia about it, and that he was ignorant of the fact that the latter represented Anderson, was hard to credit. Anderson and J. Hale Sypher, it will be recalled, had known each other for years: it was at Sypher's instance that Anderson moved to Louisiana in the first place. The fact, overlooked at the time, that Sypher consistently confused Don Weber with his brother, Emile, rendered his testimony worthless.[73]

John E. Leet was a former Republican journalist who, like Anderson, felt aggrieved that the party had not adequately rewarded him for his sterling political services. Testifying before the committee in a stiflingly hot room in the New York Custom House, he "spilled the beans" on his erstwhile associates—or as the *New York Times* put it, recounted "all they ever said or did to him." Leet's rambling, free-associative testimony depicted himself as the pivot of Louisiana politics: he edited a newspaper in Saint Tammany Parish, did "arduous duty" as a clerk in the New Orleans Custom House, and dispensed advice to the Republican politicians who crowded his desk on a daily basis. His news desk, in fact, "was a kind of Mecca for all the Louisiana statesmen." Claiming to be a confidante of Kellogg, Leet stated that the governor tried to prevent Anderson's return to East Feliciana so as to invalidate the election there. An equally close mate of Anderson, it was he, Leet, who advised the ex-supervisor to seek a written guarantee of employment from Sherman. And it was to him, Leet, that Anderson displayed the senator's signature upon receipt of the famous letter.

The prospect of Butler cross-examining a witness always created excitement. About one hundred spectators thronged the committee room, and they were not disappointed. Grilling Leet over *when* he saw the Sherman letter, exposing irreconcilable contradictions between his account and that of Anderson, Butler had the loquacious Leet stumbling for words. Hiscock then finished the demolition job. If Louisiana's Republican politicians were, as Leet asserted, "a most complete set of rascals," why did the witness spend seven years in their company, and did not the association have a demoralizing effect on him? Perhaps, Hiscock suggested, Leet's current position with the *New Orleans Times,* a Democratic newspaper, "has enabled you to recover completely, and to put you back to your original, pure, and virtuous condition." The audience laughed; Leet lost his composure.[74]

Humiliated at the hearings, ridiculed in the newspapers, and anxious about his children in plague-stricken New Orleans, Leet suffered a mental breakdown. Two days after finishing his testimony, he entered the offices of the *New York Sun* in an agitated state. He was looking for Tilden. "I'll be killed the first thing I know," he explained. "You don't know what it is to be an important witness in a great investigation. I've been shadowed. They're after me. . . . I can't sleep. I've got to watch." He then returned to his hotel room and locked himself inside. When three policemen, summoned by anxious hotel staff, arrived to ascertain his condition, Leet fired his pistol through the door. Confined overnight in a cell at the Twenty-Seventh Precinct station, "calm and violent by turns," he loosed a stream of profanity when brought before a judge at the Tombs Police Court the next morning. Friends arranged his transfer to Bloomingdale Insane Asylum. "Who are you?" he asked ex-governor Warmoth when the latter paid him a visit. "Are you a preacher, a conspirator, or an assassin, or what?"[75]

The Sherman letter, it turned out, was a chimera. The hearings, jeered the *Chicago Daily Tribune,* had produced "the impudent lying of Weber, the repeated perjuries of Anderson, the sensationalism of Mrs. Jenks, and the ravings of a maniac, who went from the committee room to an insane asylum." Potter had one more opportunity, however, to publicize the underhanded means whereby the Republican Party put its man into the White House. Thus far, the investigation had skirted the Wormley House agreement. The chairman now gave Butler free rein to probe the "corrupt bargain" that incensed so many Republicans and die-hard Tildenites. "When Butler starts on the Louisiana matter," predicted Henry Boynton of the *Cincinnati Gazette,* "Hayes will suffer." So, too, would Boynton.[76]

6

"GENERAL BUTLER IS A ROWDY"

DISCREDITING THE WORMLEY HOUSE AGREEMENT

General Butler's branch of the Potter investigation is all his own," noted the *New York Times*. The ostensible subject of the inquiry was the electoral fraud that allegedly took place in November and early December 1876. Butler, however, insisted on examining the Wormley House agreement and the MacVeagh commission, focusing on the weeks and months *after* the frauds supposedly occurred. Hiscock, Reed, and Cox objected; Potter overruled them. In attacking Hayes, Butler was doing the Democrats' work for them. He was also gratifying anti-Hayes Republicans, who, openly or tacitly, applauded his terrier-like digging. "This investigation will run all summer," Butler promised. "You have only got the shadow of the substance."[1]

The *New York Tribune*, whose editor, Whitelaw Reid, regarded Congressional Reconstruction as an abject failure and bid it good riddance, belittled Butler's quest to prove "some kind of bargain" between Hayes and certain southern Democrats. "All the facts are known that are ever likely to be known regarding the whole presidential business," it claimed, "from Oregon to Louisiana, and from Wormley's Hotel to the Columbia State House."[2]

That was true—to an extent. Shortly after Hayes took office, E. A. Burke told the *New Orleans Times* that Democrats had received "written pledges" that Hayes would allow the Packard government to fall, this being the condition for which the "opposition to the declaration of the election of Hayes . . . in the style of filibustering was withdrawn." Further details emerged at the end of March. Fretting over the president's failure to withdraw military protection from Packard and his legislature, Representatives Ellis, Gibson, and Levy met Hayes to complain of his inaction. The president told them that he had decided to send a commission to Louisiana to resolve the problem of the two rival governments. The congressmen swallowed their doubts and agreed to allow him more time. But their worries were not entirely allayed. "They very much fear that he will not keep his word to us," explained Josie Ellis, wife of the congressman. Their fear, she told her sister, was that Hayes would be "too weak to withstand the pressures brought to bear upon him by the Cabinet, and by the Republican party generally. . . . [I]t provokes me beyond measure when I think that his deceitful course will bring such bitter disappointment to our devoted and long tried people."[3]

With Hayes apparently dawdling, Congressman John Young Brown of Kentucky disclosed that he and Senator John B. Gordon of Georgia had sought "written assurances" from Charles Foster that Hayes would "restore home-rule in . . . Louisiana and South Carolina." After filling him in on the Wormley House discussions, Foster had given Brown two letters, one signed by himself and the second cosigned by Stanley Matthews, assuring him that Hayes would in fact do so. Without these assurances, Brown claimed, he would have rejoined the Democratic filibuster and attempted to defeat the electoral count. He voiced his unhappiness with Hayes's apparent procrastination. "I do not understand nor do I appreciate the delay. . . . He ought not to hesitate."[4]

On the day that Brown published the letters, Ellis gave the press a detailed account of the Wormley House meeting of February 26, 1877. Matthews had assured Ellis, Burke, and Watterson that Hayes opposed "the maintenance of State governments with troops" and "favored peace and home rule" in Louisiana and South Carolina. When Ellis pointed out the difficulty of recognizing Nicholls as Louisiana's governor when the same vote that elected Hayes also elected Packard, Matthews replied that the problem could be easily solved. Without troops and without any tax revenue, Packard's government would "starve to death." Hayes would be relieved of the necessity of choosing between Nicholls and Packard because the Republican legislature would have ceased to exist. Hayes could recognize Nicholls as the de facto governor without having to inquire into his legal title. All Matthews had asked in return was a promise from the Democrat that a Nicholls administration would guarantee "life, liberty, and property" to all Louisiana citizens; enforce the law impartially; and refrain from prosecuting Republicans for "political offences." According to Ellis, the other Republicans at the meeting—Foster, Sherman, Garfield, and Dennison—had all agreed with Matthews's presentation. Although not wholly accurate, Ellis's account divulged the essence of the Wormley House meeting a month after the event.[5]

The means whereby Hayes disposed of Packard were also reported in real time. During the commission's stay in New Orleans, it proved impossible to keep the negotiations confidential. Louisiana's Republican leaders, in an increasingly desperate effort to sway public opinion, talked freely to the press, describing their dealings with the commissioners and the deliberations of their legislative caucus. On April 30 the *New York Sun* published a blow-by-blow account, written by A. M. Gibson, of how the commission compelled Packard to resign by undermining the Republican legislature. The article disclosed that Republicans who defected to the Nicholls legislature each received pay and mileage to the amount of $1,500 ($37,000 in 2020 dollars), while some also obtained "large bonuses" from a fund raised from New Orleans businessmen. Gibson singled out Wayne MacVeagh as the commissioner who acted with the most decision, the one "determined to get the job through."[6]

Butler may well have been influenced by Gibson's article when, a few weeks later, he attacked MacVeagh in print. Replying to a letter from J. R. G. Pitkin, who complained that Hayes had removed him as US marshal without cause, he wrote that it was an "open secret" that Pitkin's successor, Jack Wharton, had assisted MacVeagh in breaking up the Packard legislature. Moreover, Butler went on, the Republicans who went over to the Nicholls legislature had been bribed to do so. While he professed a willingness to give Hayes's southern policy a fair trial, Butler had no doubt that in removing Packard, the president was "fulfilling all the bargains which his subordinates made." Pitkin gave the letter to the *New York Times,* which promptly published it.[7]

MacVeagh responded furiously. He denied any involvement in bribery—"I had no money of my own to spare"—and launched an ad hominem attack on Butler. While military governor of occupied New Orleans, he claimed, the general had appropriated a "considerable quantity of the property of others for his own use." By engaging in theft, Butler "had become the leper of our politics."[8]

MacVeagh's insistence that he had never resorted to bribery was easily disposed of. He had never claimed that Hayes's commissioners used *their own* money for bribes, Butler explained. When it came to personal insults, moreover, MacVeagh was no match for the Massachusetts congressman. Butler's riposte illustrated why he had such a fearsome reputation as a political brawler. "Let me advise you not to lose your temper in discussing political matters," lectured the general. "If you do you will prove yourself unfit to be employed to manage diplomatic affairs even near the smallest court in Europe, say of Monaco, where they have a standing army of sixty-three men only, so that you need not be afraid to go there because of any danger of war." The imputation of cowardice stemmed from MacVeagh's Civil War record. "Although you were young and able-bodied," Butler explained, "I fail to recall the number of the regiment in which you served."

Not content with delivering one kick when he could administer two, Butler then added a tasteless reference to MacVeagh's marriage to a daughter of Simon Cameron, the Republican boss of Pennsylvania. He would rather be guilty of appropriating money as a military commander, wrote the congressman, than acquire wealth by "marry[ing] into a family where I was neither wanted nor . . . respected." He promised to renew the controversy when a committee of Congress, "of which it may be my ill-fortune to be a member," launched a thorough investigation.[9]

The Republicans who took part in the Wormley House meeting maintained a nervous silence, conscious of the fact that their role in counting in Hayes and betraying Packard would not bear close scrutiny. Foster, who with Matthews had taken the lead in the matter, was the exception, issuing the first of many denials that he and the other Ohioans had bargained for the presidency. "There was no written agreement entered into," he explained. "There being no compact, it is simply impossible that Hayes should approve or disapprove of it." He and Matthews had not negotiated on behalf of the candidate and did not therefore commit him. Their assurance that the troops would be withdrawn "was simply in the nature of a belief that such would be the result of the policy which we believed the President would adopt." The *Chicago Daily Tribune* came to Foster's support, claiming that Hayes had been entirely ignorant of his and Matthews's dealings, which in any case partook "nothing in the nature of a compact or agreement." When the *New York Sun* clamored for a congressional investigation, Matthews broke his silence by insisting, "I never made any bargain with anybody about anything, at any time connected with Louisiana affairs."[10]

That did not, of course, close the matter. Over the following months, as the new president's southern policy unfolded, skeptical Republicans gave Hayes the benefit of the doubt or simply smoldered in silence. But when William Chandler published his anti-Hayes letters in December, Republican opposition boiled over. One displaced office holder fed the New Englander information about the operations of the MacVeagh commission. Another wrote Chandler that the Democrats who negotiated at Wormley

House would never have been satisfied with mere promises: they must have demanded a written assurance from Hayes "that Sherman et al. were fully accredited to treat in his behalf." This document, he believed, was in the possession of Burke, who held it as a guarantee that Hayes would fulfil his part of the bargain. Thus primed, Chandler challenged Burke to produce his written record of the Wormley House conference: "Were you present, was a memorandum made, and will you make it public?"[11]

Chandler's fresh attack on the Wormley House bargain elicited more claims of innocence from the participants. "Everything in that presidential business that I ever signed has been made public," declared Matthews. "Mr. Burke has no contract of mine." Burke, after sending Chandler a series of insulting telegrams, denied trading the presidency for Democratic control of Louisiana; he "never had an agreement signed by Stanley Matthews, Charles Foster, or anybody else." In a raucous debate in the House on February 13, 1877, Garfield, Ellis, and Foster denied that they had entered into any bargain at Wormley House or that Hayes had given any pledges. Foster explained that he had been guided by the patriotic motive of ending the electoral crisis and avoiding "internal strife and ruin." To this end he made a short speech to Congress on February 20, reiterating Hayes's intention of pursuing a conciliatory policy toward the South—that henceforth "the flag shall float over States, not provinces." Three days later Hayes sent him a brief letter, "stating that my views on the withdrawal of troops were in accordance with his own." The congressman gave the letter to A. C. Buell, editor of the *New Orleans Times,* who passed it on to Burke, who circulated it among leading southern Democrats. Foster's speech and Hayes's letter paved the way for the understanding reached at Wormley House. But Hayes "authorized no bargain, nor was any bargain made."[12]

Buell was happy to confirm Foster's account. Hayes's letter, the Ohio congressman had told him, showed that he, Foster, could speak on behalf of the presumptive president "so far as the Southern situation is concerned." It provided a "basis for a compromise between the honest Democrats of the South and the wise Republicans of the North." The meetings (plural) at Wormley House hammered out "the scope and purpose of the assurances made verbally" by Foster and Matthews. But "there was no bargain," Buell insisted. The southerners accepted the word of the two Ohioans "as a guarantee for the good faith of Hayes, without collateral security of any kind."[13]

Interviewed by a reporter for the *Washington Post,* who tracked him down at a church social, Chandler scoffed at these denials. Of course no one admitted to a bargain: "You couldn't expect the people working for Hayes to come right out and sign a contract which might sometime turn up against them. . . . They worked it smarter than that." But the circumstantial evidence pointed in one direction, and all the "dodging and equivocation" could not hide the fact that the two sides had entered into a contract. Foster's statement in the House that he gave no commitments regarding Hayes's future policy was patently false: writing to Brown a year earlier, he and Matthews had expressed their "complete confidence" as to what that policy would be, feeling themselves "authorized" to pledge Hayes's word.[14]

He first bared his teeth while grilling Thomas H. C. Smith, the appointments secretary at the Treasury Department. Butler wanted to know about James Anderson's quest for a well-paying job, his questions insinuating that the Hayes administration, with Matthews's connivance, had endeavored to keep Anderson quiet. Why had Smith failed to produce Matthews's letter of recommendation? Why had he never consulted Sherman about giving Anderson a place in the Treasury Department? Why had he continued trying to placate the ex-supervisor after the latter rejected the offer of a clerkship and Matthews had advised dropping him? What did Smith discuss with Matthews when the two men met in Cincinnati? Why, when Anderson withdrew his application, did Smith offer a position to Anderson's brother? Butler questioned Smith for hours, with both men growing increasingly ill tempered. Cox protested that Butler was bullying the witness, and "considerable temper was manifested by both gentlemen." But the examination generated more heat than light.[15]

Next in line for the Butler treatment was Henry Boynton of the *Cincinnati Gazette*. A Union veteran and former general, Boynton was a well-connected Washington correspondent and, to quote historian C. Vann Woodward, a "reformer, muckraker, and exposer of scandal." Famously combative and not devoid of self-importance, he was a useful ally and a dangerous foe. He had been deeply involved in behind-the-scenes efforts to resolve the electoral crisis in Hayes's favor and subsequently became one of the Washington reporters whom the president thought wise to cultivate.[16]

As a journalist, Boynton had eagerly anticipated the committee hearings. Testifying as a witness, however, something he had not anticipated, turned out to be a distinctly unpleasant experience. Butler knew that

Boynton had discussed Anderson with Hayes a year earlier. Quizzed on the conversation, the reporter recalled that the president, when asked why he had offered a job to a man of such dubious reputation, explained that Anderson "had risked a great deal" and was being rewarded for his services to the Republican Party. Boynton denied that Hayes had intimated that he wished to keep the ex-supervisor quiet. But under relentless questioning, he admitted having formed the impression that "Anderson's appointment had something to do with his performance in Louisiana—his manipulation of votes."[17]

Butler then asked Boynton to recount a conversation he had with John Harlan before the latter left for New Orleans in April 1877. The intent of the question was clear: he wished to demonstrate that Harlan's appointment to the Supreme Court was a reward for his political services in helping the MacVeagh commission destroy Packard's government. Boynton was acutely uncomfortable revealing the details of what he and Harlan had said to each other—the two men were political friends. Butler, however, was a pitiless inquisitor. "When constructing an argumentative question, full of his own inferences and sarcasms, he launched it out with a roar and looked at the crowd with a cunning leer, and, of course, he sometimes chuckles." Boynton, notwithstanding his long experience of national politics, turned out to possess a thin skin, or, put another way, lacked a hide of sufficient thickness. "General Butler is a rowdy," he complained, "and if the committee will not protect me I will protect myself." Butler nevertheless got what he wanted: Harlan had told the reporter that his chances of getting the judicial appointment he craved would be improved if he served on the MacVeagh commission.[18]

If Boynton could dish it out but had trouble taking it, he could count himself lucky that Butler failed to press him on his activities in Hayes's interest during the electoral crisis. The inquisitor never asked him about his role in promoting the Texas and Pacific Railway subsidy scheme. Boynton's inside knowledge, writes historian Mark Summers, "would have made a scoop devastating to the administration."[19]

These June performances were merely a warmup for the main act in August, when the Potter Committee convened in New York. In a "stiflingly close" room in the Custom House, Butler interrogated William H. Roberts, associate editor of the *New Orleans Times,* on his role as an intermediary between southern Democrats and the Hayes camp. Again, Butler's intentions were plain: he wished to prove that Hayes had plotted to destroy the Packard government in return for Democratic support during the electoral crisis. Hiscock objected to Butler's line of inquiry: How could conversations between Hayes and Roberts in December 1876 have influenced Louisiana's Returning Board? The general brushed him aside. "Nicholls and Hayes are Governor and President, and Packard is Consul to Liverpool, and Tilden is a private citizen of New York," he noted. "It is common for people to wonder when lightning strikes twice in the same place, and it was also remarkable that a similar result to this took place in Florida."[20]

A Paris-educated former Confederate colonel, Roberts proved eager to describe the behind-the-scenes maneuvering that resulted in the elimination of Louisiana's Republican government, in so doing highlighting his own role as a political fixer and go-between. Even before the Returning Board declared the result, he revealed, Louisiana Democrats anticipated its decision and began to weigh their options in the event of a Hayes presidency. Tasked by the Nicholls campaign to sound out his views on the South, Roberts journeyed to Ohio to talk with the Republican candidate. Discussing his mission with Hayes confidante Murat Halstead, editor of the *Cincinnati Commercial,* Roberts explained that they were less interested in putting Tilden in the White House than in getting Nicholls into the statehouse. "We have got to see that whatever horse loses, our horse wins," he told Halstead. He then switched to a nautical metaphor. If the Tilden ship started sinking, "we would save some of the cargo, even if we had to throw the rest overboard."[21]

Meeting Hayes on December 1, 1876, Roberts could not have been more direct: the Returning Board would declare Louisiana for Hayes, the latter would become president after a prolonged "row," and Democrats would not "make trouble" as long as they gained control of the state government. Hayes replied in friendly generalities. He assured Roberts that he was favorably disposed to the South and, if elected, would adopt a policy of "fairness and justice." Although vague about what such a policy would look like, he gave a heavy hint. "I have always believed that the intelligence of any country or any State ought to govern it," he told the editor. Roberts understood "intelligence" as a synonym for "whites." But Hayes made no commitment to abandoning Packard should the Republican gubernatorial candidate win. With Louisiana undecided and the presidency very much in play, it would have been political suicide for him to do so.[22]

Arriving in Washington, Roberts reported to Senators L. Q. C. Lamar of Mississippi and Gordon of Georgia. Hayes's comments about "fairness and justice" seemed to indicate that Democrats could capture Louisiana and South Carolina even if Tilden lost. But Lamar identified an obvious difficulty: how could Hayes abandon gubernatorial candidates Packard in Louisiana and Daniel H. Chamberlain in South Carolina if the votes in their states elected him president? "I cannot believe that he would do a thing which would compel him to unload the very party that has put him in."[23]

There things stood for more than two months. Despite many informal talks between some southern Democrats and some northern Republicans, party lines were strictly maintained while the presidential question remained undecided. In mid-February, however, when the Electoral Commission settled the dispute in favor of Hayes, the outlines of a cross-party agreement began to take shape. Hayes's surrogates were ready to promise that "bayonet rule" would end; Democrats representing Nicholls and Hampton were willing to smooth Hayes's inauguration and vow to treat Blacks fairly. The agreement sealed on February 26 at Wormley House did not explicitly commit Hayes to withdrawing military support for Packard and Chamberlain, but everyone interpreted it as doing so. This had every appearance of a bargain, Butler suggested. "It is the carrying out of an agreement," Roberts replied, "implied, tacit if you will, but it was carried out."[24]

Roberts had given Butler everything he wanted. And when the congressman moved on to the MacVeagh commission, the witness proved equally forthcoming. The inspiration for the commission, Roberts claimed, had been a proposal by a Louisiana Democrat, Major Thomas Bynum. Foster and Matthews, having worked might and main to convince southern Democrats of Hayes's sincerity, still wrestled with the problem of *how* to remove Packard. Bynum suggested sending a commission composed of Republican lawyers to Louisiana. That way Packard could be eased out—"let down easy"—rather than unceremoniously ejected. "By Jove!" Foster responded, "That is a good idea." On March 20, two weeks into his presidency, Hayes decided upon just such a device.[25]

Throughout his testimony, Roberts referred to the "fairness and justice of our case." It was a formula that Hayes and his surrogates—all Republicans who promised to end "bayonet rule"—frequently invoked. Butler now used it as a sarcastic refrain in "a long series of cunningly-devised questions." Roberts admitted that Nicholls had seized power by force, that it was a "revolutionary" government, and that "the forms of law were against us." He agreed that the Nicholls militia had taken possession of the state supreme court "by bayonets." Why then, Butler thundered, did "fairness and justice" require the destruction of the legally elected state government and the recognition of the revolutionary one? Was the MacVeagh commission concerned with "fairness and justice," or did it have a "predetermined purpose" to break up Packard's government? When Roberts replied that "fairness and justice" required the recognition of Nicholls, who carried Louisiana fairly and squarely, Butler pounced. Rising to his feet and pointing at the witness, he asked, "If, on the fairness and justice of the case (as fairness and justice are understood anywhere else but in Louisiana) these four able lawyers . . . came [to] the conclusion that Nicholls was elected and that Packard was not elected, they must also come to the conclusion that Hayes was not elected. Is that so?" Roberts could only agree—precisely the reply Butler sought.[26]

For lagniappe, Roberts served up a telling anecdote. When they met on December 1, 1877, he recalled, Hayes had asked him, "Why is it you have never gone into the Republican party—you Southern men—and endeavored to purify it?" That would be impossible, Roberts replied. It would be very much like a young girl visiting a brothel with the intention of reforming the prostitutes and their clients. "She not only couldn't do them any good, but she would lose whatever reputation she had." So much for Hayes's southern policy: Roberts told the president it never stood a chance. This is what Butler, Chandler, and Blaine also predicted.[27]

The climax of the New York hearings came during Butler's examination of "Major" E. A. Burke. If any individual knew all the secrets of the Wormley House agreement and the discussions that preceded it, Burke was that man. Gibson promised Chandler that his testimony would be sensational: what he had to say "is more explicit and involves more people than I ever expected we could bring in."

It might seem odd that Gibson, a fervent Tildenite, would give the staunchly Republican Chandler, an ally of Butler, a heads up about Burke's testimony. The fact that Burke and Chandler had conducted an acrimonious exchange of telegrams that ended with a barrage of insults makes it even odder. But politics makes strange bedfellows. When Gibson apprised the Republican operative that Burke's testimony would be "all that we have ever expected and much more," his use of the first person plural was significant. Gibson and Chandler had a bipartisan interest in discrediting Hayes.[28]

Burke, for his part, was happy to cast himself as Louisiana's savior, the man who redeemed the state from carpetbag rule amid the wreckage of the Tilden campaign. Although an outsider—born in Louisville, he did not move to New Orleans until four years after the Civil War—Edward Austin Burk had risen from obscurity to the pinnacle of Louisiana politics through brains and hard work. In 1869 he worked as a stonecutter, toiling alongside Black laborers. By 1872 he served as head of the Freight Department of the New Orleans, Jackson, and Great Northern Railroad Company and chaired the city's Democratic campaign committee. His political progress mirrored that of many aspiring Democratic leaders. Like Boss Tweed in New York, he joined a volunteer fire company and thereby gained influence among the white, predominantly immigrant, voters of his city. In 1874 those voters elected Burk administrator of improvements, a position that paid $6,000 a year and gave him control of an 185-man workforce, a rich source of political patronage. Marriage to a wealthy heiress, a planter's daughter, eased his social acceptance by the notoriously snobbish white upper class of New Orleans. He also burnished his Confederate credentials. As a nineteen-year-old in Texas in 1861, he had joined a cavalry regiment and attained the rank of second lieutenant. Adding an "e" to his surname when he moved from Galveston to New Orleans, newspapers always styled him "Major Burke." Louisiana's Republican leaders recognized Burke as able, resourceful, and aggressive—a formidable political opponent. Pitkin reckoned him the "best brain our local Democrats have."[29]

Burke had already testified before the Louisiana subcommittee, along with Congressman Ellis. The most revealing part of their testimony, buttressed by a trove of telegrams and other documents, concerned Grant. The two men recounted numerous meetings with the president in their quest to dissuade him from recognizing Packard as governor. They had not expected him to recognize Nicholls's insurgent government—a political impossibility in light of Louisiana's disputed electoral votes—but they did ask him to refrain from recognizing Packard's government. Initially, Ellis recalled, they found the president "very silent, very non-committal, very non-communicative." He would do nothing to damage Hayes's case, and he would not tolerate any violence on the part of Louisiana Democrats. Over the course of several weeks, however, Grant's distaste for Packard and sympathy for Nicholls became apparent. Ellis described it as a gradual process of "thawing out . . . the grim silent man." Grant's adopted policy, one of refusing to recognize either government and of preserving the "status quo" in Louisiana, greatly favored Nicholls, who did not need federal intervention to support his government—he had his own militia and police force—whereas Packard depended upon a regiment of soldiers to keep his government in being. Nicholls grew while Packard withered. In fact, Grant turned a blind eye to the gradual extension of the Democrat's power. To a degree that Republicans, especially, had never before appreciated, Grant had laid the groundwork for Hayes's abandonment of Packard.[30]

Burke and Ellis held nothing back when they described the negotiations that led to the Wormley House agreement. The talks began in earnest after the Electoral Commission, on February 16, awarded Louisiana's votes to Hayes and the Democratic caucus in the House, a day later, decided that the electoral count should proceed. Burke feared that the Democratic Party, in accepting Tilden's defeat, was also conceding Louisiana and South Carolina to the Republicans. He therefore encouraged a filibuster in the House of Representatives to delay the count. The purpose of the movement was less to keep Hayes out of the White House than to obtain a guarantee that the incoming administration would withdraw the troops propping up Packard and Chamberlain. The filibuster alarmed Hayes's Ohio allies, one of whom, Matthews, met Burke with a view to ending it. Burke told him that any attempt to sustain Packard would plunge Louisiana into "anarchy and strife." He sought a cast-iron assurance that Hayes would make no such attempt, that the president would, in fact, withdraw the troops guarding the statehouse, a step that would cause Packard's government to fall. Only then would Burke advise the filibuster to stop.

Three questions needed to be resolved before agreement could be reached. Matthews and Foster assured Burke that Hayes had every intention of withdrawing military support for Packard. Foster stated as much in the House on February 20 and could show a letter from Hayes endorsing his speech. But Burke and the other Louisianans worried that Hayes would be unable to deliver in the face of resistance from his own party. They sought, therefore, to bind "the Shermans, the Garfields, the Mortons, and the men of that class" to any agreement. Hence the inclusion of Sherman and Garfield in the Wormley House meeting of February 26 and the Republicans' assurance that Morton, although not present, would support the Hayes policy. The Democrats' preference was for Grant to withdraw the troops upon the completion of the electoral count, thus handing Hayes a fait accompli and sparing him an intraparty fight. This, however, they failed to secure.

The Republicans required their own assurances. Could they trust Louisiana's Democrats, once in complete control of the state government, to refrain from wreaking vengeance upon Blacks and Republicans? Would a Nicholls administration strip Black men of their right to vote or deny Black children the right to attend public schools? To allay these concerns, Burke secured a written commitment from Nicholls that there would be no violence, no bloodshed, no persecution of Republicans, and no infringement of Blacks' constitutional rights.

The Republicans also wished to avoid handing Louisiana's two Senate seats to the Democratic Party. One stood vacant, the Senate having refused to confirm Pinchback, a Black Republican. The loss of the second seat, currently occupied by J. R. West, a white Republican whose term expired in 1876, was a distasteful prospect. The Packard legislature had already elected Kellogg in place of West, but if Hayes recognized the Nicholls legislature, Senate Democrats would surely oppose seating him. Sherman wished especially to avoid a situation whereby the Nicholls legislature elected two Democrats, both of whom might present their credentials at the start of the new Congress. This eventuality, he feared, would arouse such a controversy in the Senate as to delay the confirmation of Hayes's cabinet, including Sherman's own nomination as secretary of the Treasury. To accommodate Sherman, the Democrats secured Nicholls's agreement to postpone the election of the "long term" senator until after March 10. By that date, the Republicans assumed, the Senate would have formally admitted Kellogg.[31]

Summoning Burke to testify again, this time in New York, might have appeared superfluous. But his testimony in New Orleans had been abruptly terminated on account of the yellow-fever epidemic. In New Orleans, moreover, he had been examined by two friendly Democrats, Stenger and Blackburn, and a Republican, Cox, who was friendly to Hayes. In short, he had not been subjected to a rigorous cross-examination. Butler intended to remedy that deficiency.

He questioned Burke for the better part of three days. A "slight built, nervous man, with clear blue eyes, dark hair, and a thick bushy mustache," the witness was, as his Republican foes acknowledged, an able political operator. His testimony was remarkably frank. It demolished James Anderson's credibility by revealing that the supervisor had sought $5,000 from the Democratic Party, money the Democrats would have forked out gladly had they possessed it at the time. Burke also disclosed that he observed Anderson in Moreau's restaurant while Sherman was dining there but did not see the two men speak. The presence of the Republican visiting statesmen, he thought, made all the difference to the outcome in Louisiana. Local Republicans had been despondent when the returns came in. After Sherman and Garfield arrived, however, "they never seemed to falter at any impediment."[32]

Butler's interest, however, lay elsewhere. He wished to expose the perfidy of Hayes and his surrogates in selling out the Packard government. He wanted to know the precise details of the Wormley House conference. He sought, above all, written evidence of the "bargain" whereby, as he interpreted that meeting, Burke and the Louisianans traded the presidency for Democratic control of their state. Pressed as to whether his end of the bargain involved ending the filibuster against the counting in of Hayes, Burke prevaricated. He bristled at the word "bargain" and insisted that he had not controlled the House Democrats. Under Butler's relentless questioning, however, he admitted that, having been convinced of Hayes's intention to end Packard's military protection, the Louisianans had urged an end to the filibuster. As William Levy told the House on March 1, they had received "solemn, earnest, and . . . truthful assurances from prominent members of the Republican party, high in the confidence of Mr. Hayes," that the troops would be withdrawn.[33]

Burke strenuously denied that he had in any sense betrayed Tilden. "We never swapped off Tilden. . . . We never withdrew our opposition to Mr. Hayes until after the Democratic party had abandoned Mr. Tilden." This much was true. The verdict of the Electoral Commission decided the election, and congressional Democrats agreed to accept that outcome. Burke then offered an explanation of his tactics that cast a new light on the Wormley House agreement. The House filibuster could never have prevented the timely inauguration of Hayes, he confessed. Few Democrats had the stomach for defeating the count and risking the public censure that would surely follow. "When the closing days came," Burke recalled, "many of them became restive." Agreement or no agreement, the filibuster could not have been sustained much longer: nobody wished to "plunge the country into commotion." It was a testament to Burke's skill at political poker that he extracted a firm commitment from Hayes on the basis of an empty threat. "It was a bluff game," he admitted.[34]

Butler was less successful in his quest for a "smoking gun"—a document that set down all the details of the bargain. In the early days of the Hayes administration, Burke had referred to "written pledges" from the Republican negotiators. Now, however, he insisted that all the relevant documents had already been published and that there were no more to reveal. As for the conference at Wormley House, "There was nothing committed to writing in that room." Butler refused to accept this answer. How could the Democrats have held Hayes to his promises without a written agreement? Burke kept repeating the same explanation: all that they had in writing was Hayes's letter to Foster, approving the latter's speech of February 20, and the letters of Foster and Matthews to Brown and Gordon. Butler, incredulous, asked why these worldly wise politicians would end the filibuster, at the same time pledging the good behavior of Louisiana Democrats, on the basis of verbal assurances alone. "I had the word of the President of the United States," Burke responded, "and the assurances of—." Butler cut him off. "Don't play with me. I ask about papers; you didn't take words home with you to show. You can't crawl out of that loophole. I want to know what you got from the other side."[35]

After two hours of back and forth, the same question repeated in endless variations by Butler and the same denials provided by Burke, Hiscock intervened. The examination had exhausted its usefulness, he objected; it was not the committee's purpose to test the truthfulness of the witness.

BUTLER: Pardon me, I am on this very question for the purpose of testing the truthfulness of the witness.

HISCOCK: Oh, you are not questioning that.

BUTLER: Yes! I am testing that.

HISCOCK: Questioning, I said.

BUTLER [rising to his feet and striking the table with a fist]: I do question his truthfulness, and am determined to test it.

A shocked silence descended upon the room. Burke, the blood draining from his face, stood up and faced Butler: "In what particular, sir?" Butler retorted, "I will show you that before I get through." The two men glared at each other for what seemed like minutes. A trembling Burke finally broke the silence. "Then I will answer no more questions from the General until that remark is withdrawn." The room erupted in foot-stamping applause. Potter tried to proceed with the examination, but Burke complained that he had not traveled 1,400 miles to be insulted. He again asked that Butler retract his comment. "That is a matter in which I will not protect you," Potter responded to the witness. "Then I'll protect myself," Burke shot back.[36]

Hiscock, the only member of the committee to come to Burke's defense, complained about "this eternal round of questions which travelled continuously over the same ground without reaching any point." Again Potter sided with Butler, pointing out that "a large latitude is allowed in these examinations." The general had been testing Burke's recollection, he added, not his veracity. Stenger tried to mollify Burke: he did not suppose that Butler believed the witness was being untruthful; his remark was in any case directed toward Hiscock, not Burke. The Pennsylvanian urged the witness to continue. Burke, however, was obdurate, and Butler refused to back down. "I could not conceive that fine gentlemen would make a written guarantee on their side, and carry it out, and not require something on the other side," explained the general; he *had* questioned Burke's truthfulness, "whether that come from defective memory or not." Butler therefore had nothing to withdraw. Burke, grimly silent, sipping water and smoking a cigar, had heard enough. He stalked out of the room.

Ten minutes later Burke returned. Butler, having conferred with Potter, consented to the entirety of his exchange with Hiscock being stricken from the record. His honor vindicated, the witness agreed to continue. Butler's quest for a written bargain, however, drew a blank. As the *New York Tribune* put it, he had "spent the entire day . . . in pumping a dry well."[37]

Butler was on firmer ground when he moved on to the MacVeagh commission. The details of how Hayes's hatchet men, four Republicans and a Democrat, chopped down the Packard government were already known. He was less interested in unearthing fresh information about that transaction than in underlining its sordid nature. The congressman wished to show that the demise of Louisiana's last Republican administration resulted from the treachery of Hayes and his henchmen, the hypocrisy of Louisiana's Democratic leaders, and the demoralizing influence of money. In constructing this narrative, Burke served as his foil and punching bag.

The general opened by pressing Burke on the legality of the Nicholls government: had it not seized power by force, without sanction of law? In reply, Burke denied the legality of the Packard government, which, he argued, had been installed by the illegal Returning Board. This was the answer Butler had expected, and it handily invited his follow-up question. If the Returning Board was indeed illegal, why were the Democrats so determined that their legislature should have a quorum of members who were confirmed by the Returning Board, many of whom, according to Burke, "had been returned by fraud and perjury and forgery?" How was it that "more than half of the Returning Board members at least, by the grace of God, the President, and the MacVeagh commission, [got] into the Nicholls legislature?" After much equivocation, Burke gave Butler the answer he sought. Yes, he conceded, "I am willing to admit that we were anxious to obtain a Returning-Board quorum."[38]

Butler's main targets, however, were not the Democrats who invited "fraudulently-elected" Republicans to join their legislature, but the Republicans who endorsed the red-handed Democrats of that legislature. Garfield and Sherman, he reminded Burke, had solemnly declared to the US Senate that the Democratic Party had carried Louisiana by means of violence and intimidation. Yet they assented to the Wormley House agreement. Butler then put it to him that Garfield and Sherman had either made false claims about Democratic bulldozing or "were willing to set up a government founded on bloodshed, terrorism, and murder." This was, of course, more of a speech to the audience than a question to the witness, and the latter took it as such. It was not his job, Burke responded dryly, to explain the contradiction between what these Republicans said and what they did.[39]

In all their denials of a "bargain," the Republicans who were party to the Wormley House agreement constantly reiterated one point: they had not represented Hayes, negotiated on his behalf, or consulted him in any way. All they claimed was a familiarity with their candidate's views on the southern question. It was a nice distinction, and Butler did not believe it for a minute. With his next witness, W. E. Horne, the Massachusetts congressman attempted to erase it, but in a most unusual way.

Horne was a lawyer from Texas, a Republican, and a confidante of Thomas L. Young, lieutenant governor of Ohio during the electoral crisis. Early in 1877 he resigned his position in the Treasury Department to serve as Young's eyes and ears in Washington. "Every event of importance that occurred during the day," he told Butler, "passed over the wires . . . to Governor Young." Horne did more, however, than report to Young—he also acted as a "medium of communication" between Young and Burke, a longtime acquaintance of his. Butler's supposition was that Hayes, even if not directly involved in the Washington negotiations, was kept abreast of the proceedings by the Texan, with the lieutenant governor acting as a "cutout." A telegram from Young to Horne dated February 22, 1877, appeared to support this supposition. "From the first you have understood and appreciated every political move," Young wired, "and I have taken occasion to submit your . . . telegrams to Governor Hayes." Yet when questioned about his activities, including his meetings with Hayes, Horne refused to answer, invoking his professional position as a lawyer.[40]

Horne's appearance and nonperformance provoked the worst display of temper between two committee members thus far. Hiscock accused Butler of producing the Texan in the full knowledge that he would refuse to testify; the whole performance, he alleged, had been prearranged between them. "Were you not in Mr. Butler's room last night?" the New Yorker asked Horne. As Potter rapped for order, Butler and Hiscock exchanged insults.

> BUTLER: That comes from the counsel for Hayes.
>
> HISCOCK: My motives are as pure as those of a gentleman who abandoned his own party because he is disappointed that the administration has turned his friends out of office.
>
> BUTLER: That is beneath you, and beneath me to reply.
>
> HISCOCK: That is not beneath me, and it is the motive that actuates you.
>
> BUTLER: You have lost your case, and now you lose your temper.

"Gentlemen," Potter implored, "please stop this thing. I won't have any more of it." After the kerfuffle ended, Butler asked Horne if he had recently met with Hayes. When Horne replied in the affirmative, the congressman "looked around the room with an air of triumph." But Horne had also, it transpired, met with Butler and Chandler the previous evening, lending credence to Hiscock's charge.[41]

Butler failed to prove that Hayes dictated the moves of Matthews and Foster on his behalf. He did, however, cast doubt upon the notion that the president-in-waiting was ignorant of what was being done in Washington in his name. Young had shared Horne's dispatches with Hayes. Indeed, why would Horne send Young such a flow of information unless he intended to enlighten Hayes? When it came to the Wormley House agreement itself, Butler's persistent digging unearthed a mass of hitherto unknown details. But he did not uncover the signed-and-sealed "bargain" for which he was searching. Such a document probably never existed.

This gave the Wormley House participants, and the pro-Hayes press, another opportunity for protestations of innocence and expressions of indignation. "There was not the semblance of a bargain at that conference," Ellis reiterated. Watterson pointed out that he and his fellow Democrats had been in no position to trade the White House. The decision of the Electoral Commission meant that "the coming in of Hayes was already assured." Louisiana and South Carolina "naturally and properly" sought the removal of the troops, but "there was no agreement whatever, verbal or in writing." The meeting was less a negotiation than a "pow-wow between persons who . . . were agreed on the new phase of the situation." According to the *New York Tribune*, the Republicans at Wormley House were simply confirming Hayes's intention of implementing the southern policy he had announced in his letter accepting the presidential nomination. The Democrats had acted as "patriotic Southerners" seeking to "avert civil war." There was no corrupt bargain, only an "honorable understanding."[42]

Historians, too, have downplayed the significance of the Wormley House agreement. They point out that the thesis of Butler and Chandler—that southern Democrats traded the presidency for Democratic control of Louisiana and South Carolina—is untenable because the Democrats had nothing to trade. Having placed their hopes in the Electoral Commission, a device largely of their own making, congressional Democrats were obliged to stand by its decisions. Hewitt, Randall, and other party leaders consequently abandoned any hope that Tilden might become president; all they could do was to make Hayes sweat by counting his electoral votes with agonizing slowness. "The Republicans knew that one way or another, Hayes would become president," writes Charles W. Calhoun, adding that they did not need to make any concessions to achieve that result.[43]

In diminishing the importance of the talks at Wormley House, historians have emphasized the bigger political picture. The notion that Democrats extracted a concession from Hayes in the form of a commitment to abandon Packard and Chamberlain, they argue, overlooks the fact that Hayes already intended doing precisely that. "I do not reflect on the use of military power in the past," the Ohioan wrote Carl Schurz on February 4. "But there is to be an end to that, except in emergencies which I do not think of as possible again." And this was not merely Hayes's personal predilection. Calling upon the army to uphold unstable Republican governments in the South had become politically untenable and would have ended anyway, electoral crisis or not. Grant foreshadowed Hayes's abandonment of Packard and Chamberlain with his failure to counter Democratic bulldozing in Mississippi in 1875 and, two years later, his withholding of recognition from Packard and refusal to put down Nicholls's insurrectionary government. In ending the policy of military intervention, the argument goes, Hayes was simply adhering to Grant's fait accompli. He really had no choice in the matter.[44]

There is a third reason to question the significance of what happened at Wormley House. Hayes and his supporters believed that in cutting loose the southern carpetbaggers, they could make a virtue out of necessity. Garfield, Cox, Schurz, Matthews, and Foster all believed that the Republican Party in the South as currently constituted, based almost entirely on the support of Black voters, was no longer viable. Garfield predicted that "the liberal and generous" policy advocated by Hayes would foster a political realignment whereby the parties would divide "on the great commercial and industrial questions rather than on questions of race and color." Foster advised Hayes that the appointment of one or two southerners to his cabinet would enable him to "secure a large and respectable following in the South." Matthews even predicted (preposterously) that such appointments might hasten the "disintegration of the Democratic party." All these men were convinced that the South hosted a legion of former Whigs whom the Republican Party, shorn of its carpetbaggers and cleansed of corruption, could recruit.[45]

Republican newspaper editors made the same point in unvarnished style. "We have tried for eight years to uphold Negro rule in the South, officered by carpet-baggers," complained Joseph Medill of the *Chicago Daily Tribune,* "but without exception it has resulted in failure and almost ruin to our party." Charles Nordhoff of the *New York Herald* and Reid of the *New York Tribune* had come to the same conclusion. All three men proffered the same advice: Hayes *must* jettison the last remaining "carpet-bag" governments. Reid privately voiced what many Republicans were reluctant to state in public: if it required that state governments must "be propped up by foreign bayonets," then "Negro suffrage is itself a failure." With an infusion of native white leadership, and with Blacks playing a clearly subordinate role, the party could harvest a rich crop of white voters.[46]

In order to promote this whiter, more conservative Republican Party, Hayes's advisers in the fourth estate advocated federal support for internal improvements—the kind of policy the Whig Party had championed in the 1830s and 1840s. They advocated, specifically, the passage of a bill to grant government aid to the Texas and Pacific Railway Company, which planned to construct a southern line connecting Memphis and New Orleans to San Diego. By assisting in the South's economic development, Nordhoff believed, Republicans could "make an alliance with respectable party leaders of Whig antecedents in the South."[47]

All this pointed to the fact that the Hayes, and the men upon whom he relied for advice, had already resolved to institute a new southern policy. Summarizing the dominant view today, Carol Gelderman writes that Hayes would have entered the White House, and abandoned the Republican governments of Louisiana and South Carolina, "whether or not there had been a Wormley House meeting, agreement, bargain, compromise—by whatever name it is known."[48]

But this is not how the situation appeared to people at the time. It is always tempting to write history backward and see, in hindsight, inevitability in the unfolding of events. Before it happened, few people in either party could predict with any certainty that Hayes would abandon Packard and Chamberlain. Indeed, most found it hard to believe that he would do such a thing. It could not be inferred from his letter accepting the Republican nomination, which called for "honest and capable self-government" coupled with "a hearty and generous recognition of the rights of all by all—a recognition without reserve or exception." Nor could it be inferred from the ensuing campaign, in which Hayes recommended a "bloody shirt" message that emphasized "the dread of a solid South, rebel rule etc."[49]

The nature of the disputed election made the abandonment of Packard and Chamberlain even less likely in the eyes of most Republicans and Democrats. After hearing from Sherman, Garfield, and others upon their return from New Orleans, Hayes had no doubt that Democratic bulldozing had prevented a fair election in Louisiana and that the Returning Board was entirely correct in awarding him the state. How, then, could he permit Democratic bulldozing to elect Nicholls? Foster puzzled over this. On the day the Electoral Commission decided the Louisiana case, he wrote Hayes that he "could not see how you could throw Packard overboard." As late as February 18, Sherman did not see what was coming. "I see no way out but the recognition of the Packard government," he wrote Hayes, "followed by the utmost liberality to the South."[50]

Republicans in Louisiana confidently expected Hayes to recognize Packard because, without them, Hayes would not be president. None of the visiting statesmen led them to believe otherwise; on the contrary, some, Sherman included, vowed that the national party would stand by Packard. Democrats, naturally, expressed disbelief that Hayes would oust the Republican and recognize Nicholls—to do so would violate the most basic rule of politics. As Lamar put it, "It is not the logic of elections that the man elected by one side gives his favors, or any favors, to the other side." How could Hayes fail to recognize and reward the party loyalists who had secured his victory?[51]

There is another objection to the inevitability argument. If Hayes's inauguration was unstoppable after the decisions of the Electoral Commission, and if he was already committed to withdrawing military protection from Packard and Chamberlain, why did his surrogates negotiate with the Democrats at all? And why did the Democrats negotiate with the Ohio men and filibuster? If neither side made any real concessions—in the sense of allowing something that they had previously opposed—then the Wormley House agreement was, in Woodward's words, "one of the strangest bargains in the annals of horse-swapping."[52]

Calhoun makes the argument that it was the Republicans, confident that the filibuster was a damp squib, who extracted concessions from the Democrats: the written pledges by Nicholls and his legislature that Blacks would be recognized as equal citizens and that Republicans would not be persecuted. This explanation is unpersuasive. Republicans surely knew that such guarantees could never be enforced. Their only value, perhaps, was to assuage the consciences of Sherman and Garfield, who felt troubled by the abandonment of Louisiana's Republicans; to mollify the dying but still powerful Senator Morton; and to help Hayes deflect Republican criticism when he allowed the Packard government to collapse. Was it really in return for these worthless pledges that the Republicans made a definite promise that Hayes would end military intervention, handing Louisiana and South Carolina to the Democrats?[53]

It is worth emphasizing just how extraordinary that promise was. Unbeknown to the outside world, a group of five Ohio Republicans, with the blessing of Hayes, gave a group of Democratic politicians from Louisiana a cast-iron assurance that Hayes would allow two insurrectionary governments to stand while casting aside the legally elected Republican administrations. Few incoming presidents guarantee, even to their own supporters, that a party platform will be implemented. No incoming president, with the exception of Hayes, has promised the opposition party to carry out a policy so abhorrent to their own partisans, and so contradictory to the platform on which they campaigned, that the pledge must be given in secret. "This radical change of party policy," writes historian Leon B. Richardson, "was developed without any knowledge on the part of the Republican leaders (except the Ohio group) of what was going on." When he first learned from Matthews that Hayes intended abandoning Packard, William Chandler was incredulous. "It was the first tangible evidence I had that the dishonor and dishonesty which afterward followed was contemplated."[54]

How, then, to explain the pledge? Montgomery Blair, a former Republican who had returned to the Democratic fold, was convinced that the Potter Committee ignored entirely one of the most important elements of the electoral settlement: the proposed federal subsidy to the Texas and Pacific Railway Company. "There never was any intention [on the part of Democrats] of inaugurating Tilden," he wrote Gideon Welles, his former colleague in Lincoln's cabinet. Blair was convinced that Tom Scott and Jay Gould, the promoters of the scheme, controlled the House of Representatives from start to finish. "Hayes was to help those jobbers," he publicly charged, "and the men owned by them let him be counted in over Tilden in consideration thereof. Money had everything to do with it." But the truth would never come out, Blair complained to Boynton, because too many southern Democrats had financial interests in the proposed railroad. He even suspected that Butler "was largely interested." According to the historian Woodward, the proposed subsidy played a crucial part in cementing the Compromise of 1877.[55]

The more closely historians examine the electoral crisis, however, the more skeptical they are that the Republican promise of internal improvements influenced its resolution. The men promoting the Texas and Pacific Railway bill had hoped to secure enough Democratic votes in the House to permit the counting in of Hayes. But that strategy failed: Democrats, still hoping to elect Tilden, placed their faith in the creation of the Electoral Commission. Moreover, the proposed subsidy involved such fantastic sums—it would have committed the government to lending the Texas and Pacific Railway Company $223 million over fifty years—that it stood little chance of success. The Crédit Mobilier scandal had soured public opinion on federal aid to railroads. The *New York Times* and *Chicago Daily Tribune* denounced it. Garfield and Foster voted against it. Hayes made no commitment to it. Despite the feelers put out by a number of southern Democrats, he had no interest in treating with them. Their influence was too small to be decisive, Hayes wrote Schurz: "The present House will be ruled by Tilden's caucus." The men who negotiated at Wormley House appear never to have mentioned the Texas and Pacific bill or even internal improvements in general. Both parties were focused on the inauguration of Hayes and the fate of Packard and Chamberlain.[56]

Burke confessed to Butler that his threat to defeat the electoral count by means of the House filibuster had been a "bluff game." Yet it was a bluff that worked. The filibuster seriously alarmed Sherman, Mathews, and Foster. No doubt their nerves were strained after the tension of the previous months. Their anxiety reflected, too, a yearning for "normalcy" that permeated the leaders of both parties. A good deal of the heated rhetoric during the crisis was doubtless overblown; talk of the country sliding into civil war again was mostly hot air and hysteria. Still, many Americans worried that the continual instability caused by rival governments and inconclusive elections would lead to the "Mexicanization" of US institutions. As Gregory Downs has argued, "Congressmen were motivated not just by horse-trading but by a climate of fear."[57]

Butler failed in his quest to locate a piece of paper that spelled out the details of the Wormley House agreement. But the documents he gathered, and the testimony he elicited, went a long way toward illuminating the whole murky business. The transaction reflected little credit on either side. Butler was correct, however, to train his guns on Hayes and his coterie of Ohio Republicans. What they presented as statesmanship amounted to backroom trading. What they described as conciliation was tantamount to appeasement. Butler's relentless digging revealed that what came to be known as the Compromise of 1877 hinged on the betrayal of southern Republicans, of whom the vast majority were African Americans. It was not so much a compromise, Butler argued, as a "square and profitless sellout."[58]

Hayes rejected the notion that he had been a party to any bargain. In a technical, legal sense, he was correct. He turned away persistent requests that he designate a spokesman in Washington who could speak on his behalf. He refused to elaborate upon his previous public statements, arguing that his letter accepting the Republican nomination gave sufficient indication as to his southern policy. And Hayes declined to authorize the Ohio men to give any additional assurances on his behalf, never explicitly committing himself to removing the troops propping up Packard and Chamberlain. "I see the true position to be 'hands off,'" he explained on December 31, 1876. This above-the-fray approach enabled Hayes's first biographer, Charles R. Williams, to dismiss the "bargain theory" as "silly."

Hayes "was entirely ignorant of the whole matter"; Foster and Matthews "had not professed to speak with authority, but had merely expressed, on the basis of Mr. Hayes' character and ways of thought, their confidence in his purposes toward the South."[59]

Hayes was not, however, as ignorant and uninvolved as Williams has claimed. He was kept fully informed about developments in Washington. And if he never designated a spokesman or gave any explicit commitments, he encouraged his Ohio friends to interpret his letter of acceptance broadly. "I wish you to feel authorized to speak in pretty decided terms for me whenever it seems advisable," he wrote Sherman on December 27. Three weeks later, when the Ohio men had started negotiating with the Louisiana men, he again encouraged Sherman to convey his views. "You may say that you *know* that I will stand by the friendly and encouraging words of that letter [of acceptance] and all that they imply. You cannot express that too strongly."[60]

Thus, by winks and nods, Hayes signaled to his surrogates that he would not only decline to sustain Packard but also end the policy of military intervention. At least, that is how the Ohio men interpreted such statements. Such was the depth of their distrust, and such was the strength of partisanship, that the Louisiana men found it hard to believe that Hayes would turn his back on his own party. "*He* has promised nothing," Ellis wrote his father on February 25, 1877. "I believe his friends are lying in order to drain and disarm the Democratic party." Immediately after the Wormley House meeting, however, the congressman assured Senator Thomas Bayard that he had received "the most positive and absolute assurances that the policy of the Hayes administration would be to let Packard and Chamberlain die of inanition by refusing to support them with troops. The President is committed by *actual promise* to the policy." From the Democrats' point of view, that promise was crucial. The notion that the Ohio men would have made such a promise without Hayes's tacit approval is absurd.[61]

Garfield's diary entry for February 26 is revealing. The Ohio congressman had arrived at Wormley House that evening in ignorance of the earlier discussions between Burke, Matthews, and the others. He was therefore startled to hear Matthews speak "as if it were certain that the Nicholls government would be sustained, at least that U.S. troops would not be used." He then heard Burke read out the guarantees obtained from Nicholls regarding the maintenance of Black rights and the protection of Republicans from political persecution. Burke also agreed, on Nicholls's behalf, to support the election of at least one US senator. The tenor of this exchange led Garfield to surmise that "there had been former consultations, or that a compact of some kind was meditated." But when he voiced his opposition to "anything that would be or appear to be a political bargain," the frosty response from Matthews—who was indeed concluding a political bargain—prompted him to leave the meeting early.[62]

The *New York Times* offered perhaps the fairest verdict. It adjudged both sides guilty of "want of candor." The dealings consummated at Wormley House partook "more of intrigue than bargaining," but there had clearly been an "understanding of some sort" between "personal friends of Mr. Hayes" and "certain Southern Representatives and Senators." A charitable view of the assurances given by the Republicans would assume that "Mr. Hayes had already decided upon the withdrawal of the troops." Nevertheless, there was something undeniably shady about this behind-the-scenes affair: it "cannot add to the glory of the President and his administration."[63]

Whether Hayes would have abandoned Packard and Chamberlain regardless of the Democratic filibuster and the subsequent agreement at Wormley House is unknowable. We can say with certainty, however, that the Ohio men used the electoral crisis and Burke's threat to defeat the count to make concrete and specific what had previously been abstract and vague. If Sherman and Garfield abandoned Packard reluctantly, Matthews and Foster did so gladly. As Watterson surmised, they welcomed the opportunity to "unload their party of a dead weight which had become increasingly burdensome and was becoming dangerous." Hayes gave them a green light to tell the Democrats that he would do the unloading.[64]

In consequence of the promises made at Wormley House, Hayes had little room for maneuver when he assumed the presidency. If he had already determined to end military intervention, as seems to be the case, he had no need to make any pledges—or sanction pledges made on his behalf—to southern Democrats. He might then have enjoyed more flexibility and a stronger hand in order to obtain better terms for the southern Republicans set to be jettisoned. But his prior agreement to confine US troops to barracks boxed him in. Democrats demanded that he fulfill that commitment without delay, and within two months of his inauguration, the deed was done. In truth, Hayes showed little interest in extracting concessions. He trusted to Democratic promises of good behavior and the hope that his conciliatory policy would make Republicans of white conservatives. He "pursued his set goal of appeasing the Democrats in order to secure their political support," concluded William Gillette. "Thus he had transformed a defeat into a surrender."[65]

Hayes, of course, never accepted that his southern policy entailed any dishonor. As Rayford Logan charitably put it, he tried to balance his devotion to the Constitution and his duty to uphold the Civil War amendments with his desire to end a Reconstruction policy that had failed to pacify the South and was damaging the electoral prospects of northern Republicans. He did not so much betray Black rights, Michael Fitzgerald believes, as subscribe to an excessively optimistic view of how white southerners would act in the absence of federal pressure. That unrealistic optimism, moreover, any number of influential Republicans shared. Few of them could foresee the southern horrors that lay ahead.[66]

The Potter Committee, as was by now evident, had nothing to do with ensuring the purity of the ballot box or reversing the outcome of the 1876 election. Rather, Democrats were using it to embarrass Hayes and to strengthen Tilden's case for renomination. If the results so far fell short of Democratic expectations, they had not helped the Republican Party either. But that was about to change. The Republicans were about to make the fraud issue their own.

7

OCTOBER SURPRISE

THE *NEW YORK TRIBUNE* AND THE CIPHER DISPATCHES

As Agnes Jenks reveled in her fifteen minutes of fame and Democrats waxed indignant over Sherman's theft of the presidency, a brief article in the *New York Tribune* contained an enigmatic reference to a "package of documents" that had come into the possession of Butler. "The eyes of the country are concentrated upon that package," the paper noted—an absurd claim at the time, but one that would shortly become true.[1]

The package that mysteriously landed on Butler's desk consisted of telegrams between representatives of Tilden in New York City and Democratic agents in the disputed states of Florida and South Carolina. They had been part of a much larger cache that the Western Union Telegraph Company had sent, under subpoena, to two congressional committees in December 1876. Many of the telegrams were written in a code that baffled all efforts at decryption. Republicans were convinced that these "cipher dispatches" disguised Democratic skullduggery.

They were right. One set of telegrams that *had* been translated as early as January 1877 revealed that Democrats had tried to purchase a presidential elector in Oregon. Many of the documents, moreover, had been addressed to, or sent from, 15 Gramercy Park, the New York residence of Samuel J. Tilden. Most bore the name of William T. Pelton, Tilden's nephew, who lived at the same address. But at least one of the dispatches, sent in code by "Gabble"—Oregon governor La Fayette Grover—was addressed to Tilden himself. Smarting from the public disclosure that Madison Wells had put Louisiana's Returning Board up for sale, Republicans gleefully seized on the "Gabble" dispatches. Here, they claimed, was irrefutable evidence that the Tilden campaign had endeavored to buy the presidency.[2]

Summoned to testify before a Senate committee chaired by the ailing Oliver Morton, Pelton absolved his uncle of any involvement in the telegrams that had flown back and forth between Oregon and 15 Gramercy Park. He also denied all knowledge of money being sent to Oregon—or to any of the other disputed states—for corrupt purposes. When confronted with the deciphered telegrams, Pelton took refuge in a defective memory, repeatedly failing to recall which ones he had sent and which ones he had received. Republicans shook their heads in disbelief. "The moral position of the Democrats," judged one historian, "which up to this time had been much better than the Republicans' was at once sensibly shaken." But the Oregon story, surfacing during the most intense phase of the electoral crisis, failed to arouse the attention it merited and quickly dropped out of the news.[3]

There the trail might have ended. When they were through with them, the congressional committees returned the trunkful of telegrams to Western Union. Norvin Green, the company's vice president and a Democrat, ordered the contents of the trunk destroyed. His son consigned them to a furnace and "watched every one of them burn to ashes."[4]

Unbeknown to Western Union, however, about 750 of the nearly 30,000 telegrams escaped the flames. While lying unattended in a committee room ("like a camouflaged stick of dynamite"), the dispatches had drawn the attention of George E. Bullock, a messenger in the employ of the Senate who happened to be Morton's brother-in-law. A loyal Republican, Bullock rummaged among the numerous bundles and spirited away a selection of the ones he guessed to be (not being able to read the code) the most interesting: that is to say, most potentially damaging to their Democratic authors. In May 1878, before taking up the post of US consul in Cologne, Bullock deposited these telegrams with Congressman J. L. Evans of Indiana, a friend of his, who thereupon handed them over to Assistant Postmaster General Thomas J. Brady, another staunch Republican.[5]

William Chandler had been incensed by Western Union's incineration of the cipher telegrams, convinced as he was that they masked Democratic perfidy. When he learned that Bullock had rescued hundreds and that Brady now possessed them, he took immediate steps to get them into the public domain. "I marched into [Brady's] office," Chandler recalled, "and told him . . . to bundle up those dispatches and give them to me." Some he kept for himself: he was primarily interested in the telegrams relating to Florida, where, as one of the Republican visiting statesmen, he had helped secure that state for Hayes. The rest he advised Brady to copy and send to Congressman Hiscock.[6]

In August, Whitelaw Reid, editor of the *Tribune* and Chandler's lifelong friend, found himself the recipient of about 400 telegrams, half of them in plain English, the rest in code. They came from Chandler, Hiscock, and (anonymously) Brady. The bundle of telegrams that Butler found on his desk (more than 600 of them) came from Chandler. He gave some to the general, Chandler explained, "with a view to investigation." He gave the others to Reid, "with a view to publication."[7]

But could the encoded telegrams—the ones most potentially damaging to Democrats—be decrypted? Chandler thought not. The code seemed too complex, he told Butler, and there were too many apparently arbitrary words. Butler disagreed. The arbitrary words were actually the easiest to guess, he pointed out, and his experience in the Union army had taught him that "there never was a cipher that you could not translate." Reid, too, felt confident that, with enough telegrams to work with, the code could be cracked.[8]

Tilden and Manton Marble, former editor of the *New York World* and the governor's close confidante, appeared blithely unconcerned by the possibility of exposure. The Oregon dispatches had been written in a relatively simple dictionary cipher; once the dictionary had been identified, translating them was easy. But the Florida and South Carolina dispatches were couched in a double cipher, one that used both transposition and substitution codes. They presented a fiendish challenge to any cryptanalyst.

So confident was Marble that his secrets were safe that he wrote a full-throated defense of Tilden's conduct during the electoral crisis, which the *New York Sun* published on August 5. Accusing the Hayes forces of "purchasing" the Florida and Louisiana Returning Boards, Marble praised Tilden as a crusader against corruption who, refusing to engage in a "Dutch auction" for the presidency, had placed his "absolute trust in moral forces." Written with Tilden's approval, Republicans dubbed it the "Ark and Shechinah" letter on account of a biblical allusion that typified its bombastic style.

It was an extraordinarily vituperative document. Marble described the Republican visiting statesmen as "arch-primates of treason." He suggested that Noyes's defense of his conduct in Florida "would have given that canting hypocrite, Pecksniff himself, a moral vomit." Claiming that "traces of money payments are darkly visible to the Potter Committee," he accused Republican officials of committing "high criminal offenses." These words would come back to haunt him. In September, however,

Marble was so pleased with the progress of Potter's investigation that he believed Tilden's renomination all but assured.[9]

Other Democrats, however, feared their party was taking an enormous risk in dwelling upon Republican fraud. Charles W. Woolley of Ohio had, with Marble, been up to his neck in a scheme to purchase the Florida Returning Board; he had no confidence that the secrets of their coded telegrams would remain secret. Back in May, he warned Speaker of the House Randall that authorizing another investigation into the election would be an act of folly. "It will force many of the best men in the party to either run away from the committees, to commit perjury, or by telling the truth, to disgrace themselves." The telegrams, moreover, pointed straight to "the man at Gramercy Park"; some of them, if fired by Butler, "would go through Tilden's political guts, and leave a hole as large as a minié [ball]."[10]

The Democrat from Cincinnati knew from painful experience how congressional committees could make life very uncomfortable for a witness—especially a committee that included Ben Butler. In 1868 Butler ordered Woolley locked up in the Capitol's jail for contempt of Congress. When Woolley, brought out of confinement, again refused to answer certain questions, "Butler indignantly exclaimed, 'Back to your prison, sir!'" His advice to Randall could not have been more emphatic: "investigate—don't!"[11]

Sage advice indeed. Marble's blast in the *New York Sun* prompted Chandler to write to his old friend Reid. Convinced that Marble was up to his neck in the scheme to buy a presidential elector in Oregon, he suggested that the *Tribune* "ask him to explain some of the telegrams which are among those which General Butler laid before the Potter committee at Washington the other day." Reid thought it an excellent idea.[12]

On August 17 the *Tribune* began publishing selected telegrams from Marble to Pelton, some in plain English, others in cipher. "We threw them out in editorials," Reid told the Potter Committee, "trying to make a little fun out of them." Perhaps some wide-awake *Tribune* reader might recognize the cipher or have the brains to decrypt them. This, after all, was how the *Detroit Daily Post* had obtained translations of the "Gabble" dispatches: two businessmen saw the coded messages in that paper and identified the cipher as one that they shared with their partner, J. N. H. Patrick, who had used it when acting as a Democratic agent in Oregon. Reid engaged E. S. Holden, a professor of mathematics at the US Naval Observatory, as a cryptanalyst. He also had two of the *Tribune*'s correspondents, R. G. Hassard and William G. Grosvenor, work on deciphering the telegrams.[13]

After only about two months, on October 7, the *Tribune* announced to general astonishment that it had cracked "one of the most difficult cryptograms ever devised," setting out in great detail how it had been done by the paper's staff members, who discovered the keys before Holden did. The following day it splashed the Florida dispatches, with translations, across its front page. Next came those relating to South Carolina, again with translations.[14]

Rarely has the term "smoking gun," that overused metaphor from the Watergate scandal a century later, been so apposite. In Florida it transpired that Woolley ("Fox") and Marble ("Moses") had proposed paying a member of the Returning Board $200,000, an offer that Pelton ("Denmark") rejected as too steep. When the price came down to $50,000, Pelton wired Marble, "Proposition accepted."[15] In South Carolina Smith Weed negotiated to buy control of the Returning Board for $80,000 and, accompanied by one of the venal board members, traveled to Baltimore in order to collect the money from Pelton. As with the Oregon scheme, the fact that the Florida and South Carolina plots failed owed everything to divided counsels, garbled messages, and lack of time—it was not for want of trying. The deciphered dispatches "created a tremendous sensation," historian Paul Haworth has noted. "They were read throughout the country; everyone marveled at the ingenuity of the translators."[16]

The *Tribune* milked the scoop for all it was worth. It spaced out the revelations, timing them for maximum effect on the midterm elections. It published a forty-four-page supplement that contained the most damning telegrams. Explaining the keys to the ciphers, the paper invited readers to test for themselves the accuracy of the translations. And, of course, Reid and his writers spared no sarcasm in adding to the discomfiture of the self-righteous Democrats who were now hoisted with their own petard. "Call the defense!" cried one editorial, inviting Marble and Pelton to explain the damning dispatches and, if they had any, produce evidence of Republican wrongdoing. John Hay, Lincoln's former private secretary, congratulated the editor on his handling of the story. "The funniest of all the spectacles of the day is Marble and Tilden tied helpless to the stake while the *Tribune* dances around them, enjoying the protraction of their torture."[17]

Many of Tilden's supporters felt betrayed. W. S. Dorsheimer, who had served as Tilden's lieutenant governor, poured out his disgust to Senator Francis Kernan: "This exposure with regard to Tilden sickens me. . . . You and I both pledged ourselves for him, not only as to his success but as to his character and honor. I feel mortified and ashamed to a degree I cannot express." Tilden, he believed, "was a party to these disgraceful proceedings." Writing to Senator Bayard, an aspiring candidate for the 1880 nomination, Eugene Casserly, a former senator from California, declared that Tilden could "never be . . . named for the Presidency by any sensible man." He found it all too plausible that the governor had "confided in his ass of a nephew." Bayard himself found it difficult to believe that Tilden had no knowledge of Pelton's activities. Former DNC chairman Hewitt could accept that Tilden never read his nephew's telegrams; he could not accept that he had no inkling of what Pelton was doing.[18]

His devoted admirers anxiously awaited Tilden's reply, only to be greeted with silence. Watterson, wishing to publish a response in the *Louisville Courier-Journal*, telegraphed Tilden for advice but received none. "Being thus kept in the dark, not knowing how to proceed with safety and discretion," he complained to Tilden, "I have had to adopt the always damaging policy of suppression."[19]

The other principals eventually offered their defense in coordinated letters to the *New York Herald* published on October 16. In a typically wordy and legalistic explanation, Tilden claimed that he knew nothing about the existence of the offending telegrams until he read them in the *Tribune*. No corrupt offer, he went on, "was ever authorized or sanctioned by me." Marble, whose name was all over the cipher dispatches, had a more difficult challenge. While in Florida, he admitted, he had received "many propositions that one Republican member of the Board, or both, could . . . be bought." Yet while he had reported these offers to the DNC, he had never acted on them. "I repulsed every approach of that sort, on the spot."[20]

Tilden's denials, although impossible to disprove, evoked Republican derision. "There is no man outside an insane asylum for idiots," the *Tribune* insisted, "who believe that Mr. Tilden did not know anything of dispatches in cipher passing between his house and his confidential friend, Manton Marble." Marble's own apologia strained credulity. His assertion that he was merely keeping the DNC informed was contradicted by former chairman Hewitt, who told the *Tribune* that he saw none of the dispatches and knew nothing of Pelton's activities. It was also contradicted by the telegrams themselves, which Marble could only dismiss by charging the *Tribune* with forging some and mistranslating others.[21]

Unwisely, both Tilden and Marble kept indignantly insisting that Hayes's surrogates were the real guilty parties. They claimed that promises of employment to Republican election officials "to the tune of $150,000 per annum of taxpayers' money" were tantamount to bribes. The use of patronage to reward political supporters, however, was the standard practice of both parties; cash bribes, if not illegal, were regarded as corruption plain and simple. That the Democrats' schemes proved abortive hardly mitigated their offense. As Potter commiserated to Marble, the public lacked the wit to distinguish between "mere efforts at fraud which fail and work no wrong, and successful frauds that reverse the choice of the people."[22]

The fact that Tilden had to offer a defense of his conduct at all sullied his reputation. Whether he knew about their actions or not, agents acting in his interest had engaged in the very kind of shady wheeling and dealing for which they condemned Republicans. Even if he had been as ignorant as he claimed, moreover, what did it say about Tilden's vaunted competence if he knew absolutely nothing about what was being done on his behalf by Marble and Weed, two of his closest advisers, and Pelton, his own nephew? The *Tribune*'s scoop, Reid crowed, had "placed Tilden's whole crowd on the defensive" and, no matter what denials Tilden issued, had "made an effective end of any political future he may have had."[23]

Even Tilden's coterie of ultraloyalists acknowledged the political damage. As John Bigelow confessed in the privacy of his diary, the cipher dispatches "connect so many persons more or less near to Tilden with plans to purchase the votes of Electors as to place Tilden's re-nomination in some uncertainty." Watterson, who idolized the former governor, confessed, "for the first time I am discouraged as to the outlook for the Democratic party." His own side was distracted and divided, he complained to Tilden, whereas "the Republicans deploy like a phalanx." The Potter Committee had produced the precise opposite of the intended effect. "It is enough to make a cat howl."[24]

The *Tribune*'s revelations provided a priceless opportunity for Thomas Nast, the most talented and influential political cartoonist of the day, to improve upon his caricature of Tilden. He had already highlighted the candidate's age and decrepitude by depicting him as an ancient Egyptian sarcophagus bearing Tilden's corpse-like head. On November 2 *Harper's*

Weekly published Nast's new version, with "Fox" and "Moses" now engraved on the sarcophagus, along with dollar signs, quotations from the cipher dispatches, and the ironic words "Tilden and Reform." The image was too good to use only once: Henceforth, Nast's Tilden would always be an Egyptian mummy—a dead man who could be exhumed but never revived.[25]

The dust had barely settled from the *Tribune*'s bombshell when a second explosion blackened the face of the Potter Committee. In an interview with the *Indianapolis Herald* on October 26, James Anderson announced, "I do not now believe that John Sherman wrote the letter which I attributed to him in my evidence."[26]

Explaining how he reached that startling conclusion, Anderson spun a convoluted tale that, whatever the truth of it, had Republicans chortling. Having failed to secure from Hayes a consulship in a warm climate, he recounted, he had placed his collection of incriminating documents in the hands of attorney J. R. Sypher, a cousin by marriage, who promised to fight any attempt by the State of Louisiana to extradite him from Pennsylvania. Sypher then used Anderson's inside knowledge of the East Feliciana election to help Potter, an old college chum, to launch an investigation. Anderson insisted that he had never been hostile to Hayes and had never wished to be "a machine to throw Democratic mud." But he had been forced to appear before the committee as a witness by that "unmitigated scoundrel" Sypher, who told him, falsely, that Potter would arrange his extradition to Louisiana if he refused to testify. The lawyer, he discovered subsequently, had received $3,500 from Senator Barnum, chairman of the DNC—supposedly his fee as a consulting attorney to the committee—in exchange for arranging Anderson's testimony.

As for the Sherman letter, he had believed it authentic and, after testifying in June, tried to locate the original. He then received a visit from E. L. Weber, who claimed to have it in his possession and promised, if the Democrats paid him, to produce it before the committee. Anderson sent him to Sypher, who negotiated with A. M. Gibson the terms of Weber's appearance before the committee. "They dickered for some weeks," Anderson claimed. Weber eventually settled for $10,000, with the understanding that West Feliciana Parish would drop its prosecution over his handling of schoolboard funds. Shortly before testifying, Weber showed Anderson the purported letter. Anderson had a photographic copy made and "compared the signature with that of Sherman in Brady's photograph gallery." The comparison convinced him that the document was a forgery. Sypher evidently shared that opinion, for Weber testified that he had destroyed the original a year earlier. Astonished by this volte-face, Anderson confronted Weber about it. "We had a lively time over it," he told the *New York Herald,* "and the same night he tried to kill me."[27]

What, then, of the Sherman letter's genesis? Anderson dismissed the notion that it had been concocted by Agnes Jenks: she "is no more competent to dictate such a document as she is capable of writing Hebrew." He now believed the document "to have been gotten up by Governor Kellogg" for the purpose of blackmailing Sherman into awarding federal appointments to "certain friends of his."[28]

Typically self-dramatizing, Anderson's story mixed fact and fiction in proportions that are impossible to separate. His attribution of the Sherman letter to Kellogg, however, was plainly absurd; "It is the talk of a man in his cups," commented the senator. Sypher, of course, denied that he had employed underhanded or corrupt means to secure Anderson's testimony—his client had been eager to assist the Potter inquiry. "He felt he had been injured by the visiting statesmen . . . and he was determined to pay them back." Weber had never promised to produce the Sherman letter, he added; Anderson's account of having seen it, copied it, and identified it as a forgery was a "cold, barefaced lie." Weber himself, of course, rebutted Anderson's account: "I think he was bought."[29]

For Republicans, it was hardly worth trying to disentangle truth from falsehood in the dueling narratives of Anderson and Weber. All they needed to do was sit back and enjoy the spectacle. The *National Republican*'s headline spoke for itself: "The Old Adage: 'When Rogues Fall Out.'" The *Chicago Daily Tribune* branded Anderson a "mendacious and irresponsible adventurer." Henceforth, it crowed, "the American people will . . . enjoy immunity from the Democratic cry of 'Fraud.'" Democratic newspapers denounced the Potter Committee's star witness. The *New York Herald* reminded readers that it early on warned that Anderson was a scoundrel and "that his testimony must be worthless." The *Washington Post,* the committee's most fervent supporter, complained that "avaricious Anderson" had "gone over to the enemy . . . and sold out to John Sherman."[30]

Splashing his story over its front page, the *New York Tribune* attributed Anderson's apostasy to money—not a subtle explanation, but plausible nonetheless. After he testified in June, Anderson's employer, the *Philadelphia North American,* sacked him. As long as the Potter Committee remained in session, he received a daily witness fee of three dollars, but in August, when the committee suspended its hearings, that source of income ceased. Anderson badgered his Democratic handlers to secure alternative employment, and Gibson found him a position as a proofreader on the *Washington Post* at a salary of fifteen dollars a week. But as Matthews had discovered to his cost, Anderson was an awkward customer: he regarded the pay as derisory and the work beneath his dignity. Gibson and Maddox then proposed sending him to Louisiana to hunt up witnesses for the Potter Committee, paying him ten dollars a day—anything to keep him quiet. But Anderson pressed Gibson to find him a correspondent's position on a Democratic newspaper and threatened to go over to the enemy unless he got his way. Through third parties, he approached Sherman's attorney, Samuel Shellabarger, and offered to provide an affidavit that would deny the authenticity of the Sherman letter. Shellabarger rejected the overture, but Anderson, perhaps hoping to improve his fortunes by getting back into the good graces of the Republican Party, published the affidavit anyway.[31]

Democrats also risked losing their second main witness. E. L. Weber felt badly treated. In negotiating the terms under which he would testify, Weber believed that Potter had agreed that he would appear before the subcommittee in New Orleans. But after that panel departed, he received a subpoena to testify in Washington, where he endured a savage cross-examination for which he felt utterly unprepared. He also fretted over the failure of Gibson and Maddox, his Democratic handlers, to intercede with the schoolboard of West Feliciana Parish as they had promised. By October Weber's patience was wearing thin. As long as the case dragged on, he could do nothing with his property in Saint Francisville, which included a house, a store, a printing press, and thousands of acres of land.[32]

Parish authorities had been pursuing Weber for a year. In October 1877 they indicted him for failing to account for $16,000 when he turned over his records as the outgoing treasurer of the schoolboard. In the absence of receipts to explain where the money might have gone, the board simply assumed that Weber had embezzled it. The *West Feliciana Sentinel* denied that the board was engaged in a political vendetta, but then negated the denial by describing Weber as one of "the most unconscionable thieves that were [*sic*] ever saddled upon any community." Certainly, the board adopted a hard line. When Weber supplied vouchers to account for the expenditure, members went through them with a fine-tooth comb and found fault with every uncrossed "t" and undotted "i." In November 1877

Weber suggested that a committee of arbitration examine the books and establish what, if anything, he owed. Robert M. Lusher, the Democratic state superintendent of schools, endorsed the proposal. The schoolboard, however, rejected it. In March 1878 Weber's attorney went over the accounts with the district attorney and lawyers for the schoolboard. "The fullness of your accounts . . . produce[d] a favorable impression," he reported. "I now expect the S[chool] B[oard] to come forward with proposals of compromise." But the board was in no hurry to let Weber off the hook.[33]

In September 1878 a frustrated Weber wrote Gibson for help. One of the schoolboard's attorneys, ex-governor Wickliffe, seemed favorably disposed toward him, he explained, but the district attorney and the board members were "bitterly hostile." Gibson asked Democratic congressman Ellis "if anything can be done to assist" Weber. "You are in with the boys in the Felicianas and might set them right." It is not known if Ellis interceded; if he did, it had no effect.[34]

Anderson's decision to jump the Democratic ship seems to have inspired Weber to threaten similar action. Calculating that Gibson and Maddox needed him to contradict the ex-supervisor's recent statements, he conditioned any rebuttal upon the resolution of his schoolboard case. Using Sam St. Martin as an amanuensis, he wired Gibson to demand that he settle the case "at once," after which Weber would make "such a statement as you want." He then enlisted Congressman J. H. Acklen to intercede with Gibson. Weber needed $1,000, wired Acklen. Gibson reacted badly to this peremptory demand. "I want no statement from Weber," he wired back. "If I did, I would not buy it." The ensuing exchange of telegrams lacked civility. Unless Gibson complied, Weber riposted, "you will force me to make a statement about you and others." Gibson's response was scathing: "You are wasting your time telegraphing threats to me. I am not buying statements or silence of blackmailers." Weber thereupon damned him as a liar, thief, and scoundrel. "I propose to put you in the penitentiary, where you belong."[35]

Maddox tried to mollify Weber. Parish officials had no desire to persecute him, he wrote; a local attorney was attending to his case, and Wickliffe was assisting. He would soon receive a "fair settlement." It was nevertheless evident that any final resolution of his case depended upon Weber repudiating the Republican Party and sticking to the Democratic script. "The good men" of the parish, Maddox related, believed that he had been "used by the bad men" who led his party; they trusted that he "was sincere in his desire to do the people of the parish justice." But the case dragged on.[36]

In mid-November Weber planted a story in the press signaling his intention to recant his testimony. Maddox rushed to New Orleans to prevent that happening. Two days after the planted story, the *New Orleans Daily Democrat* published an "interview" with Weber, ghosted by Maddox, that addressed his claim to have destroyed the Sherman letter—a claim he considered "the really vulnerable part" of Weber's testimony before the Potter Committee. He had destroyed the letter at the instance of Don's widow, Weber explained, in order to safeguard the family's reputation. The story might seem odd, he confessed, but it was "one of those cases where truth is stranger than fiction." The *Daily Democrat* opined that the story's very implausibility suggested that it was true. "If he had been making up a lie he would not have told an impossible lie. . . . He could easily have concocted a plausible lie."[37]

Maddox spoke with Wickliffe regarding Weber's case; so did Gibson and Carter. But on November 21 Weber again complained that "nothing had been done" and that Gibson refused to spend any money on a settlement. "I am more afraid than ever," he wrote St. Martin, "that my school-board case will be held over me." It was only in March 1879 that the schoolboard finally lifted the threat of prosecution by accepting Weber's proposal to surrender all his properties in Saint Francisville.[38]

The Democrats had succeeded in keeping Weber quiet. Or had they? At precisely the time that he was threatening to recant his testimony, St. Martin, his sidekick, approached Morris Marks, a fellow resident of Donaldsonville, and offered to expose Democratic crookedness. On December 2 he went to Marks's office in New Orleans and dictated an affidavit. He then showed it to John Ray, Sherman's attorney in New Orleans, who could hardly believe his luck. "I expect . . . to send you evidence concerning the outrageous conduct of leading Democrats in bribing witnesses before the Potter Committee," Ray wrote Sherman. "It will be startling."[39]

In Washington, arriving shortly before Christmas, St. Martin gave the document to Shellabarger and offered to testify before the Potter Committee. He now maintained that he had falsely contradicted Dula's testimony at the urging of Gibson, who paid him to do so; that the Sherman letter never existed and Weber concocted his account of destroying it; that Weber was promised $10,000 from Maddox, Carter, and Gibson to testify as he did; and that the same trio induced Black Republicans to recant their previous testimony regarding Democratic intimidation by paying them cash and pledging "immunity from future molestation" should they return to West Feliciana.

St. Martin's most explosive charge concerned Representative Stenger, chairman of the Louisiana subcommittee. The bribing of witnesses had taken place with the full knowledge of the Pennsylvania Democrat, he claimed. Not only that, but Stenger also had instructed St. Martin, whom the subcommittee employed to serve subpoenas, to withhold them from any witnesses who could not be relied on to support the Democrats' case. Instead, St. Martin should return those subpoenas and state that he had been unable to locate the intended witnesses.[40]

A young man of twenty-four years whose father had been killed at Gettysburg, St. Martin was a native French speaker who struggled to express himself in English. He held the position of town constable in Donaldsonville, a job that paid forty dollars a month plus one dollar for every arrest made. Something of a brawler—he was handy with a knife and had served jail time for wielding it—he and Weber were as thick as thieves. The latter, who had known St. Martin since he was a toddler, employed him as a bodyguard and general factotum. The two men were virtually inseparable. During the subcommittee hearings in New Orleans, Maddox recalled, St. Martin "acted as a messenger between Weber and myself."[41]

That St. Martin offered his incendiary affidavit on his own initiative is possible but unlikely. Even more implausible was his own explanation for why he chose to come forward. He claimed that after swearing falsely during the subcommittee hearings, he immediately suffered pangs of conscience and decided to make a clean breast of things, just as promptly telling Gibson, Maddox, and Carter about his change of heart. But he produced not a shred of evidence to support his claim. Gibson and his confederates unsurprisingly denied it. More telling is the fact that St. Martin took no action until November 1877 and that, up to the time he made his affidavit, was still acting as Weber's "gofer" in the latter's dealings with Maddox. Neither is there any evidence of a break between St. Martin and his mentor. Perhaps the wily Marks, who owed his position as collector of internal revenue to Sherman, induced a naïve St. Martin to make the affidavit. Or perhaps Weber persuaded him to do so in order to punish the men who had promised him so much and delivered so little, effecting this without having to retract his own testimony and admit to perjury.

One thing can be demonstrated with certainty: Weber let it be known to the Republican Party that, as D. J. M. A. Jewett reported to Sherman, "his retraction could be had for a consideration." Jewett, by his own account, rebuffed the approach, informing Weber "that his manifestly malicious perjuries were quite as serviceable to the Republican cause, as any retraction it was in his power to make." But Marks may have been more receptive; he had deeper pockets and was anxious to please Sherman. In any case, St. Martin made his affidavit a few days later. The likelihood is that he coordinated his action with Weber and that money changed hands.[42]

Sherman's attorney in Washington, however, hardly knew what to do with St. Martin. Louisiana witnesses had proven themselves notoriously untrustworthy. Wary of dealing with Weber or any of his associates, Shellabarger was loath to put the affidavit in the public domain, especially when it charged a congressman with sanctioning bribery and witness tampering. He was equally reluctant to call upon St. Martin to testify. For the next several weeks, the lawyer sat on the affidavit and kept its author at arm's length. "I have repeatedly told him that I could make no promises," he informed Sherman. The statement implied that St. Martin sought money or office.[43]

While cooling his heels, seemingly shunned by the Republicans, St. Martin sought out Maddox, who, over several meetings, urged him to repudiate his affidavit. Maddox drafted a statement in which St. Martin withdrew his bribery allegations. According to St. Martin, Maddox promised him $1,000 to sign. The negotiations ended when Shellabarger decided to send St. Martin's affidavit to Potter and ask that his allegations, including the charge against Stenger, be investigated.[44]

Clarkson Potter was by now thoroughly sick of his assignment. He could see the case against Sherman, and by implication Hayes, falling apart. Unburdening himself to Marble, he complained that "respectable men, intelligent men, thoughtful Republicans, friends of mine," had criticized him to his face as a "bitter and unscrupulous partisan." Day after day, he went on, the *New York Tribune* had misrepresented the committee, charging it with "partiality in its formation, and in the selection of subcommittees; with refusing Sherman counsel; with conducting Star Chamber proceedings, and being compelled by public opinion to open its doors; and of maligning men . . . and refusing to retract charges which they knew to be false." The committee had been hobbled from the start, he grumbled, by the reluctance of many Democrats to bring Hayes's presidential title into question; they reasoned that the party had consented to the Electoral Commission and was bound by its decision. Others were so hostile to Tilden that they opposed any effort, which they supposed the investigation to be, to assist his presidential ambitions. But Potter's keenest disappointment was the failure of the Democratic press to parry the Republican attacks. Leading papers like the *New York World* and the *New York Herald* had not taken the proceedings seriously and were lukewarm in the committee's defense. He had, Potter confessed, lost the battle for public opinion. The chairman would make no public defense of the committee because nothing he might say would convince "any of the disbelievers."[45]

Nothing would have suited him better than to close the investigation and issue a report. But his ordeal was not yet over. Republicans were clamoring for an investigation of the cipher dispatches. St. Martin's affidavit threatened to drag Gibson, Maddox, and Carter before the committee. The allegation against Stenger needed examination. Sherman's attorneys were expecting further hearings in New Orleans to question witnesses who could testify to Democratic intimidation.

Potter had not only lost control of the investigation but also risked becoming a laughing stock. In early September the *New York Tribune* reported that Democrats on the committee believed they had procured the authentic Sherman letter and intended publicizing the document in time to influence the midterm elections, which some states held in October. But the alleged original was actually a fake. "The pretense," Shellabarger told the *Tribune,* "is that the document E. L. Weber swore he found in the shoe box was a mere copy." Given that Democratic agents had induced witnesses in New Orleans to perjure themselves, Sherman commented, "It is not surprising that their next move is to be forgery." The origin of the rumor is uncertain, but Democrats suspected that it was planted by Republicans in order to make mischief.[46]

Lo and behold, Potter shortly thereafter received a letter from one "L. E. Stratton" of Brown's Station, Iowa, offering a "facsimile copy of the Sherman letter, together with other papers that I copied at the request of the Hon. John Sherman." After making enquiries, the chairman satisfied himself that no such person existed.[47]

Potter then received a package from New Orleans that enclosed a photographed copy of the by now famous, not to say infamous, Sherman letter. The provenance of this document turned out to be our old friend Agnes Jenks. On September 19 Jenks visited a carpet store on Canal Street and, seemingly by accident, dropped an envelope bearing her name on the outside. After she left without making any purchase, store employee James Maloney discovered the envelope and showed it to his two colleagues, exclaiming, "See here, boys! I've found a bonanza—here's a package addressed to Mrs. Jenks." One end of the envelope had been torn off: the documents within were fairly begging to be read. Extracting the contents, the trio could hardly fail to recognize the Sherman letter. After having them photographed, they sent Potter a list describing the documents, with an accompanying affidavit recounting the circumstances of their discovery. For the moment, Potter did nothing. The committee was due to visit Louisiana again, and he could address the matter then.[48]

The chairman arrived in New Orleans on December 30, accompanied by Congressman Cox. He quickly discovered that the trip was a waste of time. Having asked the committee in the summer to examine dozens of witnesses who could attest to bulldozing in the Felicianas, Ray withdrew the request at the last minute. The recent election, he explained, had amply demonstrated the continuing use by Democrats of violence and intimidation, actions that "most shamefully violated" the pledges of good behavior issued by the governor and legislature the previous year. A Senate committee was about to commence an investigation, making a rehearsal of the testimony regarding 1876 superfluous. Recalling witnesses from the Felicianas would be futile in any case: such persons would either swear falsely or, if they attested truthfully, would place their lives in danger. Ray pointed out that some potential witnesses in the new investigation had already been arrested or murdered to prevent them testifying.[49]

Potter thus found that he had very little to do. He and Cox examined the three carpet-store salesman about their discovery of Jenks's envelope. It transpired that she had already "lost" the package in the street several times before visiting the store, only to have it repeatedly returned to her by helpful passersby. Jenks had clearly wanted her Sherman letter to be found. Upon examining the document, however, Potter pronounced it spurious, the signature being a "forged imitation" of Sherman's. After conducting a single day of hearings, the congressmen returned to Washington, having accomplished, from the Democrats' point of view, nothing.[50]

Republicans could hardly suppress their laughter. They depicted Potter as the bumbling butt of a practical joke. When he received the package of documents from New Orleans, the *New York Tribune* chortled, the chairman "unquestionably supposed that he had struck a bonanza mine," only to discover that he been taken in by "that vivacious stateswoman who . . . will never, of her own accord, sink back into domestic obscurity." The Sherman letter, it scoffed, had "undergone more transformations than any other historical document known to man." For the benefit of readers, the writer then summarized the saga: "It has been proved by Potter's witnesses, first, that it never was written; secondly, that it was destroyed; thirdly, that it was wholly forged by Mrs. Jenks; fourthly, that it was genuine; fifthly, that the original was lying in a shoe-box along with the blacking-brushes of the late Mr. Weber; and, sixthly, that the original was safe in the breast pocket of one of the Committee, ready to be produced at the appropriate time." The farce delighted the normally dour Sherman. Democrats had been desperate to find a genuine letter, he told the *Cincinnati Enquirer*, but "it slowly broke through their minds what a thorough swindle had been played on them by a mere woman." Pleased with her trick, Jenks sent Sherman some relevant newspaper clippings. "I consider they make a fitting finale to my association with the Potter Committee," she declared.[51]

Potter denied that he had ever been taken in by the bogus letter. He knew, the *New York Sun* related, "that it was a device of Sherman's spies and detectives to entrap him." Still, it is hard to see why he needed to make a six-day roundtrip to Louisiana to establish that a document he knew to be fake was indeed so. If the main purpose of the hearings was, as Potter asserted, to examine Republican witnesses, his visit was superfluous on that account as well, for he must have known before setting out for New Orleans that Sherman's attorneys were unlikely to produce any witnesses.[52]

The absence of Republican witnesses at the truncated New Orleans hearings may, in fact, provide the most credible explanation for Potter's decision to hold the hearings at all. He could now truthfully assert that Sherman, offered an opportunity to argue his case, had declined it. The subcommittee had been willing to accommodate the Republican side by examining witnesses in their home parishes, he told the *New York Herald*, "whereupon the Republican agents finally backed down." The latter knew, he believed, that their allegations of Democratic intimidation could not be corroborated. As Potter stated in the committee's final report, Sherman's failure to produce witnesses represented a tacit admission that the 1876 election had been free and fair.[53]

The political argument over the 1876 election, however, now seemed irrelevant. It had been overtaken by events. The Democrats' blatant resort to force and fraud in the fall of 1878 grimly contradicted Potter's insistence that everything had been free and fair two years earlier. Ray did not exaggerate when he claimed that in parts of Louisiana the outrages committed by Democrats in 1878 "re-enacted with greater barbarity" the bulldozing of 1876. In the Republican stronghold of Natchitoches Parish, for example, Democrats arrested and expelled that party's leaders and compelled Blacks to cast Democratic ballots. Writing to Sherman from East Feliciana Parish, George J. Norwood, a white Republican, described how "armed desperadoes" instilled such fear that all of his party's candidates withdrew from the contest. As in 1876, Blacks could vote, but only for the Democratic ticket. Simply by sending such a letter, Norwood stated, he placed his life in danger. "I feel deeply humiliated that I cannot speak my sentiments as a free man in this *free* land."[54]

In West Feliciana Parish six weeks before the election, the body of Timothy Dalton was discovered "hanging from a tree near the Ford at Sanders Creek, on the upper Jackson road." Abducted from his home in Saint Francisville, he was "beaten nearly to death" before being lynched. Dalton, who appeared before the Potter subcommittee in New Orleans, had returned to West Feliciana from Saint James Parish with Weber's assurance that he had nothing to fear, his testimony having earned him the goodwill of local Democrats. Governor Nicholls denounced the murder and offered a reward of $500 for any information that might disclose the guilty parties. No one claimed the reward. In their customary fashion Democratic newspapers not only failed to regret Dalton's murder, they celebrated it. A prominent Republican, Dalton had been acquitted of murder in 1868. Now, gloated the *West Feliciana Sentinel*, "he met a fate he so richly deserved." The *New Orleans Daily Democrat* labeled him "a mischievous and troublesome rascal," explaining his death as payback for the misdeeds of the Republican party. "That he was hung we are not surprised."[55]

Former state legislator Joseph Armstead also discovered that recanting his previous testimony—he even denied the evidence of his own signature on Dalton's affidavit—purchased him no immunity in West Feliciana. Having returned to his family abode under what he imagined to be a tacit safe-conduct pass, he escaped through the backdoor when, on the same night that Dalton was lynched, armed whites came to his house. Once again he fled to Saint James Parish.[56]

Even the preternaturally optimistic Hayes admitted that his southern policy had failed to attract the support of conservative whites and that, in large swathes of the South, the Democratic Party showed even less disposition to tolerate Republican voters than in 1876. The Democrats increased their majority in the House of Representative largely through gains in the South, where they won all but three of seventy-three congressional districts. Hayes found the results in Louisiana and South Carolina especially troubling. "By state legislation, by frauds, by intimidation, and by violence of the most atrocious character," he confided to his diary, "colored citizens have been deprived of the right of suffrage . . . to the protection of which the [white] people of those States have been solemnly pledged."[57]

Yet with an air of Olympian detachment and unshakeable self-confidence, the president gave no thought to revising his "hands-off" policy toward the former Confederacy. He remained certain that the only protection for Blacks in the South lay in a Republican Party that could attract mass support from native whites. He certainly had no intention of employing military force again. Hayes's regret over the election results in the South, in fact, was more than counterbalanced by his delight that Ben Butler had left Congress only to lose his campaign for the governorship of Massachusetts. "The crushing defeat of Butler," he exulted, "was one of the best events that has happened since the war."[58]

Sherman, on the other hand, although no fan of Butler, was enough of a realist to recognize the bankruptcy of Hayes's policy of conciliating southern whites. "The first imperative duty of this country," he sounded off to a friend, "is to put down in some decisive way this wholesale barbarism of a people who are . . . nothing but pardoned rebels using force to seize greater political power." Garfield, too, drew the obvious conclusion: the Democrats of Louisiana and South Carolina had betrayed their promise to Hayes "that if let alone, the Negro would be fully protected."[59]

Potter had not stood for reelection, and a Republican replaced him in Congress. Before he returned to private life, however, and before he could submit his committee's report, he faced two unpleasant tasks. One was to deal with St. Martin's affidavit; the other was to respond to publication of the cipher dispatches.

If the affidavit was, as the *Chicago Daily Tribune* averred, a "bombshell in the Democratic camp," the cipher dispatches represented a barrage. Although Potter regarded the prospect of further hearings with distaste, he had no choice in the matter. St. Martin's allegations, which Shellabarger fed to the press, were so serious that they could not be ignored, especially when they impugned one of the committee members. The committee voted along party lines to examine St. Martin but to reject his affidavit.

As for the cipher dispatches, the *New York Tribune*'s translations had created such a furor that the force of public opinion, which favored a thorough congressional enquiry, could not be denied.[60]

When St. Martin appeared before the full committee in January 1879, he received a thorough going-over from Butler. The *schwerpunkt* of Butler's attack was the witness's contradictory statements regarding Stenger. A few days before he testified, and shortly after the newspapers published his affidavit, St. Martin had withdrawn his most incendiary allegation: Stenger had not, after all, told him to withhold subpoenas from uncooperative witnesses. "My instructions came from Maddox and Carter," he told the *National Republican*. "I do not wish to do Mr. Stenger . . . an injustice. And I would like to have that corrected."[61]

This belated retraction invited two obvious questions, which Butler pressed with bulldog tenacity. How could St. Martin have mistaken Stenger for Maddox, especially when he identified the former as chairman of the Louisiana subcommittee? And why, having committed the error on December 2, 1878, did he fail to correct it before Shellabarger gave his affidavit to the press in mid-January 1879, fully six weeks later? St. Martin never provided convincing explanations, and, when Butler accused him of having lied to the public, he lost his temper. "Let me tell you one thing; I don't think it is right for you to sit here and insult me," he raved. "You have the advantage of me. You wouldn't tell me outside of this room, you know." The outburst left Butler unfazed. "O, pshaw! I don't care about the word 'lie,' particularly; this was an untrue statement, a sworn untruth, stated by you under oath, and you let it go out to the public." Ignoring his petulant refusal to answer any more questions, Butler pressed St. Martin on his allegation that Stenger had had "full knowledge" of witnesses being bribed. The witness backtracked. "No, I didn't say that I had made any promises to them."[62]

The other committee members piled on and elicited more damaging contradictions. Having claimed that Gibson supplied the money for bribing witnesses, St. Martin admitted that he had never actually seen the *New York Sun* reporter distribute any cash. And having alleged that Carter also paid witnesses, he now confessed, "I didn't see him pay no money." Pressed to explain why he had refused payment to contradict Dula's testimony but contradicted it of his own volition anyway, he could only cite the befuddling influence of alcohol. Asked about his inability to remember the sums paid to each witness when, as he claimed, he had recorded the details in a memorandum, St. Martin explained that he had recently lost this document. Quizzed as to why Gibson and Maddox continued to employ him *after* he told them that he intended to expose their wrongdoing, he could give no intelligible answer.[63]

St. Martin's account of his service as a deputy sergeant at arms to the Louisiana subcommittee turned out to be absurdly inaccurate. The subcommittee's records disproved his claim that he had deliberately failed to serve a dozen subpoenas that Potter issued at the request of the Republican members. In fact, the four subpoenas he returned as "not found" had been issued at the instance of Stenger, a Democrat; all the subpoenas requested by Reed and Cox, by contrast, were served.[64]

"When a man goes upon the stand to testify," St. Martin observed, "if he goes in to lie, he must lie right, or otherwise be beat." His own testimony illustrated the truth of that assertion, although not in the way he intended. His story was so riddled with misstatements, false accusations, and contradictions that not much of it survived after two days of cross-examination. St. Martin himself seemed oblivious to that fact. "I have got as clear a conscience as any man around this table," he protested. The remark triggered a round of laughter.[65]

Republicans could derive satisfaction from St. Martin's appearance. As the *Chicago Daily Tribune* put it, although "Louisiana witnesses . . . are not entitled to full belief at any time," his testimony was particularly egregious. It further discredited E. L. Weber. It implicated Gibson, Maddox, and Carter in a scheme to induce witnesses, through bribes and promises of safety, to perjure themselves. If the Democrats were to salvage anything at all from the investigation, they needed to rebut that allegation by having Gibson, Maddox, and Carter explain themselves.[66]

These three duly appeared and, as expected, firmly denied using money to influence Weber or any other witness. They insisted, too, that their efforts to resolve Weber's dispute with the West Feliciana Parish schoolboard had been wholly altruistic and were in no wise conditioned upon his testimony before the committee, nor were they a means of keeping him quiet. If these denials were unconvincing, they were also impossible to disprove in the absence of documentary evidence. Still, their testimony gave unwitting hints that money indeed played a role in influencing witnesses. Maddox admitted to offering Weber $1,000 if he could incriminate Marks. He also related that St. Martin had stood by his allegation against Gibson, insisting that the *New York Sun* correspondent "bought him to go on the stand." Gibson's own flippant observation that he would never pay for testimony "because I do not think I would get my money's worth" might have been tongue in cheek, but he hastened to add, "even presuming that I would do such a thing." His statement that no money was paid to witnesses "so far as my knowledge goes" was a carefully crafted lawyer's response that admitted the possibility.[67]

When allegations of bribery depended upon oral testimony alone, they could never be definitely proven. In Weber's case, however, a memorandum in the Tilden papers, unsigned but clearly written by Gibson, provides more-solid evidence. Upon learning that he would be subpoenaed by the committee in Washington, Gibson recorded, Weber insisted that "certain conditions should be complied with" before he agreed to testify. Faced with the possibility that Weber would refuse to give the testimony he had promised, Gibson took it upon himself to "comply with [the] demand made," acting upon "my own judgment and . . . responsibility." These awkward circumlocutions most likely referred to money. If so, they confirm the charge made by James Anderson and St. Martin that Weber was paid for his testimony. Such payment could not have come from Gibson himself who, although handsomely remunerated by Dana, was not a wealthy man. DNC Chairman Barnum, however, might well have been the paymaster. A rich iron manufacturer, he possessed the financial wherewithal. He also had a "well-earned reputation for political dirty tricks."[68]

House Republicans enjoyed a delicious moment of schadenfreude as Congress began its new session. Amid mounting clamor for an investigation into the cipher dispatches, they prolonged Democratic agony simply by doing nothing. They were content to have the cipher dispatches, which the *New York Tribune* recycled daily, speak for themselves, pushing the onus of ordering an investigation onto the majority party. The longer the Democrats delayed, the darker the cloud became over Tilden's reputation. When the Potter Committee finally sought the House's authorization to investigate the offending telegrams, Republican members abstained from voting: they were reluctant, Reed explained with mock solemnity, to intrude upon the Democrats' private grief. "We said to them . . . that we had no dead man on our hands who needed to be buried. . . . [W]e do not propose to weep, or even to assist at the wake."[69]

When Congress finally took up the matter on January 21, 1879, Republicans could afford to gloat. Omar D. Conger of Michigan "wondered what paralysis had fallen upon the fierce Democracy" in ordering an investigation: "Another day passed and then another. . . . We sat here silently . . . , with almost irrepressible impatience . . . to wait and let the Democracy have the honor." Nobody enjoyed themselves more than Maine's Eugene Hale, one of the Republican visiting statesmen. In May 1878 he had pressed the House to authorize a "more exhaustive and searching investigation" that would cover "the one side as well as the other." Then, Potter had haughtily rebuffed him. Now, the Democrats on Potter's own committee instructed him to do just what Hale had wanted. With heavy sarcasm, he expressed his sympathy "for that simple-hearted old man in New York" and stated, with mock generosity, "I would not have him miss the opportunity of being allowed to vindicate his character."[70]

Butler, curiously, spoke against an inquiry. In May he had suggested that the committee investigate South Carolina; now in January he argued that Congress had no right to probe the actions of private individuals that, in the end, produced no crime. Such an inquiry might satisfy the public's "prurient curiosity for scandal," he asserted, but no good would come out of it. Why bring discredit upon America's republican institutions in the eyes of the world? Why "besmirch and bedim somebody who is not even a member of this House?" Better to pass over in silence "something that had better not be seen, felt, or smelled."[71]

The congressman was not known for his reticence in investigating private individuals—quite the reverse. What was he playing at? Perhaps Butler simply had no interest in the matter. He had used his place on the Potter Committee to attack Hayes's title; the cipher dispatches were irrelevant to that purpose. A second explanation, not incompatible with the first, is that Butler was in the process of transferring his allegiance from the Republican to the Democratic Party. In 1878, having decided not to seek reelection to Congress, he tried to secure the Democratic nomination for governor of Massachusetts, eventually running as an independent with the support of the Greenback Labor Party and the backing of most Democratic voters. But Republicans and anti-Butler Democrats, with an assist from Hayes, who "made Butler's political destruction an administration priority," defeated his gubernatorial bid. With plans to run again for the governorship, next time as the official Democratic candidate, Butler wanted no part in interrogating Tilden.[72]

Nevertheless, the only way for Democrats to answer Republican jeers was to authorize an inquiry. "I stand here now," thundered Abram Hewitt, "to invite the fullest investigation of those telegrams. . . . Justice to Samuel J. Tilden requires that the investigation should be made." Now a congressman from New York, he also had his own reasons for supporting an investigation. As chairman of the DNC during the presidential campaign, he had been entirely ignorant of Pelton's activities, and the cipher dispatches had never come to his attention until he read them in the *New York Tribune.* Hewitt did not wish his reputation sullied by the "mistaken zeal" of Tilden's "indiscreet friends." Whether the investigation hurt Tilden might not have worried him overmuch: his relations with the former candidate were strained. Marble and Watterson, confidantes of Tilden, had publicly arraigned Hewitt over his support for the Electoral Bill. In blaming the DNC chair for Tilden's defeat, they were publicly expressing what the candidate privately thought. Hewitt resented being made a scapegoat. The *Tribune* made merry with these tensions, suggesting that Democrats pressing for an investigation were inspired less by loyalty to Tilden than hostility to him.[73]

An unhappy Potter found himself in the position of seeking the House's permission to conduct an investigation that he opposed, having also to account for his own reluctance to initiate it. It was a case, he explained, of being damned if he did and damned if he did not. The Republican press had accused him of being a tool of Tilden and, more recently, of having fallen out with him. If he asked for an investigation of the cipher dispatches, he would be accused of acting out of "dislike and spite" and of "personally injuring Mr. Tilden." But if he resisted the investigation, critics would charge him with "protecting and whitewashing those whom the dispatches might affect." He denied having made any kind of political bargain with Tilden and insisted that his selection as chairman had nothing to do with his alleged closeness to the man. Unburdening himself, Potter complained that he had been unjustly maligned. "There has been no unworthy or partisan speech which has not been falsely put into my mouth by the press nor any mean or outrageous action which has not been falsely attributed to me."[74]

Potter's self-referential performance draw a withering review from the *Cincinnati Enquirer*'s correspondent "Gath." The congressman "almost excused himself for offering the resolution, and grew red in the face in his effort to conceal his agitation and nervousness." He left no time, moreover, to permit any of the other Democratic committee members to speak, a lapse that caused Representative McMahon to privately rebuke him.[75]

Confronted with the unavoidable, Potter proposed that the Democratic agents implicated in the bribery schemes—Pelton, Marble and Smith—should be examined in New York by a subcommittee. Readily endorsed by the Democratic majority, this arrangement ensured that Tilden's agents, perhaps even Tilden himself, would testify in a heavily Democratic city before a friendlier audience. It also enabled Potter to appoint another committee member to preside over those hearings. He had no stomach for that task. And neither did McMahon, who supported one of Tilden's rivals for the 1880 presidential nomination. So, Eppa Hunton took on the thankless task.[76]

The *New York Tribune* derided Potter's choice of location. Why New York? "Is it to spare the feelings of Messrs. Tilden and Marble? . . . Is it the purpose of the Committee to avoid the keen, bright sunlight of publicity by escaping from the National Capital to the bustle of Broadway, as a man who is hunted hides from pursuit by plunging into the midst of a crowd?" Shrewdly exploiting Democratic uncertainty over the issue, Representative Reed presented a resolution inviting Tilden to testify in his own defense, cheekily citing Hewitt's speech in Congress. The Democratic majority voted to lay it on the table. "Oh, give the old man a chance!" implored the *Tribune* in mock sympathy.[77]

Before Hunton's subcommittee departed, Potter opened hearings in Washington to establish how the cipher dispatches found their way from the offices of the Western Union Telegraph Company in January 1877 to the pages of the *New York Tribune* in October 1878. What troubled Potter and his fellow Democrats was how, out of the 29,275 dispatches that Western Union supplied to congressional committees, several hundred were "abstracted" from the pile and wound up in the hands of Thomas Brady, William Chandler, Ben Butler, Frank Hiscock, and Whitelaw Reid, Republicans all. That story, recounted earlier, need not be repeated.

What made the Republican coup doubly infuriating to Democrats was a strong suspicion that the Hayes camp had generated equally incriminating telegrams but that these had disappeared. According to the *Cincinnati Enquirer*, the late William Orton, former president of Western Union and a Republican partisan, had done everything in his power "to screen the misdeeds of the Republican managers." And it charged that the late Oliver Morton, who chaired the Senate committee that received the dispatches, had allowed Republicans free rein to enter the committee room, delve into the bundles, and carry away whatever they wished.[78]

Democratic indignation over the purloining of these private communications elicited no apologies from the purloiners. The bundles had been left in a Senate committee room, Brady nonchalantly explained, "and were considered as just so much waste paper." Republicans acquired the 700-plus dispatches, it seems, in the same way that Britain supposedly acquired its empire—in a fit of absent-mindedness. Brady again: "Anybody could look at them. I happened to find those few of my own, and I just took them." As political shenanigans go, the "abstraction" of the dispatches was small beer, and Republicans were happy, even smug, to acknowledge the peccadillo. They had pulled a fast one on their political opponents and delighted in the fact. Potter wanted to find evidence of Republican skullduggery, but the cipher dispatches offered slim pickings.[79]

Then, Western Union employee James O. Green revived Democratic hopes. He revealed that Orton had allowed Assistant Postmaster General John Tyner to remove telegrams relating to Indiana *before* the company could hand them over to Congress. About ten in number, Green recalled, they concerned "the sale of an office" whose "proceeds should go to the credit of the Republican party." He emphasized that his memory was vague and that this was "only an impression of mine." Yet despite the witness's uncertainty, the apparent loss of the telegrams, and the fact that the elections in Indiana fell outside the committee's purview, Potter subpoenaed Tyner in the hope of exposing a case of Republican corruption. The telegrams would show that Tyner and Zach Chandler, the secretary of the interior and chairman of the RNC, appointed people to federal positions on condition that they donate the equivalent of their yearly salaries to Republican Party coffers.[80]

When Tyner produced the telegrams in question and explained their contents, however, the Democratic case evaporated. What appeared to be a blatant example of selling offices for cash turned out to be nothing of the kind. True, Tyner had wired Chandler to "appoint two Indian agents" at $5,000 each. But the term "Indian agent," he claimed, was code for $5,000, the sum to be sent by the RNC to cover legitimate election expenses. Once he explained the code words, the telegrams became innocuous. Even the *New York Sun* found Tyner's account convincing. Once again, Potter had fallen flat on his face.[81]

As the subcommittee repaired to New York, Reid had his *New York Tribune* publish the cipher dispatches in a pamphlet that sold for twenty-five cents. It contained the keys and translations, supplemented with a damning commentary. When the authors of these telegrams were confronted with their coded messages, the public would be able to decide for themselves whether the translations were accurate. Tilden and his associates had a lot of explaining to do. "The sluice gates have been opened," warned the *Cincinnati Enquirer*, "and a deluge of nastiness will pour over the country."[82]

8

THE BITER BIT

SAMUEL J. TILDEN BEFORE THE POTTER COMMITTEE

As the Hunton subcommittee set about its work, "Gath" spied Samuel Tilden walking down New York's 8th Street. As he passed a row of waiting cabs, wrote the reporter, Tilden doffed his hat to any driver who recognized him and bowed with exaggerated courtesy. "The effect was that of a harmless imbecile . . . under some delusion as to who he might be." Encountering him a few months earlier, Horace White, the former editor of the *Chicago Daily Tribune*, had noted that Tilden's "vacant and limp" countenance conveyed the impression of a man who appeared "to have lost his mind."[1]

Tilden's decrepitude was a favorite theme of his political enemies. Republican malice alone, however, did not account for these cruel portraits. A lifelong hypochondriac who was constantly experimenting with self-medication, real and imagined afflictions shaped Tilden's daily life. Here was someone, Bigelow confided to his diary, "who must have a man rub him every morning for an hour or so; who must take a tonic or some other medicinal preparation before every meal; who must ride a couple of hours every day and sleep or rest an hour after it; who, as he once said to me, never knew what it was to eat a square meal in his life or to feel the joy of abounding health." Tilden's neurosis did not prevent him from attaining a respectable old age. But at sixty-three he looked pale and hunched, his voice scarcely rose above a whisper, his palsied hands trembled, and one of his eyelids drooped. Foes claimed that he betrayed symptoms of alcoholism; friends noted his "haggard and careworn" appearance. Tilden might have suffered minor strokes or may have been afflicted with Parkinson's disease. Whatever the cause, he looked like an invalid and, in Bigelow's words, ran the "danger of becoming . . . a drivelling paralytic."[2]

Despite his infirmities, Tilden had made a fortune as a corporate lawyer and acquired a formidable reputation for political acumen. His experience of elective office consisted of a single term in the New York State Assembly and two years as governor, but he had operated as a force within the Democratic Party for decades, especially after his election as chairman of the New York State Central Committee in 1866. His influence derived from vast knowledge and sheer brainpower rather than crowd-pleasing "people skills," abilities that he lacked almost entirely. A devourer of statistics and an inveterate behind-the-scenes "networker," Tilden could assess Democratic prospects in every district, knowledge that gave him a strong voice in party nominations and election campaigns. He also proved a master at cultivating favorable newspaper coverage by means of alliances with editors and money subsidies. In terms of manipulating the press, "Gath" noted, "no public man knows so much about its expenses, straits, [and] venality."[3]

As a champion of "reform" after 1870, Tilden had transcended his image as a "cold, clammy, selfish wire-puller" to become the personification of honest politics. Using his political cunning and legal skills to devastating effect, he battled corruption within his own party: smashing the Tweed Ring that had robbed New York blind, removing the corrupt judges who has assisted the plunderers, and, as governor, exposing and eliminating the Canal Ring, a combination of businessmen and politicians who had raided the state's Treasury. Having cleansed New York's Augean stables, he had vowed, if elected president, to restore honesty and integrity to the federal government.[4]

Small wonder that Tilden regarded the impending subcommittee hearings with dread. His political standing rested upon a reputation for probity, which the *New York Tribune*'s revelations now threatened to destroy. The only defense available to him was to claim total ignorance of what the Democratic agents in Oregon, Florida, and South Carolina had attempted.

The problem with this defense, however, was that the agents in question were not low-level ward heelers but senior figures in the Democratic Party, some of them Tilden's close associates. Lawyer and businessman Smith M. Weed, for example, had known Tilden for two decades; the pair served together in the New York State Assembly. Manton Marble was an intimate political colleague and a man of reputation and influence. As editor of the *New York World* between 1862 and 1876, he had enjoyed virtually unfettered access to the innermost councils of the Democratic Party. "Politicians did not direct him," writes historian Mark Summers, "they appealed, consulted, and informed." Tilden regarded Marble as a valuable ally, once lending him $45,000 to keep the *World* afloat. After selling the newspaper in 1876, Marble threw himself into Tilden's fight for the Democratic nomination and subsequent election campaign. He drafted the candidate's platform. During the electoral crisis, Marble was a frequent visitor to 15 Gramercy Park. Should Tilden win, he could expect a place in the cabinet.[5]

Tilden's connection to William T. Pelton, the son of his widowed sister Mary (who managed his household and served as a domestic companion), could scarcely be closer. Pelton and his wife had resided in Tilden's home for ten years, all the while receiving a generous allowance. During two years in Albany, the couple lived in the governor's mansion while Pelton acted as Tilden's "military secretary." During the presidential campaign, he oversaw the dissemination of pro-Tilden literature and the assignment of speakers. "Nothing could be done with Tilden for several months before the election and after it except through Pelton," a prominent Democrat told "Gath." The coded telegrams from Weed, Marble, and the other Democratic visiting statesmen had all been addressed to 15 Gramercy Park and read by Pelton.[6]

Hunton opened the New York hearings, held in a parlor of the Fifth Avenue Hotel, on February 5 at noon. Weed was the first witness. It soon became clear that the chairman, "a tall dignified Southerner with a quiet, deliberate manner," intended to conduct the proceedings with scrupulous fairness. Tilden's "want of nerve," Hunton believed, had lost the Democratic Party the presidency. He considered it no part of his duty to protect the witnesses from aggressive questioning by the two Republican members.[7]

Armed with the *Tribune* pamphlet, Hiscock and Reed gave Weed a thorough grilling over the course of six hours. Confronted with his own telegrams, Weed breezily admitted trying to buy the South Carolina Returning Board for the sum of $80,000 and arranging to meet Pelton in Baltimore to effect the transaction, the money to come from the DNC and "all to be in $1,000 or $500 bills." Pelton had kept the rendezvous but told Weed that he needed to wire DNC treasurer Edward Cooper in order for the money to be transferred. Weed likened his conduct to paying "ransom to a robber" in order to "recover stolen property." But he was at pains to exculpate Tilden: the deal fell through, he claimed, when the candidate, apprised of the plan by Cooper, ordered Pelton to drop it and return to New York. Upon their next meeting, he added, Tilden "took me to task for having entertained these propositions."[8]

Weed's attempt to vindicate Tilden, however, ran into a problem: Why, if Tilden had so decisively vetoed the bribery attempt on November 20, 1876, did Weed subsequently bring Hardy Solomon from Baltimore to New York, telling him he would raise the money from sources outside the DNC? Pressed by Hiscock, the witness explained that he had deceived Solomon (who claimed to represent the Returning Board) and had "no intention of raising the money." It was an odd explanation, to say the least.[9]

Weed also had to account for a telegram, sent from New York on November 27, agreeing to send $5,000 to his contact in South Carolina for the purpose of bribing Republican members of the state legislature. The scheme involved inducing enough Republicans to go over to the rival Democratic body, which, when it made a quorum, would override the Republican-controlled Returning Board that had certified the Hayes electors on the twenty-second and certify the Tilden electors instead. Luckily for Weed, the relevant dispatch had been written in a different cipher from the others, and the *Tribune*'s translations involved some guesswork. This enabled him to quibble and equivocate: the translation was wrong, but he could not, without the relevant cipher key, supply the correct one. In any case, he could not recall ever receiving a dispatch requesting $5,000. It was an unconvincing performance. As the *New York Times* put it, Weed "fail[ed] to remember everything which it could not otherwise be proved that he could not possibly have forgotten."[10]

When Pelton appeared the following morning, the hearing room was jammed with twenty reporters and about 150 members of the public. The spectators had come to be entertained and to cheer for their respective parties. So raucous was the applause and laughter that, during the course of another long day, Hunton more than once threatened to clear the room.[11]

Nobody proved more adept at playing to the gallery than Reed, "a fresh-looking, burly, rosy-faced man, with a quizzical expression," whose needling sarcasm discomfited Pelton and elicited guffaws from onlookers. Hiscock, "a very sad, clerical-looking gentleman," adopted a more stern, although no less sarcastic, tone. The two men gave Tilden's nephew a thorough going over. He was an easy target. Visibly nervous, he was also, unbeknown to his interrogators, a man whose life was falling apart. Now a widower with a young daughter to support, he had been turned out of Tilden's house and was living in a hotel, still dependent upon his uncle's charity, and slowly drinking himself to death.[12]

In contrast to the glib and voluble Weed, Pelton was sullen and monosyllabic. He was unable to elaborate on any of the cipher dispatches, he explained, because he no longer possessed the original key and doubted the accuracy of the *Tribune*'s translations. For example, he had no idea what Marble had meant by "Tell Russia to saddle Blackstone" and could not be sure if "Russia" referred to Tilden. Having wired Marble that he would send $50,000 to Tallahassee, he could not clarify how he had expected to raise this sum at such short notice.[13]

Pelton's obfuscation proved a gift to Reed, furnishing plentiful opportunities to demonstrate his wit. When the witness again pleaded forgetfulness, the congressman lamented that he had "given up all hope of convincing you that any of the evidence we are trying to bring out is of any importance." Stenger went to Pelton's aid—so he thought—by commenting that nobody, except perhaps "the gentleman from Maine," would remember the exact words of an encoded telegram two years after receiving it. "I am sure that if I had been engaged in such a transaction," Reed riposted, "I should have recollected something besides what has already been published in the *Tribune*." The Republicans in the audience, having been admonished to refrain from applause, showed their delight by tapping the floor with their feet.[14]

Given that Weed had confessed that he tried to bribe Republican election officials in South Carolina and had implicated Pelton in the scheme, the latter's prevarication only prolonged his agony. Hiscock had to drag the truth out of the witness, but drag it out he did. "The Colonel fairly writhed in his seat," reported the *New York Times*, "as he was driven by the Congressman's questions from one position to another." Forced to admit his role in efforts to bribe election officials, his "blunt confessions were of such astounding frankness as to elicit an audible whisper and commotion . . . among the listeners," wrote Ben Perley Poore, veteran Washington correspondent of the *Boston Morning Journal*.[15]

Pelton's memory was crystal clear, however, when it came to his uncle. Tilden knew nothing about the bribery schemes, he insisted, and had never been shown any of the telegrams that discussed them. In a voice dripping with skepticism, Reed asked the witness if he had expected "to buy a State or two without consulting him?" That was correct, replied Pelton. "After you received a pointed rebuke from your uncle in regard to South Carolina, he allowed you to have the same charge over these matters as before, didn't he?" "Yes, sir." When Reed pressed the witness on his uncle's supposed ignorance of these "wicked" proposals, he pronounced the word "uncle," the *New York Herald* noted, with "satirical unction." After Pelton admitted that he had, in fact, shared the contents of *some* telegrams with Tilden, Reed pounced again. "He never happened to call for any of those wicked ones?" Pelton treated it as a rhetorical question that called for no reply. The session ended, however, with the wretched witness falling into another of Reed's traps. In selecting the Democratic visiting statesmen, the congressman suggested, "I suppose . . . that you sent the best men you have in the party?" "Oh yes, sir," Pelton replied, "that is, well, no—not the best, but as good as any in the party." The room erupted in laughter.[16]

Pelton's abject performance evoked mock sympathy from the *New York Tribune.* It was such a "painful exhibition" that "when he was dismissed there was little or nothing left of him." Disgraced, banished from his uncle's home, and a failure in business, his alcoholism worsened. Tilden threatened to cut off his allowance unless he stopped drinking. The following year Pelton died.[17]

Few Democrats, however, were so cordially disliked by Republicans as the next day's witness, Manton Marble. As wartime editor of the *New York World,* Marble had opposed emancipation and, by condemning conscription in such vehement terms, had tacitly encouraged the New York City draft rioters in July 1863. In May 1864 he was briefly imprisoned, and the *World* temporarily suppressed, after the paper published a proclamation by Lincoln that turned out to be bogus. Marble was the victim of a hoax—by the time he discovered the error, the paper was already on sale—and the other New York editors rallied to his defense. But this show of unity had been strictly a matter of press freedom; it did not make his politics any more palatable to Republicans. During Reconstruction the *World,* under Marble's editorship, vigorously opposed Black suffrage.[18]

A more substantial political figure than either Weed or Pelton, Marble also had a whiff of the ridiculous about him. James Gordon Bennett of the *New York Herald* used to call him "Signor Mantilini Marbilini." Devoid of humor, his pomposity and self-righteousness made him an attractive target for Hiscock and Reed. His ringing defense of Tilden, published in the *New York Sun* and reprinted in pamphlet form, had been a noxious brew of magniloquence, moral rectitude, and inventive abuse. In defending his own conduct after the *Tribune* published the cipher dispatches, he had lashed out at Republicans and paraded his wounded amour propre. Yet the same man who saw himself as the personification of political integrity also, as "Gath" noted, "delight[ed] in secret missions and midnight cabals." Republicans were convinced that the cipher dispatches revealed Marble as a monumental hypocrite. "He dwelled with unction,"

Senator Blaine recalled in his memoirs, "upon the fact that the *absolute trust of Mr. Tilden and his associates in the Presidential contest had been in moral forces.*" Hiscock and Reed now flung those words in his face, sprinkling their questions with sarcastic quotations from his published statements. The audience lapped it up.[19]

Denying any wrongdoing, Marble insisted upon reading aloud telegrams that he had sent to the *Sun* and the *Herald* detailing Republican iniquities in Florida. His orotund voice grew louder as he quoted his own condemnation of the Republicans' "stupendous frauds" and "appalling villainy." But his show of righteous indignation provoked hilarity. When Hiscock objected to Marble continuing in this vein, Reed seized his moment. "No, let him go on. It is a rare privilege to hear him read his productions in his clear ringing tones. He seems to do it with a comfort and enjoyment that it would be cruelty to stop him." When the laughter died down, Marble stumbled again by asking Reed if he preferred to read the dispatch himself. The congressman declined, explaining that he could not possibly do justice to such sentences. As Marble read a second telegram, Reed beat time with his hands, interspersing the performance with mock-serious praise: "That's good! That's very good!" Marble was furious. Hunton did nothing, he later complained to a friend, "to rebuke the buffoon Reed" for his "insolent running commentary."[20]

Marble's protestations of innocence, however, flew in the face of his own telegrams. "Have just received a proposition," he wired Pelton on December 2, 1876, "to hand over . . . decision of Board and certificate of Governor for $200,000." Marble's gloss on these words was that he was merely warning Pelton that the Florida Returning Board was up for sale: "I threw up a danger signal pretty quickly." What did he mean by "danger signal," Reed asked. "I don't think that requires any explanation," replied Marble, who insisted that the proposition came from Returning Board chairman McLin, not from himself. Regardless of who suggested paying McLin, the reply Marble received from New York on December 3—"Proposition too high"—showed that Pelton, far from interpreting the dispatch as a "danger signal," took the scheme seriously.[21]

Confronted with this telegram, as well as with Pelton's statement the previous day that he had indeed sent it, Marble floundered. He did not recognize the words "proposition too high" and suggested that the *Tribune*'s translation was inaccurate. He flippantly suggested that if Pelton had testified otherwise, he was "either fatigued by the eloquence of the gentleman from New York or by the wit of the gentleman from Maine."

Reed pointed out that Pelton had testified to sending the dispatch after the committee had taken a two-hour break. "It is really too hard to saddle one man with both the scapegoat and the fatigue theory." Reed asked for what he considered the correct translation, but Marble "could not remember what the words did mean," a reply that evoked a wave of cynical chortling. Hunton tried to restore decorum by threatening to exclude the audience, forbidding further applause or laughter. He was immediately undermined by Hiscock, however, who, urging spectators to hear the witness in silence, added that "it was rather a case for mourning than for laughter"—a comment that merely evoked more laughter.[22]

Marble appeared to be digging himself into an ever-deepening hole. Shown his telegram of December 3 informing Pelton that the price of the "proposition" had come down to $50,000, he again insisted that he was only relaying information, not endorsing the payment of a bribe. Someone else, namely visiting statesman C. W. Woolley, had engaged in this dirty business. "I entered into no negotiations whatever on the subject," Marble testified. "I will allow no language implying that any plan of bribery was a plan of mine." Hiscock merely had to say, with mock solemnity, "Oh, no, sir; no sir," to set off another wave of laughter. A telegram from E. L. Parris to Henry Havemeyer, sent on December 4, contained the damning words, "Marble says plan sent you Saturday must be acted upon immediately, otherwise unavailing."[23]

Reed asked Marble to explain the reply from Pelton that arrived in Tallahassee that same day, stating: "Proposition accepted if done only once. Better consult with Woolley and act in concert." The dispatch disclosed that Marble and Woolley had been conducting parallel negotiations—the two men detested each other—and that Pelton did not wish to pay the same corrupt official twice. Marble indignantly insisted that this was not the case. He had declined to act with Woolley, and he had not responded to Pelton's telegram. "I did nothing, sir. I threw it on the fire. . . . I intercepted the dispatch and destroyed it." Reed, who had a talent for getting under Marble's skin, asked him, "How could you 'intercept' a dispatch addressed to yourself?" "You can choose any other word that suits you better," the witness snapped. "I don't propose to enter into a criticism of the English language here."[24]

Nobody, of course, could disprove Marble's claim to have ignored and destroyed Pelton's telegram. His own dispatch to Pelton on December 5, however, contradicted it. "Proposition failed," Marble had wired, words indicating that he had indeed been involved in the "proposition." He had never sent such a message, the witness averred; if Pelton had testified to the contrary, he was mistaken. The *Tribune*'s translation was wrong, he explained; it was sheer guesswork. "The words 'proposition failed' belong to the *Tribune,* and not to me." After Democrats applauded and Republicans laughed, Hunton asked Marble if he could be kind enough to give the correct translation of "Bolivia Laura." An expectant silence fell over room as the audience awaited his response. After a lengthy pause came the answer: "I am sorry to say that I can't do it." The anticlimax had the effect of a balloon bursting. "The audience broke forth into a loud, long, hearty laugh," reported the *New York Times,* "and Mr. Marble flushed for the first time during the examination."[25]

The Democrats might well have succeeded in buying McLin's vote, the dispatches revealed, had not Marble and Woolley acted independently of one another. The fact that each man used his own cipher added to the confusion: at a crucial moment in the negotiations, when time was running out, New York replied to Woolley in Marble's code and used Woolley's code in replying to Marble. The delay was fatal. "Time important," Pelton had warned. "Divided counsel may lose all." How right he was.[26]

His ordeal over, Marble complained to a friend that the *New York Tribune* would continue to treat him "as an anvil on which its . . . hammer will be daily employed." Indeed it did. In his attempt to "vindicate his high moral tone," the paper editorialized, Marble claimed that Woolley did all the corrupt bargaining in Florida, yet his refusal to admit that he had wired "proposition failed" rendered his explanation unworthy of belief. Even Tilden loyalist Bigelow, after sitting through Marble's testimony, judged that he "did not do himself much good." According to a sympathetic biographer, "it would seem that [Marble] did in fact carry through the bribe attempt, only to fail." His reputation suffered, his political ambitions evaporated, and Marble never regained his former influence in the Democratic Party.[27]

As Marble endured a pounding from Reed and Hiscock, Tilden was suffering agonies of indecision over whether he ought to testify himself. His nerves, he told Bigelow, "were very much unstrung." Bigelow wrote out a request to testify, but Tilden balked at signing and sending it. The subcommittee had not yet requested him to appear: Should he respond to an invitation or wait to be subpoenaed? Should he appear on his own volition? Should he ask the subcommittee to come to his house? Tilden was, Bigelow observed, the worst procrastinator he had ever encountered.

Hunton made up his mind for him, sending word that he should either volunteer to testify or wait to be subpoenaed; refusing an invitation from the subcommittee was not an option.[28]

Tilden entered the committee room on February 8, 1879, wearing, in the *New York Times*'s cruel words, "the expression that has been habitual to him of recent years, of being in a perpetual stupor." With trembling hands and shuffling gait, he slowly made his way to the table, removed his top hat, and sat down. Tilden was suffering from a cold; the audience, even the committee members seated close by, strained to hear his words. Democratic ward heelers, primed to cheer for him, occupied a good portion of the "uncomfortably thronged" room. Hunton, however, was bent on avoiding the circus-like atmosphere of the previous day's proceedings. He stifled the first outburst of applause and warned that any repetition would prompt him to exclude the public.[29]

The essence of Tilden's testimony, which consumed two and a half hours, was simple: He had been entirely ignorant of the misdeeds of Weed, Pelton, Marble, and others. He had nothing to do with selecting or instructing the Democratic visiting statesmen. He had made no effort to keep track of what they were doing in his name. The idea that these men were his personal emissaries "had no foundation in fact." Tilden had not even known of Weed's presence in South Carolina. He never saw any of the cipher dispatches, or even knew of their existence, until he read them in the *Tribune*. He had been unaware that his nephew had gone to Baltimore to meet Weed until Cooper told him, on November 20, 1876, that he had received a wire from Pelton requesting money. As soon as he found out about this bribery scheme, Tilden "immediately said that no such offer should be entertained; that no negotiations of that nature should be tolerated; that not a cent of money should be furnished for any such purpose; and that Colonel Pelton must be immediately telegraphed to return to New York."[30]

Hiscock and Reed questioned Tilden respectfully but with evident skepticism. It quickly became clear that they would be hard put to catch him in a lie, skilled lawyer that he was. Those very skills also, however, enabled his interlocutors to elicit answers that were evasive and even incredible. Tilden littered his replies with "may have," "might have," "do not think that," and "cannot remember." He did not perjure himself. Whether he told the truth was another matter.[31]

Reed asked Tilden about the protestations of innocence contained in the letter he sent to the *New York Herald* after the scandal of the cipher dispatches first broke. Did the letter not imply that he had been ignorant of Weed's attempted bribery in South Carolina? No, Tilden responded, he had denied knowledge of the *telegrams,* not of the transaction itself. Why had he omitted to mention that Pelton had gone to Baltimore to pursue that transaction? "It was not pertinent." Why had he left out Marble's activities in Florida? "It was not necessary."[32]

Tilden was on shakier ground when Hiscock pressed him on his claim that he had known nothing about the cipher dispatches. Had there not been a constant flow of telegrams to his home at 15 Gramercy Park? "I cannot remember." Did he not know that virtually all the dispatches sent by Weed, Marble, and Woolley had been addressed to his nephew? "I never knew to whom they addressed their dispatches. . . . I do not think that I knew [Pelton] was in any special communication with them." One of Marble's telegrams, however, had been addressed to Tilden's personal secretary, George W. Smith; had Smith shown it to him? "I do not remember anything about it." Hiscock read the telegram and repeated his question. "I may have seen it." Would not the phrase "see my dispatch to Spain" have caught his attention? "Perhaps it would; perhaps it would not." And so on.[33]

The most vulnerable aspect of Tilden's defense concerned his relationship to Pelton. How could he have been so ignorant of his nephew's antics? Why, if Tilden had instructed him to abandon his scheme to bribe the South Carolina Returning Board, did Pelton press on with other bribery proposals despite his uncle's express wishes? And why, after allegedly reprimanding his nephew for what he called "officious meddling," had Tilden continued to place his trust in him?

By Tilden's telling, he had been entirely ignorant of Pelton's activities and made little effort to enquire about what he was up to. Although they had lived in the same house, he explained, they exchanged few words because their paths rarely crossed. Pelton "generally came in after I was abed and asleep, and generally went out before seeing me in the morning." When it came to his alleged reprimand, Tilden was vague about what he actually said to Pelton but, "I have no doubt I expressed impatience." Having expressed his displeasure, "I did not imagine that he would attempt to do anything of that sort again." In any case, he added, Pelton was harmless. "He had no power . . . , he had no command of money."[34]

As to why he had been so indulgent toward this black sheep, continuing to entrust him with important political tasks, Tilden had no convincing explanation. This might have been why he took theatrical umbrage that he should be asked such a question. "You have intruded yourself into my domestic and family relations," he scolded Hiscock. Tilden then sought to change the subject by going on the offensive or, in today's parlance, resorting to "whataboutism." Pelton's actions were wrong, he conceded, but his nephew had merely been attempting to right a far greater wrong: the fact that "the presidency was being taken away from the man who had been elected by the people." Besides, none of the Democratic schemes were carried through, whereas Republican fraud had carried the day. His voice rising, Tilden struck the table with a clenched hand: "I declare before God and my country that . . . the votes and certificates of Florida and Louisiana were bought, and that the presidency was controlled by their purchase."[35]

Asked to substantiate that assertion, however, Tilden struggled. He claimed that McLin testified "that he gave a false certificate," but Hiscock told him he was in error, that McLin had sworn to nothing of the kind. Flustered, Tilden asked his fellow Democrats to back him up by producing the transcript of McLin's testimony, but they declined to go to his rescue and said nothing. Sensing his advantage, Hiscock pressed him to state what evidence of Republican wrongdoing he had possessed at the time Pelton was pursuing his bribery schemes, that is, *before* December 6, 1876. "I had no proof up to that time," he confessed, "no personal information." His entire knowledge, it turned out, had consisted of rumors reported in the newspapers.[36]

Hunton tried to help Tilden by throwing him a softball. "You state your belief that the Returning Boards of one or more States were purchased. . . . Now, it was not sold to the Democratic side, and is it not the conclusion legitimate and proper that if not purchased by the one side it was by the other?" That was a logical inference, Tilden agreed. When Reed objected to the question, Hunton laughingly asked him if he expected the chairman to overrule his own question. That is precisely what he was requesting, Reed replied. Hunton then brought Tilden's examination to a close by ruling out both question and answer. On this lighthearted note, Tilden took his hat and cane and shuffled out of the room.[37]

The verdict on Tilden's testimony split along party lines. Republicans treated his protestations of ignorance with disbelief. The *New York Tribune* wondered how Pelton, after his reprimand from Tilden, could have immediately started negotiating for the purchase of Florida, South Carolina (again), and Oregon. If the DNC had rebuffed his request for money, then he must have had "some other source of supply," implying that the impecunious nephew believed that his wealthy uncle would stump up the cash. The *New York Times* emphasized Tilden's reputation as "an active, keen, vigilant manager of his own affairs." How could Weed, Pelton, or Marble have undertaken to "pay $50,000, $80,000, $100,000, trusting to the result to justify the bargain and secure reimbursement?" Tilden must have known what Pelton was up to, the *Chicago Daily Tribune* concluded.[38]

The Democratic press took Tilden's claim of innocence at face value, although with varying degrees of conviction. In the judgement of the *Boston Globe,* the former candidate emerged "with spotless integrity." The *Louisville Courier-Journal,* edited by Watterson, whose loyalty to Tilden knew no bounds, argued that the hearings had left "not a single stain" on the New Yorker's "honorable reputation." Reid puckishly invited Democrats to match their words with action. If, as they maintained, Tilden had been defrauded of the presidency, and if they were entirely persuaded by his testimony, then "his party cannot refuse him so plain an act of justice as a second nomination."[39]

That, as Reid well knew, was unlikely to happen. Plenty of Democratic newspapers expressed dismay that men so close to Tilden could have acted in such an irresponsible and unrestrained manner, while his professed ignorance of their attempted corruption did him no credit. "Technically and legally," opined the *New York Herald,* Tilden had refuted allegations that he knew about the cipher dispatches and was involved in the bribery schemes. Still, his testimony left a "painful impression that he is a man extremely and culpably tolerant of a grossly immoral transaction in a person very near to him." He showed singular bad judgement, it added, to have retained Pelton as his agent in Washington in early 1877. There, the paper noted, his nephew had "occupied an expensive suite of rooms at a hotel, had with him a corps of assistants, and was in constant and close association with Mr. Tilden." The *Cincinnati Enquirer,* never a Tilden enthusiast, was evidently indulging in heavy-handed irony when its headlines proclaimed, "No stain on his honor, and elevated in the opinion of all candid men. . . . He stands today a citizen of the Republic of whom the Republic may well feel proud."[40]

The committee's three-part report landed with a thud on March 3, 1879. The majority report, signed by all seven Democrats, declared that through "false and fraudulent returns" by the Returning Boards of Louisiana and Florida, those two states, which had actually voted for Tilden, were dishonestly counted for Hayes; that Noyes and Sherman had encouraged those boards in their fraudulent actions; that Republicans in Louisiana had conspired to throw out the Democratic victory in East Feliciana Parish by failing to put up a Republican ticket; and that two of the signatures on Louisiana's electoral certificates had been forged, Kellogg and his private secretary, Clarke, being privy to the forgery. Tilden and not Hayes, it concluded, was "the real choice of a majority of the [presidential] electors."[41]

Potter showed his drafts to Tilden, Marble, and others, soliciting comments and suggestions. Montgomery Blair urged him to make the report sharper and more partisan, telling him that the "object of the enquiry was not, as he put it, to get laws passed to prevent fraud in future, but to arraign the authors and abettors of this fraud at the bar of public opinion . . . [and] to make the question the issue in the coming election." It seems that Potter heeded Blair's advice.[42]

The majority report focused on Louisiana, where Republicans enjoyed the worst reputation for dishonesty. The Republican frauds there, Potter argued, had many strands. They started well before the election with a rigged state census that deliberately overcounted the Black population. They continued with the appointment of partisan registrars who were instructed to turn in a Republican vote that matched the supposed number of adult male Blacks. These "pliant and despicable tools" could "register whom they pleased, and refuse whom they pleased." The frauds developed further after the election with the manufacture of affidavits procured from "ignorant and thoughtless negroes" who falsely alleged Democratic intimidation. They then culminated in a partisan, venal, and illegally constituted Returning Board that "flagrantly and outrageously abused its power" to suppress enough Democratic ballots to create a majority for the Hayes electors. Throughout the postelection phase, the Republican visiting statesmen encouraged the Returning Board in its corrupt work, giving its members to understand that they would be protected from prosecution and rewarded with federal patronage.[43]

Republican allegations of bulldozing were wholly false, Potter declared. For one thing, the Democratic Party had no incentive to engage in such acts, knowing that the Returning Board would seize upon any instances of violence and intimidation to throw out its ballots. Instead, "with the aid of barbecues and music, of promises and conciliation," Democrats persuaded an unprecedented number of Blacks to cast Democratic votes of their own free will. For another thing, much of what Republicans described as "bulldozing" consisted of inflated accounts of personal quarrels, barroom rows, drunken blustering, and "some fellow swaggering or joking in the country store." That Sherman declined an invitation to subpoena witnesses who could testify to intimidation, while more than a dozen witnesses called by Democrats retracted their previous testimony, further discredited the Republican case for rejecting so many polls. In East Feliciana Parish, where Blacks constituted a large majority and where a US Army presence afforded security, "such a state of terrorism as to prevent the casting of one Republican vote . . . was an impossibility."[44]

As for the Sherman letter, Potter admitted that the committee found no positive proof that the then-senator had ever written such a document. The chairman conceded that James Anderson's testimony was not to be trusted because that witness was a "notorious liar and vagabond." Nevertheless, whether written by Sherman or faked by someone else, a Sherman letter had definitely existed; more important, Anderson and Don Weber had *believed* it be genuine and therefore acted upon its promise of reward. Doubts about Anderson's veracity notwithstanding, Potter claimed that reliable testimony from other witnesses confirmed the basic outline of his story: that he and Weber signed false postelection protests alleging Democratic intimidation in the expectation of receiving lucrative patronage positions from a Hayes administration. The absence of Republican ballots in East Feliciana resulted from a conspiracy, aided and perhaps conceived by Anderson, to give the Returning Board a pretext for disallowing the large number of Democratic votes there. "It was this trick in East Feliciana which virtually settled the Presidential contest."[45]

Having submitted the majority report, Potter now faced the difficult and distasteful task of summarizing the hearings of the New York subcommittee. "I am spending the Sabbath," he complained to William C. Whitney, "in digging out the ox of a cipher dispatch report." He was no doubt thinking of Exodus 21:33, which defined the liability of a man who digs a pit and fails to cover it, causing an ox to fall in.[46]

Potter's thin supplemental report (it covered less than a page in the *New York Herald*) bemoaned the fact that Western Union had delivered the bulk of the telegrams to the Morton Committee rather than the Morrison Committee and suggested that Orton, the president of the company, since deceased, may have allowed his Republican sympathies to influence that decision. In any case, it enabled Republicans to abstract the 700-plus dispatches that ended up with the *New York Tribune.* In a backhanded way the report complimented the cunning involved: the Republican-related dispatches appeared innocuous because any that reflected badly on the party had been removed. Moreover, in an effort to "mislead the public," partisans had deliberately left in numerous dispatches so as not to make this cleaning-up operation too obvious. The Republican telegrams that remained, being "disjointed" and detailing "no continuous action," created a trail that led nowhere. The committee's Democrats also paid tribute to the skill of the *Tribune*'s translators. On the crucial question of the bribery schemes, the report condemned the actions of Pelton, Weed, and the other principals as "a gross wrong" that should not be justified or excused. But Tilden, it insisted, was entirely innocent of any knowledge or involvement.[47]

In contrast, the minority report, submitted by Cox, Reed, and Hiscock, placed the cipher dispatches at its front and head; to leave them out, it argued, would be akin to staging *Hamlet* without the prince. Weed and Pelton had, after all, confessed their attempts to bribe Republican election officials. Marble, anxious to maintain his "conspicuously high-toned position," had denied any wrongdoing, but the "burst of contemptuous laughter" that greeted his explanation "Mr. Marble will probably never forget." The only matter in doubt was the extent, if any, of Tilden's own involvement in the bribery schemes. On that question the three Republicans were clear: Tilden knew. They conceded that the glib and canny lawyer had avoided incriminating himself. Nevertheless, "the idea that this penniless man, Mr. Pelton, living in the house and seated at the very table of his wealthy uncle . . . should have conducted negotiations involving such large sums without word or hint to the man most closely interested, or to anybody else, cannot for a moment be entertained by candid men."[48]

The Republicans speculated that in recalling Pelton from Baltimore and chastising his nephew in the presence of Edward Cooper, Tilden was enacting a charade. As he left 15 Gramercy Park to meet Weed in Baltimore, Pelton had told the DNC treasurer to expect a wire requesting money and asked him not to tell Tilden about the impending transaction. But when he received Pelton's telegram, Cooper, purportedly shocked by the amount involved, decided to clear it with the candidate. This was most unwelcome news to Tilden, and he denounced the scheme—not, as he maintained, because it violated his moral code, but because he needed to maintain the fiction that he had no knowledge of Pelton's shady activities. The case for Tilden's innocence might be stronger, the Republicans pointed out, if Pelton had ceased his bribery efforts after this alleged reprimand. But he did not: the machinations in Florida, South Carolina, and

Florida continued for a further sixteen days, "all under the guidance of the resident nephew." Pelton had devised a system, the minority surmised, to keep his uncle "posted as to the doings of his agents, and yet left in a condition to make a general denial." To accept that Pelton's actions were those of an irresponsible fool and that Tilden knew nothing about them would be to insult the intelligence of both men. Tilden would hardly have "center[ed] all his interests in the hands of a fool."[49]

As to the alleged frauds in Louisiana, the Republicans dismissed Anderson's testimony in toto. The Anderson-Weber agreement was clearly a fake—one of a series of bogus documents, including the Sherman letter, designed to "obtain hush-money, either in the form of cash or place." The bulldozing of Republican voters was no fiction: the Black witnesses who swore to Democratic intimidation "perfectly comprehended what they were doing" when they signed their original affidavits. Summoned before the Howe Committee, they had stuck to their guns when cross-examined by Democratic senators "of great ability and legal acumen." This was the "best possible evidence of the intelligence and truth of the witnesses." True, the Potter Committee had found fourteen witnesses who went back on their previous testimony. But the fact that they had denied making those statements in the first place—a demonstrably false position—provided strong evidence that they had been coerced or bribed. Indeed, two of the witnesses whom Democrats had expected to recant, Dula and Swayze, "denounced the efforts at bribery which had been used upon them."[50]

The three Republican committeemen made short shrift of the forged signatures on Louisiana's second set of electoral certificates. The Electoral Commission, they pointed out, had accepted the first set, upon which the signatures were unquestionably genuine, not the second set. That the electors failed to sign separate certificates for president and vice president—making their lists of votes "upon one piece of paper instead of two"—was a trivial error that had no bearing on the outcome of the election in Louisiana.[51]

Many of his contemporaries regarded Ben Butler as thoroughly unreliable when it came to his word, a view shared by some historians. Still, his own separate report offered a remarkably evenhanded analysis. He wasted no time on the Sherman letter, agreeing with the three Republicans that it was a fiction. Unlike the minority report, however, he contended that Packard had a stronger claim to the governorship of Louisiana than Hayes had to the presidency, arguing that the abandonment of the legitimately elected Packard by the illegitimately elected Hayes was legally and morally indefensible. This "plague on both your houses" approach may have reflected the fact that Butler had left the Republican Party but was not yet fully accepted by the Democrats. But the Massachusetts lawyer had always displayed an independent streak, and he employed his forensic skills to follow the evidence wherever it might lead.

In Louisiana, Butler asserted, the Democrats won the election through "force and intimidation," while the Republicans reversed that victory through "fraud and guile." The Democratic Party, he noted, had regularly engaged in "flagrant acts of violence, oppression, and intimidation, accompanied even by murder," so as to render many Republicans fearful for their lives. In 1876 such methods had been mostly confined to a handful of majority Black parishes. Democrats decided, moreover, to desist from "active bulldozing" during the election campaign itself "so as to give no apparent cause to a Returning Board to reject the Democratic vote in these parishes." Republicans, for their part, seeing that no fair election could be held in those parishes, made but a desultory effort to campaign in them, concentrating instead on "collecting evidence of the bulldozing" so that the anticipated Democratic majorities could be disallowed. "What the Republicans lacked of the lion's skin they eked out with the fox's tail!"[52]

Butler had no doubt that a fair election, free of Democratic bulldozing, would have produced a Republican majority: he placed no credence in claims that Blacks in large numbers were voluntarily casting Democratic ballots. It was only right, therefore, that the Returning Board, exercising its lawful authority, rejected most of the polls in the "bulldozed parishes." In the rest of the state, moreover, "where a full campaign was made by both political parties," Packard was the clear winner.[53]

Chairman Wells, however, did not content himself with using the power of the Returning Board to counter the effects of Democratic bulldozing. Throwing out the bulldozed parishes would not elect Hayes, whose vote trailed that of Packard to the extent of giving a majority to at least one of the Tilden electors. Hayes needed every one of Louisiana's electoral votes in order to reach the winning total of 185. "The Returning Board," Butler dryly noted, "was equal to the emergency." It rejected Democratic polls in other parishes, and to justify this action, it needed further protests from supervisors and more affidavits from Republican voters, all of which were duly obtained. It then cast its net more widely still in order to elect three Republican state senators, whose votes would be necessary to elevate outgoing-governor Kellogg to the US Senate. This required "some ingenuity," but more protests and more affidavits did the trick, enabling the Returning Board "to elect some members of the legislature and defeat others." To give a patina of fairness "and not to have it appear too barefaced," the board also threw out a few polls that registered slight Republican majorities. The overall result suited the party's political requirements perfectly. "Everybody Republican was elected whom it was necessary to elect, everybody Democratic defeated whom it was necessary to defeat."[54]

It was a sad commentary on Louisiana politics, Butler observed, that Wells solicited a bribe from his own party to achieve that outcome, with neither he nor the Republicans who recommended paying him off considering the proposed transaction improper. "This inertia of conscience in Louisiana politicians," the New Englander dryly noted, "is a fact to be taken with us whenever we are dealing with their political action." In the event, no money passed hands. Nevertheless, every Republican who played a prominent role in the election, "especially the counting and returning part of it," received a federal office from the Hayes administration. Butler stopped short of endorsing the Democratic charge that these appointments were tantamount to bribery. He found no persuasive evidence that Sherman or any of the other visiting statesmen made any specific promises in this regard. Still, the men who put Louisiana in the Hayes column "all had the hopes and expectations of office . . . as strong as if they had assurances thereof."[55]

With his eye for the absurd, Butler could hardly resist commenting on the Hayes electoral certificates. When Louisiana's presidential electors realized that two of their number, Levisee and Brewster, held federal positions that disqualified them, the men resigned their government posts and were immediately reappointed as electors. Butler could not but admire this "sleight-of-hand performance." Unlike Justice Bradley, however, he considered it more serious than a technical infraction of no consequence. Equally egregious was the forging of Levisee's and Joffrion's signatures on the second set of electoral certificates. Butler ascribed the forgery to Thomas Kelly, Kellogg's messenger, acting with or without (but probably with) the governor's approval. "Anywhere outside of Louisiana politics one would naturally have supposed that the best, easiest, and honestest way of getting a man's signature . . . who lived a few hundred miles off was to send for him," he noted. "But they do things differently there."[56]

When Butler wrote, "far be it from me, humble as I am, to criticize . . . the Electoral Commission," scathing criticisms were sure to follow. This extraconstitutional body, he complained, was charged with arbitrating the presidential dispute but actually did nothing of the kind. Acting in a consistently partisan way, its Republican majority "refused to arbitrate on the justice, law, and facts of the case, but adhered to the technicalities." When confronted with the returns from Louisiana, it accepted them as they stood, ignoring any questions of fraud. The Supreme Court justices who were supposed to provide a ballast of impartiality turned out to be just as partisan as the elected politicians.[57]

Butler trained his heaviest guns on the Republicans who assented to the Wormley House agreement and on Hayes himself for carrying it out. This, indeed, had all along been his main interest in the investigation. The decisions of the Electoral Commission, he alleged, were not decisive in making Hayes president: more important was the pact concluded behind closed doors, both literally and figuratively, between a coterie of Republicans representing Hayes and a group of southern politicians representing Nicholls of Louisiana and Hampton of South Carolina. The former (Matthews, Sherman, Garfield, Foster, and Dennison) agreed that the Republican government in those two states "were to be blotted out" in return for a cessation of the Democratic filibuster in the House and the completion of the electoral count. The latter (Watterson, Levy, Ellis, and Burke) agreed to abandon Tilden's claim to the presidency because "they cared more to get control of their States, and power over the Negroes in them, than they did for the success of the Democratic party in the country."[58]

The extent to which Hayes explicitly authorized this "bargain and sale" remained unclear, Butler conceded, but it was obvious that the president "immediately carried out the arrangements which his friends had made for him." Persuading Chamberlain, the Republican claimant in South Carolina, to step aside proved easy. But eliminating Packard, who refused to surrender office, required more time and more guile. Hayes sent a commission to New Orleans—another body devoid of any constitutional warrant—with instructions to undermine the legally elected governor and legislature and replace it with an illegal state government that had seized power by force. First, the commissioners tried persuasion. When that failed, they employed "open bribery and corruption." Using money from Louisiana's taxpayers and cash from the Louisiana Lottery Company, they sought to induce "these poor colored men who had been elected to the legislature" to transfer their allegiance from Packard to Nicholls "by offers of pay and mileage," with their leaders receiving considerably more.[59]

The denouement of this tawdry scheme came when the commissioners, their efforts at persuasion and bribery unavailing, resorted to threats. Told that the soldiers who afforded them protection were about to be ordered to barracks, the members of the Packard legislature, having remained true to their Republican principles, faced the imminent prospect of being "turned over to their armed foes." Remembering all too clearly previous assassinations and massacres, "they gave up in despair and fear of murder." The US government thereby abandoned the one and only constitutional justification for intervening in the internal affairs of a state—its duty "to repress insurrection and domestic violence." Instead, acting without any legal warrant, it forced Republican legislators to join an insurrectionary government headed by a "mob executive."[60]

If Hayes and his facilitators felt any qualms about claiming Louisiana's electoral votes while destroying its Republican state government, both of them elected by the same voters, they soon shrugged them off. Hayes owed his title to the Returning Board, they reasoned, whereas Nicholls was confirmed by the legislature. But this novel argument was a transparent legal evasion, Butler reasoned, in that "the only returns from which the Nicholls legislature could count him in were the very same . . . returns of votes made by the Returning Board by which Packard was counted in." In fact, given the rule bending that the board engaged in to increase Hayes's vote, Packard had more right to be governor of Louisiana than Hayes had right to be president of the United States.[61]

Butler's conclusions could scarcely be more damning. First, Louisiana's election had been anything but "full, fair, and free." On that basis alone, he argued, Congress should have disallowed the state's electoral votes, as it had done in 1872. Such a decision would have handed the presidency to Tilden. Second, in forswearing his duty to protect a legally elected state government, Hayes had discredited himself. What made his actions "specially reprehensible" was the fact that his "purpose and motive was to carry out a corrupt political 'arrangement,' agreement, and compact on his part, made by his friends with his knowledge and acquiescence and consent." Hayes was president, although "without right and against law." It is hard to fault either Butler's argument or his conclusions. His report bears comparison with the dissent of Justice John Marshall Harlan in *Plessy v. Ferguson* for its truth-telling analysis and prophetic warnings.[62]

Appearing on the last day of the 45th Congress, when the House was in the throes of a conflict over the Army Bill, which the Democrats were refusing to pass, the Potter Committee's report received no debate. The hearings had stretched over so many months, and its findings were so thoroughly anticipated, that the report itself generated little surprise and relatively little comment. The partisan press, of course, drew predictably opposing conclusions. According to the *New York Sun,* the majority report conclusively established that the electoral votes of Florida and Louisiana were wrongly awarded to Hayes. To the *Chicago Daily Tribune,* on the other hand, the majority had relied on the discredited testimony of James Anderson, Agnes Jenks, and E. L. Weber, "whose combined oaths would not convict a starving donkey of robbing a hen-house."[63]

Reading between their lines, however, Democratic editorials betrayed dismay over the outcome of the investigation. The *Sun,* its most enthusiastic promoter, confessed that the inquiry had been undermined almost from the outset by the House's declaration that Hayes's title was unassailable. It wryly acknowledged the *New York Tribune*'s "skillful piece of newspaper enterprise" in publishing the cipher dispatches and the "fair political maneuver of the Republicans" in exploiting them. Other papers revealed their disappointment by the brevity of their comments and the alacrity with which they dropped the subject. In truth, the cipher dispatches had effectively blunted the Democrats' charge of Republican fraud.[64]

As for Tilden, the investigation, far from boosting his chances for renomination, weakened them. The *Sun* acknowledged as much when it stated that the cipher dispatches "may influence the Democracy in the choice of the next candidate for President." Two days later the paper published a lengthy interview with a "moderate opponent of Tilden" who noted that the latter was "wholly unfitted" for the job of chief executive. Tilden, he complained, had "surrounded himself with people whose moral tone was so low that bribery was easy and natural to them." Although he had condemned their acts, Tilden had "not only endured their presence but utilized their abilities."[65]

Behind closed doors, former supporters abandoned Tilden while his longstanding opponents within the party, who were numerous, felt emboldened. Charles Francis Adams, a former Republican who had enthusiastically backed Tilden in 1876, described Pelton as "little better than a circus clown who should not have been permitted to touch the outer boards." The cipher dispatches, he told Bigelow, virtually guaranteed that a Republican would gain the presidency in 1880.[66]

Tilden could afford to lose a few Boston Brahmins. But the opposition of "Honest John" Kelly, the head of Tammany Hall, New York City's Democratic organization, was much more damaging. Tilden and Kelly had been uneasy but effective allies since the downfall of Boss Tweed. In 1878, however, their political rivalry split the party. Tilden's adherents quit Tammany Hall and joined Irving Hall, a hostile faction, thus ensuring the defeat of Kelly's ticket and allowing a Republican to replace Clarkson Potter, who did not stand for reelection, in Congress. The following year Kelly opposed the renomination of Governor Lucius Robinson, Tilden's candidate, and walked out of the Democratic State Convention, taking the Tammany delegates with him. Running for governor in a three-way race, Kelly assailed "sore eyes" Robinson and the "old humbug of Cipher Alley." The Republicans thrashed the divided Democrats; Potter, who ran as Robinson's lieutenant governor, went down with the rest.[67]

The split in Democratic ranks, writes one scholar, "made a shambles of the once-powerful Tilden-led Democratic party of the state." And with confidence in his ability to deliver New York's electoral votes shattered, Tilden's chances of being renominated as the Democrats' presidential candidate evaporated. Writing to Senator Bayard, Samuel Barlow, a wealthy lawyer and staunch Democrat, danced on Tilden's political grave: "The coup de grace was given to Uncle Sammy, last week here. It is almost cruel to kill a dead man, and I have always maintained that he was wholly out of the ring long ago, but he insisted upon squirming, and so, as boys do with snakes which wriggle their tails after actual death, Kelly and his friends put an end to even the semblance of life." Tilden's political career was indeed over. As Butler put it, Tilden stood less chance of being elected president than he did of being struck by lightning.[68]

Republicans could not have hoped for a better outcome. First, the issue of electoral fraud had rebounded against their opponents. As Summers put it, the Potter Committee had found "too little directly implicating Hayes, and too much about Tilden's enterprising nephew." Hayes, in any case, was not on the 1880 Republican ticket, having pledged to serve a single term. Second, the Republican visiting statesmen, whom the Democrats had hoped to discredit, emerged from the investigation with their reputations intact. Sherman, the Democrats' principal target, claimed total vindication. Writing to Noyes, their secondary target, he noted with satisfaction that the committee's report had been greeted with a resounding silence by the Democratic press. "Neither of us should complain of any injurious result from the Potter investigation," he smugly added. "Although it was annoying, . . . I am rather gratified that it occurred." He looked forward to being nominated for president in 1880.[69]

When that nomination instead went to Garfield, Sherman was bitterly disappointed. Nevertheless, the selection of Garfield furnished more evidence that the Potter Committee had utterly failed to make the charge of fraud stick. The second-most prominent of the Republican visiting statesmen as well as a member of the Electoral Commission, Garfield did as much as anyone to secure Louisiana's electoral votes for Hayes. Thomas Hendricks, would have served as vice president had Tilden taken office, assailed the Ohioan in a speech at Indianapolis during the 1880 campaign, which the Democrats reprinted as *Garfield in Louisiana: The Disreputable Part Taken by the Republican Candidate for President in the Great Fraud of 1876*. Speech and pamphlet caused barely a ripple. The election was a squeaker, but Garfield won. Hayes took Tilden's rejection and Garfield's election as a vindication of his own victory in 1876.[70]

In the meantime, like the bad penny that always turns up, a letter from Agnes Jenks arrived for Sherman. Her husband, she reported, had been fired from his position as a messenger at the US Mint in New Orleans. Thomas had already complained to him that the job, which paid ninety dollars a month, was "not quite as lucrative" as that of a "negro door keeper." Stating ingenuously that she had never before asked him for any favors, Agnes asked Sherman to remedy the situation.

The superintendent of the mint, Henry S. Foote, apprised of Sherman's interest in the case, felt compelled to explain to the Treasury secretary why he had discharged Thomas in the first place. He had been pleased to employ Jenks, "knowing him to have been subjected to unjust and cruel harassment at the hands of . . . cruel partisan foes." But notwithstanding "recurring instances of official incapacity," Jenks had sought a promotion, and, when turned down, his wife had sent Foote's deputy an "exceedingly offensive letter, full of coarse and vehement upbraidings." The superintendent continued: "In this letter I was not spared from complaint and obloquy. . . . I found it not a little insulting and disgusting. In a week or two more, I received myself a letter of similar import . . . in which certain menacing language was embodied which would not bear recital here. Under these provocations I deemed it best to release Captain Jenks." Foote was a former governor and former US senator from Mississippi, thus a Republican of no little importance. After Sherman's intervention, however, he restored Jenks to his position. Thomas apologized for his wife's bad behavior.[71]

CONCLUSION

After compiling 3,000 pages of testimony from dozens of witnesses, none of the three reports generated by the Potter Committee could provide definitive answers to two key questions. Did John Sherman write the "Sherman letter"? Did Samuel J. Tilden attempt to buy the presidency?

The one witness who might have answered the first question, Millie Weber, Don Weber's widow, never testified. Although subpoenaed by Cox to appear before the Louisiana subcommittee, she offered her excuses—the children were sick—and failed to appear. E. L. Weber, Millie's brother-in-law, likely advised her not to testify because she would have contradicted his own testimony. Unless she committed perjury, she would have confirmed that she had neither seen the Sherman letter nor heard her husband mention such a document, thereby undermining E. L.'s patently false claim to have found and destroyed it. That the Democrats never subpoenaed Millie lends credence to this supposition.

The Anderson-Weber agreement was almost certainly a fake. James Anderson's letters to Weber, which he produced in evidence, may also have been hoaxes—all of them were "copies." The fact that Anderson produced nothing from Weber's own hand adds to the suspicion that his alleged coconspirator, conveniently dead, had never entered into the conspiracy at all. Weber appears not to have mentioned the Sherman letter to anyone. Anderson first mentioned a "written guarantee" in a letter to Thomas Jenks in June 1877, but he did not connect it to Sherman by name. He made no mention of any "written guarantee" when he met Matthews in Cincinnati, Harlan in New Orleans, or Hayes and Sherman in Washington. In October 1878 he proclaimed that he no longer believed that Sherman ever wrote such a letter but could not explain why he had formerly believed in its existence.

Sherman, of course, denied giving Anderson and Weber any written promise. Yet on his first appearance before the Potter Committee, he failed to state categorically that he had never written the letter that Anderson attributed to him. The tentative nature of his denial—he did not believe he wrote such a letter, but he could not be certain—persuaded many Democrats and some Republicans that he was indeed the author. How could he not remember whether he did or did not write the letter? His qualified denial came across as the kind of perjury-proof statement a careful lawyer would make: it covered the possibility that the document, if it existed, might turn up. Later, it is true, Sherman made a much stronger denial, but by then Agnes Jenks had testified to having faked the letter herself. Whether she did or not, her statement relieved Sherman of the need to hedge his bets. If the letter showed up, he now had a ready explanation for its existence.

On its face, Jenks's account of fabricating the letter seems absurd. If it was her own invention, why was she so anxious to find it? Why did her interest in the letter only take hold after Anderson told her husband about it? One possible explanation is that she and Don Weber concocted the letter in order to satisfy Anderson. This would explain why Weber never had resort to the letter when his life was in danger. It would explain why, writing to Millie Weber in October 1877, Jenks stated that Don Weber "had it in his pocket when he left for Bayou Sara the last time as Mr. Anderson and Captain Jenks went to the boat with him, and they were speaking of it." It might also account for why the letter vanished: knowing it to be valueless, Weber could simply have discarded it. It would not, however, account for Jenks's journey to Donaldsonville in the apparent belief that it might be found among Weber's effects, unless she was simply humoring and hoodwinking Anderson.

Ex-governor Warmoth, who knew all the dark arts of Louisiana politics, speculated that Sherman had indeed penned a note to Anderson and Weber and that Jenks, acting as courier, "put it in her pocket, and had a fictitious letter forged to appease Anderson, while she kept the original to trade with Sherman." The problem with this suggestion is that Jenks confessed to Sherman, in private, that she never possessed such a letter. When the Ohioan publicly denounced her as a blackmailer—challenging her to put up or shut up—she had nothing to produce. The conclusion is inescapable that Jenks's public testimony was as trustworthy as Anderson's—that is to say, not at all.[1]

And yet, a few scraps of evidence hint at the existence of the Sherman letter as an authentic document. We know that Anderson had a brief conversation with the senator in Moreau's restaurant. Of what passed between them we can never be certain—it was Anderson's word against Sherman's—but it is a fair bet that the supervisor asked the senator's assurance that he could count on some kind of federal employment if he stuck to his protest. Why else would Anderson seek him out? Sherman all but admitted giving assurances to Republicans risking life and limb to document Democratic bulldozing. He confessed, too, that if such men had asked for his assurance in writing, he might well have given it.

Then there are two somewhat cryptic statements by Jenks in her private letters to Sherman (addressed to Sherman's wife for the purpose of "plausible deniability"). Writing on July 9, 1878, Jenks called Sherman's attention "to the letter to Anderson and Weber saying, 'your note of even date.' If in the duplicate I sent to [Cecilia Sherman] I said 'yours of evening date' it was a mistake on my part." Her use of the word "duplicate" is striking. It implies that there *was* an original, although it fails to clarify whether that original was a genuine note from him or her own fabrication. Writing to Sherman six months later, she claimed that Michael Hahn, the state registrar of voters in 1876, "also wanted a *written* guarantee, and it is fortunate he did not get one." This statement suggests that Anderson (the crucial word here is "also") *did* ask for a written guarantee. If true, Jenks's assertion throws doubt on Sherman's denial that he never received such a request. It might also imply that Jenks, the messenger, intercepted the note to Sherman and, as she claimed in her testimony, decided not to deliver it and fabricated a false reply.[2]

Samuel Shellabarger, Sherman's private attorney, seemed to be in two minds about the letter's authenticity. In July 1878 he reported to his client that Anderson's attorney, J. R. Sypher, "expects to prove by several witnesses . . . that they saw your letter to Weber and Anderson." He quickly added that he had "no apprehension about it." Yet the tone of the letter betrays the opposite, and the phrase "your letter," without any qualifying adjective, is striking. It is worth adding that public denials of wrongdoing by politicians were—still are—more akin to Houdini-style exhibitions of escapology than evidence of the truth. These men were experienced lawyers who knew how to put up a good defense and how to appeal to a jury. Garfield's evasions during the Crédit Mobilier scandal and Blaine's defense of his conduct when the "Mulligan letters" came to light illustrate that what matters most is putting on a convincing performance. Few Republicans were naïve enough to take Sherman's denial at face value. As one of Sherman's admirers wrote to him, Anderson's testimony could not harm the Ohioan because "you only promised (if the letter is genuine) to protect him for doing his official duty."[3]

Still, the weight of evidence points to the conclusion that Sherman never wrote such a letter. No original ever materialized: the various "copies" were therefore worthless. True, some witnesses testified that Anderson had waved a document at them, but he never stated that it came from Sherman. The only witness who claimed to have read the letter, J. Hale Sypher, failed to mention it to anyone save his brother—but not to the brother who happened to be Anderson's attorney. Sypher's claim that he did not know that this brother was representing Anderson was so absurd as to render his testimony worthless.

If the provenance of the Sherman letter remains doubtful, one thing can be stated with certainty about the aftermath of the 1876 election: there were many shady transactions (and attempted transactions) that the Potter Committee never uncovered.

General Lew Wallace, one of the Republican visiting statesmen in Florida, admitted to his wife that he was appalled by what he encountered in that state:

> It is terrible the extent to which all classes go in their determination to win. Conscience offers no restraint. Nothing is so common as resort to perjury, unless it is violence—in short, I do not know whom to believe. . . . Money and intimidation can obtain the oath of white men as well as black to any required statement. A ton of affidavits could be carted into the statehouse tomorrow, and not a word of truth in them. . . . If we win, our methods are subject to impeachment for possible fraud. If the enemy win, it is the same thing exactly.

He had done his best, Wallace hastened to add, "to restrain our friends, some of whom are moved to carry the end by means resorted to by the opposition." Still, whether the visiting statesmen in Florida and Louisiana engaged in such means themselves, they provided political protection for local Republicans who did.[4]

Promises of patronage were the principal incentives for Republican election officials to swing the returns in favor of their party. But there is also evidence, albeit scanty, that money changed hands. Shortly after arriving in New Orleans, Illinois Republican C. B. Farwell informed William Henry Smith, a close friend of Hayes, that he was confident that the

Returning Board would place Louisiana in the Republican column. That confidence, Hayes biographer Ari Hoogenboom has suggested, "most likely stemmed from expenditures he made out of his own well-lined pocket." A year later Smith reminded the president that "in all delicate and important matters last year," Farwell's wealth "supplied the means when no other could be reached." Farwell also helped Kellogg secure a loan of $20,000 from the Union National Bank of Chicago shortly before the election. Kellogg, of course, denied using that money for corrupt purposes but admitted spending some of it on election expenses, a category that could cover a multitude of sins. He balked at the suggestion that he paid Louis Kenner, a member of the Returning Board, $5,000 but conceded that Kenner was reluctant to sign the board's report because he feared that he would suffer financially. Sherman certainly knew that Kenner's vote was for sale—and if Sherman knew, so did Kellogg.[5]

In short, there was much that Republicans wished to keep outside the public domain, and, in order to keep their deeds hidden, some made sure that they did *not* appear before congressional committees. Joseph R. West, for example, Louisiana's US senator during the electoral crisis, had been deeply involved in the Texas and Pacific Railway scheme, both as an incorporator of the company and as chairman of the Senate Railroad Committee. If West were called upon to testify, Agnes Jenks told Sherman, it "would not be pleasant for him." He never did testify. Grenville Dodge, former Republican congressman, famed railway engineer, and lobbyist for the Texas and Pacific Railway, absented himself from Washington when he learned that Congress was investigating the election. The prospect of being examined, he confessed to William Chandler, filled him with alarm. "The truth is that I feel that my knowledge of events that transpired after the election is so important that I do not care to run the gauntlet of an Investigating Committee." Democrats, of course, had their own dirty linen that they had no wish to air.[6]

The full extent of Democratic efforts to bribe Republican election officials is impossible to establish. The archived Tilden Papers were ruthlessly weeded by John Bigelow, Tilden's associate and biographer, to exclude anything and everything that might reflect poorly on him. Yet one missive that escaped Bigelow's pruning shears suggests that Pelton was not the only member of the Democrat's New York campaign team to have dabbled in attempted bribery. Writing to Tilden after the investigation had ended, A. M. Gibson claimed that Henry Havemeyer, the DNC's treasurer, and William C. Whitney, New York's corporation counsel, possessed a good deal of information that never became public because neither man testified before the Potter Committee. Their nonappearance was no accident, he added: powerful friends ensured that they were not summoned. According to Gibson, Whitelaw Reid "kept Whitney's name out of the *Tribune* after it was discovered that he had gone with Pelton to Baltimore." That Pelton, Havemeyer, and Whitney should have acted in concert is entirely plausible. Along with New York mayor Edward Cooper and Florida visiting statesman E. L. Parris, the trio were founding members of the Young Men's Democratic Club and were accustomed to working together. They were also close political associates of Tilden.[7]

The question of Tilden's own knowledge of Pelton's bribery schemes will never receive a definitive answer. His own denials, backed up by Weed, Marble, and Pelton, cannot be disproved. According to his testimony, Tilden's ignorance extended not only to the cipher dispatches but also to everything else that took place after the campaign. He knew nothing about the activities of the DNC, the selection of the visiting statesmen, or the doings of these men in Florida, Louisiana, South Carolina, and Oregon. And of the comings and goings of his nephew, who lived in his house, he was oblivious and, apparently, uninterested.

Circumstantial evidence and common sense, however, point to a different conclusion. Tilden was, by universal consent, a master of detail—the very opposite of the hands-off leader who remains above the fray. "He employed subordinates," writes his biographer, "but found it difficult to delegate authority, preferring to make all decisions himself." As candidate for the governorship of New York, he was in constant communication with the chairman of the state committee; he analyzed the "returns of his agents in all parts of the State with the mathematical precision of a census taker." In 1876, "with few aides," Tilden "outlined, organized, and financed" his campaign, directing the canvass with close attention to particulars.[8]

That Tilden could have been so uninformed and uninvolved about what his longtime political associates were doing on his behalf after the election defies belief. Had these schemes succeeded and secured him the presidency, his lieutenants could hardly have kept him in ignorance of the means they had employed. Weed, Marble, Woolley, and the others assumed that Pelton was acting for Tilden; Pelton acted as if money for bribes could easily be obtained. Whitney, Havemeyer, and Cooper, be it noted, were wealthy businessmen possessed of deep pockets. If his agents acted as if they had no fear of reprimand, they must have assumed that they had their candidate's tacit consent.

An entry in Bigelow's private diary, written on November 17, 1878, appears to furnish clear evidence that Tilden was indeed ignorant of Pelton's bribery schemes. The *New York Tribune*'s revelations, Bigelow recorded, came to Tilden like "a clap of thunder out of a clear sky. He was very indignant that . . . the existence of such compromising communications should have been kept from him for so long." Seemingly furious over Pelton's conduct, Tilden emphatically stated that his nephew "shall never live under the same roof again with him."[9]

But Tilden's comments to Bigelow cannot be accepted at face value. According to his own testimony, as well as that of Weed and Pelton, Tilden learned of the South Carolina bribery scheme on November 20, 1876, when he allegedly rebuked his nephew upon his return from Baltimore. Yet Pelton continued to pursue bribery schemes until December 6, acting as if the scolding by his uncle had never taken place. Pelton's role in the attempted purchase of a presidential elector in Oregon came to light in February 1877, during the hearings of the Morton Committee, but Tilden continued to employ his nephew as his principal representative in Washington. Conclusion: Tilden's anger with Pelton in November 1878 was either feigned for the benefit of Bigelow or was an expression of chagrin at having been found out. Tilden explained that he had kept Pelton on after November 20 because his nephew lacked the means to pay bribes and could do no further mischief. "He had no command of money. . . . He was not able to do anything without the concurrence of other men." But Pelton, in his own testimony, stated that he had "charge of money matters during the campaign," that although he answered to the members of the DNC, he could spend money "without any official action on their part."[10]

The Potter hearings shined an unflattering spotlight on the spoils system. A growing number of politicians in both parties recognized that the system needed reforming or even abolishing. To politicians, it had become an insufferable burden, devouring their time and energy. "I am thoroughly disgusted," Garfield complained to his diary in 1877, "with the pressure for office which knows no limits of modesty or self-restraint." More important, the system had a baleful effect on the federal civil service. The appointment of party loyalists on the basis of their political services entailed waste, inefficiency, and downright absurdity. The testimony of Florida Republican L. G. Dennis provides a typical example. Promised employment by visiting statesman E. F. Noyes, Dennis recounted how this had been fulfilled. He accepted an appointment from Hayes, he testified, but "I do not know the designation of it; I do not know what my rank was. I was connected with the Secret Service, but not on secret service." Quitting after two months, he accepted a position in the Architect's Office, although he had no knowledge of architecture. "I had no specific duty," he told Hunton. "I don't remember that I ever did anything."[11]

Advocates of civil-service reform proposed a merit system that would prevent federal employees from being appointed or removed on the basis of their political allegiance and activities. They also wished to ban the practice of having federal employees pay political "assessments" (contributions to party funds) in order to retain their positions. In 1872 the Liberal Republicans, in revolt against the Grant administration, made civil-service reform a key issue. In 1876, having drifted back to the Republican Party, former Liberals like Cox and Schurz pressed Hayes to take up the cause.[12]

Hayes posed as a civil-service reformer. He fancied himself an opponent of appointing "unfit men on partisan or personal grounds." He named arch-reformer Schurz his secretary of the interior. Once in office, Hayes issued an executive order prohibiting the collection of political "assessments" and forbidding civil servants from taking part in the "management of political organizations, caucuses, conventions, or electoral campaigns."[13]

Yet rather like Saint Augustine, who beseeched the Lord, "make me chaste, but not yet," Hayes found the spoils system too politically useful to abandon just yet. On April 22, 1877, he told his diary: "We must limit and narrow the area of patronage. We must diminish the evils of office-seeking. We must stop interference of federal officials with elections." Yet these were precisely the practices that had proved so useful, indeed essential, to his gaining the presidency.[14]

In practice, Garfield complained, Hayes's appointments were "wretched": the president had given jobs to "friends and friends of friends, removing worthy men for no reason." Moreover, the visiting statesmen and the MacVeagh commission had made liberal promises to Louisiana's Republicans. Hayes employed federal patronage to reward and silence the officials who had worked so hard to put him in the White House. In Louisiana alone, fifty-eight Republicans who had been involved in the election received federal positions, as did most of the visiting statesmen. The members of the Returning Board, the clerks who worked for the board, the election supervisors, and ousted state officials all received patronage positions. Hayes had pledged to cushion the "really good men involved" from the consequences of losing state power. But as Butler noted, the president actually appointed "every rascal, or some relative of every rascal, who had anything to do with the fraudulent returns—alleged fraudulent returns—to some office." When Butler examined Thomas H. C. Smith, he elicited the admission, "Nearly all the appointments . . . that were made when I was appointments clerk [at the Treasury Department] were made for political reasons."[15]

To Democrats, Hayes's political appointments were tantamount to bribes or the payment of hush money—a means of encouraging questionable actions and ensuring that the perpetrators held their silence. Given the fact that the Democratic Party had not controlled the federal government since 1861, such complaints might be dismissed as sour grapes. But that did not invalidate the charge. As historian Allan Nevins puts it, some of Hayes's appointments "were plainly a reward for corrupt acts." It took the murder of President Garfield by an embittered office seeker to prod Congress into taking the first steps toward creating a nonpartisan civil service.[16]

Despite their best efforts, the Democrats on the Potter Committee failed to discredit Republican allegations of bulldozing in the run-up to the 1876 election. Democrats had long charged that the production of affidavits alleging violence and intimidation amounted to a systematic effort to bend the truth or, worse, manufacture lies. They portrayed the witnesses, the vast majority of them unlettered Blacks from the country parishes, as venal, ignorant, and easily manipulated. They charged that Republican officials coached the witnesses and put words into their mouths. Historian Ella Lonn endorsed these complaints, writing in 1917 that the "evidence of dazed, ignorant Negroes, summoned from the fields for the first time in their lives to a crowded city, marched past cordons of police, and placed before a corps of stenographers, should not be overrated." Without a doubt, the men who took down the witness statements did their best to make them as strong as possible. As one of the scribes, Massachusetts-born Thomas H. Noland, put it, "We would say that he 'knew' of so and so, instead of saying that he 'heard.'"[17]

But were witnesses coached to the extent that they swore to things about which they had no knowledge or knew to be false? A rough test of the affidavits' veracity can be made by examining the same witnesses' verbal testimony when they appeared before two congressional committees, one from the Democratic-controlled House, the other from the Republican-controlled Senate, that arrived in Louisiana in mid-December 1876. Reading their testimony, one is impressed by the firmness with which they held to their stories under fierce questioning from Democrats who were skilled lawyers.[18]

These witnesses provided their evidence, moreover, despite the possibility of Democratic retaliation. J. P. Harris, in charge of the room in the Custom House where the affidavits were prepared, recalled, "where parties expected to return [to their home parishes], they seemed to be afraid to tell the truth." James Law of East Feliciana begged Harris not to let his affidavit be seen by the Democrats, otherwise "he would not live forty-eight hours." Former parish judge C. B. Wheeler of Morehouse felt especially apprehensive. His affidavit affirmed charges of violence and intimidation that he had previously denied in a November 11 sworn statement "requested" of him by local Democrats. Reluctant to name names, he explained, "I have to live in the country . . . and I think I have already sealed my fate by the affidavit I have made out."[19]

Although exaggerated regarding some parishes, the evidence from the five bulldozed parishes, related by dozens of witnesses to the Morrison and Howe Committees in the winter of 1876–77, was overwhelming. Of course, Anderson's testimony and that of E. L. Weber proved worthless. It turned out that the Blacks from the Feliciana parishes who recanted their previous testimony had been pressured and bribed. The elections of 1878 triggered a Senate investigation that documented bulldozing even more blatant and widespread than in 1876.

For Louisiana's Republicans, however, the failure of the Potter investigation to negate that evidence brought no comfort. The nation was inured to southern-atrocity stories ("waving the bloody shirt") and had become cynical about them. "General Butler's committee has invited all the soreheads in the South to come to Washington and exhibit their wounds," sneered the *New York Tribune*. "And they are coming in platoons, . . . all boasting of their services to the party, their lies, their tricks, and their rascalities, and all complaining that they have not been paid for their work." Even if the accounts of bulldozing were true—and Hayes and his supporters supposed that they were—few Republicans advocated military intervention to counteract the practice.[20]

Already in bad odor, Louisiana's Republicans emerged from the enquiry with an even worse reputation for intrigue, incompetence, mendacity, cravenness, and venality. "Their manners and morals, and the stories they tell of each other, read like a chapter of jail-yard gossip," commented one paper. To the *New York Times,* the hearings provided yet another illustration "of the utter depravity of Louisiana politics." The *New York Herald,* perhaps, offered the harshest of the many harsh verdicts. The state's Republican leaders "were men, as they themselves have shown, to whom perjury was a joke, to whom the sanctity of an election was a laughing matter, who would not be believed in any court whatever. . . . They turn out to be perjurers, thieves, murderers, highwaymen, political tricksters of the basest and most unblushing kind, traders in votes who had not, it seems, even the poor merit of fidelity to their own party, for they played only for their own hands." The most imaginative verdict came from the *New York World,* which described the "regular patent duplex back-action India-rubber conscience" of the typical Louisiana witness.[21]

Potter's investigation did nothing to enhance Democratic prospects in the 1880 presidential election, which Garfield won. It did, however, strengthen the Democrats' stranglehold on the South. Indeed, southern Democrats emerged as the main beneficiaries—arguably the *only* beneficiaries—of the Compromise of 1877. Having ended military intervention and liquidated the last Republican state governments, they ensured that every subsequent election produced Democratic governors and Democratic legislatures. Ignoring their pledges to respect the Civil War amendments, they bulldozed without restraint and eventually obliterated the region's Republican Party by disfranchising Black voters en masse. They even retained the extra congressional seats accorded the South after emancipation, notwithstanding the fact that Section 2 of the Fourteenth Amendment tied representation in Congress to a state's voting population. That section became a dead letter. So too did Section 1, the "equal protection" clause, insofar as it applied to Black Americans.

Stalwarts like Senator Blaine and Chandler condemned Hayes's abandonment of Packard in Louisiana as a dishonorable betrayal. The party as a whole, however, had little appetite for resurrecting the policy of using the military to police southern elections and prop up Republican governments. Garfield, Sherman, and the other visiting statesmen had insisted that local Republicans "do their duty"; they gave them every reason to believe that a Hayes administration would recognize Packard and the legislature elected with him. Once Hayes had been inaugurated, however, they had few qualms about jettisoning them. "Cannot the South Carolina ulcer and the Louisiana ulcer be cleansed?" one of Garfield's closest friends asked him. In excising those ulcers, Hayes carried out one of the most brutal acts of political surgery in American history.[22]

Sherman, Garfield, and the other visiting statesmen who backed Hayes's southern policy quickly adapted their consciences to necessity and ambition. Given his imminent appointment as secretary of the Treasury, Sherman quickly fell into line. He could give a "bloody shirt" speech to rival Blaine, but in between elections he busied himself with his two abiding interests: restoring the dollar to the gold standard and plotting a pathway to the White House. Garfield, a more sensitive man, was deeply troubled by Hayes's course and soon concluded that the new policy had failed. But his public defense of it and personal loyalty to Hayes helped him secure the Republican nomination in 1880 (thereby embittering Sherman, who had seen himself as Hayes's natural successor).

Hayes himself never regretted cutting loose the Republicans who had delivered him Louisiana and South Carolina. He told himself that in dispensing with Packard and Chamberlain, he was ending "bayonet rule." He told former congressman Frank Morey of Louisiana, "under that policy we had lost the State of New York and had become weaker generally in the country." With staggering naïveté, he described his goal as wiping out the "color line," abolishing sectionalism, and bringing the Civil War's disturbed aftermath to a peaceful conclusion. Stung by the charge of betrayal, Hayes told himself that the Republican Party in the South was already moribund when he took office. And, he claimed, he had done his best by the "tried and true Republicans" who had lost power there. "The possible support which can lawfully be extended to them was their appointment to office."[23]

Federal patronage, however, stretched only so far. Moreover, Hayes reduced the number of jobs available to Republicans by awarding important federal positions to Democrats in his futile quest to attract white southerners to the Republican Party. Worse, by appointing David Key, a Democrat, as postmaster general, he facilitated the ousting of Republicans from about a third of the nation's postmasterships. "I shall not forget my duty to the staunch Republicans," Hayes piously assured one of his friends. For the mass of southern Republicans, however, there was no succor and no protection—only oppression and persecution. For Don Weber, James Law, T. W. Dalton, and many others, Democratic rule brought premature and violent death.[24]

In his memoirs, published in 1893 shortly before his death, Butler made short shrift of the Hayes administration. "I took no part in the proceedings of the Republican party in seating Hayes, and had nothing to do with what I believed then and still believe was a wrong to the country in debasing the elective franchise." He made no mention of his service on the Potter Committee. By then the investigation in which he played such a prominent part had faded into obscurity. If, by exposing Democratic bulldozing and Republicans frauds, it had prompted Congress to enact prophylactic legislation to ensure free and fair elections, as Potter once hoped it might, the investigation would have had a salutary effect. But it did nothing of the kind.[25]

Democrats condemned the Republican frauds of 1876 but did not hesitate to engage in frauds themselves. Indeed, once they controlled the South's election machinery—they retained that control for one hundred years—they routinely "counted out" Republicans, Populists, and even rivals within their own party. In the North, too, electoral fraud was rampant, practiced by Democrats and Republicans alike. As for political violence, southern Democrats continued to employ it, and Republicans devised no effective remedy against it. Congressional investigations amassed testimony from victims, but they led nowhere. Federal prosecutions under the Enforcement Acts produced acquittals or, in the case of guilty verdicts, trifling sentences.[26]

In 1879, having won control of the Senate and increased their majority in the House—partly due to bulldozing in Louisiana and South Carolina—congressional Democrats made repeated attempts to prohibit the deployment of troops and the appointment of federal marshals and deputy marshals for the purpose of ensuring peace at the polling places. They even held up funding for the army itself. Hayes used his veto to block these proposals, insisting that the national government must retain the power to safeguard federal elections. His strategic decision to abjure military intervention in the South, however, enabled Democrats to achieve in practice what they failed to achieve through legislation. In 1894, moreover, a Democratic Congress repealed the Enforcements Acts in toto, removing one of the last deterrents to the mass disfranchisement of southern Blacks, a process that was completed over the next ten years.[27]

Potter's botched investigation invited much satirical commentary, some of it deserved. It certainly had elements of farce, or opéra bouffe. The Democrats' first witness, the "carpetbagger" Anderson, turned out to be an entertaining but unprincipled liar: it is hard to muster much sympathy for him. But the testimony of the southern "scalawags," which amused and disgusted in equal proportion, disclosed a serious condition. As Chandler advised Hayes, these Republicans "have no future in their states; all they can (selfishly) hope for is what consideration and patronage the administration may give them." But Hayes abandoned and betrayed them—the very people who had risked their lives to put him in the White House.[28]

One must therefore empathize with the fabulist Agnes Jenks, the mendacious E. L. Weber, and the Black witnesses who committed perjury in repudiating their previous testimony. The investigation failed utterly in its stated purpose, but it did shine a light on a critical moment in American history. "What were we?" Jenks asked a reporter from the *New Orleans Daily Democrat*. "We were the ship of state when those pirates—the MacVeagh-Harlan statesmen—boarded it. You were the foreign port. They got on board our vessel, put us in irons, and then sailed our ship of state into yours, the foreign port, and delivered us over in bondage."[29]

NOTES

INTRODUCTION

1. *New York Sun,* May 14, 1878; *New Orleans Daily Picayune,* February 26, 1879.

2. Woodward, *Reunion and Reaction,* 33.

3. *New York Sun,* June 18, 22, 1878. The "Burchard Resolution" stated that the 45th Congress had no authority to question the decision of the 44th Congress in recognizing Hayes's title to the presidency.

4. Summers, *Era of Good Stealings,* 298; Tansill, *Congressional Career of Thomas Francis Bayard,* 214.

5. *New York Herald,* June 7, 1878.

6. US Congress, House [hereafter US House], *Presidential Election Investigation,* 1:886.

7. US House, *Presidential Election Investigation,* 1:1326.

8. *Cincinnati Enquirer,* June 15, 1878.

9. US House, *Investigation of Alleged Electoral Frauds,* 38.

CHAPTER 1

1. *National Republican* (Washington, DC), June 5, 1878; James E. Anderson to John Leet, September 1, 1876, US House, *Presidential Election Investigation,* 1:950; Thomas S. Lyons testimony, ibid., 3:82–83.

2. US House, *Presidential Election Investigation,* 1:609, 684, 3:228–29. The falling out reflected the faction fight that split the state Republican Party in 1871 between supporters of Governor Henry Clay Warmoth and supporters of the "Custom House faction." The brothers conducted their feud in their respective papers, the *Dunn Leader* (E. L. Weber) and the *Semi-Weekly Republican* (D. A. Weber), both published in St. Francisville, Louisiana. Copies of the former have not survived, but see *Semi-Weekly Republican,* March 26, April 12, September 14, 17, 24, October 8, 1872.

3. US Congress, Senate [hereafter, US Senate], *Vote for Electors in Louisiana,* 155–64.

4. D. J. M. A. Jewett to Supervisor of Assumption Parish, September 25, 1876, US House, *Recent Election in Louisiana,* 1:5.

5. US Senate, *Testimony of James E. Anderson,* 1–2, 52; list of supervisors, US House, *Recent Election in Louisiana: Testimony,* 3:633–35.

6. *Clinton (LA) Patriot-Democrat,* July 30, 1875.

7. Thompson, *Clinton, Louisiana,* 167–71; *New Orleans Daily Picayune,* August 2, 11, October 2, 1874; *New Orleans Bulletin,* October 16, 1875.

8. Thompson, *Clinton, Louisiana,* 135–43; *New Orleans Daily Picayune,* August 2, 11, 1875; *New Orleans Bulletin,* October 16, 29, 1875; US House, *Recent Election in Louisiana: Testimony,* 3:246–49, 277, 281–82, 299, 353, 375–88, 394–402, 413–24, 455, 459–60.

9. Thompson, *Clinton, Louisiana,* 172–82; William Hansbury testimony, US House, *Recent Election in Louisiana: Testimony,* 3:286. See also Nelson Barton, Wesley Smith, Solomon Johnson, John C. Reilly, Resin Brown, and Bruce Pipes testimony, ibid., 314, 319–22, 347, 351, 409, 451.

10. *New Orleans Republican,* January 11, 1877; Anthony Wilson, James Law, E. A. Rigby, Monroe Meyers, and Aaron McKenzie testimony, US House, *Recent Election in Louisiana: Testimony,* 3:447, 469–70, 493–98.

11. *New Orleans Republican,* January 11, 1877; D. C. Hardee testimony, US House, *Recent Election in Louisiana: Testimony,* 3:373.

12. James De Grey and Law testimony, US House, *Recent Election in Louisiana: Testimony,* 3:465–68. Law's name appears at various times as "Law," "Laws," and "Lawes."

13. US House, *Recent Election in Louisiana: Testimony,* 3:471–72.

14. *New Orleans Daily Picayune,* January 29, 1876; Thomas Hewes testimony, US House, *Recent Election in Louisiana: Testimony,* 3:142–43; Julius Green, J. W. Dederick, Robert J. Hewlett, D. A. Weber, and W. S. D. Hamilton testimony, US Senate, *Louisiana in 1876,* 3:2387–88, 2462, 2531–35, 2566–67, 2684–85; John S. Dula testimony, US House, *Presidential Election Investigation,* 3:334–39, 356–61; Gen. C. C. Augur to Capt. G. M. Bascom, May 2, 1876; Bascom to Augur, May 2, 1876; Asst. Adjutant General O. D. Greene to Bascom, May 4, 1876; and P. G. A. Kaufman and Dederick testimony, US House, *Alleged Outrages in West Feliciana Parish,* 737–38, 759–62.

15. Statement of H. S. Perkins, May 13, 1876; and statement of Ron Johnson, May 13, 1876, Kellogg Papers; *New Orleans Daily Picayune,* May 18, 1876; W. W. Leake, H. S. Perkins, and Randolph Johnson testimony; C. C. Augur to G. M. Bascom, May 16, 1876; Bascom to O. D. Greene, May 16, 1876; and Bascom to Greene, May 17, 1876, US House, *Alleged Outrages in West Feliciana Parish,* 730, 741–46; Weber, Jefferson Carter, and J. B. Sims testimony, US Senate, *Louisiana in 1876,* 3:2572–74, 2635–38, 2640, 2664–65. According to Leake, the identities of the men who killed Aaronson were never discovered.

16. J. R. Watson and J. W. Armstead testimony, US Senate, *Louisiana in 1876,* 3:2373–75, 2434–35; Milton Jones testimony, US House, *Presidential Election Investigation,* 3:400; E. L. Weber to Kellogg, April 10, 1876; and D. A. Weber to Kellogg, July 15, 1876, Kellogg Papers.

17. L. T. Cotton testimony, US Senate, *Louisiana in 1876,* 3:2419–26.

18. Riley Norfliss, Thomas Stewart, Isaac Vessell, Daniel Johnson, John B. Rich-

ardson, Weber, G. M. Bascom, and M. F. Jamar testimony; Bascom to John R. Brooke, July 13, 1876; Jamar to Bascom, July 13, 1876; statement of Benjamin Clark, July 5, 1876; and statement of Isaac Vessell, July 26, 1876, US Senate, *Louisiana in 1876,* 3:2494–96, 2507–12, 2547–48, 2554–55, 2572, 2595–16, 2616–32; Benjamin Clark, affidavit, July 22, 1876, US House, *Recent Election in Louisiana: Testimony,* 3:217.

19. Wilkie, *Creating Freedom,* 30–31; Robert Brooks testimony, US Senate, *Louisiana in 1876,* 3:2643.

20. *New Orleans Daily Picayune,* January 29, 1876; and I. W. Dederick et al., "Report of Sub-committee of the Executive Committee of the Property-Holders, Protective Union West Feliciana," US House, *Alleged Outrages in West Feliciana Parish,* 766–68; D. A. Weber testimony, US Senate, *Louisiana in 1876,* 3:2565–68.

21. Anderson to C. C. Antoine, September 3, 1876, US Senate, *Testimony of James E. Anderson,* 109–10.

22. Anderson to Weber, September 10, 1876, US House, *Presidential Election Investigation:* 27.

23. D. J. Wedge, De Grey, and Henry Marston testimony, US House, *Recent Election in Louisiana,* 3:256, 416–17, 443–44.

24. Benjamin H. Rogers and William S. Davies testimony, US House, *Recent Election in Louisiana,* 3:242, 486–88.

25. James Lewis testimony, US House, *Recent Election in Louisiana,* 2:633.

26. J. P. Harris testimony, US House, *Recent Election in Louisiana,* 2:300–301; Thomas S. Lyons et al. to I. W. Patton, October 26, 1876, US Senate, *Electoral Vote of Louisiana,* 339–40.

27. Harris testimony, US House, *Recent Election in Louisiana: Testimony,* 2:301; Law testimony, US Senate, *Louisiana in 1876,* 3:470.

28. Harris testimony, US House, *Recent Election in Louisiana: Testimony,* 2:309; US Senate, *Testimony of James E. Anderson,* 59.

29. Lewis testimony, US House, *Recent Election in Louisiana: Testimony,* 2:632–34.

30. Lewis and Reilly testimony, US House, *Recent Election in Louisiana,* 2:632, 3:352. In addition to Packard, the team of speakers included two former Confederates, J. P. Harris and Jack Wharton; northern-born Union veteran Hugh J. Campbell; and another ex-Union soldier, James Lewis.

31. Wedge testimony, US House, *Recent Election in Louisiana,* 3:254; J. A. Norwood and D. J. Wedge to E. A. Burke, October 23, 1876, ibid., 2:464.

32. S. J. N. Smith and A. B. Payne testimony, in US House, *Recent Election in Louisiana: Testimony,* 1:148, 3:261; US Senate, *Testimony of James E. Anderson,* 60. The post of naval officer had nothing to do with commanding ships but involved auditing the transactions of the US Custom House.

33. Anderson to D. A. Weber, October 12, 1876, US House, *Presidential Election Investigation,* 1:27–28; *New Orleans Republican,* January 11, 1877.

34. Rogers and James Monahan testimony, US House, *Recent Election in Louisiana: Testimony,* 3:242–45, 438–40.

35. Alfred Hazard, J. S. Lanier, and Joseph Jones testimony, US House, *Recent*

Election in Louisiana: Testimony, 3:291, 382, 426–38; Anderson to Weber, September 10, 1876, US House, *Presidential Election Investigation,* 1:27.

36. *New Orleans Republican,* January 11, 1877; US Senate, *Testimony of James E Anderson,* 39, 50.

37. T. S. Lyons, O. P. Langworthy, John S. Lanier, et al. to I. W. Patton, October 26, 1876, US Senate, *Electoral Vote of Louisiana,* 439; E. A. Burke testimony, US House, *Recent Election in Louisiana: Testimony,* 2:464; *West Feliciana Sentinel* (St. Francisville, LA), February 3, 1877.

38. *New Orleans Republican,* October 15, 1876; John E. Leet testimony, US House, *Presidential Election Investigation,* 1:925.

39. "Speech of R. L. Gibson," *Congressional Record,* 44th Cong., 2d sess., (1877), 5(app.):46; C. B. Darrall testimony, US House, *Presidential Election Investigation,* 1:188–90; O. B. Morgan testimony, US House, *Recent Election in Louisiana: Testimony,* 1:123.

40. J. R. G. Pitkin and William P. Kellogg testimony; and Kellogg to Anderson, October 31, 1876, US House, *Presidential Election Investigation,* 1:389, 654–55; Hiram Smedley testimony, ibid., 3:192; Morgan testimony, US House, *Recent Election in Louisiana: Testimony,* 2:89.

41. Anderson to D. A. Weber, October 29, 1876, US House, *Presidential Election Investigation,* 1:27; US Senate, *Testimony of James E. Anderson,* 6, 36–37.

42. Anderson to Antoine, September 3, 1876; and Leet testimony, US House, *Presidential Election Investigation,* 1:162, 922; E. H. Flowers testimony, US House, *Recent Election in Louisiana: Testimony,* 2:148.

43. "[L. B.] Jenks on Anderson," *New York Times,* June 9, 1878; Thomas H. Jenks and Kellogg testimony, US House, *Presidential Election Investigation,* 1:288, 655; James Lawes testimony, US House, *Recent Election in Louisiana: Testimony,* 3:473.

44. *National Republican* (Washington, DC), June 5, 1878; Kellogg testimony, US House, *Presidential Election Investigation,* 1:695–99.

45. Law and Rigby testimony, US House, *Recent Election in Louisiana: Testimony,* 3:473, 489–92.

46. Green, Valentine Emery, Norfliss, and Amy Mitchell testimony, US Senate, *Louisiana in 1876,* 3:2389–90, 2442, 2496–98, 2704–7; Dawson, *Army Generals and Reconstruction,* 232.

47. J. R. G. Pitkin to W. D. Postlethwaite, October 25, 1876, US House, *Recent Election in Louisiana: Testimony,* 2:824; E. L. Weber, George A. J. Swayze, and L. F. Baugnon testimony, US House, *Presidential Election Investigation,* 3:221–22, 399, 541; W. F. Loan to Col. G. L. Norton, October 19, 1876, *West Feliciana Sentinel* (St. Francisville, LA), May 19, 1877; Cotton and Armstead testimony, US Senate, *Louisiana in 1876,* 3:2429, 2435.

48. Kaufman testimony, US House, *Alleged Outrages in West Feliciana Parish,* 759–62; J. R. Watson to Robert C. Wickliffe, October 14, 1876; and L. S. McCrindle and Kaufman testimony, US Senate, *Louisiana in 1876,* 3:2461, 2710–19; 2751–53; McCrindle testimony, US House, *Recent Election in Louisiana: Testimony,* 3:187; L. B. Jenks to [D. A. and E. L.] Weber, October 20, 1876, US House, *Presidential Election Investigation,* 1:619.

49. Burke testimony, US House, *Recent Election in Louisiana: Testimony,* 2:1004; Lyons, Charles McVea, Wedge, and I. W. Patton testimony, US House, *Presidential Election Investigation,* 3:80–82, 85–87, 128, 278–80; US Senate, *Testimony of James E. Anderson,* 9–10.

50. Patton testimony, US House, *Presidential Election Investigation,* 3:279–80.

51. James E. Anderson and Patton testimony, US House, *Presidential Election Investigation,* 1:51–52, 3:278–80; *New Orleans Republican,* January 11, 1877.

52. J. R. G. Pitkin to Alphonso Taft, November [?], 1876, Letters Received by the Department of Justice from the State of Louisiana, 1871–84, reel 3; George T. Norwood testimony, US House, *Recent Election in Louisiana: Testimony,* 3:482.

53. Isaac Guy testimony, US House, *Recent Election in Louisiana: Testimony,* 3:165; *New Orleans Republican,* January 10, 11, 1877. In 1966 Ted Tunnell argued, "It was not coercion of Negro voters that defeated the Republicans on November 7, but Negro disillusionment with eight years of Republican rule and a vigorous Democratic effort to win the Negro vote." See Tunnell, "The Negro, the Republican Party, and the Election of 1876 in Louisiana," 116. In his later work, however, he abandoned this claim, stressing instead the centrality of Democratic violence and intimidation. See Tunnell, *Crucible of Reconstruction: War, Radicalism, and Race in Louisiana, 1862–1877* (Baton Rouge: Louisiana State University Press, 1984); and *Edge of the Sword.*

54. US Senate, *Testimony of James E. Anderson,* 62; Thomas H. Jenks and Wedge testimony, US House, *Presidential Election Investigation,* 1:283, 3:129–33.

55. Dederick and Bascom testimony, US Senate, *Louisiana in 1876,* 3:2467, 2617–18; D. A. Weber to William P. Kellogg, November 6, 1876, US House, *Presidential Election Investigation,* 1:657–58; *Chicago Daily Tribune,* November 16, 1876.

56. Washington Spooner, Weber, Sebole Johnson, and Charles Fisher testimony, US Senate, *Louisiana in 1876,* 3:2404, 2417, 2569, 2575–76, 2725; US House, *Recent Election in Louisiana,* 1:83, 2:99.

57. Samuel J. Powell testimony, House, *Recent Election in Louisiana: Testimony,* 3:137–38; John H. Kennard testimony, Senate Report 701, *Louisiana in 1876,* 3:2588.

58. Act No. 98 (1872), US Senate, *Vote for Electors in Louisiana,* 161.

59. Gibson quoted in Tansill, *Congressional Career of Thomas Francis Bayard,* 125.

60. Holt, *By One Vote,* 173; Zachariah Chandler to Kellogg, November 11, 1876; and Chandler to Packard, November 11, 1876, US House, *Counting the Vote for President,* 18.

61. Holt, *By One Vote,* 194; *New York Herald,* November 10, 1876; *Chicago Daily Tribune,* November 10, 1876.

62. *New York Tribune,* November 9, 1876; *Chicago Daily Tribune,* November 10, 1876. See also A. Dumont to Zachariah Chandler, November 11, 1876, US House, *Counting the Vote for President,* 16–17.

63. *New York Tribune,* November 9, 1876; *New Orleans Republican,* November 9, 1876. These statements suggest that Kellogg might not have been aware that Anderson had returned to supervise the election. Did they also support Anderson's claim

of a Republican conspiracy to hold no election in East Feliciana? The testimony of D. J. M. A. Jewett, chairman of the Republican state registration committee, may help reconcile Anderson's allegation and Kellogg's denial. Republican leaders had no tangible plan *not* to hold elections in the bulldozed parishes, he explained, but such was the extent of violence and intimidation that "the organization of the Republican party was an impossibility." Jewett (who when he gave this testimony was politically estranged from both Kellogg and the Hayes administration) went on to state: "As the election in [East Feliciana parish] must have been a farce anyhow, I had intended to have no election there. Governor Kellogg partially overruled me in the matter and got Anderson back to the parish." See D. J. M. A. Jewett testimony, US House, *Presidential Election Investigation: Testimony,* 1:1441, 1447.

64. J. R. G. Pitkin to J. R. West, November 14, 1876, US House, *Recent Election in Louisiana: Testimony,* 2:827; J. B. Stockton to Z. Chandler, November 11, 1876, US House, *Counting the Vote for President,* 30; Alfred Hazard and William F. Norsworthy testimony, November 17, 1876, US Senate, *Electoral Vote of Louisiana,* 443–45.

65. Hugh J. Campbell testimony, US House, *Presidential Election Investigation,* 1:436.

66. Anderson, Thomas H. Jenks, Pitkin, and Campbell testimony, US House, *Presidential Election Investigation,* 1:3–6, 284–85, 399–402, 434.

67. Protest of D. A. Weber, US Congress, US Senate, *Vote for Electors in Louisiana,* 222–23; Weber and Kennard testimony, US Senate, *Louisiana in 1876,* 3:2579–81, 2588–92; Harris and Leet testimony, US House, *Presidential Election Investigation,* 1:929–30, 3:100–101. On Hearsey, see Hair, *Bourbonism and Agrarian Protest,* 24–28.

CHAPTER 2

1. John Sherman to Cecilia Sherman, November 20, 24, 1876, letter book 129, Sherman Papers.

2. Bronson, *Life and Public Services of the Hon. John Sherman,* 52–53.

3. Bronson, *Life and Public Services of the Hon. John Sherman,* ix, 59.

4. *Chicago Daily Tribune,* January 8, 1869, January 17, 1870, January 15, 1872.

5. Stealey, *Twenty Years in the Press Gallery,* 420; Bronson, *Life and Public Services of the Hon. John Sherman,* 60–61; *Cincinnati Enquirer,* November 29, 1878.

6. Holt, *By One Vote,* 179; *Washington Evening Star,* November 11, 1876.

7. *New York Tribune,* November 16, 1876.

8. S. J. N. Smith testimony, US House, *Recent Election in Louisiana: Testimony,* 1:148.

9. Charles E. Whitney and Burke testimony, US House, *Recent Election in Louisiana: Testimony,* 1:168–69, 2:459–60, 580–84.

10. Anderson and Pitkin testimony, US House, *Presidential Election Investigation,* 1:7, 402, 455–56.

11. Whitney testimony, US House, *Recent Election in Louisiana: Testimony,* 1:171; *New York Herald,* November 17, 1876.

12. Whitney testimony, US House, *Recent Election in Louisiana: Testimony,* 1:169; Anderson and Kellogg testimony, US House, *Presidential Election Investigation,* 1:17, 655–56; *New York Herald,* November 23, 1876.

13. Kellogg, Jewett, and J. F. Kelly testimony, US House, *Presidential Election Investigation,* 1:662, 1442–52, 3:171–76.

14. Anderson to Pierce Butler, November 16, 1876, US House, *Presidential Election Investigation,* 1:15.

15. John Sherman to Cecilia Sherman, November 24, 1876, letter book 129, Sherman Papers; Holt, *By One Vote,* 197–99; Garfield to Lucretia Garfield, November 15, 1876, series 3, reel 7, Garfield Papers; Watterson, *"Marse Henry,"* 1:297–98.

16. Watterson, *"Marse Henry,"* 1:297–98; *New Orleans Daily Democrat,* February 3, 1877; C. Irving Ditty testimony, US House, *Counting the Vote for President,* 278.

17. Shaw, *Crete and James,* 335–36; John Sherman to Cecilia Sherman, November 29, 1876, letter book 129, Sherman Papers.

18. Gillette, *Retreat from Reconstruction,* 104–15; Rable, "Republican Albatross," 113–21.

19. Simon, *Papers of Ulysses S. Grant,* 118; Holt, *By One Vote,* 194–96; Warren W. Bateman to Sherman, December 2, 1876, letter book 129, Sherman Papers.

20. J. Madison Wells testimony, US House, *Counting the Vote for President,* 243; *New Orleans Republican,* August 20, 25, 26, 1874. Former Republican governor Henry Warmoth delivered a fatal knife wound to a Democrat who assaulted him on the street with a cane. Two newspaper editors, one a Republican and the other a Democrat, in Natchitoches engaged in a public shoot-out on Christmas morning, 1875, with fatal consequences for the Republican. Members of the same party also quarreled violently. A duel between two Republicans in Saint James Parish left one dead and the other critically injured. Incumbent governor William P. Kellogg was assaulted by E. A Burke, and the two men exchanged bullets, both of which missed their mark. Kellogg also fended off an attack by Charles E. Nash, a Republican congressman, who tried to throttle him. On Louisiana's culture of violence, both political and personal, see Vandal, *Rethinking Southern Violence;* and Hyde, *Pistols and Politics: The Dilemma of Democracy.*

21. J. R. G. Pitkin to Alphonso Taft, December 11, 1876, Letters Received by the Department of Justice from the State of Louisiana, reel 3; U. S. Grant to William T. Sherman, November 10, 1876, Simon, *Papers of Ulysses S. Grant,* 19.

22. Grant to William T. Sherman, November 10, 1876, Simon, *Papers of Ulysses S. Grant,* 19; Wells testimony, US House, *Counting the Vote for President,* 215; John Sherman to Cecilia Sherman, November 24, 1876, letter book 129, Sherman Papers; Lowrey, "Political Career of James Madison Wells," 1007–9, 1030–90, 1097–99, 1115.

23. Simon, *Papers of Ulysses S. Grant,* 33n1; *New York Herald,* November 11, 1876; John Sherman to Rutherford B. Hayes, November 23, 1876; and Hayes to Sherman, November 27, 1876, US House, *Presidential Election Investigation,* 1:772.

24. Garfield to Lucretia, November 19, 1876, series 3, Garfield Papers.

25. Polakoff, *Politics of Inertia,* 266–67; Garfield to Lucretia, November 19, 23, 1876, series 3, Garfield Papers.

26. Garfield to Lucretia, November 24, 1876, series 3, Garfield Papers; Harris testimony, US House, *Presidential Election Investigation,* 3:102.

27. *New York Tribune,* November 29, 30, 1876; *New York Herald,* November 30, 1876; Haworth, *Hayes-Tilden Disputed Presidential Election,* 106–8.

28. John Sherman to Cecilia Sherman, November 20, 1876, letter book 129, Sherman Papers; Houdek, "James A. Garfield and Rutherford B. Hayes," 212–13. Garfield's biographer maintains, "Even before he had a chance to examine the evidence, he had already made up his mind that Hayes was entitled to the state." See Peskin, *Garfield,* 408–10.

29. Garfield diary, November 23, 1876, series 1, reel 2, Garfield Papers; Sherman to Hayes, November 23, 1876, US House, *Presidential Election Investigation,* 1:772, 792.

30. Lonn, *Reconstruction in Louisiana after 1868,* 445–50; McGinty, *Louisiana Redeemed,* 57–62. These older studies, despite expressing bias against the Republican Party, are still valuable as reference works. On November 23 Sherman informed Hayes, "The law seems conclusive that the defective ballots cannot be counted for any electors but those named on the ticket." Yet he failed to object when the Returning Board did precisely what he thought the law did not permit. See Sherman to Hayes, November 23, 1876, US House, *Presidential Election Investigation,* 1:772.

31. Watterson to Tilden, November 13, 1876, folder b26f.1, Tilden Papers; Polakoff, *Politics of Inertia,* 220.

32. Anderson to Weber, November 14, 1876; Anderson and Weber, affidavit, November 14, 1876; and Anderson testimony, US House, *Presidential Election Investigation,* 1:1–9, 403. I am classifying Anderson's letters to Weber, as well as the Anderson-Weber agreement, as "uncorroborated testimony" on the grounds that the authenticity of these documents depends upon Anderson's word alone.

33. Anderson testimony, US House, *Presidential Election Investigation,* 1:9–10.

34. Anderson to Weber, November 20, 1876; Anderson and Weber to Sherman, November 20, 1876; and Sherman to Anderson and Weber, November 20, 1876, US House, *Presidential Election Investigation,* 1:10–12.

35. Anderson-Nash agreement, November 21, 1876, and Darrall testimony, US House, *Presidential Election Investigation,* 1:18, 191–94 (quotation at 194).

36. James A. Garfield testimony, US House, *Presidential Election Investigation,* 1:797; Anon to Sherman, November 22, 1876, letter book 129, Sherman Papers; Anderson testimony, US House, *Counting the Vote for President,* 166; *New Orleans Daily Democrat,* February 4, 1877; Watterson, *"Marse Henry,"* 1:298–99.

37. James Garfield to Lucretia Garfield, November 20, 1876, series 3, reel 7, Garfield Papers.

38. Sherman to Hayes, November 23, 1876, US House, *Presidential Election Investigation,* 1:771–72.

39. Wells testimony, US House, *Counting the Vote for President,* 202; Duncan F. Kenner testimony, ibid., 376–79; Jack Wharton testimony, US House, *Presidential Election Investigation,* 1:1430.

40. Wells to Maddox, November 20, 1876, US House, *Counting the Vote for President,* 131, 178; Joseph H. Maddox testimony, ibid., 144–48; Wells to J. R. West, No-

vember 21, 1876, ibid., 180; John T. Pickett to Joseph H. Maddox, November 27, 1876, ibid., 131; Maddox to Pickett, December 1, 1876, ibid., 136; Pickett to F. C. Zacharie, December 1, 1876, ibid., 157; John T. Pickett, Maddox, Thomas C. Anderson, Wells, and Kenner testimony, ibid., 131–34, 135–59, 165–73, 192, 206, 376–84; "Speech of Senator J. R. West," February 5, 1877, *Congressional Record,* 44th Cong., 2d sess., (1877), 5(2):1257; *New York Times,* February 14, 1878.

41. US House, *Counting the Vote for President,* 202–3; US House, *Presidential Election Investigation,* 1:1431.

42. Pitkin to West, December 3, 1876, US House, *Recent Election in Louisiana,* 1:9; US House, *Presidential Election Investigation,* 1:1454.

43. L. A. Sheldon to James Garfield, December 12, 1876, reel 35, Garfield Papers; A. B. Levisee testimony, US Senate, *Louisiana in 1876,* 3:3023–41.

44. Garfield testimony, US House, *Presidential Election Investigation,* 1:797; US Senate, *Vote for Electors in Louisiana,* 7–9.

45. In private, Republicans admitted that supervisors of election had acted in a "very loose manner, and not according to the strict letter of the law," and that some had, in a "wholly unauthorize[d] manner," refused to "receive and forward certain polls." See Stephen A. Hurlbut to Garfield, December 23, 1877; and W. Townsend to Garfield, December 27, 1877, reel 35, Garfield Papers.

46. *Congressional Record,* 44th Cong., 2d sess. (1877), 5(1):54–62, 179–92, 499–504, 744–51.

47. Woodward, *Reunion and Reaction,* 164; Polakoff, *Politics of Inertia,* 279–80.

48. Butler to Garfield, January 18, 1877; J. J. McLaws to Garfield, January 18, 1877; and Garfield to Hayes, January 19, 1877, reel 35, Garfield Papers.

49. Polakoff, *Politics of Inertia,* 279–83; Holt, *By One Vote,* 220.

50. Woodward, *Reunion and Reaction,* 165–66; Holt, *By One Vote,* 224; Hunton, *Autobiography,* 175–84; Holt, *By One Vote,* 218–19.

51. Holt, *By One Vote,* 233–34; Garfield diary, February 16, 1877, series 1, reel 2, Garfield Papers. For a discussion of the bribery allegation, see Woodward, *Reunion and Reaction,* 166–74; and Rehnquist, *Centennial Crisis,* 186–200.

52. US Congress, *Proceedings of the Electoral Commission,* 1029.

53. William T. Pelton to Dear Sir, February 16, 1877, folder b.1f.8, Tilden Papers; Polakoff, *Politics of Inertia,* 158–60, 259–60, 267–71, 303–4; Woodward, *Reunion and Reaction,* 175.

54. J. R. G. Pitkin to Alphonso Taft, January 9, 1877, Simon, *Papers of Ulysses S. Grant,* 109.

55. Grant to Kellogg, January 7, 1877; J. D. Cameron to C. C. Augur, January 9, 10, 1877; Grant to Augur, January 14, 1877; and F. T. Nicholls to Burke et al., January 25, 1877, US House, *Presidential Election Investigation,* 3:603–6; Augur to Cameron, January 9, 1877, Letters Received by the Department of Justice from the State of Louisiana, reel 3.

56. Don Cameron to Augur, January 16, 1877, Letters Received by the Department of Justice from the State of Louisiana, reel 3; *New Orleans Republican,* January 10, 11, 14; US Senate, *Louisiana in 1876,* 3:2565–85.

57. William E. Chandler to William P. Kellogg, January 13, 1877; Stephen B. Pack-

ard to Chandler, January 14, 1877, box 43, Chandler Papers; Augur to Cameron, January 9, 1877, Letters Received by the Department of Justice from the State of Louisiana, reel 3. On February 15 a would-be assassin gained entry to the statehouse and shot Packard in the leg. *New Orleans Daily Democrat,* February 16, 17, 1877.

58. Augur to Cameron, January 9, 1877, Letters Received by the Department of Justice from the State of Louisiana, reel 3; Augur to E. D. Townsend, February 15, 1877, Simon, *Papers of Ulysses S. Grant,* 119.

59. Nevins, *Hamilton Fish,* 851; Rable, "Republican Albatross," 109–30.

60. E. A. Burke, E. J. Ellis, and W. M. Levy to Francis T. Nicholls, February 20, 1877, US House, *Presidential Election Investigation,* 3:616; James Longstreet to Grant, January 9, 1877, February 16, 1877, Letters Received by the Department of Justice from the State of Louisiana, reel 3; *New Orleans Daily Democrat,* February 21, 1877; Simon, *Papers of Ulysses S. Grant,* 121; Nevins, *Hamilton Fish,* 853–54; Garfield diary, February 19, 20, 1877, series 1, reel 2, Garfield Papers.

61. C. C. Sniffen to Stephen B. Packard, March 1, 1877, Letters Received by the Department of Justice from the State of Louisiana, reel 3.

62. Kellogg to John E. Leet, February 24, 1877, US House, *Presidential Election Investigation,* 1:951–52; Garfield diary, January 19, 20, 1877, series 1, reel 2, Garfield Papers.

63. Hirshon, *Farewell to the Bloody Shirt,* 22–24; Simpson, *Reconstruction Presidents,* 201–3; Calhoun, *Conceiving a New Republic,* 98–104; Holt, *By One Vote,* 124–25.

64. *New York Herald,* March 4, 1877; Haworth, *Hayes-Tilden Disputed Presidential Election,* 268–72; Woodward, *Reunion and Reaction,* 26–27, 181–218; Holt, *By One Vote,* 237–41.

65. Matthews to Packard, February 27, 1877; and Packard to Matthews, March 13, 1877, *New Orleans Daily Democrat,* March 17, 1877.

66. Hayes diary, March 16, 20, 1877, Williams, *Diary and Letters of Rutherford Birchard Hayes,* 428–29.

67. *Chicago Daily Tribune,* March 30, 1877; Webb, *Benjamin Helm Bristow,* 246–50, 267–73; McBride, *Randall Lee Gibson,* 168–69.

68. Gillette, *Retreat from Reconstruction,* 342–43; *New York Sun,* April 7, 10, 1877; John M. Harlan, undated notes [April 1877], reel 7, Harlan Papers; Harlan to Benjamin Bristow, April 9, 13, 1877, box 7, Bristow Papers.

69. *New Orleans Daily Democrat,* April 15, 17, 19, 1878.

70. *New York Herald,* April 19, 20, 1878; *New York Sun,* April 30, 1877; Gillette, *Retreat from Reconstruction,* 344–45; McGinty, *Louisiana Redeemed,* 118–24; John M. Harlan, "Federal Offices to be Filled by Presidential Appointment," n.d. [April 1877], reel 7, Harlan Papers; Pitkin testimony, US House, *Presidential Election Investigation,* 1:459–63.

71. John G. Lewis to editor, December 29, 1876, *New Orleans Republican,* February 10, 1877.

72. *Natchitoches People's Vindicator,* June 2, 1877; *West Feliciana Sentinel* (St. Francisville, LA), July 7, 14, December 1, 1877; *New Orleans Daily Democrat,* April 11, May 27, June 9, 10, July 6, 17, 1877.

73. *West Feliciana Sentinel* (St. Francisville, LA), March 10, July 21, 1877; *Woodville (MS) Republican,* March 17, 1877.

74. *New Orleans Daily Democrat,* May 8, 26, 27, June 4, 23, 1877; *West Feliciana Sentinel* (St. Francisville, LA), May 26, 1877.

75. Law testimony, US House, *Recent Election in Louisiana: Testimony,* 1:479–80; *New Orleans Daily Democrat,* May 8, 24, 26, 27, 29, June 4, 12, 23, July 1, 2, 1877; *New Orleans Republican,* May 23, 26, June 2, 9, 1877.

76. *West Feliciana Sentinel* (St. Francisville, LA), February 3, 10, 1877.

77. D. A. Weber to Stephen B. Packard, February 24, 1877, *New Orleans Republican,* March 9, 1877.

78. D. A. Weber to W. L. McMillan, March 3, 1877, US House, *Presidential Election Investigation,* 1:598.

79. *New Orleans Daily Democrat,* March 9, 10, 17, 1877; *Donaldsonville (LA) Chief,* March 10, 1877.

80. E. L. Weber to J. H. Weber, March 24, 1877, US House, *Presidential Election Investigation,* 1:596; *New Orleans Republican,* March 16, 1877.

81. *New Orleans Daily Democrat,* March 8, 1877; *West Feliciana Sentinel* (St. Francisville, LA), March 10, 17, 1877; *New Orleans Republican,* March 11, 1877.

82. E. L. Weber to W. E. Chandler, March 6, 1878, box 46, Chandler Papers; Agnes D. Jenks to Anderson, January 17, 1878, US House, *Presidential Election Investigation,* 1:75.

CHAPTER 3

1. P. B. Conn to Hayes, March 6, 1877; and Darrall and Nash to Hayes, March 13, 1877, US House, *Presidential Election Investigation,* 1:111, 113; Anderson testimony, ibid., 25.

2. Hayes diary, June 2, 1878, Williams, *Diary and Letters of Rutherford Birchard Hayes,* 485–86; Anderson testimony, US House, *Presidential Election Investigation,* 1:18–19.

3. Anderson testimony, US House, *Presidential Election Investigation,* 1:19.

4. Anderson testimony, US House, *Presidential Election Investigation,* 1:19–21.

5. Matthews testimony, US Senate, *Presidential Election in Louisiana,* 27–30. Matthews had been one of the visiting statesmen in New Orleans, although he departed on November 20.

6. Anderson testimony; Matthews to John M. Harlan, March 29, 1877; and Anderson to Matthews, April 8, 1877, US House, *Presidential Election Investigation,* 1:20–21, 111.

7. Matthews to Anderson, April 17, 22, May 7, 25, 1877; Matthews to T. C. Anderson, May 14, 1877; and Matthews to W. M. Evarts, May 14, 1877, US House, *Presidential Election Investigation,* 1:21–23; Anderson to Matthews, May 5, 10, 25, 1877, US Senate, *Testimony of James E. Anderson,* 105–6; Hoogenboom, *Presidency of Rutherford B. Hayes,* 108.

8. J. A. Straight to Hayes, May 25, 1877; and W. K. Rogers to Evarts, May 26, 1877,

US House, *Presidential Election Investigation,* 1:112–13; Anderson to Matthews, June 1, 2, 1877, US Senate, *Testimony of James E. Anderson,* 105–6.

9. Anderson and T. H. C. Smith testimony, US House, *Presidential Election Investigation,* 1:23–25, 232–37; Hayes diary, June 3, 1878, Williams, *Diary and Letters of Rutherford Birchard Hayes,* 487.

10. Anderson to Matthews, June 19, 1877; Matthews to Smith, June 22, 1877; Smith to Matthews, June 25, 1877; Anderson to Smith, July 11, 1877; and T. H. C. Smith testimony, US House, *Presidential Election Investigation,* 1:25, 230, 235–38, 247–48.

11. Anderson to Matthews, May 5, June 1, 19, 27, 1877, US House, *Presidential Election Investigation,* 1:24–26, 77–79.

12. Anderson to Matthews, April 7, June 6, 27, 1877, US House, *Presidential Election Investigation,* 1:26, 73, 78.

13. *New York Sun,* June 7, 21, 1878; Matthews testimony, US Senate, *Presidential Election in Louisiana,* 11, 15.

14. Anderson to Thomas Jenks, June 10, 1877; and Agnes Jenks, E. L. Weber, and A. J. Reynolds testimony, US House, *Presidential Election Investigation,* 1:351, 522, 593, 3:291–92.

15. Anderson to Thomas Jenks, July 24, September 23, 1877; Agnes D. Jenks to Emilie Weber, October 10, 1877; and Emilie Weber to Agnes Jenks, November 13, 1877, US House, *Presidential Election Investigation,* 1:306–9.

16. Thomas H. Jenks, affidavit, May 11, 1877, US House, *Presidential Election Investigation,* 1:351; Anderson testimony, ibid., 1:115.

17. WBF [J. E. Anderson] to *New York Sun,* July 2, 1877, US House, *Presidential Election Investigation,* 1:31; W. E. Chandler, "Memoranda of Statements Made and Letters Submitted by James E. Anderson," July 16, 1877, box 45, Chandler Papers.

18. Chandler, "Memoranda."

19. Chandler, "Memoranda."

20. Anderson testimony, US House, *Presidential Election Investigation,* 1:28.

21. *New Orleans Daily Democrat,* September 6, 1877; H. V. Boynton and Kellogg testimony, US House, *Presidential Election Investigation,* 1:388, 651.

22. Pitkin testimony, US House, *Presidential Election Investigation,* 1:466.

23. Pitkin testimony, US House, *Presidential Election Investigation,* 1:403.

24. *New Orleans Daily Democrat,* June 11, 20, 1877.

25. Pitkin testimony, US House, *Presidential Election Investigation,* 1:403–15.

26. Agnes Jenks to Kellogg, November 14, 1877; and Agnes Jenks, Kellogg, and Stephen B. Packard testimony, US House, *Presidential Election Investigation,* 1:328–29, 356, 370, 651–52, 3:44–45.

27. Agnes Jenks and John Sherman testimony, US House, *Presidential Election Investigation,* 1:342–44, 783; John Sherman, "Memorandum" [for testimony to Potter Committee], n.d. [July 1877], letter book 164, Sherman Papers.

28. *New York Times,* February 1, 2, 3, 1878.

29. Darrall testimony, US House, *Presidential Election Investigation,* 1:179; Francis Kernan to Samuel J. Tilden, February 10, 1878, folder b.15f.50–53, Tilden Papers; *Washington Post,* February 6, 1878.

30. *New York Times,* February 1, 2, 23, 1878; Sherman to Alfred Townsend, February 19, 1878, letter book 153, Sherman Papers.

31. Anderson to Agnes Jenks, February 4, 1878, letter book 153, Sherman Papers; Anderson to Emilie Weber, February 4, 1878, US House, *Presidential Election Investigation,* 3:402.

32. Morris Marks testimony, US House, *Presidential Election Investigation,* 3:416–17, 437; E. L. Weber testimony, ibid., 1:629; Rockoff, "Carpetbaggers, Jews, and Reconstruction Politics in Ascension Parish," 52–54. Weber recalled the moment differently, although less reliably: Marks himself, he claimed, knew the Sherman letter to be genuine, for Don Weber had told him about it.

33. E. L. Weber to Robert Morris, February 6, 1878, US House, *Presidential Election Investigation,* 3:372.

34. Weber to Chandler, February 14, 1878, box 46, Chandler Papers.

35. Weber to Chandler, March 6, 1878; and Chandler to Weber, March 15, 28, 1878, box 46, Chandler Papers; E. L. Weber testimony, US House, *Presidential Election Investigation,* 1:622.

36. Agnes Jenks to *New York Times,* February 3, 1878, letter book 152, Sherman Papers; *New York Times,* February 6, 1878.

37. Samuel P. Butler testimony, US House, *Presidential Election Investigation,* 1:525–26; Chandler to E. L. Weber, March 15, 1878, box 46, Chandler Papers; H. V. Boynton to Benjamin Bristow, March 29, 1878, box 8, Bristow Papers; *National Republican* (Washington, DC), June 4, 1878.

38. Alfred G. Haley testimony, US House, *Presidential Election Investigation,* 1:427–28.

39. Agnes Jenks to Cecilia Sherman, February 6, 1878, letter book 153, Sherman Papers.

40. Agnes Jenks to Cecilia Sherman, February 6, 1878; and Sherman, "Mrs. Jenks," memorandum, n.d., letter books 153, 164, Sherman Papers.

41. Jenks to Stanley Matthews, February 18, 1878; and Jenks to Cecilia Sherman, February 28, March 14, 1878, letter books 153–54, Sherman Papers.

42. Anderson to Agnes Jenks, February 4, 1878; and Jenks to John Sherman, February 28, March 25, 31, 1878, letter books 153–55, Sherman Papers; Anderson to Jenks, April 10, 1878, US House, *Presidential Election Investigation,* 1:564–65.

43. Sherman to Agnes Jenks, March 18, 1878, letter book 154, Sherman Papers.

44. *Chicago Daily Tribune,* August 27, 1877; *Anti-Monopolist* (St. Paul, MN), September 6, 1877; *New Orleans Daily Democrat,* September 6, 8, 1877; Jewett to Kellogg, February 1, 1879, US House, *Presidential Election Investigation,* 1:1421.

45. C. B. Darrall to Anderson, February 17, 27, March 3, 30, April 17, 19, 1878, US House, *Presidential Election Investigation,* 1:178–85, 201; Darrall testimony, ibid., 1:173–75, 186–88, 191, 204–9.

46. Anderson to Matthews, February 11, April 23, 1878, US Senate, *Testimony of James E. Anderson,* 107; Matthews testimony, US Senate, *Presidential Election in Louisiana,* 9.

47. Garfield diary, June 1, 1878, series 1, reel 2, Garfield Papers; *New York Sun,* June 21, 1878.

48. Anderson to Matthews, April 7, 1877, US House, *Presidential Election Investigation,* 1:73; Garfield diary, May 7, 1878, series 1, reel 2, Garfield Papers.

49. Darrall to Anderson, May 12, 1878, US House, *Presidential Election Investigation,* 1:926–27.

50. Garfield diary, October 26, 1877, series 1, reel 2, Garfield Papers; Hirshon, *Farewell to the Bloody Shirt,* 27–28, 33–40; Polakoff, *Politics of Inertia,* 319.

51. Richardson, *William E. Chandler,* 52–72, 119, 173–75.

52. Richardson, *William E. Chandler,* 76, 173, 208–10.

53. Chandler, *Letters,* 7–24; *New York Times,* December 27, 1877.

54. Chandler, *Letters,* 62, 74.

55. Pitkin to Chandler, January 10, 30, 1878; Chandler to Burke, January 28, 30, 31, 1878; and Burke to Chandler, January 29, 30, 1878, box 45, Chandler Papers; Jewett to Chandler, February 2, 1878, box 46, ibid.

56. *New York Herald,* December 24, 1877; *Cincinnati Enquirer,* January 8, 1878; Hayes diary, May 28, 1875, Williams, *Diary and Letters of Rutherford Birchard Hayes,* 269.

57. *New York Times,* January 26, February 3, 4, 8, 16, 24, 26, 1878; *Washington Post,* February 4, 11, 1878; Lowrey, "Political Career of James Madison Wells," 1111–12; McGinty, *Louisiana Redeemed,* 128–32.

58. McGinty, *Louisiana Redeemed,* 132–34; Williams, *Diary and Letters of Rutherford Birchard Hayes,* 459; Garfield diary, February 3, 4, 1878, series 1, reel 2, Garfield Papers; Wells to Sherman, February 14, 1878; Sherman to Hayes, February 9, March 8, 1878; and Sherman et al. to Thomas C. Anderson, February 11, 1878, letter books 153–54, Sherman Papers.

59. Garfield diary, February 13, 19, 1878, series 1, reel 2, Garfield Papers; *New York Times,* February 14, 15, 20, 1878; *Washington Post,* February 20, 1878; E. J. Ellis to Thomas Ellis, March 7, 1878, folder 30, box 5, Ellis Family Papers.

60. *New York Times,* February 14, 20, 1878; Chandler, *Letters,* 75.

61. *State v. Thomas C. Anderson* 30 La. Ann. 557; *New York Times,* March 14, 19, 1878; Thomas C. Anderson to Sherman, April 9, 1878, letter book 155, Sherman Papers; Hayes diary, March 28, 1878, Williams, *Diary and Letters of Rutherford Birchard Hayes,* 470.

62. *New York Times,* March 26, 1878; Hirshon, *Farewell to the Bloody Shirt,* 42–46; Calhoun, *Conceiving a New Republic,* 153.

63. Garfield diary, January 19, March 25, 1878, series 1, reel 2, Garfield Papers; *New York Tribune,* April 18, 19, 1878; H. V. Boynton to Benjamin Bristow, April 24, 29, 1878, box 8, Bristow Papers.

64. Flick, *Samuel J. Tilden,* 412–13, 423; Nevins, *Abram S. Hewitt,* 392; Bigelow, *Writings and Speeches of Samuel J. Tilden,* 2:490–91.

65. A. M. Gibson testimony, US House, *Presidential Election Investigation,* 1:1326; [Gibson] to Tilden, June 29, 1879, folder b.14.f.1-2, Tilden Papers.

66. Gibson to E. John Ellis, February 10, 1878, folder 30, box 5, Ellis Family Papers.

67. Alfred Morton to William T. Pelton, March 7, 1878, folder b.1f.8, Tilden Papers; *New York Herald,* April 25, 1878.

68. *New York Herald,* April 24, 25, 26, 1878; Haworth, *Hayes-Tilden Disputed Presidential Election,* 309; Guenther, "Potter Committee Investigation," 285–86.

69. William M. Springer to Tilden, March 10, 1878, folder b.23f.27, Tilden Papers.

70. *New York Herald,* April 24, 1878.

71. Clarkson N. Potter, May 2, 1878, folder b23f.27, Tilden Papers; *New York Tribune,* May 14, 1878; Haworth, *Hayes-Tilden Disputed Presidential Election,* 308–11.

72. *Washington Evening Star,* May 14, 15, 1878; *New York Times,* May 15, 17, 1878; *Washington Post,* May 17, 1878; *Congressional Record,* 45th Cong., 2d sess. (1878), 7(4):3440–3502.

73. *Washington Evening Star,* May 18, 1878; *New York Times,* May 18, 1878.

74. Williams, *Diary and Letters of Rutherford Birchard Hayes,* 491; Hoar, *Autobiography,* 2:44; *New Orleans Daily Democrat,* May 18, 1878.

75. *New York Herald,* April 24, 1878; *Evening Star,* May 18, 1878; *New York Tribune,* May 18, 1878.

76. Springer to Tilden, March 10, 1878, folder b.23f.27, Tilden Papers.

77. Julius L. Brown to Tilden, June 13, 1878, box 50, Marble Papers.

78. C. W. Woolley to Samuel J. Randall, May 1, 4, 1878, box 48, Randall Papers; *New York Tribune,* May 15, 1878.

79. *National Republican* (Washington, DC), May 16, 1878; *New York Herald,* May 17, 1878; *Washington Evening Star,* May 20, 1878.

80. Agnes Jenks to Sherman, April 19, 1878; Agnes Jenks to Sherman, May 18, 1878; and Thomas Jenks to Sherman, May 19, 1878, letter books 156–57, Sherman Papers; Morris Marks to E. L. Weber, May 27, 1878, US House, *Presidential Election Investigation,* 3:436.

81. L. A. Sheldon to Mrs. D. A. Weber, May 26, 1878; and Sheldon to Thomas H. Jenks, May 26, 1878, US House, *Presidential Election Investigation,* 1:622, 1328; Agnes Jenks testimony, ibid., 391.

82. E. L. Weber to William E. Chandler, May 27, 1878, box 46, Chandler Papers; Weber to Morris Marks, n.d., US House, *Presidential Election Investigation,* 1:628; E. L. Weber testimony, ibid., 622.

83. Rockoff, "Carpetbaggers, Jews, and Reconstruction Politics in Ascension Parish," 55–56; *Washington Evening Star,* June 7, 1878. The Senate confirmed Marks's appointment on June 6.

84. This description of the meeting between Anderson and Sherman is constructed from the somewhat conflicting accounts provided by Anderson, Marks, Hahn, Shellabarger, and Sherman. See *New York Sun,* May 26, 1878; *Washington Post,* May 27, 28, 1878; *New York Herald,* May 27, 1878; *Washington Evening Star,* May 27, 1878; *New York Tribune,* June 3, 1878; and Sherman and Marks testimony, US House, *Presidential Election Investigation,* 1:770, 3:410–13. Whether Marks or Anderson suggested the meeting is unclear: each claimed that the other did. We do know that Marks asked his friend A. B. Sloanaker to provide Anderson with railroad passes.

85. *New York Sun,* May 26, 1878; *Washington Post,* May 27, 1878.

86. *New Orleans Daily Democrat,* May 27, 1878; *Washington Post,* May 17, 1878; *New York Sun,* May 28, 30, 1878.

CHAPTER 4

1. *New York Tribune,* June 3, 1878; H. V. Boynton to Benjamin Bristow, March 29, April 24, 1878, box 8, Bristow Papers.

2. *New York Sun,* June 2, 1878; Flick, *Samuel J. Tilden,* 305; Bigelow, *Retrospections of an Active Life,* 281, 288–89; Nevins, *Abram S. Hewitt,* 352.

3. Robbins, "Congressional Career of William Ralls Morrison," 2–36; McCormack, *Memoirs of Gustave Koerner,* 2:72–73.

4. Vallandigham, *Life of Clement L. Vallandigham,* 50, 84; McCall, *Life of Thomas Brackett Reed,* 60.

5. *Catalogue of Phi Alpha Society* (Jacksonville: Illinois College, 1890), 47; *Springer v. United States* 102 US 586 (1881).

6. *New York Times,* July 8, 1878.

7. Fielder, *Joseph C. S. Blackburn,* 103–6.

8. Hunton, *Autobiography,* 6–8, 169–95; *Alexandria (VA) Gazette,* July 16, 1878; *New York Herald,* July 19, 20, 1878; *New York Times,* July 20, 1878.

9. Schmiel, "Career of Jacob Dolson Cox," 8, 21, 138–49, 286, 356; McFeely, *Grant,* 300–301.

10. *New York Sun,* June 2, 1878; McCall, *Life of Thomas Brackett Reed,* 21, 31–37, 57; Robinson, *Thomas B. Reed,* 257.

11. *Biographies of the Present Senators of the United States,* 393–98; *New York Sun,* June 2, 1878.

12. Hoar, *Autobiography,* 1:329–34; Trefousse, *Ben Butler,* 19–20.

13. Trefousse, *Ben Butler,* 55–56, 203; Hoar, *Autobiography,* 1:332–33; Hearn, *When the Devil Came Down to Dixie.*

14. Smith, "Let Us All Be Grateful That We Have Colored Troops That Will Fight," 22; Butler, *Butler's Book,* 491–500, 733.

15. Trefousse, *Ben Butler,* 7; Foner, *Reconstruction,* 498, 533.

16. Watterson, *"Marse Henry,"* 2:253–55; Trefousse, *Ben Butler,* 39, 49; Williams, *Diary and Letters of Rutherford Birchard Hayes,* 508.

17. Crenshaw, "Benjamin F. Butler," 28.

18. *New York Herald,* June 2, 1878; *Washington Evening Star,* June 1, 1878; *National Republican* (Washington, DC), June 3, 5, 1878.

19. US House, *Presidential Election Investigation,* 1:1–12, 14–30; *New York Times,* June 2, 3, 1878.

20. Hoar, *Autobiography,* 2:22–23; *New York Sun,* June 2, 1878.

21. *New York Sun,* June 2, 1878; *New York Times,* June 2, 1878; US House, *Presidential Election Investigation,* 1:16–17.

22. *New York Herald,* June 2, 1878; *New York Times,* June 4, 10, 1878; *Boston Post,* n.d., quoted in *Washington Post,* June 6, 1878.

23. Anderson testimony, US House, *Presidential Election Investigation,* 1:14; *New York Tribune,* June 4, 1878; *National Republican* (Washington, DC), June 3, 1878.

24. *New York Times,* June 3, 1878; *National Republican* (Washington, DC), June 4, 1878. Sherman's brother, General William T. Sherman, once stated regarding the

presidency, "I will not run if nominated and I will not serve if elected"—hence "Shermanesque statement."

25. Anderson testimony, US House, *Presidential Election Investigation,* 1:18–21.

26. *New York Herald,* June 2, 1878.

27. *New York Sun,* June 2, 1878.

28. Anderson testimony, US House, *Presidential Election Investigation,* 1:34–38.

29. W. E. Chandler to E. L. Weber, June 2, 1878, box 46, Chandler Papers.

30. Williams, *Diary and Letters of Rutherford Birchard Hayes,* 485.

31. *New York Tribune,* June 3, 1878.

32. McCall. *Life of Thomas Brackett Reed,* 21–37, 57; Anderson testimony, US House, *Presidential Election Investigation,* 1:42–56.

33. Anderson testimony, US House, *Presidential Election Investigation,* 1:49–56.

34. Anderson testimony, US House, *Presidential Election Investigation,* 1:40, 57–58.

35. *New York Tribune,* June 5, 1878.

36. Anderson testimony, US House, *Presidential Election Investigation,* 1:62–67, 72–73; *New York Times,* June 6, 1878.

37. *New York Times,* June 6, 1878; *New York Sun,* June 6, 1878.

38. *New York Tribune,* June 5, 1878; *New York Sun,* June 6, 1878; *New York Herald,* June 6, 1878; Sherman to Reed, June 5, 1878, McCall, *Life of Thomas Brackett Reed,* 61. On Weber's signature, see, for example, Weber to C. C. Antoine, April 28, 1876; and Weber to Kellogg, July 15, 1876, Kellogg Papers. The fact that the signature on the "Anderson-Weber agreement" looks nothing like Weber's suggests that Anderson had received no written communications from him, which, if the case, casts doubt on everything he claimed about Weber's participation in his schemes.

39. Anderson testimony, US House, *Presidential Election Investigation,* 1:62, 69.

40. Anderson testimony, US House, *Presidential Election Investigation,* 1:72–73.

41. William H. Seymour, Alfred A. Wilder, and George Dicks testimony, US House, *Presidential Election Investigation,* 1:218–22, 223–25 225–28; *New York Herald,* June 6, 1878; *National Republican* (Washington, DC), June 13, 1878.

42. Thomas H. Jenks testimony, US House, *Presidential Election Investigation,* 1:287, 293–94.

43. Anderson testimony, US House, *Presidential Election Investigation,* 1:52–56.

44. *New York Herald,* June 6, 1878; *New York Tribune,* June 4, 6, 1878; *New York Sun,* June 5, 6, 1878.

45. Anderson testimony, US House, *Presidential Election Investigation,* 1:8, 62, 70–71; *New York Sun,* June 2, 1878.

46. *New York Sun,* June 4, 1878.

47. Darrall testimony, US House, *Presidential Election Investigation,* 1:175–217; *New York Sun,* June 12, 1878; *New York Times,* June 12, 13, 1878; *National Republican* (Washington, DC), June 13, 1878; Garfield diary, June 1, 1878, 76–77, series 1, reel 2, Garfield Papers,

48. *New York Times,* June 6, 12, 1878; *New York Herald,* June 9, 1878.

49. US Senate, *Presidential Election in Louisiana,* 1–2, 19.

50. *New York Tribune,* June 3, 1878; *New York Times,* June 6, 10, 1878; *New York Herald,* June 10, 1878.

51. *New York Tribune,* June 6, 1878; *New Orleans Daily Picayune,* June 11, 1878.

52. *National Republican* (Washington, DC), June 6, 1878.

53. Darrall testimony, US House, *Presidential Election Investigation,* 1:190; *New York Herald,* June 5, 1878.

54. Aaron B. Levisee diary, 4:97–136, Levisee Papers.

55. Levisee testimony, US House, *Presidential Election Investigation,* 1:80–91.

56. Levisee testimony, US House, *Presidential Election Investigation,* 1:95–96; *New York Sun,* June 7, 1878.

57. US House, *Investigation of Alleged Electoral Frauds,* 50–57, 103–4.

58. Thomas S. Kelly to Clarkson N. Potter, June 9, 1878, US House, *Presidential Election Investigation,* 1:1132; Gibson, *A Political Crime,* 292.

59. James D. Kennedy and James B. Kelley testimony, US House, *Presidential Election Investigation,* 1:1114–15, 3:567–71; Gibson, *A Political Crime,* 186. In a telegram dated June 7, two days before the date of Kelly's letter, C. W. Moulton, Sherman's brother-in-law, reported, "Kelly is teaching a brass band in Lake Providence." See Moulton to Sherman, June 7, 1878, letter book 158, Sherman Papers.

60. Kellogg testimony, US House, *Presidential Election Investigation,* 1:678–82; *New York Sun,* July 13, 1878.

61. Kellogg, Kennedy, and Kelly testimony, US House, *Presidential Election Investigation,* 1:708, 1115–17, 1148; *New York Sun,* January 1, 1879.

62. Woodward, *Reunion and Reaction,* 35; Gibson, *A Political Crime,* 187; Kellogg testimony, US House, *Testimony Relating to the Star-Route Cases,* 827.

63. *Cincinnati Enquirer,* January 15, 1879.

64. W. R. Whitaker and J. Douglass testimony, US House, *Presidential Election Investigation,* 3:572–74, 574–75; *Washington Post,* January 15, 1879; *New Orleans Daily Picayune,* January 15, 20, 1879; Gibson, *A Political Crime,* 188–89; Kelly testimony, US House, *Presidential Election Investigation,* 1:1138–50.

65. Thomas W. Ferry testimony, US House, *Presidential Election Investigation,* 1:139–40; *New York Herald,* June 8, 9, 1878; Haworth, *Hayes-Tilden Disputed Presidential Election,* 115–16.

66. *New York Herald,* June 10, 1878; *New York Tribune,* June 29, 1878; *New York Times,* June 13, 1878.

67. E. John Ellis to father, February 25, 1877, folder 29, box 5, Ellis Family Papers; McJimsey, *Genteel Partisan,* 202, 206; Julius L. Brown to Manton Marble, June 13, 1878, box 50, Marble Papers; Potter to Manton Marble, September [?], 1878, box 51, ibid.

68. Williams, *Diary and Letters of Rutherford Birchard Hayes,* 484–85.

69. *New York Tribune,* June 15, 1878; *New York Sun,* June 18, 1878. The "Burchard Resolution" passed 215 to 21.

70. *New York Tribune,* June 10, 14, 1878.

71. E. W. Stoughton to Sherman, June 10, 1878; Sherman to Potter, n.d.; Sherman

to Samuel Shellabarger, July 9, 1878; and Shellabarger to Sherman, July 10, 1878, letter book 158, Sherman Papers; *New York Times*, July 10, 1878.

72. *New York Sun*, June 22, 1878; Thomas H. Jenks testimony, US House, *Presidential Election Investigation*, 1:289–90.

73. Azaniah F. Wild to James F. Brooks, February 20, 1878, letter book 152, Sherman Papers; Agnes Jenks testimony, US House, *Presidential Election Investigation*, 1:380; Hyde, *Pistols and Politics: Feuds, Factions, and the Struggle for Order*, 128–36.

74. *New Orleans Republican*, May 6, 28, 30, October 25, 1871, June 15, 1872; *Ouachita Telegraph* (Monroe, LA), June 3, 1871, April 6, 1872. Lorenzo Jenks, after what appeared to be a botched suicide attempt—-he claimed it was an accidental gunshot wound—was indicted for embezzlement. When he stood trial in New Orleans in 1872, Judge A. A. Atocha applied the statute of limitations to acquit him. But Jenks's days as an elected official were over. When Kellogg appointed him to a minor position in West Feliciana Parish, he received a petition from more than two hundred Black voters denouncing Jenks as a swindler, ballot-box stuffer, and debauchee. Even so, Jenks gained a place on the 1876 ticket as the Republican candidate for parish judge. See Andrew Duncan et al. to W. P. Kellogg, n.d., folder 41, box 6, Kellogg Papers.

75. Thomas H. Jenks, Richard B. Edgeworth, and Seymour testimony, US House, *Presidential Election Investigation*, 1:303–4, 582–83, 1078–79, 3:89–93; *New York Times*, July 3, 1878. Edgeworth placed Jenks in Seymour's office on May 11, 1877. Upon enquiring why he was there, Jenks explained: "I am here to fix that damned son of a bitch Hayes. He treated us pretty bad, didn't he?"

76. Thomas H. Jenks testimony, US House, *Presidential Election Investigation*, 1:301–17; *New York Times*, June 23, 1878.

77. *New York Sun*, June 22, 24, 1878.

CHAPTER 5

1. *New Orleans Daily Picayune*, June 23, 1878; *New York Sun*, June 24, 1878.

2. *New York Times*, February 1, 2, 3, 6, June 23, 1878; *National Republican* (Washington, DC), June 14, 1878.

3. *New York Times*, June 22, 1878; *New York Herald*, June 23, 1878; *New York Sun*, June 23; Agnes Jenks testimony, US House, *Presidential Election Investigation*, 1:321; *New York Tribune*, June 26, 1878.

4. *New York Herald*, June 23, 1878; *New York Sun*, June 23, 1878.

5. Agnes Jenks testimony, US House, *Presidential Election Investigation*, 1:320; *New York Sun*, June 23, 1878.

6. Agnes Jenks testimony, US House, *Presidential Election Investigation*, 1:321.

7. *New York Sun*, June 23, 1878; *New Orleans Daily Picayune*, June 23, 1878; *New York Times*, June 23, 1878.

8. Agnes Jenks testimony, US House, *Presidential Election Investigation*, 1:361–67.

9. *New York Times,* June 23, 1878.

10. Agnes Jenks testimony, US House, *Presidential Election Investigation,* 1:329, 365–67.

11. *New York Sun,* June 23, 25, 1878; Agnes Jenks testimony, US House, *Presidential Election Investigation,* 1:324–25, 329, 347, 354.

12. Agnes Jenks testimony, US House, *Presidential Election Investigation,* 1:328.

13. Agnes Jenks testimony, US House, *Presidential Election Investigation,* 1:322–35; *New York Times,* June 24, 1878; *New York Herald,* June 23, 1878.

14. Agnes Jenks testimony, US House, *Presidential Election Investigation,* 1:338, 344, 349–50.

15. *New York Herald,* June 24, 1878; *New York Sun,* June 25, 1878; *New Orleans Daily Democrat,* June 25, 1878; *New York Tribune,* June 25, 1878; *New Orleans Daily Picayune,* June 29, 1878; Agnes Jenks testimony, US House, *Presidential Election Investigation,* 1:358, 367.

16. Agnes Jenks testimony, US House, *Presidential Election Investigation,* 1:367, 371; *New York Sun,* June 25, 1878; *New York Times,* June 24, 1878; *Santa Barbara (CA) Weekly Press,* July 15, 1878.

17. "Women Preaching . . . / Dog Walking . . . ," Samuel Johnson Sound Bite Page, https://www.samueljohnson.com/dogwalk.html; *New York Tribune,* June 24, 1878; *Washington Post,* June 25, 1878; *New York Times,* June 24; *New York Sun,* June 23, 24, 1878.

18. *New York World,* June 24, 1878; *Santa Barbara (CA) Weekly Press,* July 15, 1878; *New York Tribune,* June 24, 1878; *New York Times,* June 25, 1878; *Washington Evening Star,* June 24, 1878.

19. *Washington Post,* June 25, 1878; *New Orleans Daily Democrat,* July 16, 1878; *New York Tribune,* June 26, 1878.

20. *New York Times,* June 24, 1878; *New York Herald,* June 24, 1878.

21. *New York Herald,* June 24, 1878; *New York Times,* June 24, 1878; *New York Sun,* June 29, 1878; Agnes Jenks testimony, US House, *Presidential Election Investigation,* 1:424.

22. *New York Herald,* June 25, 1878; *New York Tribune,* July 2, 1878; *New York Sun,* June 28, 1878; Agnes Jenks testimony, US House, *Presidential Election Investigation,* 1:378–79.

23. William E. Chandler to E. L. Weber, March 15, 1878, box 46, Chandler Papers.

24. Haley testimony, US House, *Presidential Election Investigation,* 1:430–33; *New York Times,* June 30, 1878; *National Republican* (Washington, DC), June 27, 28, 1878; *Washington Evening Star,* June 29, July 12, 1878.

25. Agnes Jenks testimony, US House, *Presidential Election Investigation,* 1:423–26; *New York Times,* June 27, 1878; *National Republican* (Washington, DC), June 27, 1878.

26. Agnes Jenks testimony, US House, *Presidential Election Investigation,* 1:424–25; *New York Times,* June 25, 27, 1878; *New York Sun,* June 25, 1878.

27. *New York Sun,* June 30, 1878.

28. Agnes Jenks testimony, US House, *Presidential Election Investigation,* 1:522–23.

29. Agnes Jenks testimony, US House, *Presidential Election Investigation,* 1:519–24, 560; *New York Sun,* June 30, 1878; *New York Times,* June 30, 1878; *New York Tribune,* July 2, 1878.

30. Agnes Jenks testimony, US House, *Presidential Election Investigation,* 1:568; *New York Times,* June 30, July 2, 1878.

31. Agnes Jenks to Sherman, July 9, 1878, letter book 159, Sherman Papers.

32. Clipping, *Public Ledger and Transcript* (Philadelphia), June 24, 1878, letter book 158; and Agnes Jenks to Sherman, May 9, 11, 15, 1878, letter book 157, Sherman Papers; *New York Herald,* June 24, 1878; *New York Tribune,* June 25, 1878; *New York Sun,* July 26, 1878.

33. *New Orleans Daily Picayune,* July 3, 1878.

34. *New York Sun,* July 3, 1878; E. L. Weber testimony, US House, *Presidential Election Investigation,* 1:589–93, 616–19.

35. *New York Times,* July 4, 1878.

36. *Washington Evening Star,* June 4, 1878; Weber to Robert Morris, February 6, 1878, US House, *Presidential Election Investigation,* 3:372; Weber to Chandler, March 6, 1878, box 46, Chandler Papers.

37. *New York Sun,* June 26, 1878.

38. E. L. Weber testimony, US House, *Presidential Election Investigation,* 1:589–92; *New York Times*, July 3, 1878.

39. E. L. Weber testimony, US House, *Presidential Election Investigation,* 1:589–92; *New York Sun,* July 3, 1878.

40. E. L. Weber testimony, US House, *Presidential Election Investigation,* 1:592.

41. E. L. Weber testimony, US House, *Presidential Election Investigation,* 1:592–600.

42. *New York Times,* July 3, 1878; *New York Tribune,* July 3, 1878.

43. [A. M. Gibson], memorandum, June 29, 1878, folder b.14.f.1–2, Tilden Papers; Summers, *Party Games,* 148, 154; "Seven Mule Barnum Gets Roasted by Mark Twain," New England Historical Society, https://www.newenglandhistoricalsociety.com/seven-mule-barnum-gets-roasted-by-mark-twain/. Gibson's authorship of this unsigned document can be inferred from its contents. Educated guesswork is also required to identify Weber.

44. Gibson testimony, US House, *Presidential Election Investigation,* 1:1325–27.

45. Samuel H. St. Martin, affidavit, December 2, 1878, *New York Herald,* January 12, 1879; ibid., January 26, 1879; Maddox testimony, US House, *Presidential Election Investigation,* 1:1303.

46. Maddox testimony, US House, *Presidential Election Investigation,* 1:1288–89. On Maddox's wartime activities, see US Senate, *Reports and Papers in the Case of Joseph H. Maddox.*

47. Lonn, *Reconstruction in Louisiana after 1868,* 91–92, 103–35; George W. Carter testimony, US House, *Presidential Election Investigation,* 1:1316–21; E. John Ellis to Tom Ellis, February 5, 1876, folder 28, box 4, Ellis Family Papers.

48. Sherman to Potter, June 21, 1878, US House, *Presidential Election Investigation,* 1:1099–1100; John Ray to Samuel Shellabarger and Jeremiah M. Wilson, July 6, 7, 1878, letter book 159, Sherman Papers. Reed was the original Republican mem-

ber of the Louisiana subcommittee, but when he returned to Maine to conduct his reelection campaign, Cox took his place.

49. E. L. Weber testimony, US House, *Presidential Election Investigation,* 3:200–206, 216–17, 227; *New York Times,* July 12, 1878.

50. E. L. Weber testimony, US House, *Presidential Election Investigation,* 3:225–34.

51. E. L. Weber testimony, US House, *Presidential Election Investigation,* 3:238–42; *New York Sun,* July 13, 1878; Tunnell, *Edge of the Sword,* 275–78.

52. *Washington Evening Star,* July 12, 1878; *New Orleans Daily Picayune,* July 12, 1878; *New Orleans Daily Democrat,* July 13, 1878; E. L. Weber testimony, US House, *Presidential Election Investigation,* 3:205, 213–18, 240.

53. Henry Reid, Andrew Duncan, Thomas Steward, T. W. Dalton, Norfliss, and Julius Green testimony, US House, *Presidential Election Investigation,* 3:272, 306, 319–21, 489–509; *New York Times,* July 17, 21, 1878.

54. Mitchell testimony, US House, *Presidential Election Investigation,* 3:471–82.

55. Steward testimony, US House, *Presidential Election Investigation,* 3:322.

56. *New Orleans Daily Democrat,* July 17, 1878; Duncan testimony, US House, *Presidential Election Investigation,* 3:318.

57. Dula testimony, US House, *Presidential Election Investigation,* 3:354–61; *New Orleans Daily Democrat,* July 18, 1878; *New York Times,* July 18, 1878.

58. Samuel H. St. Martin and E. L. Weber testimony, US House, *Presidential Election Investigation,* 3:365–71.

59. T. M. J. Clark testimony, US House, *Presidential Election Investigation,* 3:373–86; *New Orleans Daily Picayune,* July 19, 1878; *Washington Post,* July 19, 1878.

60. Swayze testimony, US House, *Presidential Election Investigation,* 3:387–99.

61. Swayze testimony, US House, *Presidential Election Investigation,* 3:391–99; *New Orleans Daily Picayune,* July 19, 1878.

62. Eliza Pinkston, affidavit, June 23, 1878, *New York Herald,* June 24, 1878.

63. John Ray to John Sherman and J. M. Wilson, July 7, 1878, letter book 159, Sherman Papers; Henry R. Smith to Sherman, July 21, 1878, *New York Times,* July 30, 1878.

64. William Williams, Charles D. Hobbs, Smedley, Henry C. Fisk, and Reynolds testimony, US House, *Presidential Election Investigation,* 3:154–63, 166–67, 182–96, 246–56, 294; *New York Sun,* July 14, 1878; *New Orleans Daily Picayune,* July 11, 14, 1878.

65. Smedley testimony, US House, *Presidential Election Investigation,* 3:184, 186.

66. *New York Times,* July 25, 1878; *New Orleans Daily Democrat,* September 25, 1878.

67. *New York Sun,* July 12, 1878; *New York Times,* July 21, 1878. The epidemic killed John Dula and P. F. Blanchard.

68. Sherman testimony, US House, *Presidential Election Investigation,* 1:765–70.

69. *New York Sun,* July 26, 1878.

70. Sherman testimony, US House, *Presidential Election Investigation,* 1:786.

71. Sherman testimony, US House, *Presidential Election Investigation,* 1:770, 780; *New York Sun,* July 26, 1878; *New York Times,* July 26, 1878.

72. Cortland Parker and Garfield testimony, US House, *Presidential Election Investigation,* 1:728, 791–803.

73. J. Hale Sypher testimony, US House, *Presidential Election Investigation,* 1:753–60, 810, 858–59; *New York Times,* July 25, 26, 1878.

74. Leet testimony, US House, *Presidential Election Investigation,* 1:914–55; *New York Sun,* August 14, 16, 17, 1878; *New York Times,* August 15, 16, 17, 1878.

75. *New York Sun,* August 17, 19, 1878; *New York Times,* August 19, 20, 21, 1878; *Washington Post,* August 19, 1878.

76. *Chicago Daily Tribune,* January 13, 1879; H. V. Boynton to Benjamin H. Bristow, April 29, 1878, box 7, Bristow Papers.

CHAPTER 6

1. *New York Times,* June 12, 1878; *Cincinnati Enquirer,* June 11, 1878.

2. *New York Tribune,* June 10, 1878.

3. Chandler, *Letters,* 67, 73; Josie Ellis to Mary E. Ellis, March 21, 1877, folder 29, box 5, Ellis Family Papers.

4. *National Republican* (Washington, DC), March 29, 1877.

5. Chandler, *Letters,* 86–87.

6. *New York Sun,* April 30, 1877. See also *New Orleans Daily Democrat,* April 5, 14, 15, 17, 19, 1878; *New York Herald,* April 19, 20, 26, 1878; and Chandler, *Letters,* 29–35.

7. Butler to J. R. G. Pitkin, May 20, 1877, *New York Times,* May 29, 1877.

8. Wayne MacVeagh to Butler, May 29, 1877, folder 8, box 8, MacVeagh Family Papers.

9. Butler to Wayne MacVeagh, May 30, 1877, *New York Times,* June 6, 1877. MacVeagh had, in fact, served in Pennsylvania's emergency militia but had never been in battle.

10. *National Republican* (Washington, DC), March 29, 1877; *Chicago Daily Tribune,* March 30, 1877; *New York Sun,* July 13, 1877.

11. J. W. Dwyer to William E. Chandler, December 31, 1877; Pitkin to Chandler, January 10, 30, 1878; and Chandler to E. A. Burke, January 28, 30, 1878, box 45, Chandler Papers.

12. *New York Times,* January 5, 1878; *Chicago Daily Tribune,* February 14, 1878; *New York Times,* February 14, 1878.

13. *Washington Post,* February 2, 1878.

14. *Washington Post,* February 1, 1878.

15. T. H. C. Smith testimony, US House, *Presidential Election Investigation,* 1:228–49; *New York Times,* June 14, 1878; *New York Tribune,* June 14, 1878.

16. Summers, *Press Gang,* 85–86, 306–7; Woodward, *Reunion and Reaction,* 30–31; Ritchie, *Press Gallery,* 113–14.

17. Boynton testimony, US House, *Presidential Election Investigation,* 1:382–87, 394.

18. *New York Times,* August 15, 1878; *New York Tribune,* June 25, 1878; Boynton testimony, US House, *Presidential Election Investigation,* 1:395.

19. Summers, *Press Gang,* 307.

20. *New York Sun,* August 14, 1878.

21. William H. Roberts testimony, US House, *Presidential Election Investigation,* 1:878–79; *New York Sun,* August 14, 1878.

22. Roberts testimony, US House, *Presidential Election Investigation,* 1:875–79; Williams, *Diary and Letters of Rutherford Birchard Hayes,* 383; *New York Times,* August 14, 1878; Woodward, *Reunion and Reaction,* 26–27; Polakoff, *Politics of Inertia,* 224–25.

23. Roberts testimony, US House, *Presidential Election Investigation,* 1:881–82; *New York Times,* August 14, 1878.

24. Roberts testimony, US House, *Presidential Election Investigation,* 1:882–86. To sweeten the deal, Democrats intimated they would support Garfield as Speaker of the House, despite Republicans being in the minority. Republicans predicted that Hayes would appoint at least one southern Democrat to his cabinet.

25. Roberts testimony, US House, *Presidential Election Investigation,* 1:902; *New York Sun,* August 15, 1878.

26. Roberts testimony, US House, *Presidential Election Investigation,* 1:902–12; *New York Tribune,* August 15, 1878; *New York Herald,* August 15, 1878; *New York Sun,* August 15, 1878.

27. Roberts testimony, US House, *Presidential Election Investigation,* 1:880; *New York Times,* August 14, 1878.

28. A. M. Gibson to W. E. Chandler, July 12, 1878, box 46, Chandler Papers.

29. *Cincinnati Enquirer,* August 31, 1878; Powers, "'Commercial Union of the Three Americas,'" 22, 31–36, 45–49; Conley, "Making of an American Imperialist," 8–26; J. R. G. Pitkin to W. E. Chandler, February 14, 1878, box 45, Chandler Papers.

30. E. John Ellis and Burke testimony, US House, *Presidential Election Investigation,* 3:595–99, 3:601–12.

31. Ellis and Burke testimony, US House, *Presidential Election Investigation,* 3:595–97, 619–21.

32. *New York Herald,* August 21, 1878; Burke testimony, US House, *Presidential Election Investigation,* 1:958, 1007.

33. Burke testimony, US House, *Presidential Election Investigation,* 1:969, 978, 989; *New York Sun,* August 21, 1878.

34. Burke testimony; and Burke to Francis T. Nicholls, February 27, 1877, US House, *Presidential Election Investigation,* 1:961, 990, 3:624–25; *New York Sun,* August 22, 1878.

35. Burke testimony, US House, *Presidential Election Investigation,* 1:979–88; *New York Tribune,* August 22, 1878.

36. The angry confrontation between Burke and Butler did not appear in the pub-

lished hearings. This account is taken from the *New York Times, New York Sun, New York Tribune,* and *New York Herald,* all of August 22, 1878.

37. *New York Tribune,* August 22, 1878.

38. Burke testimony, US House, *Presidential Election Investigation,* 1:1024–29; *New York Herald,* August 24, 1878.

39. Burke testimony, US House, *Presidential Election Investigation,* 1:1031.

40. William E. Horne testimony, US House, *Presidential Election Investigation,* 1:1019–23; Thomas L. Young to Horne, February 22, 1877, ibid., 997; Burke testimony, ibid., 970.

41. *New York Herald,* August 23, 1878; *New York Sun,* August 23, 1878. This exchange did not appear in the published hearings.

42. *New York Tribune,* June 12, 1878; *New York Sun,* July 27, 1878; *New York Times,* June 21, 1878.

43. Calhoun, *Conceiving a New Republic,* 132.

44. Bancroft, *Speeches, Correspondence, and Political Papers of Carl Schurz,* 387; Polakoff, *Politics of Inertia,* 320; Gillette, *Retreat from Reconstruction,* 333–34.

45. Garfield to Hayes, December 13, 1876, reel 118, Garfield Papers; Cox to Carl Schurz, January 26, 1877, cited in Houdek, "James A. Garfield and Rutherford B. Hayes," 250–51; Foster to Hayes, February 10, 1877, cited in Tansill, *Congressional Career of Thomas Francis Bayard,* 192; Cox to Hayes, January 31, 1877; and Matthews to Hayes, February 13, 1877, cited in Polakoff, *Politics of Inertia,* 294–95.

46. Charles Nordhoff to Charles Foster, February 15, 1877; and Joseph Medill to Richard Smith, February 17, 1877, cited in Tansill, *Congressional Career of Thomas Francis Bayard,* 193–94; Reid to James G. Blaine, April 13, 1877, cited in Cortissoz, *Life of Whitelaw Reid,* 378.

47. Woodward, *Reunion and Reaction,* 226.

48. Hoogenboom, *Presidency of Rutherford B. Hayes,* 47–48; Gelderman, *A Free Man of Color and His Hotel,* 108. See also Polakoff, *Politics of Inertia,* 294, 314; McBride, *Randall Lee Gibson,* 171–72; Trefousse, *Rutherford B. Hayes,* 92–93; Morris, *Fraud of the Century,* 234; Zuczek, *State of Rebellion,* 200; Fitzgerald, *Splendid Failure,* 206–8; Summers, *Ordeal of the Reunion,* 384; and Calhoun, *Conceiving a New Republic,* 132.

49. Polakoff, *Politics of Inertia,* 105, 115.

50. Garfield diary, January 19, 20, 1877, series 1, reel 2, Garfield Papers; Polakoff, *Politics of Inertia,* 298; Houdek, "James A. Garfield and Rutherford B. Hayes," 213–14; Hoogenboom, *Presidency of Rutherford B. Hayes,* 44.

51. Roberts testimony, US House, *Presidential Election Investigation,* 1:881–82; Charles Hill testimony, ibid., 3:58; *New York Tribune,* July 2, 1878; Richardson, *William E. Chandler,* 204.

52. Woodward, *Reunion and Reaction,* 9.

53. Calhoun, *Conceiving a New Republic,* 133–34; Richardson, *William E. Chandler,* 236.

54. Woodward, *Reunion and Reaction,* 3; Richardson, *William E. Chandler,* 206–

7; William E. Chandler testimony, US House, *Presidential Election Investigation,* 1:533.

55. Woodward, *Reunion and Reaction,* 227–28; H. V. Boynton to Benjamin Bristow, November 17, 1878, box 8, Bristow Papers; *Evening Star* (Washington, DC), June 6, 1878.

56. Polakoff, *Politics of Inertia,* 251–56; Peskin, "Was There a Compromise of 1877?," 66–69; Benedict, "Southern Democrats and the Crisis of 1876–1877," 508–9; Summers, *Era of Good Stealings,* 292–96; Hayes to Schurz, January 4, 1877, Bancroft, *Speeches, Correspondence, and Political Papers of Carl Schurz,* 355; *Chicago Daily Tribune,* February 14, 1878.

57. Polakoff, *Politics of Inertia,* 313; Downs, "Mexicanization of American Politics," 403.

58. Gillette, *Retreat from Reconstruction,* 349.

59. Williams, *Life of Rutherford Birchard Hayes,* 1:516–19, 2:67.

60. Williams, *Life of Rutherford Birchard Hayes,* 2:519, 534.

61. E. John Ellis to Pa, February 25, 1877, folder 29, box 5, Ellis Family Papers; Tansill, *Congressional Career of Thomas Francis Bayard,* 195.

62. Garfield diary, February 26, 1877, series 1, reel 2, Garfield Papers.

63. *New York Times,* August 22, 1878.

64. Watterson, *"Marse Henry,"* 1:312; Richardson, *William E. Chandler,* 214.

65. Gillette, *Retreat from Reconstruction,* 347.

66. Logan, *Betrayal of the Negro,* 3; Fitzgerald, *Splendid Failure,* 209.

CHAPTER 7

1. *New York Tribune,* June 26, 1878.

2. Alfred B. Hinman, Alfred W. Shaw, and William Stocking testimony, US Senate, *Electoral Vote of Certain States,* 434, 442–66; *National Republican* (Washington, DC), February 15, 1877; *New York Tribune,* February 16, 1877.

3. Oberholtzer, *History of the United States since the Civil War,* 306–7.

4. James O. Green testimony, US House, *Presidential Election Investigation,* 4:30.

5. Cortissoz, *Life of Whitelaw Reid:* 406–7; Richardson, *William E. Chandler,* 227; J. L. Evans, George E. Bullock, and Thomas J. Brady testimony, US House, *Presidential Election Investigation,* 4:39–41, 50–60.

6. Chandler testimony, US House, *Presidential Election Investigation,* 4:71–75; Richardson, *William E. Chandler,* 227–28.

7. Chandler testimony, US House, *Presidential Election Investigation,* 4:75.

8. Chandler testimony, US House, *Presidential Election Investigation,* 4:81. These numbers add up to more than 750 because many were copies.

9. Manton Marble, "The Electoral Commission: A Secret Chapter of Political History," *New York Sun,* August 5, 1878; McJimsey, *Genteel Partisan,* 204–6.

10. Woolley to Randall, May 1, 4, 1878, box 48, Randall Papers.

11. *Cincinnati Enquirer,* May 27, 28, 1868.

12. Chandler testimony, US House, *Presidential Election Investigation,* 4:75; Cortisozz, *Life of Whitelaw Reid,* 1:409.

13. *New York Tribune,* August 7, 23, September 4, 5, 11, 1878; Whitelaw Reid testimony, US House, *Presidential Election Investigation,* 4:111.

14. *New York Tribune,* October 7, 8, 16, 1878.

15. Manton Marble to W. T. Pelton, December 2, 3, 5, 1876; C. W. Woolley to Henry Havemeyer, December 1, 4, 1876; Havemeyer to Woolley, December 1, 1876; and Pelton to Marble, December 3, 4, 1876, Reid, *Cipher Dispatches,* 18–21.

16. Smith Weed to Havemeyer, November 13, 14, 16, 18, 1876; and Pelton to Weed, November 14, 1876, Reid, *Cipher Dispatches,* 26–30; Haworth, *Hayes-Tilden Disputed Presidential Election,* 316–21.

17. *New York Tribune,* October 12, 1878; Cortissoz, *Life of Whitelaw Reid,* 422.

18. W. S. Dorsheimer to Francis Kernan, October 11, 1878, quoted in Flick, *Samuel Jones Tilden,* 437; Bigelow, *Retrospections of an Active Life,* 401; Tansill, *Congressional Career of Thomas Francis Bayard,* 119–21, 221; Nevins, *Abram S. Hewitt,* 399.

19. Watterson to Tilden, October 14, 1878, folder b26f.1, Tilden Papers.

20. Tilden to Editor and Marble to Editor, *New York Herald,* October 16, 1878.

21. *New York Tribune,* October 9, 1878.

22. Potter to Marble, [?], 1878, box 51, Marble Papers.

23. Richardson, *William E. Chandler,* 232.

24. Bigelow, *Retrospections of an Active Life,* 397; Watterson to Tilden, November 29, 1878, folder b26f.1, Tilden Papers.

25. Thomas Nast, *Cipher Mumm(er)y,* in *Harper's Weekly,* November 2, 1878, https://www.harpweek.com/09Cartoon/BrowseByDateCartoon-Large.asp?Month=November&Date=2 (accessed October 29, 2020).

26. *National Republican* (Washington, DC), October 28, 1878.

27. *New York Times,* October 28, 1878; *New Orleans Daily Picayune,* October 30, 1878; *Washington Post,* October 31, 1878.

28. *National Republican* (Washington, DC), October 28, 1878; *Washington Post,* October 31, 1878.

29. *New York Tribune,* October 28, 1878; *Philadelphia Times,* October 29, 1878; *New Orleans Daily Picayune,* November 6, 1878; *West Feliciana Sentinel* (St. Francisville, LA), November 9, 1878; *New Orleans Daily Democrat,* November 15, 1878.

30. *National Republican* (Washington, DC), November 1, 1878; *New York Herald,* October 27, 1878; *Chicago Daily Tribune,* October 27, 1878; *Washington Post,* October 26, 1878.

31. *New York Tribune,* July 6, 1878; *New Orleans Daily Picayune,* October 26, 1878.

32. An anonymous memorandum dated June 29, 1878, probably written by A. M. Gibson, throws light on the involvement of DNC chairman W. H. Barnum and the lack of coordination between Potter and the lawyers advising him. It also hints at money payments from the DNC to Weber. See folder b14f.1–2, Tilden Papers.

33. *West Feliciana Sentinel* (St. Francisville, LA), July 7, 14, October 13, Decem-

ber 1, 15, 1877, March 16, 1878; Oliver O. Provosty to E. L. Weber, March 19, 1878, US House, *Presidential Election Investigation,* 3:405.

34. A. M. Gibson to E. J. Ellis, September 25, 1878, folder 31, box 5, Ellis Family Papers.

35. J. H. Acklen to A. M. Gibson, October 31, 1878; S. H. St. Martin to Gibson, October 31, 1878; Gibson to Acklen, November 1, 1878; Gibson to St. Martin, November 1, 1878; and St. Martin to Gibson, November 1, 1878, US House, *Presidential Election Investigation,* 1:1230–31, 1253.

36. Maddox to St. Martin, November 1, 1878, US House, *Presidential Election Investigation,* 1:1173–74.

37. St. Martin and Maddox testimony, US House, *Presidential Election Investigation,* 1:1291, 1304–5; *New Orleans Daily Democrat,* November 13, 15, 1878.

38. Weber to St. Martin, November 21, 1878, US House, *Presidential Election Investigation,* 1:1219.

39. St. Martin testimony, US House, *Presidential Election Investigation,* 1:1161–62; John Ray to Sherman, December 1, 1878, letter book 164, Sherman Papers.

40. *New York Herald,* January 12, 1879; *New Orleans Daily Picayune,* January 13, 1879.

41. St. Martin and Maddox testimony, US House, *Presidential Election Investigation,* 1:1192, 1214, 1294–95.

42. D. J. M. A. Jewett to Sherman, November 19, 1878; and Marks to Sherman, December 10, 1878, letter book 164, Sherman Papers.

43. St. Martin and Maddox testimony, US House, *Presidential Election Investigation,* 1:1164, 1293; Shellabarger to Sherman, December 26, 1878, letter book 165, Sherman Papers.

44. St. Martin and Maddox testimony, US House, *Presidential Election Investigation,* 1:1216, 1293; Shellabarger to Potter, January 17, 1879, letter book 167, Sherman Papers.

45. Clarkson N. Potter to Manton Marble, [October/November] 1878, box 50, Marble Papers.

46. *New York Tribune,* September 7, 1878; *Washington Evening Star,* September 7, 1878; *New York Sun,* January 7, 1879.

47. Statement of Clarkson N. Potter, US House, *Presidential Election Investigation,* 1:1127.

48. *New Orleans Daily Picayune,* January 1, 1879.

49. John Ray to Potter, January 1, 1879, US House, *Presidential Election Investigation,* 1:1128.

50. Henry C. Lloyd, Thomas L. Raymond, and James D. Maloney testimony, US House, *Presidential Election Investigation,* 1:1118–27.

51. *Chicago Daily Tribune,* January 7, 1879; *New York Tribune,* January 3, 8, 1879; Bronson, *Life and Public Services of Hon. John Sherman,* 42–43; Jenks to Sherman, January 11, 1879, letter book 167, Sherman Papers.

52. *New York Sun,* January 7, 1879.

53. *New York Herald,* January 11, 1879.

54. George J. Norwood to Sherman, November 18, 1878, letter book 164, Sherman Papers.

55. *West Feliciana Sentinel* (St. Francisville, LA), September 28, October 12, 1878; *New Orleans Daily Democrat,* September 25, October 2, 5, 1878.

56. St. Martin testimony, US House, *Presidential Election Investigation,* 1:1219–20.

57. Williams, *Diary and Letters of Rutherford Birchard Hayes,* 510; Hirshson, *Farewell to the Bloody Shirt,* 47–49; Simpson, *Reconstruction Presidents,* 218–19; Calhoun, *Conceiving a New Republic,* 156–58.

58. Calhoun, *Creating a New Republic,* 157; Williams, *Diary and Letters of Rutherford Birchard Hayes,* 508.

59. Houdek, "James A. Garfield and Rutherford B. Hayes," 336–37.

60. *Washington Evening Star,* January 10, 1879; *Chicago Daily Tribune,* January 11, 20, 1879; *New York Herald,* January 12, 1879; *National Republican* (Washington, DC), January 17, 1879.

61. *National Republican* (Washington, DC), January 17, 1879.

62. St. Martin testimony, US House, *Presidential Election Investigation,* 1:1118, 1168, 1241–49.

63. St. Martin testimony, US House, *Presidential Election Investigation,* 1:1166–68, 1178–80, 1191–92, 1239, 1252.

64. St. Martin testimony, US House, *Presidential Election Investigation,* 1:1123–24.

65. St. Martin testimony, US House, *Presidential Election Investigation,* 1:1178, 1201; *Washington Evening Star,* January 24, 1879.

66. *Chicago Daily Tribune,* January 13, 1879.

67. Maddox, George W. Carter, and Gibson testimony, US House, *Presidential Election Investigation,* 1:1287–1329.

68. [A. M. Gibson], memorandum, June 29, 1878, folder b.14.f.1–2, Tilden Papers; Summers, *Party Games,* 148, 154; "Seven Mule Barnum Gets Roasted by Mark Twain," New England Historical Society, https://www.newenglandhistoricalsociety.com/seven-mule-barnum-gets-roasted-by-mark-twain/.

69. *New York Tribune,* January 9, 11, 1879; *Washington Evening Star,* January 10, 1879.

70. *Congressional Record,* 45th Cong., 3d sess. (1878–79), 8(1):610.

71. *Congressional Record,* 45th Cong., 3d sess. (1878–79), 8(1):609–10; *Chicago Daily Tribune,* January 23, 1879.

72. *Cincinnati Enquirer,* August 24, 1878; *New York Tribune,* September 17, 1878; Crenshaw, "Benjamin F. Butler," 47–49, 54.

73. *Congressional Record,* 45th Cong., 3d sess. (1878–79), 8(1):611; Flick, *Samuel J. Tilden,* 401, 413.

74. *Congressional Record,* 45th Cong., 3d sess. (1878–79), 8(1):608–9.

75. *Cincinnati Enquirer,* January 22, 1879.

76. *Washington Post,* November 28, 1878, January 11, 1879; *New York Tribune,* February 1, 1879; *Cincinnati Enquirer,* January 16, February 1, 3, 1879.

77. *New York Tribune,* January 24, 25, 29, February 1, 1879.

78. *Cincinnati Enquirer,* January 29, 1879.

79. Brady testimony, US House, *Presidential Election Investigation,* 4:60–61; *New York Tribune,* January 30, 1879.

80. James O. Green testimony, US House, *Presidential Election Investigation,* 4:36; *Cincinnati Enquirer,* January 28, 1879.

81. *New York Herald,* January 27, 29, 1879; *New York Tribune,* January 30, 1879; *New York Sun,* January 30, 1879; *Cincinnati Enquirer,* January 30, 1879; J. N. Tyner testimony, US House, *Presidential Election Investigation,* 4:92.

82. *Chicago Daily Tribune,* January 23, 1879; *Cincinnati Enquirer,* January 22, 1879.

CHAPTER 8

1. *Cincinnati Enquirer,* July 9, 1878, February 6, 1879.

2. Flick, *Samuel J. Tilden,* 6, 273–74, 531–32; Bigelow, *Retrospections of an Active Life,* 208, 303, 417; Summers, *Press Gang,* 302.

3. *Cincinnati Enquirer,* June 20, 1878; Summers, *Press Gang,* 300–301; Clapp, *Forgotten First Citizen,* 278.

4. Summers, *Party Games,* 151–52; Flick, *Samuel J. Tilden,* 161–91, 213–27, 232–39, 265–74.

5. Summers, *Press Gang,* 50; Flick, *Samuel J. Tilden,* 49–50, 275, 288; Polakoff, *Politics of Inertia,* 79–80; Holt, *By One Vote,* 10–11.

6. *Cincinnati Enquirer,* February 19, 1879; Flick, *Samuel J. Tilden,* 68, 254–56, 301–2.

7. *New York Herald,* February 6, 1879; Hunton, *Autobiography,* 193.

8. Reid, *Cipher Dispatches,* 29–30; Smith M. Weed testimony, US House, *Presidential Election Investigation,* 4:116–25.

9. Weed testimony, US House, *Presidential Election Investigation,* 4:117.

10. Weed testimony, US House, *Presidential Election Investigation,* 4:148–51; Reid, *Cipher Dispatches,* 31–33; *New York Times,* February 6, 1878; *New York Tribune,* February 7, 1879.

11. *New York Herald,* February 7, 1879.

12. Grant, *Mr. Speaker!,* 85.

13. *New York Times,* February 7, 1879; *Daily Alto California* (San Francisco), February 9, 1879; William T. Pelton testimony, US House, *Presidential Election Investigation,* 4:201, 209–10.

14. *New York Herald,* February 7, 1879; *New York Times,* February 7, 1879.

15. *New York Times,* February 7, 1879; Poore, *Perley's Reminiscences,* 322–23.

16. *New York Herald,* February 7, 1879; *New York Tribune,* February 7, 1879; Pelton testimony, US House, *Presidential Election Investigation,* 4:209–20.

17. *New York Tribune,* February 7, 1879; Bigelow, *Retrospections of an Active Life,* 402; Flick, *Samuel J. Tilden,* 436.

18. McJimsey, *Genteel Partisan,* 44–53, 74.

19. *Cincinnati Enquirer,* June 20, 1878; Blaine, *Twenty Years of Congress,* 590.

20. Manton Marble testimony, US House, *Presidential Election Investigation,* 4:227–29; *New York Times,* February 8, 1879; *New York Herald,* February 8, 1879; Manton Marble to J. C. Welling, n.d., box 50, Marble Papers.

21. Marble testimony, US House, *Presidential Election Investigation,* 4:238, 260–64; Reid, *Cipher Dispatches,* 19. In his own testimony to the committee, McLin had denied soliciting a bribe. It was Marble, he claimed, who promised that the Democratic Party would provide for him if the board decided for Tilden.

22. Marble testimony, US House, *Presidential Election Investigation,* 4:238, 256–60; *New York Herald,* February 8, 1879; *New York Times,* February 8, 1879.

23. Marble testimony, US House, *Presidential Election Investigation,* 4:258; *New York Herald,* February 8, 1879.

24. Marble testimony, US House, *Presidential Election Investigation,* 4:242; *New York Herald,* February 8, 1879; *New York Times,* February 8, 1879.

25. Marble testimony, US House, *Presidential Election Investigation,* 4:243; *National Republican* (Washington, DC), February 8, 1879; *New York Times,* February 8, 1879.

26. Clark, "The Fox Goes to France," 452–54.

27. Marble to J. C. Welling, n.d., box 50, Marble Papers; *New York Tribune,* February 12, 1879; Bigelow, *Retrospections of an Active Life,* 401; McJimsey, *Genteel Partisan,* 195, 208–11.

28. Bigelow, *Retrospections of an Active Life,* 399.

29. *New York Herald,* February 9, 1879; *New York Times,* February 9, 1879; *New York Tribune,* February 10, 1879.

30. Samuel J. Tilden testimony, US House, *Presidential Election Investigation,* 4:272–74.

31. *New York Times,* February 9, 1879.

32. Tilden testimony, US House, *Presidential Election Investigation,* 4:278–80.

33. Tilden testimony, US House, *Presidential Election Investigation,* 4:281–83; Williams, *Life of Rutherford Birchard Hayes,* 2:164. Tilden's letter was, writes Williams, "disingenuous and misleading."

34. Tilden testimony, US House, *Presidential Election Investigation,* 4:275, 288.

35. Tilden testimony, US House, *Presidential Election Investigation,* 4:285–86; *New York Times,* February 9, 1879; Flick, *Samuel J. Tilden,* 434.

36. Tilden testimony, US House, *Presidential Election Investigation,* 4:285–87; *New York Times,* February 9, 1879.

37. Tilden testimony, US House, *Presidential Election Investigation,* 4:288–89.

38. *New York Tribune,* February 11, 1879; *Chicago Daily Tribune,* February 7, 1879; Williams, *Life of Rutherford Birchard Hayes,* 2:167.

39. *New York Tribune,* February 11, 1879; Cortissoz, *Life of Whitelaw Reid,* 421.

40. *New York Herald,* February 13, 1879; *Cincinnati Enquirer,* February 13, 1879.

41. US House, *Investigation of Alleged Electoral Frauds,* 65–67.

42. Montgomery Blair to Tilden, February 8, 1879, folder b6f.38–40, Tilden Papers.

43. US House, *Investigation of Alleged Electoral Frauds,* 21–37.

44. US House, *Investigation of Alleged Electoral Frauds,* 28–37.

45. US House, *Investigation of Alleged Electoral Frauds,* 30, 38, 44–46.

46. Potter to William C. Whitney, March 2, 1879, folder b.20f.37, Tilden Papers.

47. *New York Times,* March 5, 1879; *New York Herald,* March 7, 1879.

48. US House, *Investigation of Alleged Electoral Frauds,* 70–74.

49. US House, *Investigation of Alleged Electoral Frauds,* 74–75.

50. US House, *Investigation of Alleged Electoral Frauds,* 86–87.

51. US House, *Investigation of Alleged Electoral Frauds,* 89–91.

52. US House, *Investigation of Alleged Electoral Frauds,* 96.

53. US House, *Investigation of Alleged Electoral Frauds,* 117.

54. US House, *Investigation of Alleged Electoral Frauds,* 100–102.

55. US House, *Investigation of Alleged Electoral Frauds,* 100–101.

56. US House, *Investigation of Alleged Electoral Frauds,* 102–3.

57. US House, *Investigation of Alleged Electoral Frauds,* 106–7.

58. US House, *Investigation of Alleged Electoral Frauds,* 107–11. Gibson did not attend the final meeting at the Wormley House, being ill at the time.

59. US House, *Investigation of Alleged Electoral Frauds,* 111–16.

60. US House, *Investigation of Alleged Electoral Frauds,* 116.

61. US House, *Investigation of Alleged Electoral Frauds,* 114.

62. US House, *Investigation of Alleged Electoral Frauds,* 118.

63. *New York Sun,* March 5, 1879; *Chicago Daily Tribune,* March 4, 1879.

64. *New York Sun,* March 5, 1879.

65. *New York Sun,* March 5, 7, 1879.

66. Adams to Bigelow, February 16, 1879, quoted in Bigelow, *Retrospections of an Active Life,* 401; *Cincinnati Enquirer,* February 20, 1879.

67. Flick, *Samuel J. Tilden,* 445–46.

68. House, "Internal Conflict in Key States," 200–201; Samuel Barlow to Thomas Bayard, November 10, 1879, quoted in Tansill, *Congressional Career of Thomas Francis Bayard,* 242; *New York Herald,* November 9, 1879.

69. Summers, *Era of Good Stealings,* 298; Sherman, *Recollections of Forty Years,* 656–57.

70. *Garfield in Louisiana: The Disreputable Part Taken by the Republican Candidate for President in the Great Fraud of 1876* (1880); Williams, *Life of Rutherford Birchard Hayes,* 1:539.

71. Thomas H. Jenks to Sherman, February 15, 1879; Agnes D. Jenks to Sherman, February 28, 1879; and H. S. Foote to Sherman, March 6, 8, 1879, letter book 169, Sherman Papers.

CONCLUSION

1. *Cincinnati Enquirer,* July 9, 1878.

2. Jenks to Sherman, July 9, 1878, letter book 159; and Jenks to Sherman, January 11, 1879, letter book 167, Sherman Papers.

3. Shellabarger to Sherman, July 31, 1878, letter book 159; and Horace W. King to Sherman, June 7, 1878, letter book 158, Sherman Papers.

4. Wallace, *Autobiography,* 901–2.

5. Kellogg testimony, US House, *Presidential Election Investigation,* 1:665–67; Hoogenboom, *Presidency of Rutherford B. Hayes,* 29–30.

6. Woodward, *Reunion and Reaction,* 95, 134–35; Jenks to Sherman, July 9, 1878, letter book 159, Sherman Papers; Grenville M. Dodge to William E. Chandler, December 19, 1876, box 43, Chandler Papers. Democrats believed that West had bribed members of the state legislature in order to secure election to the US Senate in 1872. See E. John Ellis to Tom Ellis, January 17, February 1, 5, 1876, folder 28, box 4, Ellis Family Papers.

7. Flick, *Samuel J. Tilden,* 518–19; A. M. Gibson to Tilden, July 2, 1879, folder b.12f.24, Tilden Papers.

8. Flick, *Samuel J. Tilden,* 249, 300.

9. Bigelow, *Retrospections of an Active Life,* 397–98.

10. According to Bigelow's diary, Tilden was aware, too, that Florida's returning board had been offered to him for $100,000. See Bigelow, *Retrospections of an Active Life,* 298–99; and Summers, *Era of Good Stealings,* 291.

11. L. G. Dennis testimony, US House, *Presidential Election Investigation,* 1:556. For a list of Louisiana Republicans appointed to office, see US House, *Investigation of Alleged Electoral Frauds,* 48–49.

12. Garfield diary, March 8, 1878, series 1, reel 2, Garfield Papers.

13. Williams, *Diary and Letters of Rutherford Birchard Hayes,* 269; Hoogenboom, *Presidency of Rutherford B. Hayes,* 130.

14. Hoogenboom, *Outlawing the Spoils,* 151.

15. Schmiel, "Career of Jacob Dolson Cox," 402–3; *New York Sun,* July 21, 1878; T. H. C. Smith testimony, US House, *Presidential Election Investigation,* 1:294.

16. Nevins, *Abram S. Hewitt,* 396; Hoogenboom, *Outlawing the Spoils,* 209–52.

17. Lonn, *Reconstruction in Louisiana after 1868,* 450; Thomas H. Noland testimony, US House, *Presidential Election Investigation,* 3:582.

18. The witness testimony can be found in US House, *Recent Election in Louisiana: Testimony,* 4 parts; and US Senate, *Louisiana in 1876,* 3 vols.

19. Harris testimony, US House, *Recent Election in Louisiana: Testimony,* 2:306–7; statement of C. B. Wheeler, November 11, 1876, US Senate, *Electoral Vote of Louisiana,* 727; C. B. Wheeler, affidavit, November 20, 1876, US Senate, *Vote for Electors in Louisiana,* 443–47.

20. *New York Tribune,* June 29, 1878.

21. *Santa Barbara Weekly Press,* July 13, 1878; *New York Times,* June 13, 1878; *New York Herald,* August 13, 1878; *New York World,* June 24, 1878.

22. B. A. Hinsdale to Garfield, February 18, 1877, reel 36, Garfield Papers.

23. Frank Morey testimony, US House, *Presidential Election Investigation,* 1:849; Hayes diary, April 11, 1880, Williams, *Diary and Letters of Rutherford Birchard Hayes,* 594–95.

24. Polakoff, *Politics of Inertia,* 272.

25. Butler, *Butler's Book,* 967.

26. Goldman, *Reconstruction and Black Suffrage,* 119–34.

27. Wang, *The Trial of Democracy,* 165–77, 254–59; Perman, *Struggle for Mastery,* 37–47 passim.

28. Polakoff, *Politics of Inertia,* 264.

29. *New York Times,* July 21, 1878.

BIBLIOGRAPHY

MANUSCRIPT COLLECTIONS

Thomas F. Bayard Papers. Library of Congress, Washington, DC.

Benjamin H. Bristow Papers. Library of Congress, Washington, DC.

Benjamin F. Butler Papers. Library of Congress, Washington, DC.

William E. Chandler Papers. Library of Congress, Washington, DC.

Ellis Family Papers. Louisiana and Lower Mississippi Valley Collection. Hill Memorial Library, Louisiana State University, Baton Rouge.

James A. Garfield Papers. Library of Congress, Washington, DC. Microfilm.

John M. Harlan Papers. Library of Congress, Washington, DC.

Rutherford B. Hayes Papers. Library of Congress, Washington, DC. Microfilm.

William P. Kellogg Papers. Louisiana and Lower Mississippi Valley Collection. Hill Memorial Library, Louisiana State University, Baton Rouge.

Letters Received by the Department of Justice from the State of Louisiana, 1871–84, M940. US Department of Justice, General Records. Record Group 60. National Archives and Records Administration, Washington, DC. Microfilm.

A. B. Levisee Papers. Library of Congress, Washington, DC,

MacVeagh Family Papers. Historical Society of Pennsylvania, Philadelphia.

Manton Marble Papers. Library of Congress, Washington, DC.

Samuel J. Randall Papers. Historical Society of Pennsylvania, Philadelphia.

Whitelaw Reid Papers. Library of Congress, Washington, DC.

John Sherman Papers. Library of Congress, Washington, DC.

Samuel J. Tilden Papers. Digital Collections. New York Public Library, https://digitalcollections.nypl.org/collections/samuel-j-tilden-papers.

PUBLISHED LETTERS, DIARIES, DOCUMENTS, AND MEMOIRS

Bancroft, Frederic, ed. *Speeches, Correspondence, and Political Papers of Carl Schurz.* Vol. 3. New York: G. P. Putnam's Sons, 1913.

Bigelow, John, ed. *Letters and Literary Memorials of Samuel J. Tilden.* 2 vols. New York: Harper and Bros., 1908.

———. *Retrospections of an Active Life.* Vol. 5. Garden City, NY: Doubleday, Page, 1913.

———, ed. *The Writings and Speeches of Samuel J. Tilden.* 2 vols. New York: Harper and Bros., 1885.

Blaine, James G. Blaine. *Twenty Years of Congress.* Vol. 2. Norwich, CT: Henry Hill, 1886.

Burke, Edward A. *Statement of Facts Relating to the Election in Louisiana, November 7th, 1876.* Washington, DC, 1877.

Butler, Benjamin F. *Butler's Book: A Review of His Legal, Political and Military Career.* Boston: A. M. Thayer, 1892.

Chandler, William E. *Letters of Mr. William E. Chandler Relative to the So-called Southern Policy of President Hayes.* Concord, NH: Monitor and Statesman, 1878.

Hoar, George F. *Autobiography of Seventy Years.* 2 vols. New York: George Scribner's Sons, 1903.

Hunton, Eppa. *Autobiography of Eppa Hunton.* Richmond, VA: William Byrd, 1933.

Poore, Ben Perley. *Perley's Reminiscences of Sixty Years in the National Metropolis.* Vol. 2. Philadelphia: Hubbard Bros., 1886.

Reid, Whitelaw. *The Cipher Dispatches.* New York: Tribune Extra, 1879.

Shaw, John, ed. *Crete and James: Personal Letters of Lucretia and James Garfield.* East Lansing: Michigan State University Press, 1994.

Sherman, John. *Recollections of Forty Years in the House, Senate and Cabinet: An Autobiography.* Chicago: Werner, 1895.

Simon, John Y., ed. *The Papers of Ulysses S. Grant.* Vol. 28, *November 1, 1876–September 30, 1878.* Carbondale: Southern Illinois University Press, 2005.

Stealey, O. O. *Twenty Years in the Press Gallery.* New York: Publishers Printing, 1906.

Wallace, Lew. *An Autobiography.* Vol. 2. New York: Harper and Bros., 1906.

Watterson, Henry. *"Marse Henry": An Autobiography.* 2 vols. New York: George H. Doran, 1919.

Williams, Charles R., ed. *Diary and Letters of Rutherford Birchard Hayes.* Vol. 3. Columbus: Ohio State Archaeological and Historical Association, 1924.

PUBLIC DOCUMENTS

US Congress. *Proceedings of the Electoral Commission: The Electoral Count of 1877.* 44th Cong., 2d sess., 1877.

US Congress, House. *Alleged Outrages in West Feliciana Parish, Louisiana.* 44th Cong., 1st sess., 1877. House Rep. 816.

———. *Counting the Vote for President and Vice-President of the United States.* 44th Cong., 2d sess., 1877. House Misc. Doc. 42.

———. *Investigation of Alleged Electoral Frauds in the Late Presidential Election.* 45th Cong., 3d sess., 1879. House Rep. 140. Pt. 1.

———. *Presidential Election Investigation: Testimony Taken by the Select Committee on Alleged Frauds in the Presidential Election of 1876.* 45th Cong., 3d sess., 1879. House Misc. Doc. 31. Pts. 1–4.

———. *The Recent Election in Louisiana.* 44th Cong., 2d sess., 1877. House Rep. 156. Pts. 1–2.

———. *The Recent Election in Louisiana: Testimony.* 44th Cong., 2d sess., 1877. House Misc. Doc. 34. Pts. 1–4.

———. *Testimony Relating to the Star-Route Cases.* 48th Congress, 1st sess., 1884, House Misc. Doc. 38. Pt. 2.

———. *Use of the Army in Certain Southern States.* 44th Cong., 2d sess., 1876. House Exec. Doc. 30.

US Congress, Senate. *Electoral Vote of Certain Southern States.* 44th Cong., 2d sess., 1877. Senate Misc. Doc. 44.

———. *Electoral Vote of Louisiana.* 44th Cong., 2d sess., 1877. Senate Misc. Doc. 14.

———. *Louisiana in 1876.* 44th Cong., 2d sess., 1877. Senate Report 701. 3 vols.

———. *Louisiana in 1878.* 45th Cong., 3d sess., 1879. Senate Report 855.

———. *Presidential Election in Louisiana.* 45th Cong., 3d sess., 1879. Senate Report 867.

———. *Proceedings of the Committee on Privileges and Elections on the Contested Cases of William P. Kellogg and Henry M. Spofford as Senators from the State of Louisiana.* 46th Cong., 2d sess., 1880. Senate Misc. Doc. 79.

———. *Reports and Papers in the Case of Joseph H. Maddox.* 51st Cong., 1st sess., 1890. Senate Exec. Doc. 101.

———. *Testimony of James E. Anderson.* 45th Cong., 3d sess., 1879. Senate Misc. Doc. 50.

———. *Vote for Electors in Louisiana.* 44th Cong., 2d sess., 1877. Senate Exec. Doc. 2.

NEWSPAPERS

Alexandria (LA) Gazette
Chicago Daily Tribune
Cincinnati Enquirer
Clinton (LA) Patriot-Democrat
Donaldsonville (LA) Chief
Natchitoches (LA) People's Vindicator
National Republican (Washington, DC)

New Orleans Bulletin
New Orleans Daily Democrat
New Orleans Daily Picayune
New York Herald
New York Sun
New York Times
New York Tribune
St. Francisville (LA) Semi-Weekly Republican
Washington Evening Star
Washington Post
West Feliciana Sentinel (St. Francisville, LA)

BOOKS, ARTICLES, AND DISSERTATIONS

Benedict, Michael Les. "Southern Democrats in the Crisis of 1876–1877: A Reconsideration of *Reunion and Reaction*." *Journal of American History* 46:4 (November 1980): 489–524.

Bigelow, John. *The Life of Samuel J. Tilden*. New York: Harper and Bros., 1895.

Biographies of the Present Senators of the United States. Baltimore: Turnbull Bros., 1892.

Bronson, S. A. *Life and Public Services of the Hon. John Sherman*. Columbus, OH: H. W. Derby, 1884.

Calhoun, Charles W. *Conceiving a New Republic: The Republican Party and the Southern Question, 1869–1900*. Lawrence: University Press of Kansas, 2006.

Clapp, Margaret. *Forgotten First Citizen: John Bigelow*. New York: Little, Brown, 1947.

Clark, James C. "The Fox Goes to France: Florida, Secret Codes, and the Election of 1876." *Florida Historical Quarterly* 69:4 (April 1991): 430–56.

Conley, Kathryn K. "The Making of an American Imperialist: Major Edward Austin Burke, Reconstruction New Orleans, and the Road to Central America." M.A. thesis, University of New Orleans, 2012. UNO theses and dissertations, 1428. Earl K. Long Library, University of New Orleans, https://scholarworks.uno.edu/td/1428.

Cortissoz, Royal. *The Life of Whitelaw Reid*. Vol. 1. London: Thornton, 1921.

Crenshaw, William V. "Benjamin F. Butler: Philosophy and Politics, 1866–1879." Ph.D. diss., University of Georgia, 1976.

Davison, Kenneth E. *The Presidency of Rutherford B. Hayes*. Westport, CT: Greenwood, 1972.

Dawson, Joseph G., III. *Army Generals and Reconstruction: Louisiana, 1862–1877*. Baton Rouge: Louisiana State University Press, 1982.

Dippre, Harold C. "Corruption and the Disputed Vote of Oregon in the 1876 Election." *Oregon Historical Quarterly* 67:3 (September 1966): 257–72.

Downs, Gregory P. "The Mexicanization of American Politics: The United States' Transnational Path from Civil War to Stabilization." *American Historical Review* 112:2 (April 2012): 387–409.

Fielder, Elizabeth Rouse. *Joseph C. S. Blackburn: Soldier, Statesman, and a Friend of All.* Morley, MO: Acclaim, 2018.

Fitzgerald, Michael W. *Splendid Failure: Postwar Reconstruction in the South.* Chicago: Ivan R. Dee, 2007.

Flick, Alexander C. *Samuel J. Tilden: A Study in Political Sagacity.* New York: Dodd, Mead, 1939.

Foner, Eric. *Reconstruction: America's Unfinished Revolution, 1863–1877.* New York: Harper and Row, 1988.

Gelderman, Carol. *A Free Man of Color and His Hotel: Race, Reconstruction, and the Role of the Federal Government.* Dulles, VA: Potomac Books, 2012.

Gibson, A. M. *A Political Crime: The History of the Great Fraud.* New York: William S. Gottsberger, 1885.

Gillette, William. *Retreat from Reconstruction, 1869–1879.* Baton Rouge: Louisiana State University Press, 1979.

Goldman, Robert M. *Reconstruction and Black Suffrage: Losing the Vote in Reese and Cruikshank.* Lawrence: University Press of Kansas, 2001.

Grant, James. *Mr. Speaker! The Life and Times of Thomas B. Reed—The Man Who Broke the Filibuster.* New York: Simon and Schuster, 2011.

Guenther, Karen. "The Potter Committee Investigation of the Disputed Election of 1876." *Florida Historical Quarterly* 61:3 (January 1983): 281–96.

Hair, William Ivy. *Bourbonism and Agrarian Protest: Louisiana Politics, 1877–1900.* Baton Rouge: Louisiana State University Press, 1969.

Haworth, Paul L. *The Hayes-Tilden Disputed Presidential Election of 1876.* Cleveland: Burrow Brothers, 1906.

Hearn Chester G. *When the Devil Came Down to Dixie: Ben Butler in New Orleans.* Baton Rouge: Louisiana State University Press, 1997.

Hirshson, Stanley. *Farewell to the Bloody Shirt: Northern Republicans and the Southern Negro, 1877–1893.* Chicago: Quadrangle, 1962.

Holt, Michael F. Holt. *By One Vote: The Disputed Presidential Election of 1876.* Lawrence: University Press of Kansas, 2008.

Hoogenboom, Ari. *Outlawing the Spoils: A History of the Civil Service Reform Movement.* Urbana: University of Illinois Press, 1961.

———. *The Presidency of Rutherford B. Hayes.* Lawrence: University Press of Kansas, 1995.

Houdek, John T. "James A. Garfield and Rutherford B. Hayes: A Study in State and National Politics." Ph.D. diss., Michigan State University, 1970.

House, Albert V. "Internal Conflict in Key States in the Democratic Convention of 1880." *Pennsylvania History* 27:2 (April 1960): 188–216.

Hyde, Samuel C., Jr. *Pistols and Politics: The Dilemma of Democracy in Louisiana's Florida Parishes, 1810–1899*. Baton Rouge: Louisiana State University Press, 1996.

———. *Pistols and Politics: Feuds, Factions, and the Struggle for Order in Louisiana's Florida Parishes, 1810–1935*. Baton Rouge: Louisiana State University Press, 2018.

Kennedy, Patrick W. "Oregon and the Disputed Election of 1876." *Pacific Northwest Quarterly* 60:3 (July 1963): 135–44.

Logan, Rayford. *The Betrayal of the Negro: From Rutherford B. Hayes to Woodrow Wilson*. New York: Collier Books, 1965.

Lonn, Ella. *Reconstruction in Louisiana after 1868*. 1918. Gloucester, MA: Peter Smith, 1967.

Lowrey, Walter McGehee. "The Political Career of James Madison Wells." *Louisiana Historical Quarterly* 31 (October 1948): 994–1123.

McBride, Mary G. *Randall Lee Gibson of Louisiana: Confederate General and New South Reformer*. Baton Rouge: Louisiana State University Press, 2007.

McCall, Samuel W. *The Life of Thomas Brackett Reed*. Boston: Houghton Mifflin, 1914.

McCormack, Thomas J., ed. *Memoirs of Gustave Koerner*. 2 vols. Cedar Rapids, IA: Torch, 1909.

McFeely, William. *Grant: A Biography*. New York: W. W. Norton, 1981.

McGinty, Garnie W. *Louisiana Redeemed: The Overthrow of Carpet-Bag Rule, 1876–1880*. Gretna, LA: Pelican, 1998.

McJimsey, George T. *Genteel Partisan: Manton Marble, 1854–1917*. Ames: Iowa State University Press, 1971.

Morris, Roy, Jr. *Fraud of the Century: Rutherford B. Hayes, Samuel Tilden, and the Stolen Election of 1876*. New York: Simon and Schuster, 2003.

Muzzey, David S. *James G. Blaine: A Political Idol of Other Days*. New York: Dodd, Mead, 1934.

Nevins, Allan. *Abram S. Hewitt, with Some Account of Peter Cooper*. New York: Harper and Bros., 1935.

———. *Hamilton Fish: The Inner History of the Grant Administration*. New York: Dodd, Mead, 1936.

Oberholtzer, Ellis Paxson, *A History of the United States since the Civil War*. Vol. 3. New York: Macmillan, 1926.

Offenberger, Stanley. "The Political Career of Thomas Brackett Reed." Ph.D. diss., New York University, 1963.

Parton, James. *General Butler in New Orleans: History of the Administration of the Department of the Gulf in the Year 1862*. New York: Mason Bros., 1863.

Perman, Michael. *Struggle for Mastery: Disfranchisement in the South, 1888–1908.* Chapel Hill: University of North Carolina Press, 2001.

Peskin, Allan. *Garfield.* Kent, OH: Kent State University Press, 1978.

———. "Was There a Compromise of 1877?" *Journal of American History* 60:1 (June 1973): 63–75.

Polakoff, Keith Ian. "The Disorganized Democracy: An Institutional Study of the Democratic Party, 1872–1880." Ph.D. diss., Northwestern University, 1968.

———. *The Politics of Inertia: The Election of 1876 and the End of Reconstruction.* Baton Rouge: Louisiana State University Press, 1973.

Powers, Michael Shane. "'The Commercial Union of the Three Americas': Major Edward A. Burke and Transnational New South Visions, 1870–1928." Ph.D. diss., University of Arkansas, 2018.

Rable, George C. "Republican Albatross: The Louisiana Question, National Politics, and the Failure of Reconstruction." *Louisiana History* 23:2 (Spring 1982): 109–30.

Rehnquist, William H. *Centennial Crisis: The Disputed Election of 1876.* New York: Alfred A. Knopf, 2004.

Richardson, Leon B. *William E. Chandler: Republican.* New York: Dodd, Mead, 1940.

Ritchie, Donald A. *Press Gallery: Congress and the Washington Correspondents.* Cambridge, MA: Harvard University Press, 1991.

Robbins, David Earl. "The Congressional Career of William Ralls Morrison." Ph.D. diss., University of Illinois, 1963.

Robinson, William A. *Thomas B. Reed: Parliamentarian.* New York: Dodd, Mead, 1930.

Rockoff, Stuart. "Carpetbaggers, Jews, and Reconstruction Politics in Ascension Parish, Louisiana." *American Jewish History* 97:1 (January 2013): 52–54.

Schmiel, David E. "The Career of Jacob Dolson Cox, 1828–1900: Soldier, Scholar, Statesman." Ph.D. diss., Ohio State University, 1969.

Shofner, Jerrell H. "Florida in the Balance: The Electoral Count of 1876." *Florida Historical Quarterly* 47:2 (1968): 122–50. http://www.jstor.org/stable/30140295.

———. "Fraud and Intimidation in the Florida Election of 1876." *Florida Historical Quarterly* 47:4 (1964): 321–30. www.jstor.org/stable/30140045.

Simpson, Brooks D. *The Reconstruction Presidents.* Lawrence: University Press of Kansas, 1998.

Smith, John David Smith. "Let Us All Be Grateful That We Have Colored Troops That Will Fight." In *Black Soldiers in Blue: African American Troops in the Civil War Era,* ed. John David Smith, 1–77. Chapel Hill: University of North Carolina Press, 2002.

Smith, Theodore Clark. *The Life and Letters of James Abram Garfield.* 2 vols. 1925. Hamden, CT: Archon Books, 1968.

Steele, Janet Ellen. "From Paradise to Park Row: The Life, Opinions, and Newspapers of Charles A. Dana, 1819–1897." Ph.D. diss., Johns Hopkins University, 1986.

———. *The Sun Shines for All: Journalism and Ideology in the Life of Charles A. Dana.* Syracuse, NY: Syracuse University Press, 1993.

Summers, Mark W. *The Era of Good Stealings.* New York: Oxford University Press, 1993.

———. *The Ordeal of the Reunion: A New History of Reconstruction.* Chapel Hill: University of North Carolina Press, 2014.

———. *Party Games: Getting, Keeping, and Using Power in the Gilded Age.* Chapel Hill: University of North Carolina Press, 2004.

———. *The Press Gang: Newspapers and Politics, 1865–1878.* Chapel Hill: University of North Carolina Press, 1994.

Tansill, Charles C. *The Congressional Career of Thomas Francis Bayard,* Washington, DC: Georgetown University Press, 1946.

Taylor, Joe Gray. *Louisiana Reconstructed, 1863–1867.* Baton Rouge: Louisiana State University Press, 1974.

Thompson, Elaine V. *Clinton, Louisiana: Society, Politics, and Race Relations in a Nineteenth Century Southern Small Town.* Lafayette: University of Louisiana at Lafayette Press, 2014.

———. "Southern Small Towns: Society, Politics, and Race Relations in Clinton, Louisiana." Ph.D. diss., Rice University, 2003.

Trefousse, Hans L. *Ben Butler: The South Called Him Beast.* New York: Twayne, 1957.

———. *Rutherford B. Hayes.* New York: Times Books, 2002.

Tunnell, Ted. *Edge of the Sword: The Ordeal of Carpetbagger Marshall H. Twitchell in the Civil War and Reconstruction.* Baton Rouge: Louisiana State University Press, 2001.

———. "The Negro, the Republican Party, and the Election of 1876 in Louisiana." *Louisiana History* 7 (Spring 1966): 101–16.

Vallandigham, James K. *A Life of Clement L. Vallandigham.* Baltimore: Turnbull Bros., 1872.

Vandal, Gilles. *Rethinking Southern Violence: Homicides in Post–Civil War Louisiana, 1866–1880.* Columbus: Ohio State University Press, 2000.

Vazzano, Frank P. "The Louisiana Question Resurrected: The Potter Commission and the Election of 1876." *Louisiana History* 16:1 (Winter 1975): 39–57.

Wang, Xi. *The Trial of Democracy: Black Suffrage and Northern Republicans, 1860–1910.* Athens: University of Georgia Press, 1997.

Webb, Ross A. *Benjamin Helm Bristow: Border State Politician.* Lawrence: University Press of Kansas, 1969.

Weiss, Nathan. "The Political Theory and Practice of General Benjamin Franklin Butler." Ph.D. diss., New York University, 1961.

Wilkie, Laurie A. *Creating Freedom: Material Culture and African American Identity at Oakley Plantation, Louisiana, 1840–1950*. Baton Rouge: Louisiana State University Press, 2000.

Williams, Charles R. *The Life of Rutherford Birchard Hayes, Nineteenth President of the United States*. 2 vols. Boston: Houghton Mifflin, 1914.

Woodward, C. Vann. *Reunion and Reaction: The Compromise of 1877 and the End of Reconstruction*. Garden City, NY: Doubleday Anchor, 1956.

Zuczek, Richard. *State of Rebellion: Reconstruction in South Carolina*. Columbia: University of South Carolina Press, 1997.

INDEX

Entries in *italics* denote photographs.